Computer Systems: Modeling and Analysis

Computer Systems: Modeling and Analysis

Edited by Stan Fulcher

www.statesacademicpress.com

States Academic Press,
109 South 5th Street,
Brooklyn, NY 11249, USA

Visit us on the World Wide Web at:
www.statesacademicpress.com

ISBN: 978-1-63989-691-2

Cataloging-in-publication Data

Computer systems : modeling and analysis / edited by Stan Fulcher.
 p. cm.
Includes bibliographical references and index.
ISBN 978-1-63989-691-2
1. Computer systems. 2. Computer simulation. 3. Model-integrated computing.
I. Fulcher, Stan.
QA76 .C663 2023
004--dc23

Contents

Permissions

List of Contributors

Index

Preface

A computer system is made up of several components including input and output devices, a central processing unit (CPU), storage devices and memory. All these components work together as a single unit to produce the desired result. A computer system can be of various sizes and shapes. It can range from a high-end server to a laptop, personal desktop, smartphone, or a tablet. A system model is a tool that predicts the performance of a system under changing circumstances. System modeling refers to a process that involves developing abstract models of a system, wherein each model presents a different view of that system. It involves representing a system using some kind of graphical notation, which can be used by analysts to understand the system's functionality. The process of observing systems for troubleshooting or development purposes is known as systems analysis. Probabilistic modeling methods are applied in the study of computer systems. Models may be analyzed using queuing theory models or stochastic processes. This book aims to shed light on the modeling and analysis of computer systems. It will serve as a valuable source of reference for graduate and postgraduate students.

This book is a comprehensive compilation of works of different researchers from varied parts of the world. It includes valuable experiences of the researchers with the sole objective of providing the readers (learners) with a proper knowledge of the concerned field. This book will be beneficial in evoking inspiration and enhancing the knowledge of the interested readers.

In the end, I would like to extend my heartiest thanks to the authors who worked with great determination on their chapters. I also appreciate the publisher's support in the course of the book. I would also like to deeply acknowledge my family who stood by me as a source of inspiration during the project.

Editor

Communication-Closed Asynchronous Protocols

Andrei Damian[1], Cezara Drăgoi[2], Alexandru Militaru[1], and Josef Widder[3,4(✉)]

[1] Politehnica University Bucharest, Bucharest, Romania
[2] Inria, ENS, CNRS, PSL, Paris, France
[3] TU Wien, Vienna, Austria
`widder@forsyte.at`
[4] Interchain Foundation, Baar, Switzerland

Abstract. The verification of asynchronous fault-tolerant distributed systems is challenging due to unboundedly many interleavings and network failures (e.g., processes crash or message loss). We propose a method that reduces the verification of asynchronous fault-tolerant protocols to the verification of round-based synchronous ones. Synchronous protocols are easier to verify due to fewer interleavings, bounded message buffers etc. We implemented our reduction method and applied it to several state machine replication and consensus algorithms. The resulting synchronous protocols are verified using existing deductive verification methods.

1 Introduction

Fault tolerance protocols provide dependable services on top of unreliable computers and networks. One distinguishes asynchronous vs. synchronous protocols based on the semantics of parallel composition. Asynchronous protocols are crucial parts of many distributed systems for their better performance when compared against the synchronous ones. However, their correctness is very hard to obtain, due to the challenges of concurrency, faults, buffered message queues, and message loss and re-ordering at the network [5,19,21,26,31,35,37,42]. In contrast, reasoning about synchronous round-based semantics is simpler, as one only has to consider specific global states at round boundaries [1,8,10,11,13,17,29,32,40].

The question we address is how to connect both worlds, in order to exploit the advantage of verification in synchronous semantics when reasoning about asynchronous protocols. We consider asynchronous protocols that work in unreliable networks, which may lose and reorder messages, and where processes may crash. We focus on a class of protocols that solve state machine replication.

Due to the absence of a global clock, fault tolerance protocols implement an abstract notion of time to coordinate. The local state of a process maintains the value of the abstract time (potentially implicit), and a process timestamps the messages it sends accordingly. Synchronous algorithms do not need to implement an abstract notion of time: it is embedded in the definition of any synchronous computational model [9, 15, 18, 28], and it is called the *round number*. The key insight of our results is the existence of a correspondence between values of the abstract clock in the asynchronous systems and round numbers in the synchronous ones. Using this correspondence, we make explicit the "hidden" round-based synchronous structure of an asynchronous algorithm.

Fig. 1. Asynchronous executions without jumps

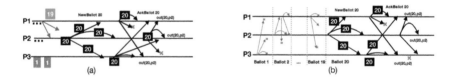

Fig. 2. Asynchronous executions with jumps

We discuss our approach using a leader election algorithm. We consider n of processes, which periodically elect collectively a new leader. These periods are called *ballots*, and in each ballot at most one leader should be elected. The protocol in Fig. 3 solves leader election. In a ballot, a process that wants to become leader proposes itself by sending a message containing its identifier me to all, and it is elected if (1) a majority of processes receive its message, (2) these receivers send a message of leadership acknowledgment to the entire network, and (3) at least one processes receives leadership acknowledgments for its leader estimate from a majority of processes. Figure 1(b) sketches an execution where process $P3$ fails to be elected in ballot 1 because the network drops all the messages sent by P3 marked with a cross. All processes timeout and there is no leader elected in ballot 1. In the second ballot, $P2$ tries to become leader, the network delivers all messages between $P1$ and $P2$ in time, the two processes form a majority, and $P2$ is elected leader of ballot 2.

The protocol is defined by the asynchronous parallel composition of n copies of the code in Fig. 3. Each process executes a loop, where each iteration defines the executors behavior in a ballot. The variable `ballot` encodes the ballot number. The function `coord()` provides a local estimate whether a process should try to become leader. Multiple processes may be selected by `coord()` as leader

Fig. 3. Control flow graph of asynchronous leader election. (Color figure online)

candidates, resulting in a race which is won by a process that is acknowledged by a majority (more than $n/2$ processes). Depending on the result of `coord()`, a process may take the leader branch on the left or the follower branch on the right. On the leader branch, a message is prepared and sent, at line 7. The message contains the ballot number, the label `NewBallot`, the leaders identity. On the other branch, a follower waits for a message from a process, which proposes itself for the current ballot number of the follower. This waiting is implemented by a loop, which terminates either on timeout or when a message is received. Next, the followers, which received a message, and the leader candidates send their leader estimate to all at lines 12 and 41, where the message contains the ballots number, the label `AckBallot`, and the leaders identity. If a processes receives more than $n/2$ messages labeled with `AckBallot` and its current ballot, it checks using `all_same(mbox, leader)` in lines 22 and 49, whether a majority of processes acknowledges the leadership of its estimate. In this case, it adds this information to the array `log` (which stores the locally elected leader of each ballot, if any) and outputs it, before it empties its mailbox and continues with the next iteration.

Figure 1(a) shows another execution of this protocol. Again, P3 sends `NewBallot` messages for ballot 1 to all processes. P3's `NewBallot` messages are delayed, and P2 times out in ballot 1, moving to ballot 2 where it is a leader candidate. The messages sent in ballot 2 are exchanged like in Fig. 1(b). Contrary to Fig. 1(b), while exchanging ballot 2 messages, the network delivers to

P2, P3's `NewBallot` message from ballot 1. However, P2 ignores it, because of the receive statement in line 14 that only accepts messages for greater or equal (`ballot`, `label`) pairs. The message from ballot 1 arrived too "late" because P2 already is in ballot 2. Thus, the messages from ballot 1 have the same effect as if they were dropped, as in Fig. 1(b). The executions are equivalent from the local perspective of the processes: By applying a "rubber band transformation" [30], one can reorder transitions, while maintaining the local control flow and the send/receive causality.

Another case of equivalent executions is given in Fig. 2. While P1 and P2 made progress, P3 was disconnected. In Fig. 2(a), while P3 is waiting for ballot 1 messages, the networks delivers a message for ballot 20. P3 receives this message in line 29 and updates `ballot` in line 35. P3 thus "jumps forward in time", acknowledging P2's leadership in ballot 20. In Fig. 2(b), P3's timeout expires in all ballots from 1 to 19, without P3 receiving any messages. Thus, it does not change its local state (except the ballot number) in these ballots. For P3, these two executions are stutter equivalent. Reducing verification to verification of executions as the ones to the right — i.e., *synchronous* executions — reduces the number of interleavings and drastically simplifies verification. In the following we discuss conditions on the code that allow such a reduction.

Communication Closure. In our example, the variables `ballot` and `label` encode abstract time: Let b and ℓ be their assigned values. Then abstract time ranges over $\mathcal{T} = \{(b, \ell) : b \in \mathbb{N}, \ell \in \{\text{NewBallot}, \text{AckBallot}\}\}$. We fix `NewBallot` to be less than `AckBallot`, and consider the lexicographical order over $\mathcal{T}$. The sequence of (b, ℓ) induced by an execution at a process is monotonically increasing; thus (b, ℓ) encodes a notion of time. A protocol is *communication-closed* if (i) each process sends only messages timestamped with the current time, and (ii) each process receives only messages timestamped with the current or a higher time value. For such protocols we show in Sect. 5 that for each asynchronous execution, there is an equivalent (processes go through the same sequence of local states) synchronous one. We use ideas from [17], but we allow reacting to future messages, which is a more permissive form of communication closure. This is essential for jumping forward, and thus for liveness in fault tolerance protocols.

The challenge is to check communication closure at the code level. For this, we rely on user-provided "tag" annotations that specify the variables and the message fields representing local time and timestamps. A system of assertions formalizes that the user-provided annotations encode time and that the protocol is communication-closed w.r.t. this definition of time. In the example, the user provides (`ballot`, `label`) for local time and `msg->bal` and `msg->lab` for timestamps. In Fig. 3, we give example assertions that we add for the send and receive conditions (i) and (ii). These assertions only consider the local state, i.e., we do not need to capture the states of other processes or the message pool. We check the assertions with the static verifier Verifast [22].

Synchronous Semantics. Central to our approach is re-writing communication-closed asynchronous protocol into synchronous ones. To formalize synchronous semantics we introduce *multi Heard-Of protocols*, mHO for short. An mHO computation is structured into a sequence of mHO-rounds that execute synchronously. Figure 4 is an example of an mHO protocol. It has two mHO-rounds: NewBallot and AckBallot. Within a round, SEND functions, resp. UPDATE functions, are executed synchronously across all processes. The *round* number r is initially 0 and it is incremented after each execution of an mHO-round. The interesting feature, which models faults and timeouts, are the heard-of sets HO [9]. For each round r and each process p, the set $HO(p, r)$ contains the set of processes from which p hears of in round r, i.e., whose messages are in the mailbox set taken as parameter by UPDATE (mbox). If the message from q to p is lost in round r, then $q \notin HO(p, r)$. Figures 1(b) and 2(b) are examples of executions of the protocol in Fig. 4. We extend the HO model [9] by allowing composition of *multiple* protocols. Verification in synchronous semantics, and thus in mHO, is simpler due to the round structure, which entails (i) no interleavings, (ii) no message buffers, and (iii) simpler invariants at the round boundaries.

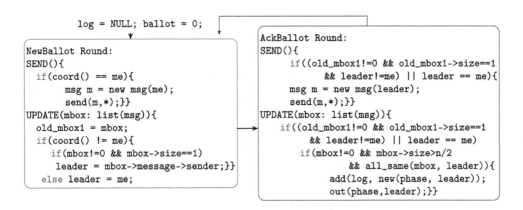

Fig. 4. Control flow graph of synchronous leader election. (Color figure online)

Rewriting to mHO. We introduce a procedure that takes as input the asynchronous protocol together with tag annotations that have been checked, and produces the protocol rewritten in mHO, e.g., Fig. 3 is rewritten into Fig. 4. The rewriting is based on the idea of matching abstract time (ballot, label) to mHO round numbers r. Roughly, mHO-round NewBallot is obtained by combining the code of the first box on each path in Fig. 3 (the red boxes) and AckBallot is obtained my combining the second box on each path (the blue ones) as follows. The three message reception loops (the code in the boxes with highlighted background) are removed, because receptions are implicit in mHO; they correspond to a non-deterministic parameter of the UPDATE function. For each round, we record the context in which it is executed, e.g., the lower box for the follower is executed only if a NewBallot message was received (more details in Sect. 6).

Verification. The specification of the running example is that if two processes find the leader election for a ballot b successful (i.e., there is log entry for b), then they agree on the leader. In general, to prove the specification, we need invariants that quantify over the ballot number b. As processes decide asynchronously, the proof of ballot 1, for some process p, must refer to the first entry of log of processes that might already be in ballot 400. As discussed in [38], in general invariants need to capture the complete message history and the complete local state of processes. The proof of the same property for the synchronous protocol requires no such invariant. Due to communication closure, no messages need to be maintained after a round terminated, that is, there is no message pool. The rewritten synchronous code has a simpler correctness proof, independent of the chosen verification method. One could use model checking [1,29,39,40], theorem prover approaches [8,11], or deductive verification [14] for synchronous systems.

For several protocols, we formalize their specification in Consensus Logic [13], we have computed the equivalent mHO protocol, and proved it correct using the existing deductive verification engine from [13].

2 Asynchronous Protocols

All processes execute the same code, written in the core language in Fig. 5. The communication between processes is done via typed messages. Message payloads, denoted M, are wrappers of primitive or composite type. We denote by $\mathcal{M}$ the set of message types. Wrappers are used to distinguish payload types. Send instructions take as input an object of some payload type and the receivers identity or $\star$ corresponding to a send to all. Receives statements are non-blocking, and return an object of payload type or NULL. Receive statements are parameterized by conditions (i.e., pointers to function) on the values in the received messages (e.g., timestamp). At most one message is received at a time. If no message has been delivered or satisfies the condition, receive returns NULL. In Fig. 3, we give the definition of the function eq, used to filter messages acknowledging the leadership of a process. The followers use also geq that checks if the received message is timestamped with a value higher or equal to the local time. We assume that each loop contains at least one send or receive statement. The iterative sequential computations are done in local functions, i.e., f($\vec{e}$). The instructions in() and out() are used to communicate with an external environment.

The semantics of a protocol $\mathcal{P}$ is the asynchronous parallel composition of n copies of the same code, one copy per process, where n is a parameter. Formally, the state of a protocol $\mathcal{P}$ is a tuple $\langle s, msg \rangle$ where: $s \in [P \rightarrow (\text{Vars} \cup \{\text{pc}\}) \rightarrow \mathcal{D}]$ is a valuation in some data domain $\mathcal{D}$ of the variables in $\mathcal{P}$, where pc is represents the current control location, where Loc is the set of all protocol locations, and $msg \subseteq \bigcup_{\text{M} \in \mathcal{M}}(P \times \mathcal{D}(\text{M}) \times P)$ is the multiset of messages in transit (the network may lose and reorder messages). Given a process $p \in P$, $s(p)$ is the local state of p, which is a valuation of p's local variables, i.e., $s(p) \in \text{Vars}_p \cup \{\text{pc}_p\} \rightarrow \mathcal{D}$. The state of a crashed process is a wildcard state that matches any state. The messages sent by a process are added to the global pool of messages msg, and

$$
\begin{array}{ll}
e := c & \text{constant} \\
\quad | \ x & \text{variable} \\
\quad | \ f(\vec{e}) & \text{operation} \\
types := \texttt{Pid} & \text{process Id} \\
\quad \texttt{M} & \text{payload type} \\
\quad \texttt{p : Pid, \ m : M} & \\
\quad \texttt{Mbox:} & \text{set of M} \\
\mathcal{P} := \Pi_{p:P}[S]_p & \text{protocol} \\
P \ \text{is the set of process identities}
\end{array}
\qquad
\begin{array}{ll}
S := \texttt{x := e} & \text{assignment} \\
\quad | \ \texttt{reset\_timeout(e)} & \text{reset a timeout} \\
\quad | \ \texttt{send(m,p)} \ | \ \texttt{send(m, \star)} & \text{send message} \\
\quad | \ \texttt{m := recv(*cond)} & \text{receive message} \\
\quad | \ \texttt{S ; S} & \text{sequence} \\
\quad | \ \text{if e then S else S} & \\
\quad | \ \text{while true S} & \\
\quad | \ \text{break} \ | \ \text{continue} & \\
\quad | \ \texttt{x = in()} & \text{client entry} \\
\quad | \ \texttt{out(e)} & \text{client output}
\end{array}
$$

Fig. 5. Syntax of asynchronous protocols.

a receive statement removes a messages from the pool. The interface operations in and out do not modify the local state of a process. An execution is an infinite sequence $s0 \ A0 \ s1 \ A1 \ldots$ such that $\forall i \geq 0$, si is a protocol state, $Ai \in A$ is a local statement, whose execution creates a transition of the form $\langle s, msg \rangle \xrightarrow{I,O} \langle s', msg' \rangle$ where $\{I, O\}$ are the observable events generated by the Ai (if any). We denote by $[\![\mathcal{P}]\!]$ the set of executions of the protocol $\mathcal{P}$.

3 Round-Based Model: mHO

Intra-procedural. mHO captures round-based distributed algorithms and is a reformulation of the model in [9]. All processes execute the same code and the computation is structured in rounds. We denote by P the set of processes and $n = |P|$ is a parameter. The central concept is the *HO*-set, where $HO(p, r)$ contains the processes from which process p has *heard of* — has received messages from — in round r; this models faults and timeouts.

Syntax. An mHO protocol consists of variable declarations, Vars is the set of variables, an initialization method init, and a non-empty sequence of rounds, called *phase*; cf. Fig. 6. A phase is a fixed-size array of rounds. Each round has a send and update method, parameterized by a type M (denoted by *round$_M$*) which

$$
\begin{array}{rl}
protocol ::= & interface \ var\_decl^* \ init \ phase \\
interface ::= & \textbf{in:} \ () \to type \ | \ \textbf{out:} \ type \to () \\
init ::= & \textbf{init:} \ () \to [P \to \text{Vars} \to \mathcal{D}] \\
phase ::= & round^+ \\
round_M ::= & \text{SEND:} \ [P \to \text{Vars}] \to [P \rightharpoonup \text{T}] \\
& \text{UPDATE:} \ [P \rightharpoonup \text{T}] \times [P \to \text{Vars}] \\
& \to [P \to \text{Vars}]
\end{array}
$$

Fig. 6. mHO syntax.

represents the message payload. The method SEND has no side effects and returns the messages to be sent based on the local state of each sender; it returns a partial map from receivers to payloads. The method UPDATE takes as input the received messages and updates the local state of a process. It may communicate with an external client via in and out. For data computations, UPDATE uses iterative control structures only indirectly via sequential functions, e.g., all_same(mbox, leader) in Fig. 3, which checks whether the payloads of all messages in mbox are equal to the local leader estimate.

Semantics. The set of executions of a mHO protocol is defined by the execution in a loop, of SEND followed by UPDATE for each round in the phase array. The initial configuration is defined by init. There are three predefined execution counters: the phase number, which is increased after a phase has been executed, the step number which tracks which mHO-round is executed in the current phase, and the round number which counts the total number of rounds executed so far and is defined by the phase times the length of the phase array, plus the step.

A protocol state is a tuple $\langle SU, s, r, msg, P, HO \rangle$ where: P is the set of processes, $SU \in \{\text{SEND}, \text{UPDATE}\}$ indicates the next transition, $s \in [P \rightarrow \text{Vars} \rightarrow \mathcal{D}]$ stores the process local states, $r \in \mathbb{N}$ is the round number, $msg \subseteq 2^{(P,\mathcal{D}(\text{M}),P)}$ stores the in-transit messages, where M is the type of the message payload, $HO \in [P \rightarrow 2^P]$ evaluates the HO-sets for the current round. After the initialization, an execution alternates SEND and UPDATE transitions. In the SEND transition, all processes send messages, which are added to a pool of messages msg, without modifying the local states. The values of the HO sets are updated non-deterministically to be a subset of P. A message is lost if the sender's identity does not belong to the HO set of the receiver. In an UPDATE transition, UPDATE is applied at each process, taking as input the set of received messages by that process in that round. If the processes communicate with an external process, then UPDATE might produce observable events o_p. These events correspond to calls to in, which returns an input value, and out that sends the value given as parameter to the client. At the end of the round, msg is purged and r is incremented. Figure 1(b) shows an execution of the mHO algorithm in Fig. 4.

Inter-procedural. The model introduced so far allows to express one protocol, e.g., a leader election protocol (e.g., Fig. 4). However, realistic systems typically combine several protocols, e.g., we can transform Fig. 4 into a replicated state machine protocol, by allowing processes to enter an atomic broadcast protocol in every ballot where a leader is elected successfully. Figure 7 sketches such an execution, where in the update of round AckBallot, a subprotocol is called; its execution is sketched with thicker edges. In the subprotocol, the leader broadcasts client requests in a loop until it loses its quorum. When a follower does not receive a message from the leader, it considers the leader crashed, and the control returns to the leader election protocol.

An inter-procedural mHO protocol differs from an intra-procedural one only in the UPDATE function: It may call another protocol and block until the call returns. An UPDATE may call at most one protocol on each path in its control flow (a sequence of calls can be implemented using multiple rounds). Thus, an inter-

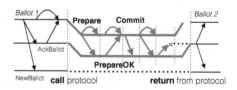

Fig. 7. Inter-procedural execution

procedural mHO protocol is a collection of non-recursive mHO protocols, with a main protocol as entry point. Different protocols exchange messages of different types.

4   Formalizing Communication Closure Using Tags

We introduce synchronization tags which are program annotations that define communication-closed rounds within an asynchronous protocol.

Definition 1 (Tag annotation). *For a protocol* $\mathcal{P}$*, a tag annotation is a tuple* $(\mathsf{SyncV}, \mathsf{tags}, \mathsf{tagm}, \preceq, \mathcal{D})$ *where:*

- $\mathcal{D} = (D_1, D_2, \ldots, D_{2m-1}, D_{2m})$*, with* $(D_i, \preceq_i, \perp_i)$ *an ordered domain with a minimal element, denoted* $\perp_i$*, for* $1 \le i \le 2m$*. The cardinality of* D_{2i} *is bounded and all* D_{2i} *are pairwise disjoint, for* $i \in [1, m]$*.*
- *relation* $\preceq$ *is the lexicographical order: the ith component is ordered by* $\preceq_i$*,*
- $\mathsf{SyncV} = (v_1, v_2, \ldots, v_{2m-1}, v_{2m})$ *is a tuple of fresh variables,*
- $\mathsf{tags} : \mathsf{Loc} \to [\mathsf{SyncV} \overset{inj}{\rightharpoonup} \mathsf{Vars}]$ *annotates each control location with a partially defined injective function, that maps* SyncV *over protocol variables,*
- $\mathsf{tagm} : \mathcal{M} \to [\mathsf{SyncV} \overset{inj}{\rightharpoonup} Fields(\mathsf{M})]$ *annotates each message type* $\mathsf{M} \in \mathcal{M}$ *with a partially defined injective function, that maps* SyncV *over the fields of* M*.*

The evaluation of a tag over $\mathcal{P}$*'s semantics is denoted* $([\![\mathsf{tags}]\!], [\![\mathsf{tagm}]\!])$*, where*

- $[\![\mathsf{tags}]\!] : \Sigma \to [\mathsf{SyncV} \to \mathcal{D}]$ *is defined over the set of local process states* $\Sigma = \bigcup_{s \in [\![\mathcal{P}]\!]} \bigcup_{p \in P} s(p)$*, such that* $[\![\mathsf{tags}]\!]_s = (d_1, \ldots, d_{|\mathsf{SyncV}|})$ *with* $d_i = [\![x]\!]_s$ *if* $x = \mathsf{tags}([\![pc]\!]_s)(v_i) \in \mathsf{Vars}$ *otherwise* $d_i = \perp_i$*, where* $s \in \Sigma$*,* $x \in \mathsf{Vars}$*,* v_i *is the* i^{th} *component in* SyncV*, and* pc *is the program counter;*
- $[\![\mathsf{tagm}]\!] : \bigcup_{\mathsf{M} \in \mathcal{M}} \mathcal{D}(\mathsf{M}) \to [\mathsf{SyncV} \to \mathcal{D} \cup \perp]$ *is a function that for any message value* $m = (m_1, \ldots, m_t)$*, in the domain of some message type* M*, associates a tuple* $[\![\mathsf{tagm}]\!]_{m:\mathsf{M}} = (d_1, \ldots, d_{|\mathsf{SyncV}|})$ *with* $d_i = m_j$ *if* $j = \mathsf{tagm}(\mathsf{M})(v_i)$ *otherwise* $d_i = \perp_i$*, where* v_i *is the* i^{th} *element in* SyncV*.*

For every $1 \le i \le m$*,* v_{2i-1} *is called a* phase *tag and* v_{2i} *is called* step *tag. Given an execution* $\pi \in [\![\mathcal{P}]\!]$*, a transition* sAs' *in* π *is tagged by* $[\![\mathsf{tagm}]\!]_m$ *if*

A *is* $send(m)$ *or* $m = recv(*cond)$*, or* A *is tagged by* $[\![\mathsf{tags}]\!]'_s$ *otherwise.*

For Fig. 3, $\mathsf{SyncV} = (v_1, v_2)$, and tags matches v_1 and v_2 with ballot and label, resp., at all control locations, i.e., a process is in step $\mathsf{NewBallot}$ of phase 3, when $\mathsf{ballot} = 3$ and $\mathsf{label} = \mathsf{NewBallot}$. For the type msg, tagm matches the field ballot and lab with v_1 and v_2, resp., i.e., a message $(3, \mathsf{NewBallot}, 5)$ is a phase 3 step $\mathsf{NewBallot}$ message. To capture that messages of type A are sent locally before messages of type B, the tagging function $\mathsf{tagm}(\mathsf{B})$ should be defined on the same synchronization variables as $\mathsf{tagm}(\mathsf{A})$.

Definition 2 (Synchronization tag). *Given a protocol* $\mathcal{P}$*, an annotation tag* $(\mathsf{SyncV}, \mathsf{tags}, \mathsf{tagm}, \mathcal{D}, \preceq)$ *is called* synchronization tag *iff:*

(I.) for any local execution $\pi = s_0 A_0 s_1 A_1 \ldots \in [\![\mathcal{P}]\!]_p$ *of a process* p*, the sequence* $[\![\mathsf{tags}]\!]_{s_0} [\![\mathsf{tags}]\!]_{s_1} [\![\mathsf{tags}]\!]_{s_2} \ldots$ *is a monotonically increasing w.r.t.* $\preceq$*.*

Moreover $\forall j, j' \in [1..m], j < j'$. *if* $[\![tags]\!]_{s_i}^{(2j-1,2j)} \neq [\![tags]\!]_{s_i+1}^{(2j-1,2j)}$ *and*
$[\![tags]\!]_{s_i}^{(2j'-1,2j')} \neq [\![tags]\!]_{s_i+1}^{(2j'-1,2j')}$ *then* $[\![tags]\!]_{s_i+1}^{(2j'-1,2j')} = (\perp_{2j'-1}, \perp_{2j'})$
where $[\![tags]\!]_{s_i}^{(2j-1,2j)}$ *is the projection of the tuple* $[\![tags]\!]_{s_i}$ *on the* $2j-1$
and $2j$ *components,*

(II.) for any local execution $\pi \in [\![\mathcal{P}]\!]_p$, *if* $s \xrightarrow{send(m,\_)} s'$ *is a transition of* π, *with*
m *a message value, then* $[\![tags]\!]_s = [\![tagm]\!]_m$ *and* $[\![tags]\!]_s = [\![tags]\!]_{s'}$,

(III.) for any local execution $\pi \in [\![\mathcal{P}]\!]_p$, *if* $s \xrightarrow{m=recv(cond)} sr$ *is a transition of* π,
with m *a value of some message type, then*
  - *if* $m \neq$ NULL *then* $[\![tags]\!]_s \preceq [\![tagm]\!]_m$, $[\![tags]\!]_s = [\![tags]\!]_{sr}$, *and*
  - *if* $m =$ NULL *then* $s = sr$,

(IV.) for any local execution $\pi \in [\![\mathcal{P}]\!]_p$, *if* $s \xrightarrow{stm} s'$ *is a transition of* π *such that*

  - $s \neq s'$ *and* $s \mid_{M,SyncV} = s' \mid_{M,SyncV}$, *that is,* s *and* s' *differ on the variables*
    that are neither of some message type nor in the image of tags,
  - *or* stm *is a* send, break, continue, *or* out(),
    then for all message type variables m *in the protocol,* $[\![tags]\!]_s = [\![tagm]\!]_m$,
    where m *is the value in the state* s *of* m, *and for any* Mbox *variables of type*
    set of messages, $[\![tags]\!]_s = [\![tagm]\!]_m$ *with* $m \in [\![Mbox]\!]_s$,

(V.) for any local execution $\pi \in [\![\mathcal{P}]\!]_p$, *if* $s_1 \xrightarrow{send(m,\_)} s_2 \xrightarrow{stm^+} s_3 \xrightarrow{send(m',\_)} s_4$
or $s_1 \xrightarrow{m=recv(*cond)} s_2 \xrightarrow{stm^+} s_3 \xrightarrow{send(m',\_)} s_4$ *are sequences of transitions*
in π, *then* $[\![tagm]\!]_m \prec [\![tagm]\!]_{m'}$, *where* stm *is any statement except* send
or recv. *Moreover, if* $s_1 \xrightarrow{m=recv(*cond)} s_2 \xrightarrow{stm^+} s_3 \xrightarrow{m'=recv(*cond')} s_4$ *in* π,
then $s_2 \mid_{Vars\backslash(M \cup SyncV)} = s_3 \mid_{Vars\backslash(M \cup SyncV)}$ *or* $[\![tags]\!]_{s_2} \prec [\![tags]\!]_{s_3}$.

A protocol $\mathcal{P}$ *is communication-closed, if there exists a synchronization tag for* $\mathcal{P}$.

Condition (I.) states that SyncV is not decreased by any local statement (it is a notion of time). Further, one synchronization pair is modified at a time, except a reset (i.e., a pair is set to its minimal value) when the value of a preceding pair is updated. Checking this, translates into checking a transition invariant, stating that the value of the synchronization tuple SyncV is increased by any assignment. To state this invariant we introduce "old synchronization variables" that maintain the value of the synchronization variables before the update.

Condition (II.) states that any message sent is tagged with a timestamp that equals the current local time. Checking it, reduces to an assert statement that expresses that for every $v \in$ SyncV, $tagm(M)(v) = tags(pc)(v)$, where M is the type of the message m which is sent, and pc is the program location of the send.

Condition (III.) states that any message received is tagged with a timestamp greater than or equal to the current time of the process. To check it, we need to consider the implementation of the functions passed as argument to a recv statement. These functions (e.g., eq and geq in Fig. 3) implement the filtering of the messages delivered by the network. We inline their code and prove Condition (III.) by comparing the tagged fields of message variables with the phase and step variables. In Fig. 3, `assert m → bal == ballot && m → lab == label` after `recv(eq(ballot, label))` checks this condition on the leader's branch.

Condition (IV.) states that if the local state of a process changes (except changes of message type variables and synchronization variables), then all locally stored messages are timestamped with the current local time. That is, future messages cannot be "used" (no variable can be written, except message type variables) before the phase and step tags are updated to match the highest timestamp. To check it, we need to prove a stronger property than the one for (III.). At each control location that writes to either variables of primitive or composite type or mailbox variables, the values of the phase (and step) variables must be equal to the phase (and step) tagged fields of all allocated message type objects. In Fig. 3, the statement `assert(equal(mbox, ballot, label))` checks this condition on the leader's branch. It is a separation logic formula that uses the inductive list definition of `mbox` which includes the content of the `mbox`.

The first four conditions imply that there is a global notion of time in the asynchronous protocol. However, this does not restrict the number of the messages exchanged between two processes with the same timestamp. mHO restricts the message exchange: for every time value (corresponding to a mHO-round), processes first send, then they receive messages, and then they perform a computation without receiving or sending more messages before time is increased. Condition (V.) ensures that the asynchronous protocol has this structure. We do a syntactic check of the code to ensure the code meets these restrictions.

Intuitively, each pair of synchronization variables identifies uniquely a mHO-protocol. To rewrite an asynchronous protocol into nested (inter-procedural) mHO-protocols, the tag of the inner protocol should include the tag of the outer one. The asynchronous code advances the time of one protocol at a time, that is, modifies one synchronization pair at a time. The only exception is when inner protocols terminate: in this case, the time of the outer protocol is advanced, while the time of the inner one is reset. Moreover, different protocols exchange different message types. To be able to order the messages exchanged by an inner protocol w.r.t. the messages exchanged by an outer protocol, the inner protocol messages should be tagged also with the synchronization variables identifying the outer one. This is actually happening in state machine replication algorithms, where the ballot (or view number), which is the tag of the outer leader election algorithm, tags also all the messages broadcast by the leader in the inner one.

5 Reducing Asynchronous Executions

We show that any execution of an asynchronous protocol that has a synchronization tag can be reduced to an indistinguishable mHO execution.

Definition 3 (Indistinguishability). *Given two executions π and π' of a protocol $\mathcal{P}$, we say a process p cannot distinguish locally between π and π' w.r.t. a set of variables W, denoted $\pi \simeq_p^W \pi'$, if the projection of both executions on the sequence of states of p, restricted to the variables in W, agree up to finite stuttering, denoted, $\pi|_{p,W} \equiv \pi'|_{p,W}$.*

Two executions π and π' are indistinguishable *w.r.t. a set of variables W, denoted $\pi \simeq^W \pi'$, iff no process can distinguish between them, i.e., $\forall p.\ \pi \simeq_p^W \pi'$.*

The reduction preserves so-called local properties [7], among which are consensus and state machine replication.

Definition 4 (Local properties). *A property ϕ is* local *if for any two executions a and b that are indistinguishable $a \models \phi$ iff $b \models \phi$.*

Theorem 1. *If there exists a synchronization tag $(\text{SyncV}, \texttt{tags}, \texttt{tagm}, \mathcal{D}, \preceq)$ for $\mathcal{P}$, then $\forall ae \in \llbracket \mathcal{P} \rrbracket$ there exists an mHO-execution se that is indistinguishable w.r.t. all variables except for M or $\text{Set}(\text{M})$ variables, therefore ae and se satisfy the same local properties.*

Proof Sketch. There are two cases to consider. Case (1): every receive transition $s \xrightarrow{m=recv(*cond)} sr$ in ae satisfies that $\llbracket \texttt{tags} \rrbracket_{sr} = \llbracket \texttt{tagm} \rrbracket_m$, i.e., all messages received are timestamped with the current local tag of the receiver. We use commutativity arguments to reorder transitions so that we obtain an indistinguishable asynchronous execution in which the transition tags are globally non-decreasing: The interesting case is if a send comes before a lower tagged receive in ae. Then the tags of the two transitions imply that the transitions concern different messages so that swapping them cannot violate send/receive causality.

We exploit that in the protocols we consider, no correct process locally keeps the tags unchanged forever (e.g., stays in a ballot forever) to arrive at an execution where the subsequence of transitions with the same tag is finite. Still, the resulting execution is not an mHO execution; e.g., for the same tag a receive may happen before a send on a different process. Condition (V.) ensures that mHO send-receive-update order is respected locally at each process. From this, together with the observation that sends are left movers, and updates are right movers, we obtain a global send-receive-update order which implies that the resulting execution is a mHO execution.

Case (2): there is a transition $s \xrightarrow{m=recv(*cond)} sr$ in ae such that $\llbracket \texttt{tags} \rrbracket_{sr} \prec \llbracket \texttt{tagm} \rrbracket_m$, that is, a process receives a message with tag k', higher than its state tag k. In mHO, a process only receives for its current round. To bring the asynchronous execution in such a form, we use Condition (IV.) and mHO semantics, where each process goes through all rounds. First, Condition (IV.) ensures that the process must update the tag variables to k' at some point t after receiving it, if it wants to use the content of the message. It ensures that the process stutters during the time instance between k and k', w.r.t. the values of the variables which are not of message type. That is, for the intermediate values of abstract time, between k and k', no messages are sent, received, and no computation is performed. We split ae at point t and add empty send instructions, receive instructions, and instructions that increment the synchronization variables, until the tag reaches k'. If we do this for each jump in ae, we arrive at an indistinguishable asynchronous execution that falls into the Case (1). □

6   Rewriting of Asynchronous to mHO

We introduce a rewriting algorithm that takes as input an asynchronous protocol $\mathcal{P}$ annotated with a synchronization tag and produces a mHO protocol whose executions are indistinguishable from the executions of $\mathcal{P}$.

Message Reception.   mHO receives all messages of a round at once, while in the asynchronous code, messages are received one by one. By Condition (V.), receive steps that belong to the same round are separated only by instructions that store the messages in the mailbox. We consider that message reception is implemented in a simple `while(true)` loop (the most inner one); cf. filled boxes in Fig. 3. Conditions (III.) and (IV.) ensure that all messages received in a loop belong to one round (the current one or the one the code will jump to after exiting the reception loop). Thus, we replace a reception loop by `havoc` and `assume` statements that subsume the possible effects of the loop, satisfying all the conditions regarding synchronization tags found in the original receive statements.

Rewriting to an Intra-proceduralmHO. When the synchronization tag is defined over a pair of variables, the rewriting will produce an intra-procedural mHO protocol. Recall that the values of synchronization variables incarnate the round number, so that each update to a pair of synchronization variables marks the beginning of a new mHO round. The difficulty is that different execution prefixes may lead to the same values of the synchronization variables. To compute mHO-rounds, the algorithm exploits the position of the updates to the synchronization variables in the control flow graph (CFG). We consider different CFG patterns, from the simplest to the most complicated one.

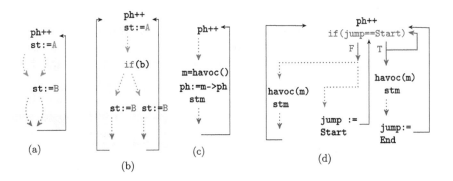

Fig. 8. Control flow graphs for rewriting. (Color figure online)

Case 1: If the CFG is like in Fig. 8(a), i.e., it consists of one loop, where the phase tag `ph` is incremented once at the beginning of each loop iteration, and for every value of the step tag `st` there is exactly one assignment in the loop body (the same on all paths). In this case, the phase tag takes the same values as the loop iteration counter (maybe shifted with some initial value). Therefore, the loop body defines the code of an mHO-phase. It is easy to structure it into two mHO-rounds: the code of round A is the part of the CFG from the beginning of the loop's body up to the second assignment of the st variable, and round B is the rest of the code up to the end of the loop body.

Case 2: The CFG is like in Fig. 8(b). It differs from Case 1 in that the same value is assigned to st in different branches. Each of this assignments marks the beginning of a mHO round B, which thus has multiple entry points. In mHO, a round only has one entry point. To simulate the multiple entry points in mHO, we store in auxiliary variables the values of the conditions along the paths that led to the entry point. In the figure, the code of round A is given by the red box, and the code of round B by the condition in the first blue box, expressed on the auxiliary variable, followed by the respective branches in the blue box.

In our example in Fig. 3, the assignment label = AckBallot appears in the leader and the follower branch. Followers send and receive AckBallot messages only if they have received a NewBallot. The rewrite introduces old_mbox1 in the mHO protocol in Fig. 4 to store this information. Also, we eliminate the variables ballot and label; they are subsumed by the phase and round number of mHO.

Case 3: Let us assume that the CFG is like in Fig. 8(c). It differs from Case 1 because the phase tag ph is assigned twice. We rewrite it into asynchronous code that falls into Case 1 or 2. The resulting CFG is sketched in Fig. 8(d), with only one assignment to ph at the beginning of the loop.

If the second assignment changes the value of ph, then there is a jump. In case of a jump, the beginning of a new phase does not coincide with the first instruction of the loop. Thus there might be multiple entry points for a phase. We introduce (non-deterministic) branching in the control flow to capture different entry points: In case there is no jump, the green followed by the purple edge are executed within the same phase. In case of a jump, the rewritten code allows the green and the purple paths to be executed in different phases; first the green, and then the purple in a later phase. We add empty loops to simulate the phases that are jumped over. As a pure non-deterministic choice at the top of the loop would be too imprecise, we use the variable jump to make sure that the purple edge is executed only once prior to green edge. In case of multiple assignments, we perform this transformation iteratively for each assignment.

The protocol in Fig. 4 is obtained using two optimizations of the previous construction: First we do not need empty loops. They are subsumed by the mHO semantics as all local state changes are caused by some message reception. Thus, an empty loop is simulated by the execution of a phase with empty HO sets. Second, instead of adding jump variables, we reuse the non-deterministic value of mbox. This is possible as the jump is preconditioned by a cardinality constraint on the mbox, and the green edge is empty (assignments to ballot and label correspond to ph++ and reception loops have been reduced to havoc statements).

Nesting. Cases 1–3 capture loops without nesting. Nested loops are rewritten into inter-procedural mHO protocols, using the structure of the tag annotations from Sect. 4. Each loop is rewritten into one protocol, starting with the most inner loop using the procedure above. For each outer loop, it first replaces the nested loop with a call to the computed mHO protocol, and then applies the same rewriting procedure. Interpreting each loop as a protocol is pessimistic, and our rewriting may generate deeper nesting than necessary. Inner loops appearing on different branches may belong to the same sub-protocol, so that these different loops exchange messages. If `tags` associates different synchronization variables to different loops then the rewriting builds one (sub-)protocol for each loop. Otherwise, the rewriting merges the loops into one mHO protocol. To soundly merge several loops into the same mHO protocol, the rewrite algorithm identifies the context in which the inner loop is executed.

Theorem 2. *Given an asynchronous protocol $\mathcal{P}$ annotated with a synchronization tag $(\mathrm{SyncV}, \mathtt{tags}, \mathtt{tagm}, \mathcal{D}, \preceq)$, the rewriting returns an inter-procedural mHO protocol $\mathcal{P}^{mHO}$ whose executions are indistinguishable from the executions of $\mathcal{P}$.*

7 Experimental Results

We implemented the rewriting procedure in a prototype tool ATHOS (https:// github.com/alexandrumc/async-to-sync-translation). We applied it to several fault-tolerant distributed protocols. Figure 9 summarizes our results.

Verification of Synchronization Tags. The tool takes protocols in a C embedding of the language from Sect. 2 as input. We use a C embedding to be able to use Verifast [22] for checking the conditions in Sect. 4, i.e., the communication closure of an asynchronous protocol. Verifast is a deductive verification tool based on separation logic for sequential programs. Therefore, communication closure is specified in separation logic in our tool. To reason about sending and receiving messages, we inline every `recv(*cond)` and use predefined specifications for `send` and `recv`. We consider only the prototype and the specification of these functions.

The user specifies in a configuration file the synchronization tag by (i) defining the number of (nested) protocols, (ii) for each protocol, the phase and step variables, and (iii) for each messages type the fields that encode the timestamp, i.e., the phase and step number. Figure 9 gives the names of phase and step variables of our benchmarks. For now, we manually insert the specification to be proven, i.e., the `assert` statements that capture Conditions (I.) to (V.) in Sect. 4. In Fig. 9, column Async gives the size in LoC of the input asynchronous protocol, +CC gives the size in LoC of the input annotated with the checks for communication closure (Conditions (I.) to (V.)) and their proofs.

Protocol	Tags	Async	+CC	Sync
Consensus [6, Fig.6]	$ph = r_p$ $st=$ {Phase1, Phase2, Phase3, Phase4}	332	661	251
Two phase commit	$ph = $ i, $st=$ {Query, Vote, Commit, Ack}	342	596	242
Figure 3*,V	$ph = $ ballot, $st = $ {NewBallot, AckBallot}	255	576	110
ViewChange* [34]	$ph1 = $ **view**, $st1 = $ {StartViewChange, DoViewChange, StartView}	352	720	172
Normal-Op^V [34]	$ph = $ op_number $st = $ {Prepare, PrepareOK, Commit}	266	628	182
Multi-Paxos*,V [25]	$ph1 = $ ballot, $st1 = $ {NewBallot, AckBallot, NewLog} $ph2 = $ op_number, $st2 = $ {Prepare, PrepareOK, Commit}	1646	621	405

Fig. 9. Benchmarks. The superscript * identifies protocols that jump over phases. The superscript V marks protocols whose synchronous counterpart we verified.

Benchmarks. Our tool has rewritten several challenging benchmarks: the algorithm from [6, Fig.6] solves consensus using a failure detector. The algorithm jumps to a specific decision round, if a special decision message is received. Multi-Paxos is the Paxos algorithm from [25] over sequences, without fast paths, where the classic path is repeated as long as the leader is stable. Roughly, it does a leader election similar to our running example (NewBallot is *Phase1a*), except that the last all-to-all round is replaced by one back-and-forth communication between the leader and its quorum: the leader receives $n/2$ acknowledgments that contain also the log of its followers (*Phase1b*). The leader computes the maximal log and sends it to all (*Phase1aStart*). In a subprotocol, a stable leader accepts client requests, and broadcasts them one by one to its followers. The broadcast is implemented by three rounds, *Phase2aClassic*, *Phase2bClassic*, *Learn*, and is repeated as long as the leader is stable. ViewChange is a leader election algorithm similar to the one in ViewStamped [34]. Normal-Op is the subprotocol used in ViewStamped to implement the broadcasting of new commands by a stable leader. The last column of Fig. 9 gives the size of the mHO protocol computed by the rewriting. The implementation uses pycparser [3], to obtain the abstract syntax tree of the input protocol.

Verification. We verified the safety specification (agreement) of the mHO counterparts of the running example (Fig. 3), Normal-Op, and Multi-Paxos, by deductive verification: We encoded the specification of these algorithms, i.e., atomic broadcast, consensus, leader election, and the transition relation in Consensus Logic CL [13]. CL is a specification logic that allows us to express global properties of synchronous systems, and it contains expressions for processes, values, sets, cardinalities, and set comprehension. The verification conditions are soundly discarded by using an SMT solver. We used Z3 [33] in our experiments.

For Multi-Paxos we did a modular proof. First we prove the correctness of the sub-protocol Normal-Op which implements a loop of atomic broadcasts (executed in case of a stable leader). Then we prove the leader election outer loop correct, by replacing the subprotocol Normal-Op with its specification.

8 Related Work and Conclusions

Verification of asynchronous protocols received a lot of attention in the past years. Mechanized verification techniques like IronFleet [21] and Verdi [41] were the first to address verification of state machine replication. Later, Disel [38] proposes a logic to make the reasoning less protocol-specific, with the tradeoff of proofs that use the entire message history. At the other end of the spectrum, model checking based techniques [2,4,20,23,24] are fully automated but more restricted regarding the protocols they apply to. In between, semi-automated verification techniques based on deductive verification like natural proofs [12], Ivy [36], and PSync [14] try to minimize the user input for similar benchmarks.

We propose a technique that reduces the verification of an asynchronous protocol to a synchronous one, which simplifies the verification task no matter which method is chosen. We verified the resulting synchronous protocols with deductive verification based on [14]. Our technique uses the notion of communication closure [17], which we believe is the essence of any explicit or implicit synchrony in the system. We formalized a more general notion of communication closure that allows jumping over rounds, which is a catch-up mechanism essential to resynchronize and ensure liveness. Previous reduction techniques focus on shared memory systems [16,27], in contrast we focus on message passing concurrency.

The closest approaches are the results in [4,24] and [2,20], which also explore the synchrony of the system. Compared to these approaches, our technique allows more general behaviors, e.g., reasoning about stable leaders is possible because communication closure includes (for the first time) unbounded jumps. Also, we reduce to a stronger synchronous model, a round-based one instead of a peer to peer one, where interleavings w.r.t. actions of other rounds are removed.

As future work, we will address the relation between communication closure and specific network assumptions, e.g., FIFO channels, and a current limitation of communication closure which is reacting on messages from the past. For instance, recovery protocols react to such messages.

References

1. Aminof, B., Rubin, S., Stoilkovska, I., Widder, J., Zuleger, F.: Parameterized model checking of synchronous distributed algorithms by abstraction. In: Dillig, I., Palsberg, J. (eds.) VMCAI 2018. LNCS, vol. 10747, pp. 1–24. Springer, Cham (2018). https://doi.org/10.1007/978-3-319-73721-8_1
2. Bakst, A., von Gleissenthall, K., Kici, R.G., Jhala, R.: Verifying distributed programs via canonical sequentialization. PACMPL **1**(OOPSLA), 110:1–110:27 (2017)
3. Bendersky, E.: pycparser. https://github.com/eliben/pycparser. Accessed 7 Nov 2018

4. Bouajjani, A., Enea, C., Ji, K., Qadeer, S.: On the completeness of verifying message passing programs under bounded asynchrony. In: Chockler, H., Weissenbacher, G. (eds.) CAV 2018, Part II. LNCS, vol. 10982, pp. 372–391. Springer, Cham (2018). https://doi.org/10.1007/978-3-319-96142-2_23

5. Chandra, T.D., Griesemer, R., Redstone, J.: Paxos made live: an engineering perspective. In: PODC, pp. 398–407 (2007)

6. Chandra, T.D., Toueg, S.: Unreliable failure detectors for reliable distributed systems. J. ACM **43**(2), 225–267 (1996)

7. Chaouch-Saad, M., Charron-Bost, B., Merz, S.: A reduction theorem for the verification of round-based distributed algorithms. In: Bournez, O., Potapov, I. (eds.) RP 2009. LNCS, vol. 5797, pp. 93–106. Springer, Heidelberg (2009). https://doi.org/10.1007/978-3-642-04420-5_10

8. Charron-Bost, B., Debrat, H., Merz, S.: Formal verification of consensus algorithms tolerating malicious faults. In: Défago, X., Petit, F., Villain, V. (eds.) SSS 2011. LNCS, vol. 6976, pp. 120–134. Springer, Heidelberg (2011). https://doi.org/10.1007/978-3-642-24550-3_11

9. Charron-Bost, B., Schiper, A.: The heard-of model: computing in distributed systems with benign faults. Distrib. Comput. **22**(1), 49–71 (2009)

10. Chou, C., Gafni, E.: Understanding and verifying distributed algorithms using stratified decomposition. In: PODC, pp. 44–65 (1988)

11. Debrat, H., Merz, S.: Verifying fault-tolerant distributed algorithms in the heard-of model. In: Archive of Formal Proofs 2012 (2012)

12. Desai, A., Garg, P., Madhusudan, P.: Natural proofs for asynchronous programs using almost-synchronous reductions. In: Proceedings of the 2014 ACM International Conference on Object Oriented Programming Systems Languages & Applications, OOPSLA 2014, Part of SPLASH 2014, Portland, OR, USA, 20–24 October 2014, pp. 709–725 (2014)

13. Drăgoi, C., Henzinger, T.A., Veith, H., Widder, J., Zufferey, D.: A logic-based framework for verifying consensus algorithms. In: McMillan, K.L., Rival, X. (eds.) VMCAI 2014. LNCS, vol. 8318, pp. 161–181. Springer, Heidelberg (2014). https://doi.org/10.1007/978-3-642-54013-4_10

14. Drăgoi, C., Henzinger, T.A., Zufferey, D.: PSync: a partially synchronous language for fault-tolerant distributed algorithms. In: POPL, pp. 400–415 (2016)

15. Dwork, C., Lynch, N., Stockmeyer, L.: Consensus in the presence of partial synchrony. JACM **35**(2), 288–323 (1988)

16. Elmas, T., Qadeer, S., Tasiran, S.: A calculus of atomic actions. In: Proceedings of the 36th ACM SIGPLAN-SIGACT Symposium on Principles of Programming Languages, POPL 2009, Savannah, GA, USA, 21–23 January 2009, pp. 2–15 (2009)

17. Elrad, T., Francez, N.: Decomposition of distributed programs into communication-closed layers. Sci. Comput. Program. **2**(3), 155–173 (1982)

18. Gafni, E.: Round-by-round fault detectors: unifying synchrony and asynchrony (extended abstract). In: PODC, pp. 143–152 (1998)

19. García-Pérez, Á., Gotsman, A., Meshman, Y., Sergey, I.: Paxos consensus, deconstructed and abstracted. In: Ahmed, A. (ed.) ESOP 2018. LNCS, vol. 10801, pp. 912–939. Springer, Cham (2018). https://doi.org/10.1007/978-3-319-89884-1_32

20. von Gleissenthall, K., Gökhan Kici, R., Bakst, A., Stefan, D., Jhala, R.: Pretend synchrony: synchronous verification of asynchronous distributed programs. PACMPL **3**(POPL), 59:1–59:30 (2019)

21. Hawblitzel, C., et al.: IronFleet: proving safety and liveness of practical distributed systems. Commun. ACM **60**(7), 83–92 (2017)

22. Jacobs, B., Smans, J., Piessens, F.: A quick tour of the verifast program verifier. In: Ueda, K. (ed.) APLAS 2010. LNCS, vol. 6461, pp. 304–311. Springer, Heidelberg (2010). https://doi.org/10.1007/978-3-642-17164-2_21

23. Konnov, I.V., Lazic, M., Veith, H., Widder, J.: A short counterexample property for safety and liveness verification of fault-tolerant distributed algorithms. In: POPL, pp. 719–734 (2017)

24. Kragl, B., Qadeer, S., Henzinger, T.A.: Synchronizing the asynchronous. In: CONCUR, pp. 21:1–21:17 (2018)

25. Lamport, L.: Generalized consensus and paxos. Technical report, March 2005. https://www.microsoft.com/en-us/research/publication/generalized-consensus-and-paxos/

26. Lesani, M., Bell, C.J., Chlipala, A.: Chapar: certified causally consistent distributed key-value stores. In: POPL, pp. 357–370 (2016)

27. Lipton, R.J.: Reduction: a method of proving properties of parallel programs. Commun. ACM 18(12), 717–721 (1975)

28. Lynch, N.: Distributed Algorithms. Morgan Kaufman, San Francisco (1996)

29. Marić, O., Sprenger, C., Basin, D.: Cutoff bounds for consensus algorithms. In: Majumdar, R., Kunčak, V. (eds.) CAV 2017, Part II. LNCS, vol. 10427, pp. 217–237. Springer, Cham (2017). https://doi.org/10.1007/978-3-319-63390-9_12

30. Mattern, F.: On the relativistic structure of logical time in distributed systems. In: Parallel and Distributed Algorithms, pp. 215–226 (1989)

31. Moraru, I., Andersen, D.G., Kaminsky, M.: There is more consensus in Egalitarian parliaments. In: SOSP, pp. 358–372 (2013)

32. Moses, Y., Rajsbaum, S.: A layered analysis of consensus. SIAM J. Comput. 31(4), 989–1021 (2002)

33. de Moura, L., Bjørner, N.: Z3: an efficient SMT solver. In: Ramakrishnan, C.R., Rehof, J. (eds.) TACAS 2008. LNCS, vol. 4963, pp. 337–340. Springer, Heidelberg (2008). https://doi.org/10.1007/978-3-540-78800-3_24

34. Oki, B.M., Liskov, B.: Viewstamped replication: a general primary copy. In: PODC, pp. 8–17 (1988)

35. Ongaro, D., Ousterhout, J.K.: In search of an understandable consensus algorithm. In: 2014 USENIX Annual Technical Conference, USENIX ATC 2014, pp. 305–319 (2014)

36. Padon, O., McMillan, K.L., Panda, A., Sagiv, M., Shoham, S.: Ivy: safety verification by interactive generalization. In: PLDI, pp. 614–630 (2016)

37. Rahli, V., Guaspari, D., Bickford, M., Constable, R.L.: Formal specification, verification, and implementation of fault-tolerant systems using EventML. ECEASST 72 (2015)

38. Sergey, I., Wilcox, J.R., Tatlock, Z.: Programming and proving with distributed protocols. PACMPL 2(POPL), 28:1–28:30 (2018)

39. Stoilkovska, I., Konnov, I., Widder, J., Zuleger, F.: Verifying safety of synchronous fault-tolerant algorithms by bounded model checking. In: Vojnar, T., Zhang, L. (eds.) TACAS 2019, Part II. LNCS, vol. 11428, pp. 357–374. Springer, Cham (2019). https://doi.org/10.1007/978-3-030-17465-1_20

40. Tsuchiya, T., Schiper, A.: Verification of consensus algorithms using satisfiability solving. Distrib. Comput. 23(5–6), 341–358 (2011)

41. Wilcox, J.R., et al.: Verdi: a framework for implementing and formally verifying distributed systems. In: PLDI, pp. 357–368 (2015)

42. Woos, D., Wilcox, J.R., Anton, S., Tatlock, Z., Ernst, M.D., Anderson, T.E.: Planning for change in a formal verification of the RAFT consensus protocol. In: CPP, pp. 154–165 (2016)

2

Checking Robustness Against Snapshot Isolation

Sidi Mohamed Beillahi$^{(\boxtimes)}$, Ahmed Bouajjani, and Constantin Enea

Université de Paris, IRIF, CNRS, Paris, France
{beillahi,abou,cenea}@irif.fr

Abstract. Transactional access to databases is an important abstraction allowing programmers to consider blocks of actions (transactions) as executing in isolation. The strongest consistency model is *serializability*, which ensures the atomicity abstraction of transactions executing over a sequentially consistent memory. Since ensuring serializability carries a significant penalty on availability, modern databases provide weaker consistency models, one of the most prominent being *snapshot isolation*. In general, the correctness of a program relying on serializable transactions may be broken when using weaker models. However, certain programs may also be insensitive to consistency relaxations, i.e., all their properties holding under serializability are preserved even when they are executed over a weak consistent database and without additional synchronization.

In this paper, we address the issue of verifying if a given program is *robust against snapshot isolation*, i.e., all its behaviors are serializable even if it is executed over a database ensuring snapshot isolation. We show that this verification problem is polynomial time reducible to a state reachability problem in transactional programs over a sequentially consistent shared memory. This reduction opens the door to the reuse of the classic verification technology for reasoning about weakly-consistent programs. In particular, we show that it can be used to derive a proof technique based on Lipton's reduction theory that allows to prove programs robust.

1 Introduction

Transactions simplify concurrent programming by enabling computations on shared data that are isolated from other concurrent computations and resilient to failures. Modern databases provide transactions in various forms corresponding to different tradeoffs between consistency and availability. The strongest consistency level is achieved with *serializable* transactions [21] whose outcome in concurrent executions is the same as if the transactions were executed atomically in some order. Since serializability carries a significant penalty on availability, modern databases often provide weaker consistency models, one of the most prominent being *snapshot isolation* (SI) [5]. Then, an important issue is to ensure that the level of consistency needed by a given program coincides with the one that is guaranteed by its infrastructure, i.e., the database it uses. One way to tackle this issue is to investigate the problem of checking *robustness* of programs against consistency relaxations: Given a program P and two consistency models S and W such that S is stronger than W, we say that P is robust for S against W if for every two implementations I_S and I_W of S and W respectively, the set of computations of P when running with I_S is the same as its set of computations when running with I_W. This means that P is not sensitive to the consistency relaxation from S to W, and therefore it is possible to reason about the behaviors of P assuming that it is running over S, and no additional synchronization is required when P runs over the weak model W such that it maintains all its properties satisfied with S.

In this paper, we address the problem of verifying robustness of transactional programs for serializability, against *snapshot isolation*. Under snapshot isolation, any transaction t reads values from a snapshot of the database taken at its start and t can commit only if no other committed transaction has written to a location that t wrote to, since t started. Robustness is a form of program equivalence between two versions of the same program, obtained using two semantics, one more permissive than the other. It ensures that this permissiveness has no effect on the program under consideration. The difficulty in checking robustness is to apprehend the extra behaviors due to the relaxed model w.r.t. the strong model. This requires a priori reasoning about complex order constraints between operations in arbitrarily long computations, which may need maintaining unbounded ordered structures, and make robustness checking hard or even undecidable.

Our first contribution is to show that verifying robustness of transactional programs against snapshot isolation can be reduced in polynomial time to the reachability problem in concurrent programs under sequential consistency (SC). This allows (1) to avoid explicit handling of the snapshots from where transactions read along computations (since this may imply memorizing unbounded information), and (2) to leverage available tools for verifying invariants/reachability problems on concurrent programs. This also implies that the robustness problem is decidable for finite-state programs, PSPACE-complete when the number of sites is fixed, and EXPSPACE-complete otherwise. This is the first result on the decidability and complexity of the problem of verifying robustness in the context of transactional programs. The problem of verifying robustness has been considered in the literature for several models, including eventual and causal consistency [6,10–12,20]. These works provide (over- or under-)approximate analyses for checking robustness, but none of them provides precise (sound and complete) algorithmic verification methods for solving this problem.

Based on this reduction, our second contribution is a proof methodology for establishing robustness which builds on Lipton's reduction theory [18]. We use the theory of movers to establish whether the relaxations allowed by SI are harmless, i.e., they don't introduce new behaviors compared to serializability.

We applied the proposed verification techniques on 10 challenging applications extracted from previous work [2,6,11,14,16,19,24]. These techniques were enough for proving or disproving the robustness of these applications.

Complete proofs and more details can be found in [4].

```
        p1:                   p2:
t1: [r1 = y //0 || t2: [r2 = x //0
       x = 1]               y = 1]
```

$$[r1 = y; x = 1] \quad\underset{\text{conflict}}{\overset{\text{conflict}}{\longrightarrow}}\quad [r2 = x; y = 1]$$

(a) Write Skew (WS).   (b) A WS execution trace.

Fig. 1. Examples of non-robust programs illustrating the difference between SI and serializability. *causal dependency* means that a read in a transaction obtains its value from a write in another transaction. *conflict* means that a write in a transaction is not visible to a read in another transaction, but it would affect the read value if it were visible. Here, *happens-before* is the union of the two.

2 Overview

In this section, we give an overview of our approach for checking robustness against snapshot isolation. While serializability enforces that transactions are atomic and conflicting transactions, i.e., which read or write to a common location, *cannot* commit concurrently, SI [5] allows that conflicting transactions commit in parallel as long as they don't contain a write-write conflict, i.e., write on a common location. Moreover, under SI, each transaction reads from a snapshot of the database taken at its start. These relaxations permit the "anomaly" known as Write Skew (WS) shown in Fig. 1a, where an anomaly is a program execution which is allowed by SI, but not by serializability. The execution of Write Skew under SI allows the reads of x and y to return 0 although this cannot happen under serializability. These values are possible since each transaction is executed locally (starting from the initial snapshot) without observing the writes of the other transaction.

Execution Trace. Our notion of program robustness is based on an abstract representation of executions called *trace*. Informally, an execution trace is a set of events, i.e., accesses to shared variables and transaction begin/commit events, along with several standard dependency relations between events recording the data-flow. The transitive closure of the union of all these dependency relations is called *happens-before*. An execution is an anomaly if the happens-before of its trace is cyclic. Figure 1b shows the happens-before of the Write Skew anomaly. Notice that the happens-before order is cyclic in both cases.

Semantically, every transaction execution involves two main events, the issue and the commit. The issue event corresponds to a sequence of reads and/or writes where the writes are visible only to the current transaction. We interpret it as a single event since a transaction starts with a database snapshot that it updates in isolation, without observing other concurrently executing transactions. The commit event is where the writes are propagated and made visible to all processes. Under serializability, the two events coincide, i.e., they are adjacent in the execution. Under SI, this is not the case and in between the issue and the commit of the same transaction, we may have issue/commit events from concurrent transactions. When a transaction commit does not occur immediately after its issue, we say that the underlying transaction is *delayed*. For example, the following execution of WS corresponds to the happens-before cycle in Fig. 1b where the write to x was committed after t_2 finished, hence, t_1 was delayed:

$begin(p_1, t_1)ld(p_1, t_1, y, 0)isu(p_1, t_1, x, 1)$ $com(p_1, t_1)$
$begin(p_2, t_2)ld(p_2, t_2, x, 0)isu(p_2, t_2, y, 1)com(p_2, t_2)$

Above, $begin(p_1, t_1)$ stands for starting a new transaction t_1 by process p_1, ld represents read (load) actions, while isu denotes write actions that are visible only to the current transaction (not yet committed). The writes performed during t_1 become visible to all processes once the commit event $com(p_1, t_1)$ takes place.

Reducing Robustness to SC Reachability. The above SI execution can be mimicked by an execution of the same program under serializability modulo an instrumentation that simulates the delayed transaction. The local writes in the issue event are simulated by writes to auxiliary registers and the commit event is replaced by copying the values from the auxiliary registers to the shared variables (actually, it is not necessary to simulate the commit event; we include it here for presentation reasons). The auxiliary registers are visible only to the delayed transaction. In order that the execution be an anomaly (i.e., not possible under serializability without the instrumentation) it is required that the issue and the commit events of the delayed transaction are linked by a chain of happens-before dependencies. For instance, the above execution for WS can be simulated by:

$begin(p_1, t_1)ld(p_1, t_1, y, 0)st(p_1, t_1, r_x, 1)$ $st(p_1, t_1, x, r_x)$
$begin(p_2, t_2)ld(p_2, t_2, x, 0)isu(p_2, t_2, y, 1)com(p_2, t_2)$

The write to x was delayed by storing the value in the auxiliary register r_x and the happens-before chain exists because the read on y that was done by t_1 is conflicting with the write on y from t_2 and the read on x by t_2 is conflicting with the write of x in the simulation of t_1's commit event. On the other hand, the following execution of Write-Skew without the read on y in t_1:

$begin(p_1, t_1)st(p_1, t_1, r_x, 1)$ $st(p_1, t_1, x, r_x)$
$begin(p_2, t_2)ld(p_2, t_2, x, 0)isu(p_2, t_2, y, 1)com(p_2, t_2)$

misses the conflict (happens-before dependency) between the issue event of t_1 and t_2. Therefore, the events of t_2 can be reordered to the left of t_1 and obtain an equivalent execution where $st(p_1, t_1, x, r_x)$ occurs immediately after $st(p_1, t_1, r_x, 1)$. In this case, t_1 is not anymore delayed and this execution is possible under serializability (without the instrumentation).

If the number of transactions to be delayed in order to expose an anomaly is unbounded, the instrumentation described above may need an unbounded number of auxiliary registers. This would make the verification problem hard or even undecidable. However, we show that it is actually enough to delay a single transaction, i.e., a program admits an anomaly under SI iff it admits an anomaly containing a single delayed transaction. This result implies that the number of auxiliary registers needed by the instrumentation is bounded by the number of program variables, and that checking robustness against SI can be reduced in linear time to a reachability problem under serializability (the reachability problem encodes the existence of the chain of happens-before dependencies mentioned above). The proof of this reduction relies on a nontrivial characterization of anomalies.

Proving Robustness Using Commutativity Dependency Graphs. Based on the reduction above, we also devise an approximated method for checking robustness based on the concept of mover in Lipton's reduction theory [18]. An event is a left (resp., right) mover if it commutes to the left (resp., right) of another event (from a different process) while preserving the computation. We use the notion of mover to characterize happens-before dependencies between transactions. Roughly, there exists a happens-before dependency between two transactions in some execution if one doesn't commute to the left/right of the other one. We define a commutativity dependency graph which summarizes the happens-before dependencies in all executions of a given program between transactions t as they appear in the program, transactions $t \setminus \{w\}$ where the writes of t are deactivated (i.e., their effects are not visible outside the transaction), and transactions $t \setminus \{r\}$ where the reads of t obtain non-deterministic values. The transactions $t \setminus \{w\}$ are used to simulate issue events of delayed transactions (where writes are not yet visible) while the transactions $t \setminus \{r\}$ are used to simulate commit events of delayed transactions (which only write to the shared memory). Two transactions a

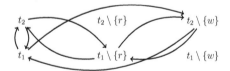

Fig. 2. Commutativity dependency graph of WS where the read of y is omitted.

and b are linked by an edge iff a *cannot* move to the right of b (or b cannot move to the left of a), or if they are related by the program order (i.e., issued in some order in the same process). Then a program is robust if for every transaction t, this graph *doesn't* contain a path from $t \setminus \{w\}$ to $t \setminus \{r\}$ formed of transactions that don't write to a variable that t writes to (the latter condition is enforced by SI since two concurrent transactions cannot commit at the same time when they write to a common variable). For example, Fig. 2 shows the commutativity dependency graph of the modified WS program where the read of y is removed from t_1. The fact that it doesn't contain any path like above implies that it is robust.

3   Programs

A program is parallel composition of *processes* distinguished using a set of identifiers $\mathbb{P}$. Each process is a sequence of *transactions* and each transaction is a
sequence of *labeled instructions*. Each transaction starts with a `begin` instruction and finishes with a `commit` instruction. Each other instruction is either an
assignment to a process-local *register* from a set $\mathbb{R}$ or to a *shared variable* from
a set $\mathbb{V}$, or an `assume` statement. The read/write assignments use values from a
data domain $\mathbb{D}$. An assignment to a register $\langle reg \rangle := \langle var \rangle$ is called a *read* of the
shared-variable $\langle var \rangle$ and an assignment to a shared variable $\langle var \rangle := \langle reg\text{-}expr \rangle$
is called a *write* to $\langle var \rangle$ ($\langle reg\text{-}expr \rangle$ is an expression over registers whose syntax we leave unspecified since it is irrelevant for our development). The `assume`
$\langle bexpr \rangle$ blocks the process if the Boolean expression $\langle bexpr \rangle$ over registers is
false. They are used to model conditionals as usual. We use `goto` statements
to model an arbitrary control-flow where the same label can be assigned to
multiple instructions and multiple `goto` statements can direct the control to the
same label which allows to mimic imperative constructs like loops and conditionals. To simplify the technical exposition, our syntax includes simple read/write
instructions. However, our results apply as well to instructions that include SQL
(select/update) queries. The experiments reported in Sect. 7 consider programs
with SQL based transactions.

   The semantics of a program under SI is defined as follows. The shared variables are stored in a central memory and each process keeps a replicated copy
of the central memory. A process starts a transaction by discarding its local
copy and fetching the values of the shared variables from the central memory.
When a process commits a transaction, it merges its local copy of the shared
variables with the one stored in the central memory in order to make its updates
visible to all processes. During the execution of a transaction, the process stores
the writes to shared variables only in its local copy and reads only from its
local copy. When a process merges its local copy with the centralized one, it is
required that there were no concurrent updates that occurred after the last fetch
from the central memory to a shared variable that was updated by the current
transaction. Otherwise, the transaction is aborted and its effects discarded.
   More precisely, the semantics of a program $\mathcal{P}$ under SI is defined as a labeled
transition system $[\mathcal{P}]_{\text{SI}}$ where transactions are labeled by the set of events

$$\mathbb{E}\text{v} = \{\text{begin}(p, t), \text{ld}(p, t, x, v), \text{isu}(p, t, x, v), \text{com}(p, t) : p \in \mathbb{P}, t \in \mathbb{T}^2, x \in \mathbb{V}, v \in \mathbb{D}\}$$

where `begin` and `com` label transitions corresponding to the start and the commit of a transaction, respectively. `isu` and `ld` label transitions corresponding to
writing, resp., reading, a shared variable during some transaction.

   An execution of program $\mathcal{P}$, under snapshot isolation, is a sequence of events
$ev_1 \cdot ev_2 \cdot \ldots$ corresponding to a run of $[\mathcal{P}]_{\text{CM}}$. The set of executions of $\mathcal{P}$ under
SI is denoted by $\mathbb{E}\text{x}_{\text{SI}}(\mathcal{P})$.

4   Robustness Against SI

A *trace* abstracts the order in which shared-variables are accessed inside a transaction and the order between transactions accessing different variables. Formally, the trace of an execution ρ is obtained by (1) replacing each sub-sequence of transitions in ρ corresponding to the same transaction, but excluding the com transition, with a single "macro-event" $\mathsf{isu}(p,t)$, and (2) adding several standard relations between these macro-events $\mathsf{isu}(p,t)$ and commit events $\mathsf{com}(p,t)$ to record the data-flow in ρ, e.g. which transaction wrote the value read by another transaction. The sequence of $\mathsf{isu}(p,t)$ and $\mathsf{com}(p,t)$ events obtained in the first step is called a *summary of* ρ. We say that a transaction t in ρ performs an *external read* of a variable x if ρ contains an event $\mathsf{ld}(p,t,x,v)$ which is not preceded by a write on x of t, i.e., an event $\mathsf{isu}(p,t,x,v)$. Also, we say that a transaction t *writes* a variable x if ρ contains an event $\mathsf{isu}(p,t,x,v)$, for some v.

The *trace* $\mathsf{tr}(\rho) = (\tau, \mathsf{PO}, \mathsf{WR}, \mathsf{WW}, \mathsf{RW}, \mathsf{STO})$ of an execution ρ consists of the summary τ of ρ along with the *program order* PO, which relates any two issue events $\mathsf{isu}(p,t)$ and $\mathsf{isu}(p,t')$ that occur in this order in τ, *write-read* relation WR (also called *read-from*), which relates any two events $\mathsf{com}(p,t)$ and $\mathsf{isu}(p',t')$ that occur in this order in τ such that t' performs an external read of x, and $\mathsf{com}(p,t)$ is the last event in τ before $\mathsf{isu}(p',t')$ that writes to x (to mark the variable x, we may use $\mathsf{WR}(x)$), the *write-write* order WW (also called store-order), which relates any two store events $\mathsf{com}(p,t)$ and $\mathsf{com}(p',t')$ that occur in this order in τ and write to the same variable x (to mark the variable x, we may use $\mathsf{WW}(x)$), the *read-write* relation RW (also called *conflict*), which relates any two events $\mathsf{isu}(p,t)$ and $\mathsf{com}(p',t')$ that occur in this order in τ such that t reads a value that is overwritten by t', and the *same-transaction* relation STO, which relates the issue event with the commit event of the same transaction. The read-write relation RW is formally defined as $\mathsf{RW}(x) = \mathsf{WR}^{-1}(x); \mathsf{WW}(x)$ (we use ; to denote the standard composition of relations) and $\mathsf{RW} = \bigcup_{x \in \mathbb{V}} \mathsf{RW}(x)$. If a transaction t reads the initial value of x then $\mathsf{RW}(x)$ relates $\mathsf{isu}(p,t)$ to $\mathsf{com}(p',t')$ of any other transaction t' which writes to x (i.e., $(\mathsf{isu}(p,t), \mathsf{com}(p',t')) \in \mathsf{RW}(x)$) (note that in the above relations, p and p' might designate the same process).

Since we reason about only one trace at a time, to simplify the writing, we may say that a trace is simply a sequence τ as above, keeping the relations PO, WR, WW, RW, and STO implicit. The set of traces of executions of a program $\mathcal{P}$ under SI is denoted by $\mathbb{Tr}(\mathcal{P})_{\mathsf{SI}}$.

Serializability Semantics. The semantics of a program under serializability can be defined using a transition system where the configurations keep a single shared-variable valuation (accessed by all processes) with the standard interpretation of read and write statements. Each transaction executes in isolation. Alternatively, the serializability semantics can be defined as a restriction of $[\mathcal{P}]_{\mathsf{SI}}$ to the set of executions where each transaction is *immediately* delivered when it starts, i.e., the start and commit time of transaction coincide $t.st = t.ct$. Such executions are called *serializable* and the set of serializable executions of a program $\mathcal{P}$ is denoted by $\mathbb{Ex}_{\mathsf{SER}}(\mathcal{P})$. The latter definition is easier to reason about when relating executions under snapshot isolation and serializability, respectively.

Serializable Trace. A trace tr is called *serializable* if it is the trace of a serializable execution. Let $\mathbb{T}r_{\mathsf{SER}}(\mathcal{P})$ denote the set of serializable traces. Given a serializable trace $tr = (\tau, \mathsf{PO}, \mathsf{WR}, \mathsf{WW}, \mathsf{RW}, \mathsf{STO})$ we have that every event $\mathsf{isu}(p, t)$ in τ is immediately followed by the corresponding $\mathsf{com}(p, t)$ event.

Happens Before Order. Since multiple executions may have the same trace, it is possible that an execution ρ produced by snapshot isolation has a serializable trace $tr(\rho)$ even though $\mathsf{isu}(p, t)$ events may not be immediately followed by $\mathsf{com}(p, t)$ actions. However, ρ would be equivalent, up to reordering of "independent" (or commutative) transitions, to a serializable execution. To check whether the trace of an execution is serializable, we introduce the *happens-before* relation on the events of a given trace as the transitive closure of the union of all the relations in the trace, i.e., $\mathsf{HB} = (\mathsf{PO} \cup \mathsf{WW} \cup \mathsf{WR} \cup \mathsf{RW} \cup \mathsf{STO})^+$.

Finally, the happens-before relation between events is extended to transactions as follows: a transaction t_1 *happens-before* another transaction $t_2 \neq t_1$ if the trace tr contains an event of transaction t_1 which happens-before an event of t_2. The happens-before relation between transactions is denoted by HB_t and called *transactional happens-before*. The following characterizes serializable traces.

Theorem 1 ([1,23]). *A trace tr is serializable iff HB_t is acyclic.*

A program is called robust if it produces the same set of traces as the serializability semantics.

Definition 1. *A program $\mathcal{P}$ is called* robust *against* SI *iff* $\mathbb{T}r_{\mathsf{SI}}(\mathcal{P}) = \mathbb{T}r_{\mathsf{SER}}(\mathcal{P})$.

Since $\mathbb{T}r_{\mathsf{SER}}(\mathcal{P}) \subseteq \mathbb{T}r_{\mathsf{X}}(\mathcal{P})$, the problem of checking robustness of a program $\mathcal{P}$ is reduced to checking whether there exists a trace $tr \in \mathbb{T}r_{\mathsf{SI}}(\mathcal{P}) \setminus \mathbb{T}r_{\mathsf{SER}}(\mathcal{P})$.

5 Reducing Robustness Against SI to SC Reachability

A trace which is not serializable must contain at least an issue and a commit event of the same transaction that don't occur one after the other even after reordering of "independent" events. Thus, there must exist an event that occur between the two which is related to both events via the happens-before relation, forbidding the issue and commit to be adjacent. Otherwise, we can build another trace with the same happens-before where events are reordered such that the issue is immediately followed by the corresponding commit. The latter is a serializable trace which contradicts the initial assumption. We define a program instrumentation which mimics the delay of transactions by doing the writes on auxiliary variables which are not visible to other transactions. After the delay of a transaction, we track happens-before dependencies until we execute a transaction that does a "read" on one of the variables that the delayed transaction writes to (this would expose a read-write dependency to the commit event of the delayed transaction). While tracking happens-before dependencies we cannot execute a transaction that writes to a variable that the delayed transaction writes to since SI forbids write-write conflicts between concurrent transactions.

Concretely, given a program $\mathcal{P}$, we define an instrumentation of $\mathcal{P}$ such that $\mathcal{P}$ is not robust against SI iff the instrumentation reaches an error state under serializability. The instrumentation uses auxiliary variables in order to simulate a *single* delayed transaction which we prove that it is enough for deciding robustness. Let $\mathsf{isu}(p, t)$ be the issue event of the only delayed transaction. The process p that delayed t is called the *Attacker*. When the attacker finishes executing the delayed transaction it stops. Other processes that execute transactions afterwards are called *Happens-Before Helpers*.

The instrumentation uses two copies of the set of shared variables in the original program to simulate the delayed transaction. We use primed variables x' to denote the second copy. Thus, when a process becomes the attacker, it will only write to the second copy that is not visible to other processes including the happens-before helpers. The writes made by the other processes including the happens-before helpers are made visible to all processes.

When the attacker delays the transaction t, it keeps track of the variables it accessed, in particular, it stores the name of one of the variables it writes to, x, it tracks every variable y that it reads from and every variable z that it writes to. When the attacker finishes executing t, and some other process wants to execute some other transaction, the underlying transaction must contain a write to a variable y that the attacker reads from. Also, the underlying transaction must not write to a variable that t writes to. We say that this process has joined happens-before helpers through the underlying transaction. While executing this transaction, we keep track of each variable that was accessed and the type of operation, whether it is a read or write. Afterward, in order for some other transaction to "join" the happens-before path, it must not write to a variable that t writes to so it does not violate the fact that SI forbids write-write conflicts, and it has to satisfy one of the following conditions in order to ensure the continuity of the happens-before dependencies: (1) the transaction is issued by a process that has already another transaction in the happens-before dependency (program order dependency), (2) the transaction is reading from a shared variable that was updated by previous transaction in the happens-before dependency (write-read dependency), (3) the transaction writes to a shared variable that was read by a previous transaction in the happens-before dependency (read-write dependency), or (4) the transaction writes to a shared variable that was updated by a previous transaction in the happens-before dependency (write-write dependency). We introduce a flag for each shared variable to mark the fact that the variable was read or written by a previous transaction.

Processes continue executing transactions as part of the chain of happens-before dependencies, until a transaction does a read on the variable x that t wrote to. In this case, we reached an error state which signals that we found a cycle in the transactional happens-before relation.

The instrumentation uses four varieties of flags: a) global flags (i.e., HB, $a_{\mathsf{tr_A}}$, $a_{\mathsf{st_A}}$), b) flags local to a process (i.e., $p.a$ and $p.hbh$), and c) flags per shared variable (i.e., $x.event$, $x.event'$, and $x.eventI$). We will explain the meaning of these flags along with the instrumentation. At the start of the execution, all flags are initialized to null ($\bot$).

Whether a process is an attacker or happens-before helper is not enforced syntactically by the instrumentation. It is set non-deterministically during the execution using some additional process-local flags. Each process chooses to set to true at most one of the flags $p.a$ and $p.hbh$, implying that the process becomes an attacker or happens-before helper, respectively. At most one process can be an attacker, i.e., set $p.a$ to true. In the following, we detail the instrumentation for read and write instructions of the attacker and happens-before helpers.

5.1 Instrumentation of the Attacker

Figure 3 lists the instrumentation of the write and read instructions of the attacker. Each process passes through an initial phase where it executes transactions that are visible immediately to all the other processes (i.e., they are not delayed), and then non-deterministically it can choose to delay a transaction at which point it sets the flag $a_{\mathsf{tr_A}}$ to true. During the delayed transaction it chooses non-deterministically a write instruction to a variable x and stores the name of this variable in the flag $a_{\mathsf{st_A}}$ (line (5)). The values written during the delayed transaction are stored in the primed variables and are visible only to the current transaction, in case the transaction reads its own writes. For example, given a variable z, all writes to z from the original program are transformed into writes to the primed version z' (line (3)). Each time, the attacker writes to z, it sets the flag $z.event' = 1$. This flag is used later by transactions from happens-before helpers to avoid writing to variables that the delayed transaction writes to.

$[\![\mathsf{l}_1\colon r := x;\ \mathsf{goto}\ \mathsf{l}_2;]\!]_\mathsf{A} =$
// **Read before the delayed transaction**
l_1: assume $a_{\mathsf{tr_A}} = \bot$; goto l_{x1};
l_{x1}: $r := x$; goto l_2;
// **Read in the delayed transaction**
l_1: assume $a_{\mathsf{tr_A}} \neq \bot \wedge p.a \neq \bot$; goto l_{x2};
l_{x2}: $r := x'$; goto l_{x3};
l_{x3}: $x.event := \mathsf{Id}$; goto l_{x4}; (1)
l_{x4}: assume $\mathsf{HB} = \bot$; goto l_{x5};
l_{x5}: $\mathsf{HB} := \mathsf{true}$; goto l_2; (2)
l_{x4}: assume $\mathsf{HB} \neq \bot$; goto l_2;

$[\![\mathsf{l}_1\colon x := e;\ \mathsf{goto}\ \mathsf{l}_2;]\!]_\mathsf{A} =$
// **Write before the delayed transaction**
l_1: assume $a_{\mathsf{tr_A}} = \bot$; goto l_{x1};
l_{x1}: $x := e$; goto l_2;
// **Write in the delayed transaction**
l_1: assume $a_{\mathsf{tr_A}} \neq \bot \wedge p.a \neq \bot$; goto l_{x2};
l_{x2}: $x' := e$; goto l_{x3}; (3)
l_{x3}: $x.event' := 1$; goto l_2; (4)
// **Special write in the delayed transaction**
l_1: assume $a_{\mathsf{st_A}} = x.event = \bot \wedge a_{\mathsf{tr_A}} \neq \bot$; goto l_{x4};
l_{x4}: $x' := e$; goto l_{x5};
l_{x5}: $a_{\mathsf{st_A}} := \text{`}x\text{`}$; goto l_{x6}; (5)
l_{x8}: $x.event' := 1$; goto l_2;

Fig. 3. Instrumentation of the Attacker. We use 'x'' to denote the name of the shared variable x.

A read on a variable, y, in the delayed transaction takes her value from the primed version, y'. In every read in the delayed transaction, we set the flag $y.event$ to ld (line (1)) to be used latter in order for a process to join the happens-before helpers. Afterward, the attacker starts the happens-before path, and it sets the variable HB to true (line (2)) to mark the start of the happens. When the flag HB is set to true the attacker stops executing new transactions.

5.2   Instrumentation of the Happens-Before Helpers

The remaining processes, which are not the attacker, can become a happens-before helper. Figure 4 lists the instrumentation of write and read instructions of a happens-before helper. In a first phase, each process executes the original code until the flag a_{tr_A} is set to true by the attacker. This flag signals the "creation" of the secondary copy of the shared-variables, which can be observed only by the attacker. At this point, the flag HB is set to true, and the happens-before helper process chooses non-deterministically a first transaction through which it wants to join the set of happens-before helpers, i.e., continue the happens-before dependency created by the existing happens-before helpers. When a process chooses a transaction, it makes a pledge (while executing the **begin** instruction) that during this transaction it will either read from a variable that was written to by another happens-before helper, write to a variable that was accessed (read or written) by another happens-before helper, or write to a variable that was read from in the delayed transaction. When the pledge is met, the process sets the flag $p.hbh$ to true (lines (7) and (11)). The execution is blocked if a process does not keep its pledge (i.e., the flag $p.hbh$ is null) at the end of the transaction. Note that the first process to join the happens-before helper has to execute a transaction t which writes to a variable that was read from in the delayed transaction since this is the only way to build a happens-before between t, and the delayed transaction (PO is not possible since t is not from the attacker, WR is not possible since t does not see the writes of the delayed transaction, and WW is not possible since t cannot write to a variable that the delayed transaction writes to). We use a flag $x.event$ for each variable x to record the type (read ld or write st) of the last access made by a happens-before helper (lines (8) and (10)). During the execution of a transaction that is part of the happens-before dependency, we must ensure that the transaction does not write to variable y where $y.even'$ is set to 1. Otherwise, the execution is blocked (line 9).

The happens-before helpers continue executing their instructions, until one of them reads from the shared variable x whose name was stored in a_{st_A}. This establishes a happens-before dependency between the delayed transaction and a "fictitious" store event corresponding to the delayed transaction that could be executed just after this read of x. The execution doesn't have to contain this store event explicitly since it is always enabled. Therefore, at the end of every transaction, the instrumentation checks whether the transaction read x. If it is the case, then the execution stops and goes to an error state to indicate that this is a robustness violation. Notice that after the attacker stops, the only processes that are executing transactions are happens-before helpers, which is justified since when a process is not from a happens-before helper it implies that we cannot construct a happens-before dependency between a transaction of this process and the delayed transaction which means that the two transactions commute which in turn implies that this process's transactions can be executed before executing the delayed transaction of the attacker.

5.3   Correctness

The role of a process in an execution is chosen non-deterministically at runtime. Therefore, the final instrumentation of a given program $\mathcal{P}$, denoted by $[\![\mathcal{P}]\!]$, is obtained by replacing each labeled instruction $\langle linst \rangle$ with the concatenation of the instrumentations corresponding to the attacker and the happens-before helpers, i.e., $[\![\langle linst \rangle]\!] ::= [\![\langle linst \rangle]\!]_{\mathsf{A}} \ [\![\langle linst \rangle]\!]_{\mathsf{HbH}}$

The following theorem states the correctness of the instrumentation.

Theorem 2. $\mathcal{P}$ *is not robust against* SI *iff* $[\![\mathcal{P}]\!]$ *reaches the error state.*

If a program is not robust, this implies that the execution of the program under SI results in a trace where the happens-before is cyclic. Which is possible only if the program contains at least one delayed transaction. In the proof of this theorem, we show that is sufficient to search for executions that contain a single delayed transaction.

Notice that in the instrumentation of the attacker, the delayed transaction must contain a read and write instructions on different variables. Also, the transactions of the happens-before helpers must not contain a write to a variable that the delayed transaction writes to. The following corollary states the complexity of checking robustness for finite-state programs[1] against snapshot isolation. It is a direct consequence of Theorem 2 and of previous results concerning the reachability problem in concurrent programs running over a sequentially-consistent memory, with a fixed [17] or parametric number of processes [22].

$[\![\mathsf{l}_1: r := x;\ \mathsf{goto}\ \mathsf{l}_2;]\!]_{\mathsf{HbH}} =$

// Read before the delayed transaction

$\mathsf{l}_1:$ assume $\mathsf{HB} =\bot\ \wedge p.a =\bot$; goto l_{x1};

$\mathsf{l}_{x1}:\ r := x;\ \mathsf{goto}\ \mathsf{l}_2;$

// Read after the delayed transaction

$\mathsf{l}_1:$ assume $\mathsf{HB} \neq\bot$; goto l_{x2};

$\mathsf{l}_{x2}:\ r := x;\ \mathsf{goto}\ \mathsf{l}_{x3};$

$\mathsf{l}_{x3}:$ assume $x.eventI = \mathsf{st} \wedge p.hbh =\bot$; goto l_{x4};

$\mathsf{l}_{x4}:\ p.hbh := \mathsf{true};\ \mathsf{goto}\ \mathsf{l}_2;$ (7)

$\mathsf{l}_{x3}:$ assume $x.event =\bot$; goto l_{x5};

$\mathsf{l}_{x5}:\ x.event := \mathsf{ld};\ \mathsf{goto}\ \mathsf{l}_2;$ (8)

$\mathsf{l}_{x3}:$ assume $x.event \neq\bot \vee p.hbh \neq\bot$; goto l_2;

$[\![\mathsf{l}_1: x := e;\ \mathsf{goto}\ \mathsf{l}_2;]\!]_{\mathsf{HbH}} =$

// Write before the delayed transaction

$\mathsf{l}_1:$ assume $\mathsf{HB} =\bot \wedge a_{\mathsf{tr}_{\mathsf{A}}} =\bot$; goto l_{x1};

$\mathsf{l}_{x1}:\ x := e;\ \mathsf{goto}\ \mathsf{l}_2;$

(6) **// Write after the delayed transaction**

$\mathsf{l}_1:$ assume $\mathsf{HB} \neq\bot \wedge p.a =\bot$; goto l_{x2};

$\mathsf{l}_{x2}:$ assume $x.event' \neq\bot$; assume false; (9)

$\mathsf{l}_{x2}:$ assume $x.event' =\bot$; goto l_{x3};

$\mathsf{l}_{x3}:\ x := e;\ \mathsf{goto}\ \mathsf{l}_{x4};$

$\mathsf{l}_{x4}:\ x.event := \mathsf{st};\ \mathsf{goto}\ \mathsf{l}_{x5};$ (10)

$\mathsf{l}_{x5}:$ assume $x.eventI \neq\bot \wedge p.hbh =\bot$; goto l_{x6};

$\mathsf{l}_{x6}:\ p.hbh := \mathsf{true};\ \mathsf{goto}\ \mathsf{l}_2;$ (11)

$\mathsf{l}_{x5}:$ assume $x.eventI =\bot \vee p.hbh \neq\bot$; goto l_2;

Fig. 4. Instrumentation of happens-before helpers.

---

[1] Programs with a bounded number of variables taking values from a bounded domain.

Corollary 1. *Checking robustness of finite-state programs against snapshot isolation is PSPACE-complete when the number of processes is fixed and EXPSPACE-complete, otherwise.*

The instrumentation can be extended to SQL (select/update) queries where a statement may include expressions over a finite/infinite set of variables, e.g., by manipulating a set of flags x.event for each statement instead of only one.

6   Proving Program Robustness

As a more pragmatic alternative to the reduction in the previous section, we define an approximated method for proving robustness which is inspired by Lipton's reduction theory [18].

Movers. Given an execution $\tau = ev_1 \cdot \ldots \cdot ev_n$ of a program $\mathcal{P}$ under serializability (where each event ev_i corresponds to executing an entire transaction), we say that the event ev_i *moves right (resp., left)* in τ if $ev_1 \cdot \ldots \cdot ev_{i-1} \cdot ev_{i+1} \cdot ev_i \cdot ev_{i+2} \cdot \ldots \cdot ev_n$ (resp., $ev_1 \cdot \ldots \cdot ev_{i-2} \cdot ev_i \cdot ev_{i-1} \cdot ev_{i+1} \cdot \ldots \cdot ev_n$) is also a valid execution of $\mathcal{P}$, the process of ev_i is different from the process of ev_{i+1} (resp., ev_{i-1}), and both executions reach to the same end state σ_n. For an execution τ, let $\mathsf{instOf}_\tau(ev_i)$ denote the transaction that generated the event ev_i. A transaction t of a program $\mathcal{P}$ is a *right (resp., left) mover* if for all executions τ of $\mathcal{P}$ under serializability, the event ev_i with $\mathsf{instOf}(ev_i) = t$ moves right (resp., left) in τ.

If a transaction t is not a right mover, then there must exist an execution τ of $\mathcal{P}$ under serializability and an event ev_i of τ with $\mathsf{instOf}(ev_i) = t$ that does not move right. This implies that there must exist another ev_{i+1} of τ which caused ev_i to not be a right mover. Since ev_i and ev_{i+1} do not commute, then this must be because of either a write-read, write-write, or a read-write dependency. If $t' = \mathsf{instOf}(ev_{i+1})$, we say that t is not a right mover because of t' and some dependency that is either write-read, write-write, or read-write. Notice that when t is not a right mover because of t' then t' is not a left mover because of t.

We define $\mathsf{M_{WR}}$ as a binary relation between transactions such that $(t, t') \in \mathsf{M_{WR}}$ when t is *not* a right mover because of t' and a write-read dependency. We define the relations $\mathsf{M_{WW}}$ and $\mathsf{M_{RW}}$ corresponding to write-write and read-write dependencies in a similar way.

Read/Write-free Transactions. Given a transaction t, we define $t \setminus \{r\}$ as a variation of t where all the reads from shared variables are replaced with non-deterministic reads, i.e., $\langle reg \rangle := \langle var \rangle$ statements are replaced with $\langle reg \rangle := \star$ where $\star$ denotes non-deterministic choice. We also define $t \setminus \{w\}$ as a variation of t where all the writes to shared variables in t are disabled. Intuitively, recalling the reduction to SC reachability in Sect. 5, $t \setminus \{w\}$ simulates the delay of a transaction by the Attacker, i.e., the writes are not made visible to other processes, and $t \setminus \{r\}$ approximates the commit of the delayed transaction which only applies a set of writes.

Commutativity Dependency Graph. Given a program $\mathcal{P}$, we define the commutativity dependency graph as a graph where vertices represent transactions and their read/write-free variations. Two vertices which correspond to the original transactions in $\mathcal{P}$ are related by a program order edge, if they belong to the same process. The other edges in this graph represent the "non-mover" relations $\mathsf{M_{WR}}$, $\mathsf{M_{WW}}$, and $\mathsf{M_{RW}}$.

Given a program $\mathcal{P}$, we say that the commutativity dependency graph of $\mathcal{P}$ contains a *non-mover cycle* if there exist a set of transactions $t_0, t_1, \ldots, t_n$ of $\mathcal{P}$ such that the following hold:

(a) $(t_0'', t_1) \in \mathsf{M_{RW}}$ where t_0'' is the write-free variation of t_0 and t_1 does not write to a variable that t_0 writes to;

(b) for all $i \in [1, n]$, $(t_i, t_{i+1}) \in (\mathsf{PO} \cup \mathsf{M_{WR}} \cup \mathsf{M_{WW}} \cup \mathsf{M_{RW}})$, t_i and t_{i+1} do not write to a shared variable that t_0 writes to;

(c) $(t_n, t_0') \in \mathsf{M_{RW}}$ where t_0' is the read-free variation of t_0 and t_n does not write to a variable that t_0 writes to.

A non-mover cycle approximates an execution of the instrumentation defined in Sect. 5 in between the moment that the Attacker delays a transaction t_0 (which here corresponds to the write-free variation t_0'') and the moment where t_0 gets committed (the read-free variation t_0').

The following theorem shows that the acyclicity of the commutativity dependency graph of a program implies the robustness of the program. Actually, the notion of robustness in this theorem relies on a slightly different notion of trace where store-order and write-order dependencies take into account values, i.e., store-order relates only writes writing different values and the write-order relates a read to the oldest write (w.r.t. execution order) writing its value. This relaxation helps in avoiding some harmless robustness violations due to for instance, two transactions writing the same value to some variable.

Theorem 3. *For a program $\mathcal{P}$, if the commutativity dependency graph of $\mathcal{P}$ does not contain non-mover cycles, then $\mathcal{P}$ is robust.*

7 Experiments

To test the applicability of our robustness checking algorithms, we have considered a benchmark of 10 applications extracted from the literature related to weakly consistent databases in general. A first set of applications are open source projects that were implemented to be run over the Cassandra database, extracted from [11]. The second set of applications is composed of: TPC-C [24], an on-line transaction processing benchmark widely used in the database community, Small-Bank, a simplified representation of a banking application [2], FusionTicket, a movie ticketing application [16], Auction, an online auction application [6], and Courseware, a course registration service extracted from [14,19].

Table 1. An overview of the analysis results. CDG stands for commutativity dependency graph. The columns PO and PT show the number of proof obligations and proof time in second, respectively. T stands for trivial when the application has only read-only transactions.

Application	#Transactions	Robustness	Reachability analysis		CDG Analysis	
			PO	PT	PO	PT
Auction	4	✓	70	0.3	20	0.5
Courseware	5	✗	59	0.37	na	na
FusionTicket	4	✓	72	0.3	34	0.5
SmallBank	5	✗	48	0.28	na	na
TPC-C	5	✓	54	0.7	82	3.7
Cassieq-Core	8	✓	173	0.55	104	2.9
Currency-Exchange	6	✓	88	0.35	26	3.5
PlayList	14	✓	99	4.63	236	7.3
RoomStore	5	✓	85	0.3	22	0.5
Shopping-Cart	4	✓	58	0.25	T	T

A first experiment concerns the reduction of robustness checking to SC reachability. For each application, we have constructed a client (i.e., a program composed of transactions defined within that application) with a fixed number of processes (at most 3) and a fixed number of transactions (between 3 and 7 transactions per process). We have encoded the instrumentation of this client, defined in Sect. 5, in the Boogie programming language [3] and used the Civl verifier [15] in order to check whether the assertions introduced by the instrumentation are violated (which would represent a robustness violation). Note that since clients are of fixed size, this requires no additional assertions/invariants (it is an instance of bounded model checking). The results are reported in Table 1. We have found two of the applications, Courseware and SmallBank, to *not* be robust against snapshot isolation. The violation in Courseware is caused by transactions RemoveCourse and EnrollStudent that execute concurrently, RemoveCourse removing a course that has no registered student and EnrollStudent registering a new student to the same course. We get an invalid state where a student is registered for a course that was removed. SmallBank's violation contains transactions Balance, TransactSaving, and WriteCheck. One process executes WriteCheck where it withdraws an amount from the checking account after checking that the sum of the checking and savings accounts is bigger than this amount. Concurrently, a second process executes TransactSaving where it withdraws an amount from the saving account after checking that it is smaller than the amount in the savings account. Afterwards, the second process checks the contents of both the checking and saving accounts. We get an invalid state where the sum of the checking and savings accounts is negative.

Since in the first experiment we consider fixed clients, the lack of assertion violations doesn't imply that the application is robust (this instantiation of our reduction can only be used to reveal robustness violations). Thus, a second experiment concerns the robustness proof method based on commutativity dependency graphs (Sect. 6). For the applications that were not identified as non-robust by the previous method, we have used Civl to construct their commutativity dependency graphs, i.e., identify the "non-mover" relations M_{WR}, M_{WW}, and M_{RW} (Civl allows to check whether some code fragment is a left/right mover). In all cases, the graph didn't contain non-mover cycles, which allows to conclude that the applications are robust.

The experiments show that our results can be used for finding violations and proving robustness, and that they apply to a large set of interesting examples. Note that the reduction to SC and the proof method based on commutativity dependency graphs are valid for programs with SQL (select/update) queries.

8 Related Work

Decidability and complexity of robustness has been investigated in the context of relaxed memory models such as TSO and Power [7,9,13]. Our work borrows some high-level principles from [7] which addresses the robustness against TSO. We reuse the high-level methodology of characterizing minimal violations according to some measure and defining reductions to SC reachability using a program instrumentation. Instantiating this methodology in our context is however very different, several fundamental differences being:

- SI and TSO admit different sets of relaxations and SI is a model of transactional databases.
- We use a different notion of measure: the measure in [7] counts the number of events between a write issue and a write commit while our notion of measure counts the number of delayed transactions. This is a first reason for which the proof techniques in [7] don't extend to our context.
- Transactions induce more complex traces: two transactions might be related by several dependency relations since each transaction may contain multiple reads and writes to different locations. In TSO, each action is a read or a write to some location, and two events are related by a single dependency relation. Also, the number of dependencies between two transactions depends on the execution since the set of reads/writes in a transaction evolves dynamically.

Other works [9,13] define decision procedures which are based on the theory of regular languages and do not extend to infinite-state programs like in our case.

As far as we know, our work provides the first results concerning the decidability and the complexity of robustness checking in the context of transactions. The existing work on the verification of robustness for transactional programs

```
p1:                  p2:
t1: [ if (x > y)     t2: [ if (y > x)
      r1 = x - y ||        r2 = y - x
      x = y ]              y = x ]
```

Fig. 5. A robust program.

provide either over- or under-approximate analyses. Our commutativity dependency graphs are similar to the static dependency graphs used in [6,10–12], but they are more precise, i.e., reducing the number of false alarms. The static dependency graphs record happens-before dependencies between transactions based on a syntactic approximation of the variables accessed by a transaction. For example, our techniques are able to prove that the program in Fig. 5 is robust, while this is not possible using static dependency graphs. The latter would contain a dependency from transaction t_1 to t_2 and one from t_2 to t_1 just because syntactically, each of the two transactions reads both variables and may write to one of them. Our dependency graphs take into account the semantics of these transactions and do not include this happens-before cycle. Other over- and under-approximate analyses have been proposed in [20]. They are based on encoding executions into first order logic, bounded-model checking for the under-approximate analysis, and a sound check for proving a cut-off bound on the size of the happens-before cycles possible in the executions of a program, for the over-approximate analysis. The latter is strictly less precise than our method based on commutativity dependency graphs. For instance, extending the TPC-C application with additional transactions will make the method in [20] fail while our method will succeed in proving robustness (the three transactions are for adding a new product, adding a new warehouse based on the number of customers and warehouses, and adding a new customer, respectively).

Finally, the idea of using Lipton's reduction theory for checking robustness has been also used in the context of the TSO memory model [8], but the techniques are completely different, e.g., the TSO technique considers each update in isolation and doesn't consider non-mover cycles like in our commutativity dependency graphs.

References

1. Adya, A.: Weak consistency: a generalized theory and optimistic implementations for distributed transactions. Ph.D. thesis (1999)
2. Alomari, M., Cahill, M.J., Fekete, A., Röhm, U.: The cost of serializability on platforms that use snapshot isolation. In: Alonso, G., Blakeley, J.A., Chen, A.L.P. (eds.) Proceedings of the 24th International Conference on Data Engineering, ICDE 2008, 7–12 April 2008, Cancún, Mexico, pp. 576–585. IEEE Computer Society (2008)
3. Barnett, M., Chang, B.-Y.E., DeLine, R., Jacobs, B., Leino, K.R.M.: Boogie: a modular reusable verifier for object-oriented programs. In: de Boer, F.S., Bonsangue, M.M., Graf, S., de Roever, W.-P. (eds.) FMCO 2005. LNCS, vol. 4111, pp. 364–387. Springer, Heidelberg (2006). https://doi.org/10.1007/11804192_17
4. Beillahi, S.M., Bouajjani, A., Enea, C.: Checking robustness against snapshot isolation. CoRR, abs/1905.08406 (2019)
5. Berenson, H., Bernstein, P.A., Gray, J., Melton, J., O'Neil, E.J., O'Neil, P.E.: A critique of ANSI SQL isolation levels. In: Carey, M.J., Schneider, D.A. (eds.) Proceedings of the 1995 ACM SIGMOD International Conference on Management of Data, San Jose, California, USA, 22–25 May 1995, pp. 1–10. ACM Press (1995)

6. Bernardi, G., Gotsman, A.: Robustness against consistency models with atomic visibility. In: Desharnais, J., Jagadeesan, R. (eds.) 27th International Conference on Concurrency Theory, CONCUR 2016, 23–26 August 2016, Québec City, Canada. LIPIcs, vol. 59, pp. 7:1–7:15. Schloss Dagstuhl - Leibniz-Zentrum fuer Informatik (2016)
7. Bouajjani, A., Derevenetc, E., Meyer, R.: Checking and enforcing robustness against TSO. In: Felleisen, M., Gardner, P. (eds.) ESOP 2013. LNCS, vol. 7792, pp. 533–553. Springer, Heidelberg (2013). https://doi.org/10.1007/978-3-642-37036-6_29
8. Bouajjani, A., Enea, C., Mutluergil, S.O., Tasiran, S.: Reasoning about TSO programs using reduction and abstraction. In: Chockler, H., Weissenbacher, G. (eds.) CAV 2018. LNCS, vol. 10982, pp. 336–353. Springer, Cham (2018). https://doi.org/10.1007/978-3-319-96142-2_21
9. Bouajjani, A., Meyer, R., Möhlmann, E.: Deciding robustness against total store ordering. In: Aceto, L., Henzinger, M., Sgall, J. (eds.) ICALP 2011. LNCS, vol. 6756, pp. 428–440. Springer, Heidelberg (2011). https://doi.org/10.1007/978-3-642-22012-8_34
10. Brutschy, L., Dimitrov, D., Müller, P., Vechev, M.T.: Serializability for eventual consistency: criterion, analysis, and applications. In: Castagna, G., Gordon, A.D. (eds.) Proceedings of the 44th ACM SIGPLAN Symposium on Principles of Programming Languages, POPL 2017, Paris, France, 18–20 January 2017, pp. 458–472. ACM (2017)
11. Brutschy, L., Dimitrov, D., Müller, P., Vechev, M.T.: Static serializability analysis for causal consistency. In: Foster, J.S., Grossman, D. (eds.) Proceedings of the 39th ACM SIGPLAN Conference on Programming Language Design and Implementation, PLDI 2018, Philadelphia, PA, USA, 18–22 June 2018, pp. 90–104. ACM (2018)
12. Cerone, A., Gotsman, A.: Analysing snapshot isolation. J. ACM 65(2), 11:1–11:41 (2018)
13. Derevenetc, E., Meyer, R.: Robustness against power is PSpace-complete. In: Esparza, J., Fraigniaud, P., Husfeldt, T., Koutsoupias, E. (eds.) ICALP 2014. LNCS, vol. 8573, pp. 158–170. Springer, Heidelberg (2014). https://doi.org/10.1007/978-3-662-43951-7_14
14. Gotsman, A., Yang, H., Ferreira, C., Najafzadeh, M., Shapiro, M.: 'cause i'm strong enough: reasoning about consistency choices in distributed systems. In: Bodík, R., Majumdar, R. (eds.) Proceedings of the 43rd Annual ACM SIGPLAN-SIGACT Symposium on Principles of Programming Languages, POPL 2016, St. Petersburg, FL, USA, 20–22 January 2016, pp. 371–384. ACM (2016)
15. Hawblitzel, C., Petrank, E., Qadeer, S., Tasiran, S.: Automated and modular refinement reasoning for concurrent programs. In: Kroening, D., Păsăreanu, C.S. (eds.) CAV 2015. LNCS, vol. 9207, pp. 449–465. Springer, Cham (2015). https://doi.org/10.1007/978-3-319-21668-3_26
16. Holt, B., Bornholt, J., Zhang, I., Ports, D.R.K., Oskin, M., Ceze, L.: Disciplined inconsistency with consistency types. In: Aguilera, M.K., Cooper, B., Diao, Y. (eds.) Proceedings of the Seventh ACM Symposium on Cloud Computing, Santa Clara, CA, USA, 5–7 October 2016, pp. 279–293. ACM (2016)
17. Kozen, D.: Lower bounds for natural proof systems. In: 18th Annual Symposium on Foundations of Computer Science, Providence, Rhode Island, USA, October 31–1 November 1977, pp. 254–266. IEEE Computer Society (1977)
18. Lipton, R.J.: Reduction: a method of proving properties of parallel programs. Commun. ACM 18(12), 717–721 (1975)

19. Nagar, K., Jagannathan, S.: Automated detection of serializability violations under weak consistency. In: Schewe, S., Zhang, L. (eds.) 29th International Conference on Concurrency Theory, CONCUR 2018, 4–7 September 2018, Beijing, China. LIPIcs, vol. 118, pp. 41:1–41:18. Schloss Dagstuhl - Leibniz-Zentrum fuer Informatik (2018)
20. Nagar, K., Jagannathan, S.: Automatic detection of serializability violations under weak consistency. In: 29th International Conference on Concurrency Theory (CONCUR 2018), September 2018
21. Papadimitriou, C.H.: The serializability of concurrent database updates. J. ACM **26**(4), 631–653 (1979)
22. Rackoff, C.: The covering and boundedness problems for vector addition systems. Theoret. Comput. Sci. **6**, 223–231 (1978)
23. Shasha, D.E., Snir, M.: Efficient and correct execution of parallel programs that share memory. ACM Trans. Program. Lang. Syst. **10**(2), 282–312 (1988)
24. TPC: Technical report, Transaction Processing Performance Council, February 2010. http://www.tpc.org/tpc_documents_current_versions/pdf/tpc-c_v5.11.0.pdf

3

On the Complexity of Checking Consistency for Replicated Data Types

Ranadeep Biswas[1]([✉]), Michael Emmi[2], and Constantin Enea[1]

[1] Université de Paris, IRIF, CNRS, 75013 Paris, France
{ranadeep,cenea}@irif.fr
[2] SRI International, New York, NY, USA
michael.emmi@sri.com

Abstract. Recent distributed systems have introduced variations of familiar abstract data types (ADTs) like counters, registers, flags, and sets, that provide high availability and partition tolerance. These *conflict-free replicated data types* (CRDTs) utilize mechanisms to resolve the effects of concurrent updates to replicated data. Naturally these objects weaken their consistency guarantees to achieve availability and partition-tolerance, and various notions of *weak consistency* capture those guarantees.

In this work we study the tractability of CRDT-consistency checking. To capture guarantees precisely, and facilitate symbolic reasoning, we propose novel logical characterizations. By developing novel reductions from propositional satisfiability problems, and novel consistency-checking algorithms, we discover both positive and negative results. In particular, we show intractability for replicated flags, sets, counters, and registers, yet tractability for replicated growable arrays. Furthermore, we demonstrate that tractability can be redeemed for registers when each value is written at most once, for counters when the number of replicas is fixed, and for sets and flags when the number of replicas and variables is fixed.

1 Introduction

Recent distributed systems have introduced variations of familiar abstract data types (ADTs) like counters, registers, flags, and sets, that provide high availability and partition tolerance. These *conflict-free replicated data types* (CRDTs) [33] efficiently resolve the effects of concurrent updates to replicated data. Naturally they weaken consistency guarantees to achieve availability and partition-tolerance, and various notions of *weak consistency* capture such guarantees [8,11,29,35,36].

In this work we study the tractability of CRDT consistency checking; Fig. 1 summarizes our results. In particular, we consider *runtime verification*: deciding

Data Types	Complexity
Add-Wins Set, Remove-Wins Set	NP-complete
Enable-Wins Flag, Disable-Wins Flag	NP-complete
Sets & Flags — with bounded domains	PTIME
Last-Writer-Wins Register (LWW)	NP-complete
Multi-Value Register (MVR)	NP-complete
Registers – with unique values	PTIME
Replicated Counters	NP-complete
Counters – with bounded replicas	PTIME
Replicated Growable Array (RGA)	PTIME

Fig. 1. The complexity of consistency checking for various replicated data types. We demonstrate intractability and tractability results in Sects. 3 and 4, respectively.

whether a given execution of a CRDT is consistent with its ADT specification. This problem is particularly relevant as distributed-system testing tools like Jepsen [25] are appearing; without efficient, general consistency-checking algorithms, such tools could be limited to specialized classes of errors like node crashes.

Our setting captures executions across a set of replicas as per-replica sequences of operations called *histories*. Roughly speaking, a history is *consistent* so long as each operation's return value can be justified according to the operations that its replica has observed so far. In the setting of CRDTs, the determination of a replica's observations is essentially an implementation choice: replicas are only obliged to observe their own operations, and the predecessors of those it has already observed. This relatively-weak constraint on replicas' observations makes the CRDT consistency checking problem unique.

Our study proceeds in three parts. First, to precisely characterize the consistency of various CRDTs, and facilitate symbolic reasoning, we develop novel logical characterizations to capture their guarantees. Our logical models are built on a notion of *abstract execution*, which relates the operations of a given history with three separate relations: a *read-from* relation, governing the observations from which a given operation constitutes its own return value; a *happens-before* relation, capturing the causal relationships among operations; and a *linearization* relation, capturing any necessary arbitration among non-commutative effects which are executed concurrently, e.g., following a *last-writer-wins* policy. Accordingly, we capture data type specifications with logical axioms interpreted over the read-from, happens-before, and linearization relations of abstract executions, reducing the consistency problem to: does there exist an abstract execution over the given history which satisfies the axioms of the given data type?

Second, we demonstrate the intractability of several replicated data types by reduction from propositional satisfiability (SAT) problems. In particular, we consider the 1-in-3 SAT problem [19], which asks for a truth assignment to the variables of a given set of clauses such that exactly one literal per clause is assigned true. Our reductions essentially simulate the existential choice of a truth assignment with the existential choice of the read-from and happens-before relations of an abstract execution. For a given 1-in-3 SAT instance, we construct a history of replicas obeying carefully-tailored synchronization protocols, which is consistent exactly when the corresponding SAT instance is positive.

Third, we develop tractable consistency-checking algorithms for individual data types and special cases: replicated growing arrays; multi-value and last-writer-wins registers, when each value is written only once; counters, when replicas are bounded; and sets and flags, when their sizes are also bounded. While the algorithms for each case are tailored to the algebraic properties of the data types they handle, they essentially all function by constructing abstract executions incrementally, processing replicas' operations in prefix order.

The remainder of this article is organized around our three key contributions:

1. We develop novel logical characterizations of consistency for the replicated register, flag, set, counter, and array data types (Sect. 2);
2. We develop novel reductions from propositional satisfiability problems to consistency checking to demonstrate intractability for replicated flags, sets, counters, and registers (Sect. 3); and
3. We develop tractable consistency-checking algorithms for replicated growable arrays, registers, when written values are unique, counters, when replicas are bounded, and sets and flags, when their sizes are also bounded (Sects. 4–6).

Section 7 overviews related work, and Sect. 8 concludes.

2 A Logical Characterization of Replicated Data Types

In this section we describe an axiomatic framework for defining the semantics of replicated data types. We consider a set of method names $\mathbb{M}$, and that each method $\mathsf{m} \in \mathbb{M}$ has a number of arguments and a return value sampled from a data domain $\mathbb{D}$. We will use operation labels of the form $\mathsf{m}(a) \overset{i}{\Rightarrow} b$ to represent the call of a method $\mathsf{m} \in \mathbb{M}$, with argument $a \in \mathbb{D}$, and resulting in the value $b \in \mathbb{D}$. Since there might be multiple calls to the same method with the same arguments and result, labels are tagged with a unique identifier i. We will ignore identifiers when unambiguous.

The interaction between a data type implementation and a client is represented by a *history* $h = \langle \mathsf{Op}, \mathsf{ro} \rangle$ which consists of a set of operation labels Op and a partial *replica order* ro ordering operations issued by the client on the same replica. Usually, ro is a union of sequences, each sequence representing the operations issued on the same replica, and the *width* of ro, i.e., the maximum number of mutually-unordered operations, gives the number of replicas in a given history.

To characterize the set of histories $h = \langle \mathsf{Op}, \mathsf{ro} \rangle$ admitted by a certain replicated data type, we use *abstract executions* $e = \langle \mathsf{rf}, \mathsf{hb}, \mathsf{lin} \rangle$, which include:

- a *read-from* binary relation rf over operations in Op, which identifies the set of updates needed to "explain" a certain return value, e.g., a write operation explaining the return value of a read,
- a strict partial *happens-before* order hb, which includes ro and rf, representing the causality constraints in an execution, and
- a strict total *linearization* order lin, which includes hb, used to model conflict resolution policies based on timestamps.

In this work, we consider replicated data types which satisfy *causal consistency* [26], i.e., updates which are related by cause and effect relations are observed by all replicas in the same order. This follows from the fact that the happens-before order is constrained to be a partial order, and thus transitive (other forms of weak consistency don't pose this constraint). Some of the replicated data types we consider in this paper do *not* consider resolution policies based on timestamps and in those cases, the linearization order can be ignored.

 READFROM(R)

$\forall o_1, o_2.\ \mathsf{rf}(o_1, o_2) \Rightarrow R(o_1, o_2)$

READFROMMAXIMAL(R)

$\forall o_1, o_2, o_3.\ \mathsf{rf}(o_1, o_2) \wedge R(o_3, o_2) \Rightarrow$
$\neg \mathsf{hb}(o_1, o_3) \vee \neg \mathsf{hb}(o_3, o_2)$

READALLMAXIMALS(R)

$\forall o_1, o_2.\ \mathsf{hb}(o_1, o_2) \wedge R(o_1, o_2)$
$\Rightarrow \exists o_3.\ \mathsf{hb}^*(o_1, o_3) \wedge \mathsf{rf}(o_3, o_2)$

CLOSEDRF(R)

$\forall o_1, o_2, o_3.\ R(o_1, o_2) \wedge \mathsf{hb}(o_1, o_3)$
$\wedge\ \mathsf{rf}(o_3, o_2) \Rightarrow \mathsf{rf}(o_1, o_2)$

RETVALSET(X, v, Y)

$\forall o_1.\ \mathsf{meth}(o_1) = X \wedge \mathsf{ret}(o_1) = v$
$\Leftrightarrow \exists o_2.\ \mathsf{rf}(o_2, o_1) \wedge \mathsf{meth}(o_2) = Y$
$\wedge\ \mathsf{arg}(o_1) = \mathsf{arg}(o_2)$

RETVALCOUNTER

$\forall o_1.\ \mathsf{meth}(o_1) = \mathsf{read}$
$\Rightarrow \mathsf{ret}(o_1) = |\{o_2 : \mathsf{meth}(o_2) = \mathsf{inc} \wedge \mathsf{rf}(o_2, o_1)\}|$
$-\ |\{o_2 : \mathsf{meth}(o_2) = \mathsf{dec} \wedge \mathsf{rf}(o_2, o_1)\}|$

LINLWW

$\forall o_1, o_2, o_3.\ \mathsf{rf}(o_1, o_2) \wedge \mathsf{meth}(o_3) = \mathsf{write}$
$\wedge\ \mathsf{arg}_1(o_3) = \mathsf{arg}(o_2) \wedge \mathsf{hb}(o_3, o_2) \Rightarrow \mathsf{lin}(o_3, o_1)$

RETVALREG

$\forall o_1, v.\mathsf{meth}(o_1) = \mathsf{read} \wedge v \in \mathsf{ret}(o_1) \Rightarrow \exists! o_2.\mathsf{rf}(o_2, o_1) \wedge \mathsf{meth}(o_2) = \mathsf{write} \wedge \mathsf{arg}_2(o_2) = v$

Fig. 2. The axiomatic semantics of replicated data types. Quantified variables are implicitly distinct, and $\exists! o$ denotes the existence of a unique operation o.

A *replicated data type* is defined by a set of first-order axioms Φ characterizing the relations in an abstract execution. A history h is *admitted* by a data type when there exists an abstract execution e such that $\langle h, e \rangle \models \Phi$. The satisfaction relation $\models$ is defined as usual in first order logic. The *admissibility problem* is the problem of checking whether a history h is admitted by a given data type.

In the following, we define the replicated data types with respect to which we study the complexity of the admissibility problem. The axioms used to define them are listed in Figs. 2 and 3. These axioms use the function symbols meth-od, arg-ument, and ret-urn interpreted over operation labels, whose semantics is self-explanatory.

2.1 Replicated Sets and Flags

The Add-Wins Set and Remove-Wins Set [34] are two implementations of a replicated set with operations $add(x)$, $remove(x)$, and $contains(x)$ for adding, removing, and checking membership of an element x. Although the meaning of these methods is self-evident from their names, the result of conflicting concurrent operations is not evident. When concurrent $add(x)$ and $remove(x)$ operations are delivered to a certain replica, the Add-Wins Set chooses to keep the element x in the set, so every subsequent invocation of $contains(x)$ on this replica returns $true$, while the Remove-Wins Set makes the dual choice of removing x from the set.

The formal definition of their semantics uses abstract executions where the read-from relation associates sets of $add(x)$ and $remove(x)$ operations to $contains(x)$ operations. Therefore, the predicate $ReadOk(o_1, o_2)$ is defined by

$$meth(o_1) \in \{add, remove\} \land meth(o_2) = contains \land arg(o_1) = arg(o_2)$$

and the Add-Wins Set is defined by the following set of axioms:

$$\textsc{ReadFrom}(\mathsf{ReadOk}) \land \textsc{ReadFromMaximal}(\mathsf{ReadOk}) \land$$
$$\textsc{ReadAllMaximals}(\mathsf{ReadOk}) \land \textsc{RetvalSet}(contains, true, add)$$

ReadFromMaximal says that every operation read by a $contains(x)$ is maximal among its hb-predecessors that add or remove x while ReadAllMaximals says that all such maximal hb-predecessors are read. The RetvalSet instantiation ensures that a $contains(x)$ returns $true$ iff it reads-from at least one $add(x)$.

The definition of the Remove-Wins Set is similar, except for the parameters of RetvalSet, which become RetvalSet(contains, $false$, remove), i.e., a $contains(x)$ returns $false$ iff it reads-from at least one $remove(x)$.

The Enable-Wins Flag and Disable-Wins Flag are implementations of a set of flags with operations: $enable(x)$, $disable(x)$, and $read(x)$, where $enable(x)$ turns the flag x to true, $disable(x)$ turns x to false, while $read(x)$ returns the state of the flag x. Their semantics is similar to the Add-Wins Set and Remove-Wins Set, respectively, where $enable(x)$, $disable(x)$, and $read(x)$ play the role of $add(x)$, $remove(x)$, and $contains(x)$, respectively. Their axioms are defined as above.

2.2 Replicated Registers

We consider two variations of replicated registers called Multi-Value Register (MVR) and Last-Writer-Wins Register (LWW) [34] which maintain a set of registers and provide $write(x,v)$ operations for writing a value v on a register x and $read(x)$ operations for reading the content of a register x (the domain of values is kept unspecified since it is irrelevant). While a $read(x)$ operation of

MVR returns *all* the values written by concurrent writes which are maximal among its happens-before predecessors, therefore, leaving the responsibility for solving conflicts between concurrent writes to the client, a read(x) operation of LWW returns a single value chosen using a conflict-resolution policy based on timestamps. Each written value is associated to a timestamp, and a read operation returns the most recent value w.r.t. the timestamps. This order between timestamps is modeled using the linearization order of an abstract execution.

Therefore, the predicate ReadOk(o_1, o_2) is defined by

$$\mathsf{meth}(o_1) = \mathsf{write} \wedge \mathsf{meth}(o_2) = \mathsf{read} \wedge \mathsf{arg}_1(o_1) = \mathsf{arg}(o_2) \wedge \mathsf{arg}_2(o_1) \in \mathsf{ret}(o_2)$$

(we use $\mathsf{arg}_1(o_1)$ to denote the first argument of a write operation, i.e., the register name, and $\mathsf{arg}_2(o_1)$ to denote its second argument, i.e., the written value) and the MVR is defined by the following set of axioms:

$$\textsc{ReadFrom}(\mathsf{ReadOk}) \wedge \textsc{ReadFromMaximal}(\mathsf{ReadOk}) \wedge$$
$$\textsc{ReadAllMaximals}(\mathsf{ReadOk}) \wedge \textsc{RetvalReg}$$

where RetvalReg ensures that a read(x) operation reads from a write(x,v) operation, for each value v in the set of returned values[1].

LWW is obtained from the definition of MVR by replacing ReadAllMaximals with the axiom LinLWW which ensures that every write$(x,\_)$ operation which happens-before a read(x) operation is linearized before the write$(x,\_)$ operation from where the read(x) takes its value (when these two write operations are different). This definition of LWW is inspired by the "bad-pattern" characterization in [6], corresponding to their causal convergence criterion.

2.3 Replicated Counters

The replicated counter datatype [34] maintains a set of counters interpreted as integers (the counters can become negative). This datatype provides operations inc(x) and dec(x) for incrementing and decrementing a counter x, and read(x) operations to read the value of the counter x. The semantics of the replicated counter is quite standard: a read(x) operation returns the value computed as the difference between the number of inc(x) operations and dec(x) operations among its happens-before predecessors. The axioms defined below will enforce the fact that a read(x) operation reads-from all its happens-before predecessors which are inc(x) or dec(x) operations.

Therefore, the predicate ReadOk(o_1, o_2) is defined by

$$\mathsf{meth}(o_1) \in \{\mathsf{inc}, \mathsf{dec}\} \wedge \mathsf{meth}(o_2) = \mathsf{read} \wedge \mathsf{arg}(o_1) = \mathsf{arg}(o_2)$$

and the replicated counter is defined by the following set of axioms:

$$\textsc{ReadFrom}(\mathsf{ReadOk}) \wedge \textsc{ClosedRF}(\mathsf{ReadOk}) \wedge \textsc{RetvalCounter}.$$

---

[1] For simplicity, we assume that every history contains a set of write operations writing the initial values of variables, which precede every other operation in replica order.

RᴇᴀᴅFʀᴏᴍRGA

$\forall o_2.\ \text{meth}(o_2) = \text{addAfter} \Rightarrow \text{arg}_1(o_2) = \circ\ \lor$
$$\exists o_1.\ \text{meth}(o_1) = \text{addAfter} \land \text{arg}_2(o_1) = \text{arg}_1(o_2) \land \text{rf}(o_1, o_2)$$
$\land\ \text{meth}(o_2) = \text{remove} \Rightarrow \exists o_1.\ \text{meth}(o_1) = \text{addAfter} \land \text{arg}_2(o_1) = \text{arg}(o_2) \land \text{rf}(o_1, o_2)$
$\land\ \text{meth}(o_2) = \text{read} \Rightarrow \forall v \in \text{ret}(o_2)\ \exists o_1.\text{meth}(o_1) = \text{addAfter} \land \text{arg}_2(o_1) = v \land \text{rf}(o_1, o_2)$

RᴇᴛᴠᴀʟRGA

$\forall o_1, o_2.\ \text{meth}(o_1) = \text{read} \land \text{meth}(o_2) = \text{addAfter} \land \text{hb}(o_2, o_1) \land \text{arg}_2(o_2) \notin \text{ret}(o_1)$
$$\Rightarrow \exists o_3.\ \text{meth}(o_3) = \text{remove} \land \text{arg}(o_3) = \text{arg}_2(o_2) \land \text{rf}(o_3, o_1)$$

LɪɴRGA

$\forall o_1, o_2.\ \big(\text{meth}(o_1) = \text{meth}(o_2) = \text{addAfter} \land \text{arg}_1(o_1) = \text{arg}_1(o_2)\ \land$
$\exists o_3, o_4, o_5.\ \text{meth}(o_3) = \text{meth}(o_4) = \text{addAfter} \land \text{rf}^*_{\text{addAfter}}(o_1, o_3) \land \text{rf}^*_{\text{addAfter}}(o_2, o_4) \land$
$\text{meth}(o_5) = \text{read} \land \text{arg}_2(o_4) <_{o_5} \text{arg}_2(o_3)\big) \Rightarrow \text{lin}(o_1, o_2)$

Fig. 3. Axioms used to define the semantics of RGA.

2.4 Replicated Growable Array

The Replicated Growing Array (RGA) [32] is a replicated list used for text-editing applications. RGA supports three operations: addAfter(a,b) which adds the character b immediately after the occurrence of the character a assumed to be present in the list, remove(a) which removes a assumed to be present in the list, and read() which returns the list contents. It is assumed that a character is added at most once[2]. The conflicts between concurrent addAfter operations that add a character immediately after the same character is solved using timestamps (i.e., each added character is associated to a timestamp and the order between characters depends on the order between the corresponding timestamps), which in the axioms below are modeled by the linearization order.

Figure 3 lists the axioms defining RGA. RᴇᴀᴅFʀᴏᴍRGA ensures that:

- every addAfter(a,b) operation reads-from the addAfter(_,a) adding the character a, except when $a = \circ$ which denotes the "root" element of the list[3],
- every remove(a) operation reads-from the operation adding a, and
- every read operation returning a list containing a reads-from the operation addAfter(_,a) adding a.

Then, RᴇᴛᴠᴀʟRGA ensures that a read operation o_1 happening-after an operation adding a character a reads-from a remove(a) operation when a doesn't occur in the list returned by o_1 (the history must contain a remove(a) operation because otherwise, a should have occurred in the list returned by the read).

Finally, LɪɴRGA models the conflict resolution policy by constraining the linearization order between addAfter(a,_) operations adding some character

---

[2] In a practical context, this can be enforced by tagging characters with replica identifiers and sequence numbers.

[3] This element is not returned by read operations.

immediately after the same character a. As a particular case, LINRGA enforces that addAfter(a,b) is linearized before addAfter(a,c) when a read operation returns a list where c precedes b (addAfter(a,b) results in the list $a \cdot b$ and applying addAfter(a,c) on $a \cdot b$ results in the list $a \cdot c \cdot b$). However, this is not sufficient: assume that the history contains the two operations addAfter(a,b) and addAfter(a,c) along with two operations remove(b) and addAfter(b,d). Then, a read operation returning the list $a \cdot c \cdot d$ must enforce that addAfter(a,b) is linearized before addAfter(a,c) because this is the only order between these two operations that can lead to the result $a \cdot c \cdot d$, i.e., executing addAfter(a,b), addAfter(b,d), remove(b), addAfter(a,c) in this order. LINRGA deals with any scenario where arbitrarily-many characters can be removed from the list: $\mathsf{rf}^*_{\mathsf{addAfter}}$ is the reflexive and transitive closure of the projection of rf on addAfter operations and $<_{o_5}$ denotes the order between characters in the list returned by the read operation o_5.

3   Intractability for Registers, Sets, Flags, and Counters

In this section we demonstrate that checking the consistency is intractable for many widely-used data types. While this is not completely unexpected, since some related consistency-checking problems like sequential consistency are also intractable [20], this contrasts recent tractability results for checking strong consistency (i.e., linearizability) of common non-replicated data types like sets, maps, and queues [15]. In fact, in many cases we show that intractability even holds if the number of replicas is fixed.

Our proofs of intractability follow the general structure of Gibbons and Korach's proofs for the intractability of checking sequential consistency (SC) for atomic registers with read and write operations [20]. In particular, we reduce a specialized type of NP-hard propositional satisfiability (SAT) problem to checking whether histories are admitted by a given data type. While our construction borrows from Gibbons and Korach's, the adaptation from SC to CRDT consistency requires a significant extension to handle the consistency relaxation represented by abstract executions: rather than a direct sequencing of threads' operations, CRDT consistency requires the construction of three separate relations: read-from, happens-before, and linearization.

Technically, our reductions start from the 1-in-3 SAT problem [19]: given a propositional formula $\bigwedge_{i=1}^m (\alpha_i \vee \beta_i \vee \gamma_i)$ over variables $x_1, \dots, x_n$ with only positive literals, i.e., $\alpha_i, \beta_i, \gamma_i \in \{x_1, \dots, x_n\}$, does there exist an assignment to the variables such that exactly one of $\alpha_i, \beta_i, \gamma_i$ per clause is assigned *true*? The proofs of Theorems 1 and 2 reduce 1-in-3 SAT to CRDT consistency checking.

Theorem 1. *The admissibility problem is NP-hard when the number of replicas is fixed for the following data types: Add-Wins Set, Remove-Wins Set, Enable-Wins Flag, Disable-Wins Flag, Multi-Value Register, and Last-Writer-Wins Register.*

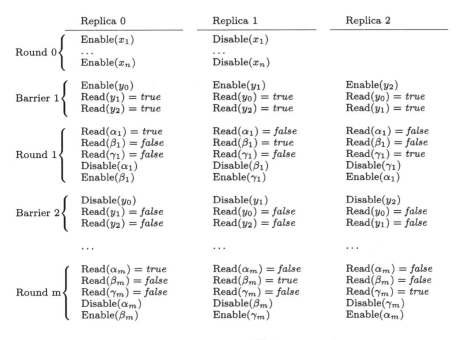

	Replica 0	Replica 1	Replica 2
Round 0	Enable(x_1) ... Enable(x_n)	Disable(x_1) ... Disable(x_n)	
Barrier 1	Enable(y_0) Read(y_1) = $true$ Read(y_2) = $true$	Enable(y_1) Read(y_0) = $true$ Read(y_2) = $true$	Enable(y_2) Read(y_0) = $true$ Read(y_1) = $true$
Round 1	Read(α_1) = $true$ Read(β_1) = $false$ Read(γ_1) = $false$ Disable(α_1) Enable(β_1)	Read(α_1) = $false$ Read(β_1) = $true$ Read(γ_1) = $false$ Disable(β_1) Enable(γ_1)	Read(α_1) = $false$ Read(β_1) = $false$ Read(γ_1) = $true$ Disable(γ_1) Enable(α_1)
Barrier 2	Disable(y_0) Read(y_1) = $false$ Read(y_2) = $false$	Disable(y_1) Read(y_0) = $false$ Read(y_2) = $false$	Disable(y_2) Read(y_0) = $false$ Read(y_1) = $false$
	...	...	...
Round m	Read(α_m) = $true$ Read(β_m) = $false$ Read(γ_m) = $false$ Disable(α_m) Enable(β_m)	Read(α_m) = $false$ Read(β_m) = $true$ Read(γ_m) = $false$ Disable(β_m) Enable(γ_m)	Read(α_m) = $false$ Read(β_m) = $false$ Read(γ_m) = $true$ Disable(γ_m) Enable(α_m)

Fig. 4. The encoding of a 1-in-3 SAT problem $\bigwedge_{i=1}^{m}(\alpha_i \vee \beta_i \vee \gamma_i)$ over variables $x_1, \ldots, x_n$ as a 3-replica history of a flag data type. Besides the flag variable x_j for each propositional variable x_j, the encoding adds per-replica variables y_j for synchronization barriers.

Proof. We demonstrate a reduction from the 1-in-3 SAT problem. For a given problem $p = \bigwedge_{i=1}^{m}(\alpha_i \vee \beta_i \vee \gamma_i)$ over variables $x_1, \ldots, x_n$, we construct a 3-replica history h_p of the flag data type — either enable- or disable-wins — as illustrated in Fig. 4. The encoding includes a flag variable x_j for each propositional variable x_j, along with a per-replica flag variable y_j used to implement synchronization barriers. Intuitively, executions of h_p proceed in $m + 1$ rounds: the first round corresponds to the assignment of a truth valuation, while subsequent rounds check the validity of each clause given the assignment. The reductions to sets and registers are slight variations on this proof, in which the Read, Enable, and Disable operations are replaced with Contains, Add, and Remove, respectively, and Read and Writes of values 1 and 0, respectively.

It suffices to show that the constructed history h_p is admitted if and only if the given problem p is satisfiable. Since the flag data type does not constrain the linearization relation of its abstract executions, we regard only the read-from and happens-before components. It is straightforward to verify that the happens-before relations of h_p's abstract executions necessarily order:

1. every pair of operations in distinct rounds — due to barriers; and
2. every operation in a given round, over all replicas, without interleaving the operations of distinct replicas within the same round — since a replica's reads in a given round are only consistent with the other replicas' after the re-enabling and -disabling of flag variables.

In other words, replicas appear to execute atomically per round, in a round-robin fashion. Furthermore, since all operations in a given round happen before the operations of subsequent rounds, the values of flag variables are consistent across rounds —i.e., as read by the first replica to execute in a given round — and determined in the initial round either by conflict resolution — i.e., enable- or disable-wins — or by happens-before, in case conflict resolution would have been inconsistent with subsequent reads.

In the "if" direction, let $r \in \{0, 1, 2\}^m$ be the positions of positively-assigned variables in each clause, e.g., $r_i = 0$ implies $\alpha_i = \textit{true}$ and $\beta_i = \gamma_i = \textit{false}$. We construct an abstract execution e_r in which the happens-before relation sequences the operations of replica r_i before those of $r_i + 1 \bmod 3$, and in turn before $r_i + 2 \bmod 3$. In other words, the replicas in round i appear to execute in left-to-right order from starting with the replica r_i, whose reads correspond to the satisfying assignment of $(\alpha_i \vee \beta_i \vee \gamma_i)$. The read-from relation of e_r relates each $\text{Read}(x_j) = \textit{true}$ operation to the most recent $\text{Enable}(x_j)$ operation in happens-before order, which is unique since happens-before sequences the operations of all rounds; the case for $\text{Read}(x_j) = \textit{false}$ and $\text{Disable}(x_j)$ is symmetric. It is then straightforward to verify that e_r satisfies the axioms of the enable- or disable-wins flag, and thus h_p is admitted.

In the "only if" direction, let e be an abstract execution of h_p, and let $r \in \{0, 1, 2\}^m$ be the replicas first to execute in each round according to the happens-before order of e. It is straightforward to verify that the assignment in which a given variable is set to true iff the replica encoding its positive assignment in some clause executes first in its round, i.e.,

$$x_j = \begin{cases} \textit{true} & \text{if } \exists i.(r_i = 0 \wedge \alpha_i = x_j) \vee (r_i = 1 \wedge \beta_i = x_j) \vee (r_i = 2 \wedge \gamma_i = x_j) \\ \textit{false} & \text{otherwise,} \end{cases}$$

is a satisfying assignment to p.   □

Theorem 1 establishes intractability of consistency for the aforementioned sets, flags, and registers, independently from the number of replicas. In contrast, our proof of Theorem 2 for counter data types depends on the number of replicas, since our encoding requires two replicas per propositional variable. Intuitively, since counter increments and decrements are commutative, the initial round in the previous encoding would have fixed all counter values to zero. Instead, the next encoding isolates initial increments and decrements to independent replicas. The weaker result is indeed tight since checking counter consistency with a fixed number of replicas is polynomial time, as Sect. 5 demonstrates.

Theorem 2. *The admissibility problem for the Counter data type is NP-hard.*

Proof. We demonstrate a reduction from the 1-in-3 SAT problem. For a given problem $p = \bigwedge_{i=1}^m (\alpha_i \vee \beta_i \vee \gamma_i)$ over variables $x_1, \ldots, x_n$, we construct a history h_p of the counter data type over $2n + 3$ replicas, as illustrated in Fig. 5.

Besides the differences imposed due to the commutativity of counter increments and decrements, our reduction follows the same strategy as in the proof of

Theorem 1: the happens-before relation of h_p's abstract executions order every pair of operations in distinct rounds (of Replicas 0–2), and every operation in a given (non-initial) round. As before, Replicas 0–2 appear to execute atomically per round, in a round-robin fashion, and counter variables are consistent across rounds. The key difference is that here abstract executions' happens-before relations only relate the operations of either Replica $2j+1$ or $2j+2$, for each $j = 1, \ldots, n$, to operations in subsequent rounds: the other's operations are never observed by other replicas. Our encoding ensures that exactly one of each is observed by ensuring that the counter y is incremented exactly n times — and relying on the fact that every variable appears in some clause, so that a read that observed neither or both would yield the value zero, which is inconsistent with h_p. Otherwise, our reasoning follows the proof of Theorem 1, in which the read-from relation selects all increments and decrements of the same counter variable in happens-before order.   □

4   Polynomial-Time Algorithms for Registers and Arrays

We show that the problem of checking consistency is polynomial time for RGA, and even for LWW and MVR under the assumption that each value is written at most once, i.e., for each value v, the input history contains at most one write operation write(x,v). Histories satisfying this assumption are called *differentiated*. The latter is a restriction motivated by the fact that practical implementations of these datatypes are data-independent [38], i.e., their behavior doesn't depend on the concrete values read or written and any potential buggy behavior can be exposed in executions where each value is written at most once. Also, in a testing environment, this restriction can be enforced by tagging each value with a replica identifier and a sequence number.

In all three cases, the feature that enables polynomial time consistency checking is the fact that the read-from relation becomes fixed for a given history, i.e., if the history is consistent, then there exists exactly one read-from relation rf that satisfies the READFROM- and RETVAL- axioms, and rf can be derived syntactically from the operation labels (using those axioms). Then, our axiomatic characterizations enable a consistency checking algorithm which roughly, consists in instantiating those axioms in order to compute an abstract execution.

The consistency checking algorithm for RGA, LWW, and MVR is listed in Algorithm 1. It computes the three relations rf, hb, and lin of an abstract execution using the datatype's axioms. The history is declared consistent iff there exist satisfying rf and hb relations, and the relations hb and lin computed this way are acyclic. The acyclicity requirement comes from the definition of abstract executions where hb and lin are required to be partial/total orders. While an abstract execution would require that lin is a total order, this algorithm computes a partial linearization order. However, any total order compatible with this partial linearization would satisfy the axioms of the datatype.

ComputeRF computes the read-from relation rf satisfying the READFROM- and RETVAL- axioms. In the case of LWW and MVR, it defines rf as the set

	Replica 0	Replica $2j+1$	Replica $2j+2$
Round 0 $\Big\{$		$\text{Inc}(y)$ $\text{Inc}(x_j)$	$\text{Inc}(y)$ $\text{Dec}(x_j)$
	$\text{Read}(y) = n$		

		Replica 1	Replica 2
Barrier 1 $\Big\{$	$\text{Inc}(z)$ $\text{Read}(z) = 3$	$\text{Inc}(z)$ $\text{Read}(z) = 3$	$\text{Inc}(z)$ $\text{Read}(z) = 3$
Round 1 $\Bigg\{$	$\text{Read}(\alpha_1) = 1$ $\text{Read}(\beta_1) = -1$ $\text{Read}(\gamma_1) = -1$ $\text{Dec}(\alpha_1); \text{Dec}(\alpha_1)$ $\text{Inc}(\beta_1); \text{Inc}(\beta_1)$	$\text{Read}(\alpha_1) = -1$ $\text{Read}(\beta_1) = 1$ $\text{Read}(\gamma_1) = -1$ $\text{Dec}(\beta_1); \text{Dec}(\beta_1)$ $\text{Inc}(\gamma_1); \text{Inc}(\gamma_1)$	$\text{Read}(\alpha_1) = -1$ $\text{Read}(\beta_1) = -1$ $\text{Read}(\gamma_1) = 1$ $\text{Dec}(\gamma_1); \text{Dec}(\gamma_1)$ $\text{Inc}(\alpha_1); \text{Inc}(\alpha_1)$
Barrier 2 $\Big\{$	$\text{Dec}(z)$ $\text{Read}(z) = 0$	$\text{Dec}(z)$ $\text{Read}(z) = 0$	$\text{Dec}(z)$ $\text{Read}(z) = 0$
	$\cdots$	$\cdots$	$\cdots$
Round m $\Bigg\{$	$\text{Read}(\alpha_m) = 1$ $\text{Read}(\beta_m) = -1$ $\text{Read}(\gamma_m) = -1$ $\text{Dec}(\alpha_m); \text{Dec}(\alpha_m)$ $\text{Inc}(\beta_m); \text{Inc}(\beta_m)$	$\text{Read}(\alpha_m) = -1$ $\text{Read}(\beta_m) = 1$ $\text{Read}(\gamma_m) = -1$ $\text{Dec}(\beta_m); \text{Dec}(\beta_m)$ $\text{Inc}(\gamma_m); \text{Inc}(\gamma_m)$	$\text{Read}(\alpha_m) = -1$ $\text{Read}(\beta_m) = -1$ $\text{Read}(\gamma_m) = 1$ $\text{Dec}(\gamma_m); \text{Dec}(\gamma_m)$ $\text{Inc}(\alpha_m); \text{Inc}(\alpha_m)$
Barrier $m+1$ $\Big\{$	$\text{Inc}(z)$ or $\text{Dec}(z)$ $\text{Read}(z) = 3$ or 0	$\text{Inc}(z)$ or $\text{Dec}(z)$ $\text{Read}(z) = 3$ or 0	$\text{Inc}(z)$ or $\text{Dec}(z)$ $\text{Read}(z) = 3$ or 0
Round $m+1$ $\{$	$\text{Read}(y) = n$		

Fig. 5. The encoding of a 1-in-3 SAT problem $\bigwedge_{i=1}^{m}(\alpha_i \vee \beta_i \vee \gamma_i)$ over variables $x_1, \ldots, x_n$ as the history of a counter over $2n+3$ replicas. Besides the counter variables x_j encoding propositional variables x_j, the encoding adds a variable y encoding the number of initial increments and decrements, and a variable z to implement synchronization barriers.

of all pairs formed of write(x,v) and read(x) operations where v belongs to the return value of the read. By RETVAL_, each read(x) operation must be associated to at least one write$(x,\_)$ operation. Also, the fact that each value is written at most once implies that this rf relation is uniquely defined, e.g., for LWW, it is not possible to find two write operations that could be rf related to the same read operation. In general, if there exists no rf relation satisfying these axioms, then ComputeRF returns a distinguished value $\perp$ to signal a consistency violation. Note that the computation of the read-from for LWW and MVR is quadratic time[4] since the constraints imposed by the axioms relate only to the operation labels, the methods they invoke or their arguments. The case of RGA is slightly more involved because the axiom RETVALRGA introduces more read-from constraints based on the happens-before order which includes ro and the rf itself. In this case, the computation of rf relies on a fixpoint computation, which converges in at most quadratic time (the maximal size of rf), described in Algorithm 2. Essentially, we use the axiom READFROMRGA to populate the

---

[4] Assuming constant time lookup/insert operations (e.g., using hashmaps), this complexity is linear time.

Input: A differentiated history $h = \langle \mathsf{Op}, \mathsf{ro} \rangle$ and a datatype T.
Output: *true* iff h satisfies the axioms of T.
1 $\mathsf{rf} \leftarrow \mathsf{ComputeRF}(h, \mathrm{READFROM}[T], \mathrm{RETVAL}[T]$);
2 **if** $\mathsf{rf} = \bot$ **then return** *false*;
3 $\mathsf{hb} \leftarrow (\mathsf{ro} \cup \mathsf{rf})^+$;
4 **if** hb *is cyclic or* $\langle h, \mathsf{rf}, \mathsf{hb} \rangle \not\models \mathrm{READFROMMAXIMAL}[T] \wedge \mathrm{READALLMAXIMALS}[T]$
   then
5 | **return** *false*;
6 $\mathsf{lin} \leftarrow \mathsf{hb}$;
7 $\mathsf{lin} \leftarrow \mathsf{LinClosure}(\mathsf{hb}, \mathrm{LIN}[T])$;
8 **if** lin *is cyclic* **then return** *false*;
9 **return** *true*;

Algorithm 1. Consistency checking for RGA, LWW, and MVR. RE...[T] refers to an axiom of T, or *true* when T lacks such an axiom. The relation R^+ denotes the transitive closure of R.

read-from relation and then, apply the axiom $\mathrm{RETVALRGA}$ iteratively, using the read-from constraints added in previous steps, until the computation converges.

After computing the read-from relation, our algorithm defines the happens-before relation hb as the transitive closure of ro union rf. This is sound because none of the axioms of these datatypes enforce new happens-before constraints, which are not already captured by ro and rf. Then, it checks whether the hb defined this way is acyclic and satisfies the datatype's axioms that constrain hb, i.e., $\mathrm{READFROMMAXIMAL}$ and $\mathrm{READALLMAXIMALS}$ (when they are present).

Finally, in the case of LWW and RGA, the algorithm computes a (partial) linearization order that satisfies the corresponding $\mathrm{LIN}\_$ axioms. Starting from an initial linearization order which is exactly the happens-before, it computes new constraints by instantiating the universally quantified axioms LINLWW and LINRGA. Since these axioms are not "recursive", i.e., they don't enforce linearization order constraints based on other linearization order constraints, a standard instantiation of these axioms is enough to compute a partial linearization order such that any extension to a total order satisfies the datatype's axioms.

Theorem 3. *Algorithm 1 returns true iff the input history is consistent.*

The following holds because Algorithm 1 runs in polynomial time — the rank depends on the number of quantifiers in the datatype's axioms. Indeed, Algorithm 1 represents a least fixpoint computation which converges in at most a quadratic number of iterations (the maximal size of rf).

Corollary 1. *The admissibility problem is polynomial time for RGA, and for LWW and MVR on differentiated histories.*

Input: A history $h = \langle \mathsf{Op}, \mathsf{ro} \rangle$ of RGA.
Output: An rf satisfying READFROMRGA $\wedge$ RETVALRGA, if exists; $\perp$ o/w

1   rf $\leftarrow \{(o_1, o_2) : \mathsf{meth}(o_1) = \mathsf{addAfter}, \mathsf{meth}(o_2) \in$
   $\{\mathsf{addAfter}, \mathsf{remove}, \mathsf{read}\}, \mathsf{arg}_2(o_1) = \mathsf{arg}_1(o_2) \vee \mathsf{arg}_2(o_1) \in \mathsf{ret}(o_2)\}$;
2   **if** $\langle h, \mathsf{rf} \rangle \not\models$ READFROMRGA **then return** $\perp$;
3   **while** *true* **do**
4      $\mathsf{rf}_1 \leftarrow \emptyset$;
5   **foreach** $o_1, o_2 \in \mathsf{Op}$ s.t. $\langle o_2, o_1 \rangle \in (\mathsf{rf} \cup \mathsf{ro})^+$ and $\mathsf{meth}(o_1) = \mathsf{read}$ and
      $\mathsf{meth}(o_2) = \mathsf{addAfter}$ and $\mathsf{arg}_2(o_2) \notin \mathsf{ret}(o_1)$ **do**
6   **if** $\exists o_3 \in \mathsf{Op}$ s.t. $\mathsf{meth}(o_3) = \mathsf{remove}$ and $\mathsf{arg}(o_3) = \mathsf{arg}_2(o_2)$ **then**
7           $\mathsf{rf}_1 \leftarrow \mathsf{rf}_1 \cup \{\langle o_3, o_1 \rangle\}$;
8   **else**
9   **return** $\perp$;
10   **if** $\mathsf{rf}_1 \subseteq \mathsf{rf}$ **then break**;
11   **else** $\mathsf{rf} \leftarrow \mathsf{rf} \cup \mathsf{rf}_1$;
12 **return** rf;

Algorithm 2. The procedure ComputeRF for RGA.

5   Polynomial-Time Algorithms for Replicated Counters

In this section, we show that checking consistency for the replicated counter datatype becomes polynomial time assuming the number of replicas in the input history is fixed (i.e., the width of the replica order ro is fixed). We present an algorithm which constructs a valid happens-before order (note that the semantics of the replicated counter doesn't constrain the linearization order) incrementally, following the replica order. At any time, the happens-before order is uniquely determined by a *prefix mapping* that associates to each replica a *prefix* of the history, i.e., a set of operations which is downward-closed w.r.t. replica order (i.e., if it contains an operation it contains all its ro predecessors). This models the fact that the replica order is included in the happens-before and therefore, if an operation o_1 happens-before another operation o_2, then all the ro predecessors of o_1 happenbefore o_2. The happens-before order can be extended in two ways: (1) adding an operation issued on the replica i to the prefix of replica i, or (2) "merging" the prefix of a replica j to the prefix of a replica i (this models the delivery of an operation issued on replica j and all its happens-before predecessors to the replica i). Verifying that an extension of the happens-before is valid, i.e., that the return values of newly-added read operations satisfy the RETVALCOUNTER axiom, doesn't depend on the happens-before order between the operations in the prefix associated to some replica (it is enough to count the inc and dec operations in that prefix). Therefore, the algorithm can be seen as a search in the space of prefix mappings. If the number of replicas in the input history is fixed, then the number of possible prefix mappings is polynomial in the size of the history, which implies that the search can be done in polynomial time.

Let $h = (\mathsf{Op}, \mathsf{ro})$ be a history. To simplify the notations, we assume that the replica order is a union of sequences, each sequence representing the operations

---

Input: History $h = (\mathsf{Op}, \mathsf{ro})$, prefix map m, and set *seen* of invalid prefix maps
Output: *true* iff there exists read-from and happens-before relations rf and hb
such that $m \subseteq \mathsf{hb}$, and $\langle h, \mathsf{rf}, \mathsf{hb}\rangle$ satisfies the counter axioms.

1 **if** m *is complete* **then return** *true*;
2 **foreach** *replica* i **do**
3   **foreach** *replica* $j \neq i$ **do**
4          $m' \leftarrow m[i \leftarrow m(i) \cup m(j)]$;
5   **if** $m' \notin$ *seen* **and** $\mathsf{checkCounter}(h, m', \textit{seen})$ **then**
6   **return** *true*;
7   *seen* $\leftarrow$ *seen* $\cup \{m'\}$;
8   **if** $\exists o_1. \ \mathsf{ro}^1(\mathsf{last}_i(m), o_1)$ **then**
9   **if** $\mathsf{meth}(o_1) = \mathsf{read}$ *and*
        $\mathsf{arg}(o_1) = x \wedge \mathsf{ret}(o_1) \neq |\{o \in m[i] | o = \mathsf{inc}(x)\}| - |\{o \in m[i] | o = \mathsf{dec}(x)\}|$
        then
10   **return** *false*;
11         $m' \leftarrow m[i \leftarrow m(i) \cup \{o_1\}]$;
12   **if** $m' \notin$ *seen* **and** $\mathsf{checkCounter}(h, m', \textit{seen})$ **then**
13   **return** *true*;
14   *seen* $\leftarrow$ *seen* $\cup \{m'\}$;
15 **return** *false*;

Algorithm 3. The procedure $\mathsf{checkCounter}$, where ro^1 denotes immediate ro-successor, and $f[a \leftarrow b]$ updates function f with mapping $a \mapsto b$.

issued on the same replica. Therefore, each operation $o \in \mathsf{Op}$ is associated with a replica identifier $\mathsf{rep}(o) \in [1..n_h]$, where n_h is the number of replicas in h.

A *prefix* of h is a set of operation $\mathsf{Op}' \subseteq \mathsf{Op}$ such that all the ro predecessors of operations in Op' are also in Op', i.e., $\forall o \in \mathsf{Op}. \ \mathsf{ro}^{-1}(o) \in \mathsf{Op}$. Note that the union of two prefixes of h is also a prefix of h. The *last operation* of replica i in a prefix Op' is the ro-maximal operation o with $\mathsf{rep}(o) = i$ included in Op'. A prefix Op' is called *valid* if $(\mathsf{Op}', \mathsf{ro}')$, where ro' is the projection of ro on Op', is admitted by the replicated counter.

A *prefix map* is a mapping m which associates a prefix of h to each replica $i \in [1..n_h]$. Intuitively, a prefix map defines for each replica i the set of operations which are "known" to i, i.e., happen-before the last operation of i in its prefix. Formally, a prefix map m is *included* in a happens-before relation hb, denoted by $m \subseteq \mathsf{hb}$, if for each replica $i \in [1..n_h]$, $\mathsf{hb}(o, o_i)$ for each operation in $o \in m(i) \setminus \{o_i\}$, where o_i is the last operation of i in $m(i)$. We call o_i the *last operation* of i in m, and denoted it by $\mathsf{last}_i(m)$. A prefix map m is *valid* if it associates a valid prefix to each replica, and *complete* if it associates the whole history h to each replica i.

Algorithm 3 lists our algorithm for checking consistency of replicated counter histories. It is defined as a recursive procedure $\mathsf{checkCounter}$ that searches for a sequence of valid extensions of a given prefix map (initially, this prefix map is empty) until it becomes complete. The axiom RETVALCOUNTER is enforced whenever extending the prefix map with a new **read** operation (when the last operation of a replica i is "advanced" to a **read** operation). The following theorem states of the correctness of the algorithm.

Theorem 4. checkCounter$(h, \emptyset, \emptyset)$ *returns true iff the input history is consistent.*

When the number of replicas is fixed, the number of prefix maps becomes polynomial in the size of the history. This follows from the fact that prefixes are uniquely defined by their **ro**-maximal operations, whose number is fixed.

Corollary 2. *The admissibility problem for replicated counters is polynomial-time when the number of replicas is fixed.*

6 Polynomial-Time Algorithms for Sets and Flags

While Theorem 1 shows that the admissibility problem is NP-complete for replicated sets and flags even if the number of replicas is fixed, we show that this problem becomes polynomial time when additionally, the number of values added to the set, or the number of flags, is also fixed. Note that this doesn't limit the number of operations in the input history which can still be arbitrarily large. In the following, we focus on the Add-Wins Set, the other cases being very similar.

We propose an algorithm for checking consistency which is actually an extension of the one presented in Sect. 5 for replicated counters. The additional complexity in checking consistency for the Add-Wins Set comes from the validity of **contains**(x) return values which requires identifying the maximal predecessors in the happens-before relation that add or remove x (which are not necessarily the maximal **hb**-predecessors all-together). In the case of counters, it was enough just to count happens-before predecessors. Therefore, we extend the algorithm for replicated counters such that along with the prefix map, we also keep track of the **hb**-maximal **add**(x) and **remove**(x) operations for each element x and each replica i. When extending a prefix map with a **contains** operation, these **hb**-maximal operations (which define a witness for the read-from relation) are enough to verify the RETVALSET axiom. Extending the prefix of a replica with an **add** or **remove** operation (issued on the same replica), or by merging the prefix of another replica, may require an update of these **hb**-maximal predecessors.

When the number of replicas and elements are fixed, the number of read-from maps is polynomial in the size of the history — recall that the number of operations associated by a read-from map to a replica and set element is bounded by the number of replicas. Combined with the number of prefix maps being polynomial when the number of replicas is fixed, we obtain the following result.

Theorem 5. *Checking whether a history is admitted by the Add-Wins Set, Remove-Wins Set, Enable-Wins Flag, or the Disable-Wins Flag is polynomial time provided that the number of replicas and elements/flags is fixed.*

7 Related Work

Many have considered consistency models applicable to CRDTs, including causal consistency [26], sequential consistency [27], linearizability [24], session consistency [35], eventual consistency [36], and happens-before consistency [29]. Burckhardt et al. [8,11] propose a unifying framework to formalize these models. Many have also studied the complexity of verifying data-type agnostic notions of consistency, including serializability, sequential consistency and linearizability [1,2,4,18,20,22,30], as well as causal consistency [6]. Our definition of the replicated LWW register corresponds to the notion of causal convergence in [6]. This work studies the complexity of the admissibility problem for the replicated LWW register. It shows that this problem is NP-complete in general and polynomial time when each value is written only once. Our NP-completeness result is stronger since it assumes a fixed number of replicas, and our algorithm for the case of unique values is more general and can be applied uniformly to MVR and RGA. While Bouajjani et al. [5,14] consider the complexity for individual linearizable collection types, we are the first to establish (in)tractability of individual replicated data types. Others have developed effective consistency checking algorithms for sequential consistency [3,9,23,31], serializability [12,17,18,21], linearizability [10,16,28,37], and even weaker notions like eventual consistency [7] and sequential happens-before consistency [13,15]. In contrast, we are the first to establish precise polynomial-time algorithms for runtime verification of replicated data types.

8 Conclusion

By developing novel logical characterizations of replicated data types, reductions from propositional satisfiability checking, and tractable algorithms, we have established a frontier of tractability for checking consistency of replicated data types. As far as we are aware, our results are the first to characterize the asymptotic complexity consistency checking for CRDTs.

References

1. Alur, R., McMillan, K.L., Peled, D.A.: Model-checking of correctness conditions for concurrent objects. Inf. Comput. **160**(1–2), 167–188 (2000). https://doi.org/10.1006/inco.1999.2847
2. Bingham, J.D., Condon, A., Hu, A.J.: Toward a decidable notion of sequential consistency. In: Rosenberg, A.L., auf der Heide, F.M. (eds.) SPAA 2003: Proceedings of the Fifteenth Annual ACM Symposium on Parallelism in Algorithms and Architectures, San Diego, California, USA, (part of FCRC 2003), 7–9 June 2003, pp. 304–313. ACM (2003). https://doi.org/10.1145/777412.777467
3. Bingham, J., Condon, A., Hu, A.J., Qadeer, S., Zhang, Z.: Automatic verification of sequential consistency for unbounded addresses and data values. In: Alur, R., Peled, D.A. (eds.) CAV 2004. LNCS, vol. 3114, pp. 427–439. Springer, Heidelberg (2004). https://doi.org/10.1007/978-3-540-27813-9_33

4. Bouajjani, A., Emmi, M., Enea, C., Hamza, J.: Verifying concurrent programs against sequential specifications. In: Felleisen, M., Gardner, P. (eds.) ESOP 2013. LNCS, vol. 7792, pp. 290–309. Springer, Heidelberg (2013). https://doi.org/10.1007/978-3-642-37036-6_17

5. Bouajjani, A., Emmi, M., Enea, C., Hamza, J.: On reducing linearizability to state reachability. Inf. Comput. **261**(Part), 383–400 (2018). https://doi.org/10.1016/j.ic.2018.02.014

6. Bouajjani, A., Enea, C., Guerraoui, R., Hamza, J.: On verifying causal consistency. In: Castagna, G., Gordon, A.D. (eds.) Proceedings of the 44th ACM SIGPLAN Symposium on Principles of Programming Languages, POPL 2017, Paris, France, 18–20 January 2017, pp. 626–638. ACM (2017). http://dl.acm.org/citation.cfm?id=3009888

7. Bouajjani, A., Enea, C., Hamza, J.: Verifying eventual consistency of optimistic replication systems. In: Jagannathan, S., Sewell, P. (eds.) The 41st Annual ACM SIGPLAN-SIGACT Symposium on Principles of Programming Languages, POPL 2014, San Diego, CA, USA, 20–21 January 2014, pp. 285–296. ACM (2014). https://doi.org/10.1145/2535838.2535877

8. Burckhardt, S.: Principles of eventual consistency. Found. Trends Program. Lang. **1**(1–2), 1–150 (2014). https://doi.org/10.1561/2500000011

9. Burckhardt, S., Alur, R., Martin, M.M.K.: Checkfence: checking consistency of concurrent data types on relaxed memory models. In: Ferrante, J., McKinley, K.S. (eds.) Proceedings of the ACM SIGPLAN 2007 Conference on Programming Language Design and Implementation, San Diego, California, USA, 10–13 June 2007, pp. 12–21. ACM (2007). https://doi.org/10.1145/1250734.1250737

10. Burckhardt, S., Dern, C., Musuvathi, M., Tan, R.: Line-up: a complete and automatic linearizability checker. In: Zorn, B.G., Aiken, A. (eds.) Proceedings of the 2010 ACM SIGPLAN Conference on Programming Language Design and Implementation, PLDI 2010, Toronto, Ontario, Canada, 5–10 June 2010, pp. 330–340. ACM (2010). https://doi.org/10.1145/1806596.1806634

11. Burckhardt, S., Gotsman, A., Yang, H., Zawirski, M.: Replicated data types: specification, verification, optimality. In: Jagannathan, S., Sewell, P. (eds.) The 41st Annual ACM SIGPLAN-SIGACT Symposium on Principles of Programming Languages, POPL 2014, San Diego, CA, USA, 20–21 January 2014, pp. 271–284. ACM (2014). https://doi.org/10.1145/2535838.2535848

12. Cohen, A., O'Leary, J.W., Pnueli, A., Tuttle, M.R., Zuck, L.D.: Verifying correctness of transactional memories. In: Proceedings of the 7th International Conference on Formal Methods in Computer-Aided Design, FMCAD 2007, Austin, Texas, USA, 11–14 November 2007, pp. 37–44. IEEE Computer Society (2007). https://doi.org/10.1109/FAMCAD.2007.40

13. Emmi, M., Enea, C.: Monitoring weak consistency. In: Chockler, H., Weissenbacher, G. (eds.) CAV 2018, Part I. LNCS, vol. 10981, pp. 487–506. Springer, Cham (2018). https://doi.org/10.1007/978-3-319-96145-3_26

14. Emmi, M., Enea, C.: Sound, complete, and tractable linearizability monitoring for concurrent collections. PACMPL **2**(POPL), 25:1–25:27 (2018). https://doi.org/10.1145/3158113

15. Emmi, M., Enea, C.: Weak-consistency specification via visibility relaxation. PACMPL **3**(POPL), 60:1–60:28 (2019). https://dl.acm.org/citation.cfm?id=3290373

16. Emmi, M., Enea, C., Hamza, J.: Monitoring refinement via symbolic reasoning. In: Grove, D., Blackburn, S. (eds.) Proceedings of the 36th ACM SIGPLAN Conference on Programming Language Design and Implementation, Portland, OR, USA, 15–17 June 2015, pp. 260–269. ACM (2015). https://doi.org/10.1145/2737924.2737983

17. Emmi, M., Majumdar, R., Manevich, R.: Parameterized verification of transactional memories. In: Zorn, B.G., Aiken, A. (eds.) Proceedings of the 2010 ACM SIGPLAN Conference on Programming Language Design and Implementation, PLDI 2010, Toronto, Ontario, Canada, 5–10 June 2010, pp. 134–145. ACM (2010). https://doi.org/10.1145/1806596.1806613

18. Farzan, A., Madhusudan, P.: Monitoring atomicity in concurrent programs. In: Gupta, A., Malik, S. (eds.) CAV 2008. LNCS, vol. 5123, pp. 52–65. Springer, Heidelberg (2008). https://doi.org/10.1007/978-3-540-70545-1_8

19. Garey, M.R., Johnson, D.S.: Computers and Intractability: A Guide to the Theory of NP-Completeness. W. H. Freeman, New York (1979)

20. Gibbons, P.B., Korach, E.: Testing shared memories. SIAM J. Comput. **26**(4), 1208–1244 (1997). https://doi.org/10.1137/S0097539794279614

21. Guerraoui, R., Henzinger, T.A., Jobstmann, B., Singh, V.: Model checking transactional memories. In: Gupta, R., Amarasinghe, S.P. (eds.) Proceedings of the ACM SIGPLAN 2008 Conference on Programming Language Design and Implementation, Tucson, AZ, USA, 7–13 June 2008, pp. 372–382. ACM (2008). https://doi.org/10.1145/1375581.1375626

22. Hamza, J.: On the complexity of linearizability. In: Bouajjani, A., Fauconnier, H. (eds.) NETYS 2015. LNCS, vol. 9466, pp. 308–321. Springer, Cham (2015). https://doi.org/10.1007/978-3-319-26850-7_21

23. Henzinger, T.A., Qadeer, S., Rajamani, S.K.: Verifying sequential consistency on shared-memory multiprocessor systems. In: Halbwachs, N., Peled, D. (eds.) CAV 1999. LNCS, vol. 1633, pp. 301–315. Springer, Heidelberg (1999). https://doi.org/10.1007/3-540-48683-6_27

24. Herlihy, M., Wing, J.M.: Linearizability: a correctness condition for concurrent objects. ACM Trans. Program. Lang. Syst. **12**(3), 463–492 (1990). https://doi.org/10.1145/78969.78972

25. Kingsbury, K.: Jepsen: Distributed systems safety research (2016). https://jepsen.io

26. Lamport, L.: Time, clocks, and the ordering of events in a distributed system. Commun. ACM **21**(7), 558–565 (1978). https://doi.org/10.1145/359545.359563

27. Lamport, L.: How to make a multiprocessor computer that correctly executes multiprocess programs. IEEE Trans. Comput. **28**(9), 690–691 (1979). https://doi.org/10.1109/TC.1979.1675439

28. Lowe, G.: Testing for linearizability. Concurr. Comput. Pract. Exp. **29**(4) (2017). https://doi.org/10.1002/cpe.3928

29. Manson, J., Pugh, W., Adve, S.V.: The java memory model. In: Palsberg, J., Abadi, M. (eds.) Proceedings of the 32nd ACM SIGPLAN-SIGACT Symposium on Principles of Programming Languages, POPL 2005, Long Beach, California, USA, 12–14 January 2005, pp. 378–391. ACM (2005). https://doi.org/10.1145/1040305.1040336

30. Papadimitriou, C.H.: The serializability of concurrent database updates. J. ACM **26**(4), 631–653 (1979). https://doi.org/10.1145/322154.322158

31. Qadeer, S.: Verifying sequential consistency on shared-memory multiprocessorsby model checking. IEEE Trans. Parallel Distrib. Syst. **14**(8), 730–741 (2003). https://doi.org/10.1109/TPDS.2003.1225053

32. Roh, H., Jeon, M., Kim, J., Lee, J.: Replicated abstract data types: building blocks for collaborative applications. J. Parallel Distrib. Comput. **71**(3), 354–368 (2011). https://doi.org/10.1016/j.jpdc.2010.12.006

33. Shapiro, M., Preguiça, N., Baquero, C., Zawirski, M.: Conflict-free replicated data types. In: Défago, X., Petit, F., Villain, V. (eds.) SSS 2011. LNCS, vol. 6976, pp. 386–400. Springer, Heidelberg (2011). https://doi.org/10.1007/978-3-642-24550-3_29

34. Shapiro, M., Preguiça, N.M., Baquero, C., Zawirski, M.: Convergent and commutative replicated data types. Bull. EATCS **104**, 67–88 (2011). http://eatcs.org/beatcs/index.php/beatcs/article/view/120

35. Terry, D.B., Demers, A.J., Petersen, K., Spreitzer, M., Theimer, M., Welch, B.B.: Session guarantees for weakly consistent replicated data. In: Proceedings of the Third International Conference on Parallel and Distributed Information Systems (PDIS 1994), Austin, Texas, USA, 28–30 September 1994, pp. 140–149. IEEE Computer Society (1994). https://doi.org/10.1109/PDIS.1994.331722

36. Terry, D.B., Theimer, M., Petersen, K., Demers, A.J., Spreitzer, M., Hauser, C.: Managing update conflicts in bayou, a weakly connected replicated storage system. In: Jones, M.B. (ed.) Proceedings of the Fifteenth ACM Symposium on Operating System Principles, SOSP 1995, Copper Mountain Resort, Colorado, USA, 3–6 December 1995, pp. 172–183. ACM (1995). https://doi.org/10.1145/224056.224070

37. Wing, J.M., Gong, C.: Testing and verifying concurrent objects. J. Parallel Distrib. Comput. **17**(1–2), 164–182 (1993). https://doi.org/10.1006/jpdc.1993.1015

38. Wolper, P.: Expressing interesting properties of programs in propositional temporal logic. In: Conference Record of the Thirteenth Annual ACM Symposium on Principles of Programming Languages, St. Petersburg Beach, Florida, USA, January 1986, pp. 184–193. ACM Press (1986). https://doi.org/10.1145/512644.512661

4

Verification of Threshold-Based Distributed Algorithms by Decomposition to Decidable Logics

Idan Berkovits[1]([✉]), Marijana Lazić[2,3], Giuliano Losa[4], Oded Padon[5], and Sharon Shoham[1]

[1] Tel Aviv University, Tel Aviv-Yafo, Israel
berkovits@mail.tau.ac.il
[2] TU Wien, Vienna, Austria
[3] TU Munich, Munich, Germany
[4] University of California, Los Angeles, USA
[5] Stanford University, Stanford, USA

Abstract. Verification of fault-tolerant distributed protocols is an immensely difficult task. Often, in these protocols, *thresholds* on set cardinalities are used both in the process code and in its correctness proof, e.g., a process can perform an action only if it has received an acknowledgment from at least half of its peers. Verification of threshold-based protocols is extremely challenging as it involves two kinds of reasoning: first-order reasoning about the unbounded state of the protocol, together with reasoning about sets and cardinalities. In this work, we develop a new methodology for decomposing the verification task of such protocols into *two* decidable logics: EPR and BAPA. Our key insight is that such protocols use thresholds in a restricted way as a means to obtain certain properties of "intersection" between sets. We define a language for expressing such properties, and present two translations: to EPR and BAPA. The EPR translation allows verifying the protocol while assuming these properties, and the BAPA translation allows verifying the correctness of the properties. We further develop an algorithm for automatically generating the properties needed for verifying a given protocol, facilitating fully automated deductive verification. Using this technique we have verified several challenging protocols, including Byzantine one-step consensus, hybrid reliable broadcast and fast Byzantine Paxos.

1 Introduction

Fault-tolerant distributed protocols play an important role in the avionic and automotive industries, medical devices, cloud systems, blockchains, etc. Their unexpected behavior might put human lives at risk or cause a huge financial loss. Therefore, their correctness is of ultimate importance.

Ensuring correctness of distributed protocols is a notoriously difficult task, due to the unbounded number of processes and messages, as well as the non-deterministic behavior caused by the presence of faults, concurrency, and message delays. In general, the problem of verifying such protocols is undecidable.

This imposes two directions for attacking the problem: (i) developing fully-automatic verification techniques for *restricted* classes of protocols, or (ii) designing deductive techniques for a wide range of systems that *require user assistance*. Within the latter approach, recently emerging techniques [29] leverage decidable logics that are supported by mature automated solvers to significantly reduce user effort, and increase verification productivity. Such logics bring several key benefits: (i) their solvers usually enjoy stable performance, and (ii) whenever annotations provided by the user are incorrect, the automated solvers can provide a counterexample for the user to examine.

Deductive verification based on decidable logic requires a logical formalism that satisfies two conflicting criteria: the formalism should be expressive enough to capture the protocol, its correctness properties, its inductive invariants, and ultimately its verification conditions. At the same time, the formalism should be decidable and have an effective automated tool for checking verification conditions.

In this paper we develop a methodology for deductive verification of *threshold-based* distributed protocols using decidable logic, well-established decidable logics to settle the tension explained above.

In threshold-based protocols, a process may take different actions based on the number of processes from which it received certain messages. This is often used to achieve fault-tolerance. For example, a process may take a certain step once it has received an acknowledgment from a strict majority of its peers, that is, from more than $n/2$ processes, where n is the total number of processes. Such expressions as $n/2$, are called *thresholds*, and in general they can depend on additional parameters, such as the maximal number of crashed processes, or the maximal number of Byzantine processes.

Verification of such protocols requires two flavors of reasoning, as demonstrated by the following example. Consider the Paxos [20] protocol, in which each process proposes a value and all must agree on a common proposal. The protocol tolerates up to t process crashes, and ensures that every two processes that decide agree on the decided value. The protocol requires $n > 2t$ processes, and each process must obtain confirmation messages from $n - t$ processes before making a decision. The protocol is correct due to, among others, the fact that if $n > 2t$ then any two sets of $n - t$ processes have a process in common. To verify this protocol we need to express (i) relationships between an unbounded number of processes and values, which typically requires quantification over uninterpreted domains ("every two processes"), and (ii) properties of sets of certain cardinalities ("any two sets of $n - t$ processes intersect"). Crucially, these two types of reasoning are intertwined, as the sets of processes for which we need to capture cardinalities may be defined by their relations with other state components ("messages from at least $n - t$ processes"). While uninterpreted first-order logic (FOL) seems like the natural fit for the first type of reasoning, it is seemingly a poor fit for the second type, since it cannot express set cardinalities and the arithmetic used to define thresholds. Typically, logics that combine both types of reasoning are either undecidable or not flexible enough to capture protocols as intricate as the ones we consider.

The approach we present relies on the observation that threshold-based protocols and their correctness proofs use set cardinality thresholds in a restricted way as a means to obtain certain properties between sets, and that these properties can be expressed in FOL via a suitable encoding. In the example above, the important property is that every two sets of cardinality at least $n - t$ have a non-empty intersection. This property can be encoded in FOL by modeling sets of cardinality at least $n - t$ using an uninterpreted sort along with a membership relation between this sort and the sort for processes. However, the validity of the property under the assumption that $n > 2t$ cannot be verified in FOL.

The key idea of this paper is, hence, to decompose the verification problem of threshold-based protocols into the following problems: (i) Checking protocol correctness assuming certain intersection properties, which can be reduced to verification conditions expressed in the Effectively Propositional (EPR) fragment of FOL [25,35]. (ii) Checking that sets with cardinalities adhering to the thresholds satisfy the intersection properties (under the protocol assumptions), which can be reduced to validity checks in quantifier-free Boolean Algebra with Presburger Arithmetic (BAPA) [19]. Both BAPA and EPR are decidable logics, and are supported by mature solvers.

A crucial step in employing this decomposition is finding suitable intersection properties that are strong enough to imply the protocol's correctness (i.e., imply the FOL verification conditions), and are also implied by the precise definitions of the thresholds and the protocol's assumptions. Thus, these intersection properties can be viewed as *interpolants* between the FOL verification conditions and the thresholds in the context of the protocol's assumptions. We present fully automated procedures to find such intersection property interpolants, either eagerly or lazily.

The main contributions of this paper are[1]:

1. We define a threshold intersection property (TIP) language for expressing properties of sets whose cardinalities adhere to certain thresholds; TIP is expressive enough to capture the properties required to prove the correctness of challenging threshold-based protocols.
2. We develop two encodings of TIP, one in BAPA, and another in EPR. These encodings facilitate decomposition of protocol verification into decidable EPR and (quantifier-free) BAPA queries.
3. We show that there are only finitely many TIP formulas (up to equivalence) that are valid for any given protocol. Moreover, we present an effective algorithm for computing all TIP formulas valid for a given protocol, as well as an algorithm for lazily finding a set of TIP formulas that suffice to prove a given protocol.
4. Put together, we obtain an effective deductive verification approach for threshold-based protocols: the user models the protocol and its inductive invariants in EPR using a suitable encoding of thresholds, and defines the

---

[1] An extended version of this paper, which includes additional details and proofs, appears in [3].

thresholds and the protocol's assumptions using arithmetic; verification is carried out automatically via decomposition to well-established decidable logics.
5. We implement the approach, leveraging mature existing solvers (Z3 and CVC4), and evaluate it by verifying several challenging threshold-based protocols with sophisticated thresholds and assumptions. Our evaluation shows the effectiveness and flexibility of our approach in modeling and verifying complex protocols, including the feasibility of automatically inferring threshold intersection properties.

2   Preliminaries

Transition Systems in FOL. We model distributed protocols as transition systems expressed in many-sorted FOL. A state of the system is a first-order (FO) structure $s = (\mathcal{D}, \mathcal{I})$ over a vocabulary Σ that consists of sorted constant, function and relation symbols, s.t. s satisfies a finite set of *axioms* Θ in the form of closed formulas over Σ. $\mathcal{D}$ is the *domain* of s mapping each sort to a set of objects (elements), and $\mathcal{I}$ is the *interpretation function*. A FO *transition system* is a tuple (Σ, Θ, I, TR), where Σ and Θ are as above, I is a closed formula over Σ that defines the *initial states*, and TR is a closed formula over $\Sigma \uplus \Sigma'$ that defines the *transition relation* where Σ describes the source state of a transition and $\Sigma' = \{a' \mid a \in \Sigma\}$ describes the target state. We require that TR does not modify any symbol that appears in Θ. The set of reachable states is defined as usual. In practice, we define FO transition systems using a modeling language with a convenient syntax [29].

Properties and Inductive Invariants. A *safety property* is expressed by a closed FO formula P over Σ. The system is *safe* if all of its reachable states satisfy P. A closed FO formula Inv over Σ is an *inductive invariant* for a transition system (Σ, Θ, I, TR) and property P if the following formulas, called the *verification conditions*, are valid (equivalently, their negations are unsatisfiable): (i) $\Theta \rightarrow (I \rightarrow Inv)$, (ii) $\Theta \rightarrow (Inv \wedge TR \rightarrow Inv')$ and (iii) $\Theta \rightarrow (Inv \rightarrow P)$, where Inv' results from substituting every symbol in Inv by its primed version. We also use inductive invariants to verify arbitrary first-order LTL formulas via the reduction of [30,31].

Effectively Propositional Logic (EPR). The effectively-propositional (EPR) fragment of FOL is restricted to formulas without function symbols and with a quantifier prefix $\exists^*\forall^*$ in prenex normal form. Satisfiability of EPR formulas is decidable [25]. Moreover, EPR formulas enjoy the *finite model property*, i.e., φ is satisfiable iff it has a finite model. We consider a straightforward extension of EPR that maintains these properties and is supported by solvers such as Z3 [5]. The extension allows function symbols and quantifier alternations as long as the formula's *quantifier alternation graph*, denoted $QA(\varphi)$, is acyclic. For φ in negation normal form, $QA(\varphi)$ is a directed graph where the set of vertices is the set of sorts and the set of edges is defined as follows: every function symbol introduces edges from its arguments' sorts to its image's sort, and every existential quantifier $\exists x$ that resides in the scope of universal quantifiers introduces edges from the sorts of the universally quantified variables to the sort of x. The quantifier alternation graph is extended to sets of formulas as expected.

Boolean Algebra with Presburger Arithmetic (BAPA). Boolean Algebra with Presburger Arithmetic (BAPA) [19] is a FO theory defined over two sorts: int (for integers), and set (for subsets of a finite universe). The language is defined as follows:

$$F:: = B_1 = B_2 \mid L_1 = L_2 \mid L_1 < L_2 \mid F_1 \wedge F_2 \mid F_1 \vee F_2 \mid \neg F \mid \exists x.F \mid \forall x.F \mid \exists u.F \mid \forall u.F$$
$$B:: = x \mid \emptyset \mid \mathbf{a} \mid B_1 \cup B_2 \mid B_1 \cap B_2 \mid B^c \qquad L:: = u \mid K \mid \mathbf{n} \mid i \mid L_1 + L_2 \mid K \cdot L \mid |B|$$

where L defines linear integer terms, where u denotes an integer variable, $k \in K$ defines an (interpreted) integer constant symbol $\ldots, -2, -1, 0, 1, 2 \ldots$, $\mathbf{n}$ is an integer constant symbol that represents the size of the finite set universe, i is an uninterpreted integer constant symbol (as opposed to the constant symbols from K), and $|b|$ denotes set cardinality; B defines set terms, where x denotes a set variable, $\emptyset$ is a (interpreted) set constant symbol that represents the empty set, and $\mathbf{a}$ is an uninterpreted set constant symbol; and F defines the set of BAPA formulas, where $\ell_1 = \ell_2$ and $\ell_1 < \ell_2$ are atomic arithmetic formulas and $b_1 = b_2$ is an atomic set formula. (Other set constraints such as $b_1 \subseteq b_2$ can be encoded in the usual way). In the sequel, we also allow arithmetic terms of the form $\frac{\ell}{k}$ where $k \in K$ is a positive integer and $\ell \in L$, as any formula that contains such terms can be translated to an equivalent BAPA formula by multiplying by k.

A BAPA structure is $s_B = (\mathcal{D}, \mathcal{I})$ where the domain $\mathcal{D}$ maps sort int to the set of all integers and maps sort set to the set of all subsets of a finite universe U, called the *universal set*. The semantics of terms and formulas is as expected, where the interpretation of the complement operation is defined with respect to U (e.g., $\mathcal{I}(\emptyset^c) = U$), and the integer constant $\mathbf{n}$ is interpreted to the size of U, i.e. $\mathcal{I}(\mathbf{n}) = |U|$.

Both validity and satisfiability of BAPA formulas (with arbitrary quantification) are decidable [19], and the quantifier-free fragment is supported by CVC4 [2].

3 First-Order Modeling of Threshold-Based Protocols

Next we explain our modeling of threshold-based protocols as transition systems in FOL (Note that FOL cannot directly express set cardinality constraints). The idea is to capture each threshold by a designated sort, such that elements of this sort represent sets of nodes that satisfy the threshold. Elements of the threshold sort are then used instead of the actual threshold in the description of the protocol and in the verification conditions. For verification to succeed, some properties of the sets satisfying the cardinality threshold must be captured in FOL. This is done by introducing additional assumptions (formally, axioms of the transition system) expressed in FOL, as discussed in Sect. 4.

1　Input: v_p	1　sort node, value, set$_{n-t}$, set$_{\frac{n+3t+1}{2}}$, set$_{\frac{n-t+1}{2}}$
2　**broadcast** v_p to all processes	2　$\cdots$
3　**wait until** $n - t$ messages have been received	3　**assume** $\exists q$: set$_{n-t}$. $\forall m$: node. $member(m,q) \to$
4	4　$\exists u$: value. $rcv\_msg(n,m,u)$
5　**if** there exists v s.t. more than $\frac{n+3t}{2}$	5　**if** $\exists v$: value, q : set$_{\frac{n+3t+1}{2}}$. $\forall m$: node.
6　　messages contain value v **then**	6　　$member(m,q) \to rcv\_msg(n,m,v)$ **then**
7　　DECIDE(v)	7　　$decision(n,v) :=$ true
8　**if** there exists exactly one v s.t. more than	8　**if** $\exists! v$: value. $\exists q$: set$_{\frac{n-t+1}{2}}$. $\forall m$: node.
9　　$\frac{n-t}{2}$ messages contain value v **then**	9　　$member(m,q) \to rcv\_msg(n,m,v)$ **then**
10　　$v_p := v$	10　　$v_p := v$
11　**call** underlying$-$consensus(v_p)	11　$und\_cons(n,v_p) :=$ true

Fig. 1. Bosco: a one-step asynchronous Byzantine consensus algorithm [39], and an excerpt RML (relational modeling language) code of the main transition. Note that we overload the *member* relation for all threshold sorts. The formula $\exists! x.\, \varphi(x)$ is a shorthand for exists and unique.

Running Example. We illustrate our approach using the example of Bosco— an asynchronous Byzantine fault-tolerant (BFT) consensus algorithm [39]. Its modeling in first-order logic using our technique appears alongside an informal pseudo-code in Fig. 1.

In the BFT consensus problem, each node proposes a value and correct nodes must decide on a unique proposal. BFT consensus algorithms typically require at least two communication rounds to reach a decision. In Bosco, nodes execute a preliminary communication step which, under favorable conditions, reaches an early decision, and then call an underlying BFT consensus algorithm to ensure reaching a decision even if these conditions are not met. Bosco is safe when **n > 3t**; it guarantees that a preliminary decision will be reached if all nodes are non-faulty and propose the same value when **n > 5t** (weakly one-step condition), and even if some nodes are faulty, as long as all non-faulty nodes propose the same value, when **n > 7t** (strongly one-step condition).

Bosco achieves consensus by ensuring that (a) no two correct nodes decide differently in the preliminary step, and (b) if a correct node decides value v in the preliminary step then every correct process calls the underlying BFT consensus algorithm with proposal v. Property (a) is ensured by the fact that a node decides in the preliminary step only if more than $\frac{n+3t}{2}$ nodes proposed the same value. When **n > 3t**, two sets of cardinality greater than $\frac{n+3t}{2}$ have at least one non-faulty node in common, and therefore no two different values can be proposed by more than $\frac{n+3t}{2}$ nodes. Similarly, we can derive property (b) from the fact that a set of more than $\frac{n+3t}{2}$ nodes and a set of **n − t** nodes intersect in $\frac{\mathbf{n}+\mathbf{t}}{2}$ nodes, which, after removing t nodes which may be faulty, still leaves us with more than $\frac{\mathbf{n}-\mathbf{t}}{2}$ nodes, satisfying the condition in line 9.

3.1   Threshold-Based Protocols

Parameters and Resilience Conditions. We consider protocols whose definitions depend on a set of *parameters*, *Prm*, divided into *integer parameters*, Prm_I, and *set parameters*, Prm_S. Prm_I always includes $\mathbf{n}$, the total number of nodes (assumed to be finite). Protocol correctness is ensured under a set of assumptions Γ called *resilience conditions*, formulated as BAPA formulas over *Prm* (this means that all the uninterpreted constants appearing in Γ are from *Prm*). In Bosco, $Prm_I = \{\mathbf{n}, \mathbf{t}\}$, where $\mathbf{t}$ is the maximal number of Byzantine failures tolerated by the algorithm, and $Prm_S = \{\mathbf{f}\}$, where $\mathbf{f}$ is the set of Byzantine nodes; $\Gamma = \{\mathbf{n} \geq 3\mathbf{t} + 1, |\mathbf{f}| \leq \mathbf{t}\}$.

Threshold Conditions. Both the description of the protocol and the inductive invariant may include conditions that require the size of some set of nodes to be "at least t", "at most t", and so on, where the threshold t is of the form $t = \frac{\ell}{k}$, where k is a positive integer, and ℓ is a ground BAPA integer term over *Prm* (we do not allow comparing sizes of two sets – we observe that it is not needed for threshold-based protocols). We denote the set of thresholds by T. For example, in Bosco, $T = \{\mathbf{n} - \mathbf{t}, \frac{\mathbf{n}+3\mathbf{t}+1}{2}, \frac{\mathbf{n}-\mathbf{t}+1}{2}\}$.

Wlog we assume that all conditions on set cardinalities are of the form "at least t" since every condition can be written this way, possibly by introducing new thresholds:

$$|X| > \frac{\ell}{k} \equiv |X| \geq \frac{\ell+1}{k} \qquad |X| \leq \frac{\ell}{k} \equiv |X^c| \geq \frac{k \cdot \mathbf{n} - \ell}{k} \qquad |X| < \frac{\ell}{k} \equiv |X| \leq \frac{\ell-1}{k}$$

3.2   Modeling in FOL

FO Vocabulary for Modeling Threshold-Based Protocols. We describe the protocol's states (e.g., pending messages, votes, etc.) using a core FO vocabulary Σ_C that includes sort node and additional sorts and symbols. Parameters *Prm* are *not* part of the FO vocabulary used to model the protocol. Also, we do not model set cardinality directly. Instead, we encode the cardinality thresholds in FOL by defining a FO vocabulary Σ_T^{Prm}:

- For every threshold t we introduce a *threshold sort* set$_t$ with the intended meaning that elements of this sort are sets of nodes whose size is at least t.
- Each sort set$_t$ is equipped with a binary relation symbol *member$_t$* between sorts node and set$_t$ that captures the membership relation of a node in a set.
- For each set parameter $\mathbf{a} \in Prm_S$ we introduce a unary relation symbol *member$_\mathbf{a}$* over sort node that captures membership of a node in the set $\mathbf{a}$.

We then model the protocol as a transition system (Σ, Θ, I, TR) where $\Sigma = \Sigma_C \uplus \Sigma_T^{Prm}$.

We are interested only in states (FO structures over Σ) where the interpretation of the threshold sorts and membership relations is according to their intended meaning in a corresponding BAPA structure. Formally, these are T-extensions, defined as follows:

Definition 1. *We say that a FO structure $s_C = (\mathcal{D}_C, \mathcal{I}_C)$ over Σ_C and a BAPA structure $s_B = (\mathcal{D}_B, \mathcal{I}_B)$ over Prm are compatible if $\mathcal{D}_B(\text{set}) = \mathcal{P}(\mathcal{D}_C(\text{node}))$, where $\mathcal{P}$ is the powerset operator. For such compatible structures and a set of thresholds T over Prm, the T-extension of s_C by s_B is the structure $s = (\mathcal{D}, \mathcal{I})$ over Σ defined as follows:*

$\mathcal{D}(\text{s}) = \mathcal{D}_C(\text{s})$ *for every sort* s *in* Σ_C $\qquad \mathcal{I}(a) = \mathcal{I}_C(a)$ *for every* a *in* Σ_C

$\mathcal{D}(\text{set}_t) = \{A \subseteq \mathcal{D}_C(\text{node}) \mid |A| \geq \mathcal{I}_B(t)\} \qquad \mathcal{I}(member_{\mathbf{a}}) = \mathcal{I}_B(\mathbf{a})$

$\mathcal{I}(member_t) = \{(e, A) \mid e \in \mathcal{D}_C(\text{node}), A \in \mathcal{D}(\text{set}_t), e \in A\}$

Note that for the T-extension s to be well defined as a FO structure, we must have that $\mathcal{D}(\text{set}_t) \neq \emptyset$ for every threshold $t \in T$. This means that a T-extension by s_B only exists if $\{A \subseteq \mathcal{D}(\text{node}) \mid |A| \geq \mathcal{I}_B(t)\} \neq \emptyset$. This is ensured by the following condition:

Definition 2 (Feasibility). *T is Γ-feasible if $\Gamma \models t \leq \mathbf{n}$ for every $t \in T$.*

Expressing Threshold Constraints. Cardinality constraints can be expressed in FOL over the vocabulary $\Sigma = \Sigma_C \uplus \Sigma_T^{Prm}$ using quantification. To express that $|\{n : \text{node} \mid \varphi(n, \bar{u})\}| \geq t$, i.e., that there are at least t nodes that satisfy the FO formula φ over Σ_C (where $\bar{u}$ are free variables in φ), we use the following first-order formula over Σ: $\exists q : \text{set}_t. \forall n : \text{node}. \, member_t(n, q) \rightarrow \varphi(n, \bar{u})$. Similarly, to express the property that a node is a member of a set parameter $\mathbf{a}$ (e.g., to check if $n \in \mathbf{f}$, i.e., a node is faulty) we use the FO formula $member_{\mathbf{a}}(n)$. For example, in Fig. 1, line 5 (right) uses the FO modeling to express the condition in line 5 (left). This modeling is sound in the following sense:

Lemma 1 (Soundness). *Let $s_C = (\mathcal{D}_C, \mathcal{I}_C)$ be a FO structure over Σ_C, $s_B = (\mathcal{D}_B, \mathcal{I}_B)$ a compatible BAPA structure over Prm s.t. $s_B \models \Gamma$ and T a Γ-feasible set of thresholds over Prm. Then there exists a (unique) T-extension s of s_C by s_B. Further:*

1. *For every $\mathbf{a} \in Prm_S$ and FO valuation ι: $s, \iota \models member_{\mathbf{a}}(n)$ iff $\iota(n) \in \mathcal{I}_B(\mathbf{a})$,*
2. *For every $t \in T$, formula φ, and FO valuation ι: $s, \iota \models \exists q : \text{set}_t. \forall n : \text{node}. \, member_t(n, q) \rightarrow \varphi(n, \bar{u})$ iff $|\{e \in \mathcal{D}(\text{node}) \mid s_C, \iota[n \mapsto e] \models \varphi(n, \bar{u})\}| \geq \mathcal{I}_B(t)$.*

Definition 3. *A first-order structure s over Σ is threshold-faithful if it is a T-extension of some s_C by some $s_B \models \Gamma$ (as in Lemma 1).*

Incompleteness. Lemma 1 ensures that the FO modeling can be soundly used to verify the protocol. It also ensures that the modeling is precise on threshold-faithful structures (Def. 1). Yet, the FO transition system is not restricted to such states, hence it *abstracts* the actual protocol. To have any hope to verify the protocol, we must capture *some* of the intended meaning of the threshold sorts and relations. This is obtained by adding FO axioms to the FO transition system. Soundness is maintained as long as the axioms hold in all threshold-faithful structures. We note that the set of *all* such axioms is not recursively enumerable– this is where the essential incompleteness of our approach lies.

4   Decomposition via Threshold Intersection Properties

In this section, we identify a set of properties we call *threshold intersection properties*. When captured via FO axioms, these properties suffice for verifying many threshold-based protocols (all the ones we considered). Importantly, these are properties of sets adhering to the thresholds that do not involve the protocol state. As a result, they can be expressed both in FOL and in BAPA. This allows us to decompose the verification task into: (i) checking that certain threshold properties are valid in all threshold-faithful structures by checking that they are implied by Γ (carried out using quantifier free BAPA), and (ii) checking that the verification conditions of the FO transition-system with the same threshold properties taken as axioms are valid (carried out in first-order logic, and in EPR if quantifier alternations are acyclic).

4.1   Threshold Intersection Property Language

Threshold properties are expressed in the *threshold intersection property language* (TIP). TIP is essentially a subset of BAPA, specialized to have the properties listed above.

Syntax. We define TIP as follows, with $t \in T$ a threshold (of the form $\frac{\ell}{k}$) and $\mathbf{a} \in Prm_S$:

$$F ::= B \neq \emptyset \mid B^c = \emptyset \mid g_{\geq t}(B) \mid F_1 \wedge F_2 \mid \forall x : g_{\geq t}.F$$
$$B ::= \mathbf{a} \mid \mathbf{a}^c \mid x \mid x^c \mid \emptyset \mid \emptyset^c \mid B_1 \cap B_2$$

TIP restricts the use of set cardinality to *threshold guards* $g_{\geq t}(b)$ with the meaning $|b| \geq t$. No other arithmetic atomic formulas are allowed. Comparison atomic formulas are restricted to $b \neq \emptyset$ and $b^c = \emptyset$. Quantifiers must be guarded, and negation, disjunction and existential quantification are excluded. We forbid set union and restrict complementation to atomic set terms. We refer to such formulas as *intersection properties* since they express properties of intersections of (atomic) sets.

Example 1. In Bosco, the following property captures the fact that the intersection of a set of at least $\mathbf{n} - \mathbf{t}$ nodes and a set of more than $\frac{\mathbf{n}+3\mathbf{t}}{2}$ nodes consists of at least $\frac{\mathbf{n}-\mathbf{t}}{2}$ non-faulty nodes. This is needed for establishing correctness of the protocol.

$$\forall x : g_{\geq \mathbf{n}-\mathbf{t}}. \forall y : g_{\geq \frac{\mathbf{n}+3\mathbf{t}+1}{2}}. g_{\geq \frac{\mathbf{n}-\mathbf{t}+1}{2}}(x \cap y \cap \mathbf{f}^c)$$

Semantics. As TIP is essentially a subset of BAPA, we define its semantics by translating its formulas to BAPA, where most constructs directly correspond to BAPA constructs, and guards are translated to cardinality constraints:

$$\mathcal{B}(g_{\geq \frac{\ell}{k}}(b)) \stackrel{\text{def}}{=} k \cdot |b| \geq \ell \qquad \mathcal{B}(\forall x : g. \ \varphi) \stackrel{\text{def}}{=} \forall x. \ \neg \mathcal{B}(g(x)) \vee \mathcal{B}(\varphi)$$

The notions of structures, satisfaction, equivalence, validity, satisfiability, etc. are inherited from BAPA. In particular, given a set of BAPA resilience conditions Γ over the parameters *Prm*, we say that a TIP formula φ is Γ-valid, denoted $\Gamma \models \varphi$, if $\Gamma \models \mathcal{B}(\varphi)$.

If Γ is quantifier-free (which is the typical case), Γ-validity of TIP formulas can be checked via validity checks of quantifier-free BAPA formulas, supported by mature solvers. Note that Γ-validity of a formula of the form $\forall x : g_{\geq t_1}. \ |x \cap b| \geq t_2$ is equivalent to $\Gamma \models \forall u. \ u \geq t_1 \rightarrow u + |b| - n \geq t_2$, allowing replacing quantification over sets by quantification over integers, thus improving performance of existing solvers.

4.2 Translation to FOL

To verify threshold-based protocols, we translate TIP formulas to FO axioms, using the threshold sorts and relations. To translate $g_{\geq t}(b)$, we follow the principle in (Sect. 3.2):

$$\mathcal{FO}(\neg \varphi) = \neg \mathcal{FO}(\varphi) \qquad\qquad \mathcal{FO}(n \in b^c) = \neg \mathcal{FO}(n \in b)$$
$$\mathcal{FO}(\varphi_1 \wedge \varphi_2) = \mathcal{FO}(\varphi_1) \wedge \mathcal{FO}(\varphi_2) \qquad \mathcal{FO}(n \in \emptyset) = \textit{false}$$
$$\mathcal{FO}(\forall x : g. \varphi) = \forall x : \mathsf{set}_g. \mathcal{FO}(\varphi) \qquad \mathcal{FO}(n \in \mathbf{a}) = \textit{member}_{\mathbf{a}}(n)$$
$$\mathcal{FO}(n \in b_1 \cap b_2) = \mathcal{FO}(n \in b_1) \wedge \mathcal{FO}(n \in b_2) \qquad \mathcal{FO}(n \in x) = \textit{member}_t(n, x)$$
$$\mathcal{FO}(b \neq \emptyset) = \exists n : \mathsf{node}. \mathcal{FO}(n \in b) \qquad\qquad \text{where } x \text{ is guarded by } t$$
$$\mathcal{FO}(b^c = \emptyset) = \forall n : \mathsf{node}. \mathcal{FO}(n \in b)$$
$$\mathcal{FO}(g_{\geq t}(b)) = \exists x : \mathsf{set}_t. \forall n : \mathsf{node}. \textit{member}_t(n, x) \rightarrow \mathcal{FO}(n \in b)$$

We lift $\mathcal{FO}$ to sets of formulas: $\mathcal{FO}(\Delta) = \{\mathcal{FO}(\varphi) \mid \varphi \in \Delta\}$.

Next, we state the soundness of the translation, which intuitively means that $\mathcal{FO}(\varphi)$ is "equivalent" to φ over threshold-faithful FO structures (Definition 1). This justifies adding $\mathcal{FO}(\varphi)$ as a FO axiom whenever φ is Γ-valid.

Theorem 1 (Translation soundness). *Let $s_C = (\mathcal{D}_C, \mathcal{I}_C)$ be a first-order structure over Σ_C, $s_B = (\mathcal{D}_B, \mathcal{I}_B)$ a compatible BAPA structure over Prm, and s the T-extension of s_C by s_B. Then for every closed TIP formula φ, we have $s_B \models \varphi \Leftrightarrow s \models \mathcal{FO}(\varphi)$.*

Corollary 1. *For every closed TIP formula φ such that $\Gamma \models \varphi$, we have that $\mathcal{FO}(\varphi)$ is satisfied by every threshold-faithful first-order structure.*

5   Automatically Inferring Threshold Intersection Properties

To apply the approach described in Sects. 3 and 4, it is crucial to find suitable threshold properties. That is, given the resilience conditions Γ and a FO transition system modeling the protocol, we need to find a set Δ of TIP formulas such that (i) $\Gamma \models \varphi$ for every $\varphi \in \Delta$, and (ii) the VCs of the transition system with the axioms $\mathcal{FO}(\Delta)$ are valid.

In this section, we address the problem of automatically inferring such a set Δ. In particular, we prove that for any protocol that satisfies a natural condition, there are finitely many Γ-valid TIP formulas (up to equivalence), enabling a complete automatic inference algorithm. Furthermore, we show that (under certain reasonable conditions formalized in this section), the FO axioms resulting from the inferred TIP properties have an *acyclic* quantifier alternation graph, facilitating protocol verification in EPR.

Notation. For the rest of this section, we fix a set Prm of parameters, a set Γ of resilience conditions over Prm, and a set T of thresholds. Note that $b \neq \emptyset \equiv g_{\geq 1}(b)$ and $b^c = \emptyset \equiv g_{\geq \mathbf{n}}(b)$. Therefore, for uniformity of the presentation, given a set T of thresholds, we define $\hat{T} \stackrel{\text{def}}{=} T \cup \{1, \mathbf{n}\}$ and replace atomic formulas of the form $b \neq \emptyset$ and $b^c = \emptyset$ by the corresponding guard formulas. As such, the only atomic formulas are of the form $g_{\geq t}(b)$ where $t \in \hat{T}$. Note that guards in quantifiers are still restricted to $g_{\geq t}$ where $t \in T$. Given a set Prm_S, we also denote $\hat{Prm}_S = Prm_S \cup \{\mathbf{a}^c \mid \mathbf{a} \in Prm_S\}$.

5.1   Finding Consequences in the Threshold Intersection Property Language

In this section, we present AIP– an algorithm for inferring all Γ-valid TIP formulas. A naïve (non-terminating) algorithm would iteratively check Γ-validity of every TIP formula. Instead, AIP prunes the search space relying on the following condition:

Definition 4. T *is Γ-non-degenerate if for every $t \in T$ it holds that $\Gamma \not\models t \leq 0$.*

If $\Gamma \models t \leq 0$ then t is degenerate in the sense that $g_{\geq t}(b)$ is always Γ-valid, and $\forall x : g_{\geq t}.\ g_{\geq t'}(x \cap b)$ is never Γ-valid unless t' is also degenerate. We observe that we can (i) push conjunctions outside of formulas (since $\forall$ distributes over $\wedge$), and assuming non-degeneracy, (ii) ignore terms of the form x^c:

Lemma 2. *If T is Γ-feasible and Γ-non-degenerate, then for every Γ-valid φ in TIP, there exist $\varphi_1, \ldots, \varphi_m$ s.t. $\varphi \equiv \bigwedge_{i=1}^{m} \varphi_i$ and for every $1 \leq i \leq m$, φ_i is of the form:*

$$\forall x_1 : g_{\geq t_1} \ldots \forall x_q : g_{\geq t_q}.\ g_{\geq t}(x_1 \cap \ldots \cap x_q \cap a_1 \ldots \cap a_k)$$

where $q + k > 0$, $t_1, \ldots, t_q \in T$, $t \in \hat{T}$, $a_1, \ldots, a_k \in \mathring{Prm}_S$, and the a_i's are distinct.

We refer to φ_i of the form above as *simple*, and refer to $g_{\geq t}$ as its *atomic guard*.

By Lemma 2, it suffices to generate all *simple* Γ-valid formulas. Next, we show that this can be done more efficiently by pruning the search space based on a subsumption relation that is checked syntactically avoiding Γ-validity checks.

Definition 5 (Subsumption). *For every $h_1, h_2 \in \hat{T} \cup \mathring{Prm}_S$, we denote $h_1 \sqsubseteq_\Gamma h_2$ if one of the following holds: (1) $h_1 = h_2$, or (2) $h_1, h_2 \in \hat{T}$ and $\Gamma \models h_1 \geq h_2$, or (3) $h_1 \in \mathring{Prm}_S$, $h_2 \in \hat{T}$ and $\Gamma \models |h_1| \geq h_2$.*

For $h_1, h_2 \in \hat{T}$ and $h_3 \in \mathring{Prm}_S$, $h_1 \sqsubseteq_\Gamma h_2$ means that $\Gamma \models \forall x : g_{\geq h_1}.\ g_{\geq h_2}(x)$, and $h_3 \sqsubseteq_\Gamma h_2$ means that $\Gamma \models g_{\geq h_2}(h_3)$. We lift the relation $\sqsubseteq_\Gamma$ to act on simple formulas:

Definition 6. *Given simple formulas*

$$\alpha = \forall x_1 : g_{\geq h_1} \ldots \forall x_q : g_{\geq h_q}.\ g_{\geq t}(x_1 \cap \ldots \cap x_q \cap h_{q+1} \ldots \cap h_k)$$
$$\beta = \forall x_1 : g_{\geq h'_1} \ldots \forall x_{q'} : g_{\geq h'_{q'}}.\ g_{\geq t'}(x_1 \cap \ldots \cap x_{q'} \cap h'_{q'+1} \ldots \cap h'_{k'})$$

we say that $\alpha \sqsubseteq_\Gamma \beta$ if (i) $t \sqsubseteq_\Gamma t'$, and (ii) there exists an injective function $f : \{1, \ldots, k'\} \to \{1, \ldots, k\}$ s.t. for any $1 \leq i \leq k'$ it holds that $h'_i \sqsubseteq_\Gamma h_{f(i)}$.

Lemma 3. *Let α, β be simple formulas such that $\alpha \sqsubseteq_\Gamma \beta$. If $\Gamma \models \alpha$ then $\Gamma \models \beta$.*

Corollary 2. *If no simple formula with q quantifiers is Γ-valid then no simple formula with more than q quantifiers is Γ-valid.*

Algorithm 1 depicts AIP that generates all Γ-valid simple formulas, relying on Lemma 3. AIP uses a naïve search strategy; different strategies can be used (e.g. [26]). Based on Corollary 2, AIP terminates if for some number of quantifiers no Γ-valid formula is discovered.

Algorithm 1. Algorithm for Inferring Intersection Properties (AIP)

Input: Prm_S, T, Γ

1   set checked_true = checked_false = [ ] ;
2   **foreach** $q = 0, 1, \ldots$ **do**
3   **foreach** *simple formula φ over T and Prm_S with q quantifiers* **do**
4   **if** *exists $\psi \in$ checked_true s.t. $\psi \sqsubseteq_\Gamma \varphi$* **then**   yield φ ;
5   **else if** *exists $\psi \in$ checked_false s.t. $\varphi \sqsubseteq_\Gamma \psi$* **then**   continue ;
6   **else if** $\Gamma \models \varphi$ **then**   yield φ ; add φ to checked_true ;
7   **else**   add φ to checked_false ;
8   **if** *no formulas were added to checked_true* **then**   terminate ;

Lemma 4 (Soundness). *Every formula φ that is returned by the algorithm is Γ-valid.*

Lemma 5 (Completeness). *If T is Γ-feasible and Γ-non-degenerate, then for every Γ-valid TIP formula φ there exist $\varphi_1 \ldots \varphi_m$ s.t. $\varphi \equiv \bigwedge_{i=1}^{m} \varphi_i$ and AIP yields every φ_i.*

Next, we characterize the cases in which there are finitely many Γ-valid TIP formulas, up to equivalence, and thus, AIP is guaranteed to terminate.

Definition 7. *T is Γ-sane if for every $t_1, t_2 \in T$, $\Gamma \not\models t_1 \leq 0 \vee t_2 > \mathbf{n} - 1$. (T, Prm_S) is Γ-sane if, in addition, for every $t_1 \in T$, $a \in \hat{Prm}_S$, $\Gamma \not\models t_1 \leq 0 \vee |a| = \mathbf{n}$.*

Theorem 2. *Assume that T is Γ-feasible. Then the following conditions are equivalent: (1) There are finitely many Γ-valid simple formulas. (2) There are finitely many Γ-valid TIP formulas, up to equivalence. (3) T is Γ-sane.*

Corollary 3 (Termination). *If T is Γ-feasible and Γ-sane, AIP terminates.*

5.2 From TIP to Axioms in EPR

The set of simple formulas generated by AIP, Δ, is translated to FOL axioms as described in Sect. 4.2. Next, we show how to ensure that the quantifier alternation graph (Sect. 2) of $\mathcal{FO}(\Delta)$ is acyclic. A simple formula induces quantifier alternation edges in $QA(\mathcal{FO}(\varphi))$ from the sorts of its universal quantifiers to the sort of its atomic guard $g_{\geq t}$ (or if $t = 1$ to the node sort). Therefore, from Lemma 3, for a Γ-valid φ, cycles in $QA(\mathcal{FO}(\varphi))$ may only occur if they occur in the graph obtained by $\sqsubseteq_\Gamma$. Furthermore, if $QA(\mathcal{FO}(\varphi))$ is not acyclic, then the atomic guard must be equal to one of the quantifier guards. We refer to such a formula as a *cyclic formula*. We show that, under the following assumption, we can eliminate all cyclic formulas from Δ.

Definition 8. *T is Γ-acyclic if for every $t_1, t_2 \in T$, if $\Gamma \models t_1 = t_2$ then $t_1 = t_2$.*

Intuitively, if T is not Γ-acyclic, then it has (at least) two "equivalent" thresholds, making one of them redundant. If that is the case, we can alter the protocol and its proof so that one of these guards is eliminated and the other one is used instead.

Theorem 3. *Let T be Γ-feasible and Γ-acyclic and (T, Prm_S) be Γ-sane. Let Δ be the set returned by AIP, and $\Delta' = \{\varphi \in \Delta \mid \varphi \text{ is acyclic}\}$. Then the VCs of the FO transition system with axioms $\mathcal{FO}(\Delta)$ are valid iff they are valid with axioms $\mathcal{FO}(\Delta')$. Further, $QA(\mathcal{FO}(\Delta'))$ is acyclic.*

5.3 Finding Minimal Properties Required for a Protocol

If Δ consists of *all* acyclic Γ-valid TIP formulas returned by AIP, using $\mathcal{FO}(\Delta)$ as FO axioms leads to divergence of the verifier. To overcome this, we propose two variants.

Minimal Equivalent. Δ_{min}. Some of the formulas in $\mathcal{FO}(\Delta)$ are implied by others, making them redundant. We remove such formulas using a greedy procedure that for every $\varphi_i \in \Delta$, checks whether $\mathcal{FO}(\Delta \setminus \{\varphi_i\}) \models \mathcal{FO}(\varphi_i)$, and if so, removes φ_i from Δ. Note that if $QA(\mathcal{FO}(\Delta))$ is acyclic, the check translates to (un)satisfiability in EPR.

This procedure results in $\Delta_{min} \subseteq \Delta$ s.t. $\mathcal{FO}(\Delta_{min}) \models \mathcal{FO}(\Delta)$ and no strict subset of Δ_{min} satisfies this condition. That is, Δ_{min} is a local minimum for that property.

Interpolant. Δ_{int}. There may exist $\Delta_{int} \subseteq \Delta$ s.t. $\mathcal{FO}(\Delta_{int}) \not\models \mathcal{FO}(\Delta)$ but $\mathcal{FO}(\Delta_{int})$ suffices to prove the first-order VCs, and enables to discharge the VCs more efficiently. We compute such a set Δ_{int} iteratively. Initially, $\Delta_{int} = \emptyset$. In each iteration, we check the VCs. If a counterexample to induction (CTI) is found, we add to Δ_{int} a formula from Δ not satisfied by the CTI. In this approach, Δ is not pre-computed. Instead, AIP is invoked lazily to generate candidate formulas in reaction to CTIs.

6   Evaluation

We evaluate the approach by verifying several challenging threshold-based distributed protocols that use sophisticated thresholds: we verify the safety of Bosco [39] (presented in Sect. 3) under its 3 different resilience conditions, the safety and liveness (using the liveness to safety reduction presented in [30]) of Hybrid Reliable Broadcast [40], and the safety of Byzantine Fast Paxos [23]. Hybrid Reliable Broadcast tolerates four different types of faults, while Fast Byzantine Paxos is a fast-learning [21,22] Byzantine fault-tolerant consensus protocol; fast-learning protocols are notorious because two such algorithms, Zyzzyva [17] and FaB [28], were recently revealed incorrect [1] despite having been published at major systems conferences.

Implementation. We implemented both algorithms described in Sect. 5.3. $\text{AIP}_{\text{EAGER}}$ eagerly constructs Δ by running AIP, and then uses EPR reasoning to remove redundant formulas (whose FO representation is implied by the FO representation of others). To reduce the number of EPR validity checks used during this minimization step, we implemented an optimization that allows us to prove redundancy of TIP formulas internally based on an extension of the notion of subsumption from Sect. 5. AIP_{LAZY} computes a subset of Δ while using AIP in a lazy fashion, guided by CTIs obtained from attempting to verify the FO transition system. Our implementations use CVC4 to discharge BAPA queries, and Z3 to discharge EPR queries. Verification of first-order transition systems is performed using Ivy, which internally uses Z3 as well. All experiments reported were performed on a laptop running 64-bit Windows 10, with a Core-i5 2.2 GHz CPU, using Z3 version 4.8.4, CVC4 version 1.7, and the latest version of Ivy.

Figure 2 lists the protocols we verified and the details of the evaluation. Each experiment was repeated 10 times, and we report the mean time (μ) and standard

Protocol	T	Γ	AIP$_{\text{EAGER}}$						AIP$_{\text{LAZY}}$						
			V	I	Q	t_C	$\Delta_{\text{EAGER}}^{\text{Protocol}}$	t_v	$\Delta_{\text{LAZY}}^{\text{Protocol}}$	V	I	CTI	Q	t_I	t_v
Bosco	$t_1=\mathbf{n}-t$ $t_2=\frac{\mathbf{n}+3t+1}{2}$ $t_3=\frac{\mathbf{n}-t-1}{2}$	$\mathbf{n}>3t$ $\lvert f\rvert\le t$	$\frac{23}{39}$	$\frac{21}{1216}$	6	$3s$	$g_1(f^c)$ $\forall x{:}g_1.y{:}g_1.z{:}g_2.g_3.(x\cap y\cap z)\neq\emptyset$	$\mu(12s)$ $\sigma(4s)$	$g_1(f^c)$ $\forall x{:}g_1.y{:}g_1.y{:}g_2.g_3.(x\cap y\cap f^c)$ $\forall x{:}g_2.y{:}g_2.x{:}g_3.x\cap y\cap f^c\neq\emptyset$	24	6	18	2	$\mu(3m)$ $\sigma(1m)$	$\mu(4s)$ $\sigma(0.4s)$
Bosco Weakly One-step	$''$	$\mathbf{n}>5t$ $\lvert f\rvert\le t$	$\frac{16}{51}$	$\frac{24}{1204}$	6	$3s$	$\Delta_{\text{EAGER}}^{\text{Bosco}}$ $\forall x{:}g_1.g_2(x)$	$\mu(13m)$ $\sigma(14m)$	$\Delta_{\text{LAZY}}^{\text{Bosco}}$ $\forall x{:}g_1.g_2(x)$	32	7	19	2	$\mu(13m)$ $\sigma(9m)$	$\mu(9s)$ $\sigma(2s)$
Bosco Strongly One-step	$''$	$\mathbf{n}>7t$ $\lvert f\rvert\le t$	$\frac{26}{63}$	$\frac{24}{2407}$	8	$8s$	$\Delta_{\text{EAGER}}^{\text{Bosco}}$ $\forall x{:}g_1.g_1.g_2(x\cap y)$	T.O.	$\Delta_{\text{LAZY}}^{\text{Bosco}}$ $\forall x{:}g_1.g_2(x\cap f^c)$	34	9	20	2	$\mu(23m)$ $\sigma(8m)$	$\mu(16s)$ $\sigma(13s)$
Hybrid Reliable Broadcast	$t_1=t_a+t_s+1$ $t_2=\mathbf{n}-t_c-t_a$ $-t_s-t_i$	$\mathbf{n}>t_c+3t_a+$ $2t_s+2t_i$ $\lvert f_x\rvert\le t_x$ $f_x\cap f_y=\emptyset$ for $x\neq y$ $x,y\in\{a,c,i,s\}$	$\frac{25}{63}$	$\frac{34}{1877}$	2	$37s$	$g_2(f_c^c\cap f_a^c\cap f_s^c\cap f_i^c)$ $\forall x{:}g_1.x\cap f_a^c\cap f_s^c\neq\emptyset$ $\forall x{:}g_2.g_1(x\cap f_a^c\cap f_i^c)$	$\mu(35s)$ $\sigma(0.3s)$	$\Delta_{\text{EAGER}}^{\text{Hybrid Reliable Broadcast}}$	63	15	45	1	$\mu(15m)$ $\sigma(1.5m)$	$\mu(43s)$ $\sigma(1s)$
Byzantine Fast Paxos	$t_1=\mathbf{n}-t$ $t_2=\mathbf{n}-q$ $t_3=\mathbf{n}-2t-q$ $t_4=t+1$	$\mathbf{n}>2q+3t$ $t\ge q$ $q\ge0$ $\lvert b\rvert\le t$	$\frac{22}{79}$	$\frac{44}{3695}$	6	$6s$	$g_1(b^c)$ $\forall x{:}g_2.g_1(x)$ $\forall x{:}g_1.g_4.x\cap y\neq\emptyset$ $\forall x{:}g_2.g_3.g_4.(x\cap y)$ $\forall x{:}g_1.y{:}g_1.z{:}g_2.g_3.(x\cap y\cap z)$	T.O.	$g_1(b^c)$ $\forall x{:}g_2.g_1(x)$ $\forall x{:}g_3.x\neq\emptyset$ $\forall x{:}g_4.x\neq\emptyset$ $\forall x{:}g_3(x\cap b^c)$ $\forall x{:}g_1.g_1.g_4(x\cap y)$	44	11	19	2	$\mu(36m)$ $\sigma(21m)$	$\mu(28m)$ $\sigma(19m)$

Fig. 2. Protocols verified using our technique. For each protocol, T is the set of thresholds and Γ is the resilience condition. AIP$_{\text{EAGER}}$ lists metrics for the procedure of finding all Γ-valid TIP formulas (taking time t_C), and verifying the transition system using the resulting properties (taking time t_v). Obtaining a minimal subset that FO-implies the rest takes negligible time, so we did not include it in the table. The properties are given in $\Delta_{\text{EAGER}}^{\text{Protocol}}$, where g_i denotes $g_{\ge t_i}$. In addition to the run times, $\mathbf{V}$ shows $\frac{c}{v}$, where c is the number of Γ-valid simple formulas that were checked using the BAPA solver (CVC4), and v is the total number of Γ-valid simple formulas. Namely, $v - c$ simple formulas were inferred to be valid via subsumption. $\mathbf{I}$ reports the analogous metric for Γ-invalid). $\mathbf{Q}$ reports the maximal number of quantifiers considered (for which all formulas were Γ-invalid). AIP$_{\text{LAZY}}$ lists metrics for the procedure of finding a set of Γ-valid TIP formulas sufficient to prove the protocol based on counterexamples. The resulting set is listed in $\Delta_{\text{LAZY}}^{\text{Protocol}}$, and t_I lists the total Ivy runtime, with the standard deviation specified below. $\mathbf{V}$ (resp. $\mathbf{I}$) lists the number of Γ-valid (resp. Γ-invalid) simple formulas considered before the final set was reached. $\mathbf{CTI}$ lists the number of counterexample iterations required, and $\mathbf{Q}$ lists the maximal number of quantifiers of any TIP formula considered. Finally, t_v lists the time required to verify the first-order transition system assuming the obtained set of properties. T.O. indicates that a time out of 1 h was reached.

deviation (σ). The figure's caption explains the presented information, and we discuss the results below.

Aip$_{\text{EAGER}}$ For all protocols, running A$_{\text{IP}}$ took less than 1 min (column $\mathbf{t_C}$), and generated all Γ-valid simple TIP formulas. We observe that for most formulas, (in)validity is deduced from other formulas by subsumption, and less than 2%–5% of the formulas are actually checked using a BAPA query. With the optimization of the redundancy check, minimization of the set is performed in negligible time. The resulting set, Δ_{EAGER}, contains 3–5 formulas, compared to 39–79 before minimization.

Due to the optimization described in Sect. 4 for the BAPA validity queries, the number of quantifiers in the TIP formulas that are checked by A$_{\text{IP}}$ does not affect the time needed to compute the full Δ. For example, Bosco under the Strongly One-step resilience condition contains Γ-valid simple TIP formulas with up to 7 quantifiers (as $\mathbf{n} > 7\mathbf{t}$ and $t_1 = \mathbf{n} - \mathbf{t}$), but A$_{\text{IP}}$ does not take significantly longer to find Δ. Interestingly, in this example the Γ-valid TIP formulas with more than 3 quantifiers are implied (in FOL) by formulas with at most 3 quantifiers, as indicated by the fact that these are the only formulas that remain in $\Delta_{\text{EAGER}}^{\text{Bosco Strongly One-step}}$.

Aip$_{\text{LAZY}}$ With the lazy approach based on CTIs, the time for finding the set of TIP formulas, Δ_{LAZY}, is generally longer. This is because the run time is dominated by calls to Ivy with FO axioms that are too weak for verifying the protocol. However, the resulting Δ_{LAZY} has a significant benefit: it lets Ivy prove the protocol much faster compared to using Δ_{EAGER}. Comparing $\mathbf{t_V}$ in A$_{\text{IP EAGER}}$ vs. A$_{\text{IP LAZY}}$ shows that when the former takes a minute, the latter takes a few seconds, and when the former times out after 1 h, the latter terminates, usually in under 1 min. Comparing the formulas of Δ_{EAGER} and Δ_{LAZY} reveals the reason. While the FO translation of both yields EPR formulas, the formulas resulting from Δ_{EAGER} contain more quantifiers and generate much more ground terms, which degrades the performance of Z3.

Another advantage of the lazy approach is that during the search, it avoids considering formulas with many quantifiers unless those are actually needed. Comparing the 3 versions of Bosco we see that A$_{\text{IP LAZY}}$ is not sensitive to the largest number of quantifiers that may appear in a Γ-valid simple TIP formula. The downside is that A$_{\text{IP LAZY}}$ performs many Ivy checks in order to compute the final Δ_{LAZY}. The total duration of finding CTIs varies significantly (as demonstrated under the column $\mathbf{t_I}$), in part because it is very sensitive to the CTIs returned by Ivy, which are in turn affected by the random seed used in the heuristics of the underlying solver.

Finally, Δ_{LAZY} provides more insight into the protocol design, since it presents minimal assumptions that are required for protocol correctness. Thus, it may be useful in designing and understanding protocols.

7   Related Work

Fully Automatic Verification of Threshold-Based Protocols. Algorithms modeled as Threshold automata (TA) [14] have been studied in [13,16], and verified using an automated tool ByMC [15]. The tool also automatically synthesizes thresholds as arithmetic expressions [24]. Reachability properties of TAs for more general thresholds are studied in [18]. There have been recent advances in verification of synchronous threshold-based algorithms using TAs [41], and of asynchronous randomized algorithms where TAs support coin tosses and an unbounded number of rounds [4]. Still, this modeling is very restrictive and not as faithful to the pseudo-code as our modeling.

Another approach for full automation is to use sound and incomplete procedures for deduction and invariant search for logics that combine quantifiers and set cardinalities [8,10]. However, distributed systems of the level of complexity we consider here (e.g., Byzantine Fast Paxos) are beyond the reach of these techniques.

Verification of Distributed Protocols Using Decidable Logics. Padon et al. [33] introduced an interactive approach for the safety verification of distributed protocols based on EPR using the Ivy [29] verification tool. Later works extended the approach to more complex protocols [32], their implementations [42], and liveness properties [30,31]. Those works verified some threshold protocols using ad-hoc first-order modeling and axiomatization of threshold-intersection properties, whereas we develop a systematic methodology. Moreover, the axioms were not mechanically verified, except in [42], where a simple intersection property—intersection of two sets with more than $\frac{n}{2}$ nodes—requires a proof by induction over n. The proof relies on a user provided induction hypothesis that is automatically checked using the FAU decidable fragment [9]. This approach requires user ingenuity even for a simple intersection property, and we expect that it would not scale to the more complex properties required for e.g. Bosco or Fast Byzantine Paxos. In contrast, our approach completely automates both verification and inference of threshold-intersection properties required to verify protocol correctness.

Dragoi et al. [6] propose a decidable logic supporting cardinalities, uninterpreted functions, and universal quantifiers for verifying consensus algorithms expressed in the partially synchronous Heard-Of Model. As in this paper, the user is expected to provide an inductive invariant. The PSync framework [7] extends the approach to protocol implementations. Compared to our approach, the approach of Dragoi et al. is less flexible due to the specialized logic used and the restrictions of the Heard-Of Model.

Our approach decomposes verification into EPR and BAPA. Piskac [34] presents a decidable logic that combines BAPA and EPR, with some restrictions. The verification conditions of the protocols we consider are outside the scope of this fragment since they include cardinality constraints in the scope of quantifiers. Furthermore, this logic is not supported by mature solvers. Instead of looking for a specialized logic per protocol, we rely on a decomposition which allows more flexibility.

Recently, [11] presented an approach for verifying asynchronous algorithms by reduction to synchronous verification. This technique is largely orthogonal and complementary to our approach, which is focused on the challenge of cardinality thresholds.

Verification using interactive theorem provers. We are not aware of works based on interactive theorem provers that verified protocols with complex thresholds as we do in this work (although doing so is of course possible). However, many works used interactive theorem provers to verify related protocols, e.g., [12, 27, 36–38, 43] (the most related protocols use either $\frac{n}{2}$ or $\frac{2n}{3}$ as the only thresholds, other protocols do not involve any thresholds). The downside of verification using interactive theorem provers is that it requires tremendous human efforts and skills. For example, the Verdi proof of Raft included 50,000 lines of proof in Coq for 500 lines of code [44].

8 Conclusion

This paper proposes a new deductive verification approach for threshold-based distributed protocols by decomposing the verification problem into two well-established decidable logics, BAPA and EPR, thus allowing greater flexibility compared to monolithic approaches based on domain-specific, specialized logics. The user models their protocol in EPR, defines the thresholds and resilience conditions using arithmetic in BAPA, and provides an inductive invariant. An automatic procedure infers threshold intersection properties expressed in TIP that are both (1) sound w.r.t. the resilience conditions (checked in quantifier-free BAPA) and (2) sufficient to discharge the VCs (checked in EPR). Both logics are supported by mature solvers, and allow providing the user with an understandable counterexample in case verification fails.

Our evaluation, which includes notoriously tricky fast-learning consensus protocols, shows that threshold intersection properties are inferred in a matter of minutes. While this may be too slow for interactive use, we expect improvements such as memoization and parallelism to provide response times of a few seconds in an iterative, interactive setting. Another potential future direction is combining our inference algorithm with automated invariant inference algorithms.

Acknowledgements. We thank the anonymous referees for insightful comments which improved this paper. This publication is part of a project that has received funding from the European Research Council (ERC) under the European Union's Horizon 2020 research and innovation programme (grant agreement No [759102-SVIS] and [787367-PaVeS]). The research was partially supported by Len Blavatnik and the Blavatnik Family foundation, the Blavatnik Interdisciplinary Cyber Research Center, Tel Aviv University, the Israel Science Foundation (ISF) under grant No. 1810/18, the United States-Israel Binational Science Foundation (BSF) grant No. 2016260 and the Austrian Science Fund (FWF) through Doctoral College LogiCS (W1255-N23).

References

1. Abraham, I., Gueta, G., Malkhi, D., Alvisi, L., Kotla, R., Martin, J.P.: Revisiting Fast Practical Byzantine Fault Tolerance (2017)

2. Bansal, K., Reynolds, A., Barrett, C., Tinelli, C.: A new decision procedure for finite sets and cardinality constraints in SMT. In: Olivetti, N., Tiwari, A. (eds.) IJCAR 2016. LNCS (LNAI), vol. 9706, pp. 82–98. Springer, Cham (2016). https://doi.org/10.1007/978-3-319-40229-1_7

3. Berkovits, I., Lazić, M., Losa, G., Padon, O., Shoham, S.: Verification of threshold-based distributed algorithms by decomposition to decidable logics. CoRR abs/1905.07805 (2019). http://arxiv.org/abs/1905.07805

4. Bertrand, N., Konnov, I., Lazic, M., Widder, J.: Verification of Randomized Distributed Algorithms under Round-Rigid Adversaries. HAL hal-01925533, November 2018. https://hal.inria.fr/hal-01925533

5. de Moura, L., Bjørner, N.: Z3: an efficient SMT solver. In: Ramakrishnan, C.R., Rehof, J. (eds.) TACAS 2008. LNCS, vol. 4963, pp. 337–340. Springer, Heidelberg (2008). https://doi.org/10.1007/978-3-540-78800-3_24

6. Drăgoi, C., Henzinger, T.A., Veith, H., Widder, J., Zufferey, D.: A logic-based framework for verifying consensus algorithms. In: McMillan, K.L., Rival, X. (eds.) VMCAI 2014. LNCS, vol. 8318, pp. 161–181. Springer, Heidelberg (2014). https://doi.org/10.1007/978-3-642-54013-4_10

7. Dragoi, C., Henzinger, T.A., Zufferey, D.: PSync: A partially synchronous language for fault-tolerant distributed algorithms. In: Proceedings of the 43rd Annual ACM SIGPLAN-SIGACT Symposium on Principles of Programming Languages, POPL 2016, St. Petersburg, FL, USA, January 20–22, 2016, vol. 51, no. 1, pp. 400–415 (2016). https://dblp.uni-trier.de/rec/bibtex/conf/popl/DragoiHZ16?q=speculative%20AQ4%20Byzantine%20fault%20tolerance

8. Dutertre, B., Jovanović, D., Navas, J.A.: Verification of fault-tolerant protocols with sally. In: Dutle, A., Muñoz, C., Narkawicz, A. (eds.) NFM 2018. LNCS, vol. 10811, pp. 113–120. Springer, Cham (2018). https://doi.org/10.1007/978-3-319-77935-5_8

9. Ge, Y., de Moura, L.: Complete instantiation for quantified formulas in satisfiabiliby modulo theories. In: Bouajjani, A., Maler, O. (eds.) CAV 2009. LNCS, vol. 5643, pp. 306–320. Springer, Heidelberg (2009). https://doi.org/10.1007/978-3-642-02658-4_25

10. v. Gleissenthall, K., Bjørner, N., Rybalchenko, A.: Cardinalities and universal quantifiers for verifying parameterized systems. In: Proceedings of the 37th ACM SIGPLAN Conference on Programming Language Design and Implementation, PLDI 2016, pp. 599–613. ACM (2016)

11. von Gleissenthall, K., Kici, R.G., Bakst, A., Stefan, D., Jhala, R.: Pretend synchrony: synchronous verification of asynchronous distributed programs. PACMPL 3(POPL), 59:1–59:30 (2019). https://dl.acm.org/citation.cfm?id=3290372

12. Hawblitzel, C., Howell, J., Kapritsos, M., Lorch, J.R., Parno, B., Roberts, M.L., Setty, S.T.V., Zill, B.: Ironfleet: proving practical distributed systems correct. In: Proceedings of the 25th Symposium on Operating Systems Principles, SOSP 2015, Monterey, CA, USA, 4–7 October 2015, pp. 1–17 (2015). https://doi.org/10.1145/2815400.2815428,

13. Konnov, I., Lazic, M., Veith, H., Widder, J.: Para^2: Parameterized path reduction, acceleration, and SMT for reachability in threshold-guarded distributed algorithms. Form. Methods Syst. Des. **51**(2), 270–307 (2017). https://link.springer.com/article/10.1007/s10703-017-0297-4
14. Konnov, I., Veith, H., Widder, J.: On the completeness of bounded model checking for threshold-based distributed algorithms: reachability. Inf. Comput. **252**, 95–109 (2017)
15. Konnov, I., Widder, J.: ByMC: byzantine model checker. In: Margaria, T., Steffen, B. (eds.) ISoLA 2018. LNCS, vol. 11246, pp. 327–342. Springer, Cham (2018). https://doi.org/10.1007/978-3-030-03424-5_22
16. Konnov, I.V., Lazic, M., Veith, H., Widder, J.: A short counterexample property for safety and liveness verification of fault-tolerant distributed algorithms. In: Proceedings of the 44th ACM SIGPLAN Symposium on Principles of Programming Languages, POPL 2017, Paris, France, 18–20 January 2017, pp. 719–734 (2017)
17. Kotla, R., Alvisi, L., Dahlin, M., Clement, A., Wong, E.: Zyzzyva: speculative Byzantine fault tolerance. SIGOPS Oper. Syst. Rev. **41**(6), 45–58 (2007)
18. Kukovec, J., Konnov, I., Widder, J.: Reachability in parameterized systems: all flavors of threshold automata. In: CONCUR. LIPIcs, vol. 118, pp. 19:1–19:17. Schloss Dagstuhl - Leibniz-Zentrum fuer Informatik (2018)
19. Kuncak, V., Nguyen, H.H., Rinard, M.: An algorithm for deciding BAPA: boolean algebra with presburger arithmetic. In: Nieuwenhuis, R. (ed.) CADE 2005. LNCS (LNAI), vol. 3632, pp. 260–277. Springer, Heidelberg (2005). https://doi.org/10.1007/11532231_20
20. Lamport, L.: The Part-time Parliament 16(2), 133–169 (1998–2005). https://doi.org/10.1145/279227.279229
21. Lamport, L.: Lower bounds for asynchronous consensus. In: Schiper, A., Shvartsman, A.A., Weatherspoon, H., Zhao, B.Y. (eds.) Future Directions in Distributed Computing. LNCS, vol. 2584, pp. 22–23. Springer, Heidelberg (2003). https://doi.org/10.1007/3-540-37795-6_4
22. Lamport, L.: Lower bounds for asynchronous consensus. Distrib. Comput. **19**(2), 104–125 (2006)
23. Lamport, L.: Fast byzantine paxos, 17 November 2009. uS Patent 7,620,680
24. Lazic, M., Konnov, I., Widder, J., Bloem, R.: Synthesis of distributed algorithms with parameterized threshold guards. In: OPODIS (2017, to appear). http://forsyte.at/wp-content/uploads/opodis17.pdf
25. Lewis, H.R.: Complexity results for classes of quantificational formulas. Comput. Syst. Sci. **21**(3), 317–353 (1980)
26. Liffiton, M.H., Previti, A., Malik, A., Marques-Silva, J.: Fast, flexible mus enumeration. Constraints **21**(2), 223–250 (2016)
27. Liu, Y.A., Stoller, S.D., Lin, B.: From clarity to efficiency for distributed algorithms. ACM Trans. Program. Lang. Syst. **39**(3), 121–1241 (2017). https://doi.org/10.1145/2994595
28. Martin, J.P., Alvisi, L.: Fast Byzantine consensus. IEEE Trans. Dependable Secure Comput. **3**(3), 202–215 (2006)
29. McMillan, K.L., Padon, O.: Deductive verification in decidable fragments with ivy. In: Podelski, A. (ed.) SAS 2018. LNCS, vol. 11002, pp. 43–55. Springer, Cham (2018). https://doi.org/10.1007/978-3-319-99725-4_4
30. Padon, O., Hoenicke, J., Losa, G., Podelski, A., Sagiv, M., Shoham, S.: Reducing liveness to safety in first-order logic. PACMPL **2**(POPL), 26:1–26:33 (2018)

31. Padon, O., Hoenicke, J., McMillan, K.L., Podelski, A., Sagiv, M., Shoham, S.: Temporal prophecy for proving temporal properties of infinite-state systems. In: FMCAD, pp. 1–11. IEEE (2018)

32. Padon, O., Losa, G., Sagiv, M., Shoham, S.: Paxos made EPR: decidable reasoning about distributed protocols. PACMPL 1(OOPSLA), 1081–10831 (2017)

33. Padon, O., McMillan, K.L., Panda, A., Sagiv, M., Shoham, S.: Ivy: safety verification by interactive generalization. In: Krintz, C., Berger, E. (eds.) Proceedings of the 37th ACM SIGPLAN Conference on Programming Language Design and Implementation, PLDI 2016, Santa Barbara, CA, USA, 13–17 June 2016, pp. 614–630. ACM (2016)

34. Piskac, R.: Decision procedures for program synthesis and verification (2011). http://infoscience.epfl.ch/record/168994

35. Piskac, R., de Moura, L., Bjrner, N.: Deciding effectively propositional logic using DPLL and substitution sets. J. Autom. Reason. **44**(4), 401–424 (2010)

36. Rahli, V., Guaspari, D., Bickford, M., Constable, R.L.: Formal specification, verification, and implementation of fault-tolerant systems using eventml. ECEASST 72 (2015). https://doi.org/10.14279/tuj.eceasst.72.1013

37. Rahli, V., Vukotic, I., Völp, M., Esteves-Verissimo, P.: Velisarios: Byzantine fault-tolerant protocols powered by Coq. In: Ahmed, A. (ed.) ESOP 2018. LNCS, vol. 10801, pp. 619–650. Springer, Cham (2018). https://doi.org/10.1007/978-3-319-89884-1_22

38. Sergey, I., Wilcox, J.R., Tatlock, Z.: Programming and proving with distributed protocols. PACMPL **2**(POPL), 28:1–28:30 (2018)

39. Song, Y.J., van Renesse, R.: Bosco: one-step Byzantine asynchronous consensus. In: Taubenfeld, G. (ed.) DISC 2008. LNCS, vol. 5218, pp. 438–450. Springer, Heidelberg (2008). https://doi.org/10.1007/978-3-540-87779-0_30

40. Srikanth, T., Toueg, S.: Simulating authenticated broadcasts to derive simple fault-tolerant algorithms. Dist. Comp. **2**, 80–94 (1987)

41. Stoilkovska, I., Konnov, I., Widder, J., Zuleger, F.: Verifying safety of synchronous fault-tolerant algorithms by bounded model checking. In: Vojnar, T., Zhang, L. (eds.) TACAS 2019. LNCS, vol. 11428, pp. 357–374. Springer, Cham (2019). https://doi.org/10.1007/978-3-030-17465-1_20

42. Taube, M., et al.: Modularity for decidability of deductive verification with applications to distributed systems. In: PLDI, pp. 662–677. ACM (2018)

43. Wilcox, J.R., et al.: Verdi: a framework for implementing and formally verifying distributed systems. In: Proceedings of the 36th ACM SIGPLAN Conference on Programming Language Design and Implementation, Portland, OR, USA, 15–17 June 2015, pp. 357–368 (2015). https://doi.org/10.1145/2737924.2737958

44. Woos, D., Wilcox, J.R., Anton, S., Tatlock, Z., Ernst, M.D., Anderson, T.E.: Planning for change in a formal verification of the raft consensus protocol. In: Proceedings of the 5th ACM SIGPLAN Conference on Certified Programs and Proofs, Saint Petersburg, FL, USA, 20–22 January 2016, pp. 154–165 (2016). https://doi.org/10.1145/2854065.2854081

Verifying Asynchronous Event-Driven Programs Using Partial Abstract Transformers

Peizun Liu[1(✉)], Thomas Wahl[1],
and Akash Lal[2]

[1] Northeastern University, Boston, USA
lpzun@ccs.neu.edu
[2] Microsoft Research, Bangalore, India

Abstract. We address the problem of analyzing asynchronous event-driven programs, in which concurrent agents communicate via unbounded message queues. The safety verification problem for such programs is undecidable. We present in this paper a technique that combines *queue-bounded exploration* with a *convergence test*: if the sequence of certain abstractions of the reachable states, for increasing queue bounds k, converges, we can prove any property of the program that is preserved by the abstraction. If the abstract state space is finite, convergence is *guaranteed*; the challenge is to catch the point k_{max} where it happens. We further demonstrate how simple invariants formulated over the *concrete* domain can be used to eliminate spurious *abstract* states, which otherwise prevent the sequence from converging. We have implemented our technique for the P programming language for event-driven programs. We show experimentally that the sequence of abstractions often converges fully automatically, in hard cases with minimal designer support in the form of sequentially provable invariants, and that this happens for a value of k_{max} small enough to allow the method to succeed in practice.

1 Introduction

Asynchronous event-driven (AED) programming refers to a style of programming multi-agent applications. The agents communicate shared work via messages. Each agent waits for a message to arrive, and then processes it, possibly sending messages to other agents, in order to collectively achieve a goal. This programming style is common for distributed systems as well as low-level designs such as device drivers [11]. Getting such applications right is an arduous task, due to the inherent concurrency: the programmer must defend against all possible interleavings of messages between agents. In response to this challenge, recent years have seen multiple approaches to verifying AED-like programs, e.g. by delaying send actions, or temporarily bounding their number (to keep queue sizes small) [7,10], or by reasoning about a small number of representative execution schedules, to avoid interleaving explosion [5].

In this paper we consider the P language for AED programming [11]. A P program consists of multiple state machines running in parallel. Each machine has a local store, and a message queue through which it receives events from other machines. P allows the programmer to formulate safety specifications via a statement that asserts some predicate over the local state of a single machine. Verifying such reachability properties of course requires reasoning over global system behavior and is, for unbounded-queue P programs, undecidable [8].

The unboundedness of the reachable state space does not prevent the use of testing tools that try to explore as much of the state space as possible [3,6,11,13] in the quest for bugs. Somewhat inspired by this kind of approach, the goal of this paper is a verification technique that can (sometimes) *prove* a safety property, despite exploring only a finite fraction of that space. Our approach is as follows. Assuming that the machines' queues are the only source of unboundedness, we consider a bound k on the queue size, and exhaustively compute the reachable states R_k of the resulting finite-state problem, checking the local assertion Φ along the way. We then increase the queue bound until (an error is found, or) we reach some point $k_{\max}$ of *convergence*: a point that allows us to conclude that increasing k further is not required to prove Φ.

What kind of "convergence" are we targeting? We design a sequence $(\overline{R}_k)_{k=0}^{\infty}$ of abstractions of each reachability set over a *finite* abstract state space. Due to the monotonicity of sequence $(\overline{R}_k)_{k=0}^{\infty}$, this ensures convergence, i.e. the existence of $k_{\max}$ such that $\overline{R}_K = \overline{R}_{k_{\max}}$ for all $K \geq k_{\max}$. Provided that an abstract state satisfies Φ exactly if all its concretizations do, we have: if all abstract states in $\overline{R}_{k_{\max}}$ comply with Φ, then so do all reachable concrete states of P—we have proved the property.

We implement this strategy using an abstraction function α with a finite co-domain that leaves the local state of a machine unchanged and maintains the *first occurrence* of each event in the queue; repeat occurrences are dropped. This abstraction preserves properties over the local state and the head of the queue, i.e. the visible (to the machine) part of the state space, which is typically sufficient to express reachability properties.

The second major step in our approach is the detection of the point of convergence of $(\overline{R}_k)_{k=0}^{\infty}$: We show that, for the *best abstract transformer* $\overline{Im}$ [9,27, see Sect. 4.2], if $\overline{Im}(\overline{R}_k) \subseteq \overline{R}_k$, then $\overline{R}_K = \overline{R}_k$ for all $K \geq k$. In fact, we have a stronger result: under an easy-to-enforce condition, it suffices to consider abstract *dequeue operations*: all others, namely enqueue and local actions, never lead to abstract states in $\overline{R}_{k+1} \setminus \overline{R}_k$. The best abstract transformer for dequeue actions is efficiently implementable for a given P program.

It is of course possible that the convergence condition $\overline{Im}(\overline{R}_k) \subseteq \overline{R}_k$ never holds (the problem is undecidable). This manifests in the presence of a *spurious* abstract state in the image produced by $\overline{Im}$, i.e. one whose concretization does not contain any reachable state. Our third contribution is a technique to assist users in eliminating such states, enhancing the chances for convergence. We have observed that spurious abstract states are often due to violations of simple *machine invariants*: invariants that do not depend on the behavior of other machines. By their nature, they can be proved using a cheap sequential analysis.

We can eliminate an abstract state (e.g. produced by $\overline{Im}$) if *all* its concretizations violate a machine invariant. In this paper, we propose a domain-specific temporal logic to express invariants over machines with event queues and, more importantly, an algorithm that decides the above *abstract queue invariant checking* problem, by reducing it efficiently to a plain model checking problem. We have used this technique to ensure the convergence in "hard" cases that otherwise defy convergence of the abstract reachable states sequence.

We have implemented our technique for the P language and empirically evaluated it on an extensive set of benchmark programs. The experimental results support the following conclusions: (i) for our benchmark programs, the sequence of abstractions often converges fully automatically, in hard cases with minimal designer support in the form of separately dischargeable invariants; (ii) almost all examples converge at a small value of $k_{\max}$; and (iii) the overhead our technique adds to the bounding technique is small: the bulk is spent on the exhaustive bounded exploration itself.

Proofs and other supporting material can be found in the Appendix of [23].

2   Overview

We illustrate the main ideas of this paper using an example in the P language. A machine in a P program consists of multiple states. Each state defines an entry code block that is executed when the machine enters the state. The state also defines handlers for each event type e that it is prepared to receive. A handler can either be **on e do foo** (executing foo on receiving e), or **ignore e** (dequeuing and dropping e). A state can also have a **defer e** declaration; the semantics is that a machine dequeues the first non-deferred event in its queue. As a result, a queue in a P program is not strictly FIFO. This relaxation is an important feature of P that helps programmers express their logic compactly [11]. Figure 1 shows a P program named *PiFl*, in which a Sender (eventually) floods a Receiver's queue with PING events. This queue is the only source of unboundedness in *PiFl*.

A critical property for P programs is *(bounded) responsiveness*: the receiving machine must have a handler (e.g. on, defer, ignore) for every event arriving at the queue head; otherwise the event will come as a "surprise" and crash the machine. To prove responsiveness for *PiFl*, we have to demonstrate (among others) that in state Ignore_it, the DONE event is never at the head of the Receiver's queue. We cannot perform exhaustive model checking, since the set of reachable states is infinite. Instead, we will compute a conservative abstraction of this set that is precise enough to rule out DONE events at the queue head in this state.

We first define a suitable abstraction function α that collapses repeated occurrences of events to each event's first occurrence. For instance, the queue

$$Q = \text{PRIME.PRIME.PRIME.DONE.PING.PING.PING.PING} \tag{1}$$

```
1    event PRIME, DONE, PING;
2
3    machine Sender {                           20        state Ping_it {
4      var receiver: machine;                   21          entry {
5      start state Init {                        22            send receiver, PING; goto Ping_it;
6        entry {                                 23          }
7          receiver = new Receiver();            24        }
8        }                                       25    }
9        goto Prime_it;                          26
10     }                                         27    machine Receiver {
11     state Prime_it {                          28        start state Init {
12       entry {                                 29          defer PRIME;
13         var i:int;                            30          on DONE goto Ignore_it;
14         while (i < 3) { // 3x PRIME           31        }
15           send receiver, PRIME; i = i + 1;    32
16         }                                     33        state Ignore_it {
17         send receiver, DONE; goto Ping_it;    34          ignore PRIME, PING;
18       }                                       35        }
19     }                                         36    }
```

Fig. 1. *PiFl*: a Ping-Flood scenario. The Sender and the Receiver communicate via events of types PRIME, DONE, and PING. After sending some PRIME events and one DONE, the Sender floods the Receiver with PINGs. The Receiver initially **defers** PRIMEs. Upon receiving DONE it enters a state in which it **ignores** PING.

will be abstracted to $\overline{Q} = \alpha(Q) = $ PRIME.DONE.PING. The *finite* number of possible abstract queues is $1 + 3 + 3 \cdot 2 + 3 \cdot 2 \cdot 1 = 16$. The abstraction preserves the head of the queue. This and the machine state has enough information to check responsiveness.

We now generate the sequence $\overline{R}_k$ of abstractions of the reachable states sets R_k for queue size bounds $k = 0, 1, 2, \ldots$, by computing each finite set R_k, and then $\overline{R}_k$ as $\alpha(R_k)$. The obtained monotone sequence $(\overline{R}_k)_{k=0}^{\infty}$ over a finite domain will eventually converge, but we must prove that it has. This is done by applying the *best abstract transformer* $\overline{Im}$, restricted to dequeue operations (defined in Sect. 4.2), to the current set $\overline{R}_k$, and confirming that the result is contained in $\overline{R}_k$.

As it turns out, the confirmation fails for the *PiFl* program: $k = 5$ marks the first time set $\overline{R}_k$ repeats, i.e. $\overline{R}_4 = \overline{R}_5$, so we are motivated to run the convergence test. Unfortunately we find a state $\overline{s} \in \overline{Im}(\overline{R}_5) \setminus \overline{R}_5$, preventing convergence. Our approach now offers two remedies to this dilemma. One is to refine the queue abstraction. In our implementation, function α is really α_p, for a parameter p that denotes the size of the *prefix* of the queue that is kept unchanged by the abstraction. For example, for the queue from Eq. (1) we have $\alpha_4(Q) = $ PRIME.PRIME.PRIME.DONE $\mid$ PING, where $\mid$ separates the prefix from the "infinite tail" of the abstract queue. This (straightforward) refinement maintains finiteness of the abstraction and increases precision, by revealing that the queue starts with three PRIME events. Re-running the analysis for the *PiFl* program with $p = 4$, at $k = 5$ we find $\overline{Im}(\overline{R}_5) \subseteq \overline{R}_5$, and the proof is complete.

The second remedy to the failed convergence test dilemma is more powerful but also less automatic. Let's revert to prefix $p = 0$ and inspect the abstract state $\overline{s} \in \overline{Im}(\overline{R}_5) \setminus \overline{R}_5$ that foils the test. We find that it features a DONE event followed by a PRIME event in the Receiver's queue. A simple static analysis of the Sender's machine in isolation shows that it permits no path from the **send** DONE to the **send** PRIME statement. The behavior of other machines is irrelevant for this invariant; we call it a *machine invariant*. We pass the invariant to our tool via the command line using the expression

$$\mathsf{G}\,(\textsc{Done} \Rightarrow \mathsf{G}\,\neg\textsc{Prime}) \tag{2}$$

in a temporal-logic like notation called QuTL (Sect. 5.1), where G universally quantifies over all queue entries. Our tool includes a QuTL checker that determines that **every concretization** of $\bar{s}$ violates property (2), concluding that $\bar{s}$ is spurious and can be discarded. This turns out to be sufficient for convergence.

3 Queue-(Un)Bounded Reachability Analysis

Communicating Queue Systems. We consider P programs consisting of a fixed and known number n of machines communicating via event passing through unbounded FIFO queues.[1] For simplicity, we assume the machines are created at the start of the program; dynamic creation at a later time can be simulated by having the machine **ignore** all events until it receives a special creation event.

We model such a program as a *communicating queue system* (CQS). Formally, given $n \in \mathbb{N}$, a CQS P^n is a collection of n *queue automata* (QA) $P_i = (\Sigma, \mathcal{L}_i, Act_i, \Delta_i, \ell_i^I)$, $1 \leq i \leq n$. A QA consists of a finite queue alphabet Σ shared by all QA, a finite set $\mathcal{L}_i$ of local states, a finite set Act_i of action labels, a finite set $\Delta_i \subseteq \mathcal{L}_i \times (\Sigma \cup \{\varepsilon\}) \times Act_i \times \mathcal{L}_i \times (\Sigma \cup \{\varepsilon\})$ of transitions, and an initial local state $\ell_i^I \in \mathcal{L}_i$. An action label $act \in Act_i$ is of the form

- $act \in \{deq, loc\}$, denoting an action *internal* to P_i (no other QA involved) that either *dequeues* an event (deq), or updates its *local* state (loc);   **or**
- $act = !(e, j)$, for $e \in \Sigma$, $j \in \{1, \ldots, n\}$, denoting a *transmission*, where P_i (the *sender*) adds event e to the end of the queue of P_j (the *receiver*).

The individual QA of a CQS model machines of a P program; hence we refer to QA states as *machine states*. A transmit action is the only communication mechanism among the QA.

Semantics. A *machine state* m of a QA is of the form $(\ell, \mathcal{Q}) \in \mathcal{L} \times \Sigma^*$; state $m^I = (\ell^I, \varepsilon)$ is *initial*. We define machine transitions corresponding to internal actions as follows (transmit actions are defined later at the global level):

$$\frac{(\ell, \varepsilon) \overset{loc}{\to} (\ell', \varepsilon) \in \Delta}{(\ell, \mathcal{Q}) \to (\ell', \mathcal{Q})} \quad \text{for } \ell, \ell' \in \mathcal{L}, \mathcal{Q} \in \Sigma^* \qquad \textbf{(local)}$$

$$\frac{(\ell, e) \overset{deq}{\to} (\ell', \varepsilon) \in \Delta}{(\ell, e\mathcal{Q}) \to (\ell', \mathcal{Q})} \quad \text{for } \ell, \ell' \in \mathcal{L}, e \in \Sigma, \mathcal{Q} \in \Sigma^* \qquad \textbf{(dequeue)}$$

---

[1] The P language permits unbounded machine creation, a feature that we do not allow here and that is not used in any of the benchmarks we are aware of.

A *(global) state* s of a CQS is a tuple $\langle(\ell_1, \mathcal{Q}_1), \dots, (\ell_n, \mathcal{Q}_n)\rangle$ where $(\ell_i, \mathcal{Q}_i) \in \mathcal{L}_i \times \Sigma^*$ for $i \in \{1, \dots, n\}$. State $s^I = \langle(\ell_1^I, \varepsilon), \dots, (\ell_n^I, \varepsilon)\rangle$ is initial. We extend the machine transition relation $\rightarrow$ to states as follows:

$$\langle(\ell_1, \mathcal{Q}_1), \dots, (\ell_n, \mathcal{Q}_n)\rangle \rightarrow \langle(\ell_1', \mathcal{Q}_1'), \dots, (\ell_n', \mathcal{Q}_n')\rangle$$

if there exists $i \in \{1, \dots, n\}$ such that one of the following holds:

(internal) $(\ell_i, \mathcal{Q}_i) \rightarrow (\ell_i', \mathcal{Q}_i')$, and for all $k \in \{1, \dots, n\} \setminus \{i\}$, $\ell_k = \ell_k'$, $\mathcal{Q}_k = \mathcal{Q}_k'$;
(transmission) there exists $j \in \{1, \dots, n\}$ and $e \in \Sigma$ such that:

1. $(\ell_i, \varepsilon) \xrightarrow{!(e,j)} (\ell_i', \varepsilon) \in \Delta_i$;
2. $\mathcal{Q}_j' = \mathcal{Q}_j e$;
3. $\ell_k' = \ell_k$ for all $k \in \{1, \dots, n\} \setminus \{i\}$; and
4. $\mathcal{Q}_k' = \mathcal{Q}_k$ for all $k \in \{1, \dots, n\} \setminus \{j\}$.

The execution model of a CQS is strictly interleaving. That is, in each step, one of the two above transitions **(internal)** or **(transmission)** is performed for a nondeterministically chosen machine i.

Queue-Bounded and Queue-Unbounded Reachability. Given a CQS P^n, a state $s = \langle(\ell_1, \mathcal{Q}_1), \dots, (\ell_n, \mathcal{Q}_n)\rangle$, and a number k, the *queue-bounded reachability problem* (for s and k) determines whether s is *reachable under queue bound* k, i.e. whether there exists a path $s_0 \rightarrow s_1 \dots \rightarrow s_z$ such that $s_0 = s^I$, $s_z = s$, and for $i \in \{0, \dots, z\}$, all queues in state s_i have at most k events. Queue-bounded reachability for k is trivially decidable, by making enqueue actions for queues of size k *blocking* (the sender cannot continue), which results in a finite state space. We write $R_k = \{s : s \text{ is reachable under queue bound } k\}$.

Queue-bounded reachability will be used in this paper as a tool for solving our actual problem of interest: Given a CQS P^n and a state s, the *Queue-UnBounded reachability Analysis (QUBA) problem* determines whether s is reachable, i.e. whether there exists a (queue-unbounded) path from s^I to s. The QUBA problem is undecidable [8]. We write $R (= \bigcup_{k \in \mathbb{N}} R_k)$ for the set of reachable states.

4 Convergence via Partial Abstract Transformers

In this section, we formalize our approach to detecting the convergence of a suitable sequence of *observations* about the states R_k reachable under k-bounded semantics. We define the observations as abstractions of those states, resulting in sets $\overline{R}_k$. We then investigate the convergence of the sequence $(\overline{R}_k)_{k=0}^{\infty}$.

4.1 List Abstractions of Queues

Our abstraction function applies to queues, as defined below. Its action on machine and system states then follows from the hierarchical design of a CQS. Let $|\mathcal{Q}|$ denote the number of events in $\mathcal{Q}$, and $\mathcal{Q}[i]$ the ith event in $\mathcal{Q}$ $(0 \leq i < |\mathcal{Q}|)$.

Definition 1. *For a parameter $p \in \mathbb{N}$, the **list abstraction** function $\alpha_p : \Sigma^* \mapsto \Sigma^*$ is defined as follows:*

1. $\alpha_p(\varepsilon) = \varepsilon$.
2. *For a non-empty queue $\mathcal{Q} = P \cdot e$,*

$$\alpha_p(\mathcal{Q}) = \begin{cases} \alpha_p(P) & \text{if there exists } j \text{ s.t. } p \leq j < |P| \text{ and } \mathcal{Q}[j] = e \\ \alpha_p(P) \cdot e & \text{otherwise} \end{cases} . \quad (3)$$

Intuitively, α_p abstracts a queue by leaving its first p events unchanged (an idea also used in [16]). Starting from position p it keeps only the first occurrence of each event e in the queue, if any; repeat occurrences are dropped.[2] The preservation of existence and order of the first occurrences of all present events motivates the term *list abstraction*. An alternative is an abstraction that keeps only the *set* (not: list) of queue elements from position p, i.e. it ignores multiplicity *and order*. This is by definition less precise than the list abstraction and provided no efficiency advantages in our experiments. An abstraction that keeps only the queue head proved cheap but too imprecise.

The motivation for parameter p is that many protocols proceed in *rounds* of repeating communication patterns, involving a bounded number of message exchanges. If p exceeds that number, the list abstraction's loss of information may be immaterial.

We write an abstract queue $\overline{\mathcal{Q}} = \alpha_p(\mathcal{Q})$ in the form $pref \,|\, suff$ s.t. $p = |pref|$, and refer to $pref$ as $\overline{\mathcal{Q}}$'s prefix (shared with $\mathcal{Q}$), and $suff$ as $\overline{\mathcal{Q}}$'s suffix.

Example 2. *The queues $\mathcal{Q} \in \{bbbba, bbba, bbbaa\}$ are α_2-**equivalent**: $\alpha_2(\mathcal{Q}) = bb \,|\, ba$.*

We extend α_p to act on a machine state via $\alpha_p(\ell_i, \mathcal{Q}_i) = (\ell_i, \alpha_p(\mathcal{Q}_i))$, on a state via $\alpha_p(s) = \langle (\ell_1, \alpha_p(\mathcal{Q}_1)), \ldots, (\ell_n, \alpha_p(\mathcal{Q}_n)) \rangle$, and on a set of states pointwise via $\alpha_p(S) = \{\alpha_p(s) : s \in S\}$.

Discussion. The abstract state space is finite since the queue prefix is of fixed size, and each event in the suffix is recorded at most once (the event alphabet is finite). The sets of reachable abstract states grow monotonously with increasing queue size bound k, since the sets of reachable concrete states do:

$$k_1 \leq k_2 \;\;\Rightarrow\;\; R_{k_1} \subseteq R_{k_2} \;\;\Rightarrow\;\; \alpha_p(R_{k_1}) \subseteq \alpha_p(R_{k_2}) .$$

Finiteness and monotonicity guarantee convergence of the sequence of reachable abstract states.

We say the abstraction function α_p *respects* a property of a state if, for any two α_p-equivalent states (see Example 2), the property holds for both or for neither. Function α_p respects properties that refer to the local-state part of a machine, and to the first $p + 1$ events of its queue (which are preserved by α_p). In addition, the property may look beyond the prefix and refer to the existence of events in the queue, but not their frequency or their order after the first occurrence.

---

[2] Note that the head of the queue is always preserved by α_p, even for $p = 0$.

The rich information preserved by the abstraction (despite being finite-state) especially pays off in connection with the **defer** feature in the P language, which allows machines to delay handling certain events at the head of a queue [11]. The machine identifies the first non-deferred event in the queue, a piece of information that is precisely preserved by the list abstraction (no matter what p).

Definition 3. *Given an abstract queue* $\overline{Q} = e_0 \ldots e_{p-1} \mid e_p \ldots e_{z-1}$, *the **concretization function** $\gamma_p \colon \Sigma^* \to 2^{\Sigma^*}$ maps $\overline{Q}$ to the* language *of the regular expression*

$$RE_p(\overline{Q}) := e_0 \ldots e_{p-1} e_p \{e_p\}^* e_{p+1} \{e_p, e_{p+1}\}^* \ldots e_{z-1} \{e_p, \ldots, e_{z-1}\}^* , \qquad (4)$$

i.e. $\gamma_p(\overline{Q}) := \mathcal{L}(RE_p(\overline{Q}))$.

As a special case, $RE_p(\varepsilon) = \varepsilon$ and so $\gamma_p(\varepsilon) = \mathcal{L}(\varepsilon) = \{\varepsilon\}$ for the empty queue. We extend γ_p to act on abstract (machine or global) states in a way analogous to the extension of α_p, by moving it inside to the queues occurring in those states.

4.2 Abstract Convergence Detection

Recall that finiteness and monotonicity of the sequence $(\overline{R}_k)_{k=0}^\infty$ guarantee its convergence, so nothing seems more suggestive than to compute the limit. We summarize our overall procedure to do so in Algorithm 1. The procedure iteratively increases the queue bound k and computes the concrete and (per α_p-projection) the abstract reachability sets R_k and $\overline{R}_k$. If, for some k, an error is detected, the procedure terminates (Lines 4–5; in practice implemented as an on-the-fly check).

Algorithm 1. Queue-unbounded reachability analysis

Input: CQS with transition relation $\to$, $p \in \mathbb{N}$, property Φ respected by α_p.
1: **compute** R_0; $\overline{R}_0 := \alpha_p(R_0)$
2: **for** $k := 1$ **to** ∞ **do**
3:    **compute** R_k; $\overline{R}_k := \alpha_p(R_k)$
4:    **if** $\exists r \in R_k : r \not\models \Phi$ **then**
5:      **return** "error reachable with queue bound k"
6:    **if** $|\overline{R}_k| = |\overline{R}_{k-1}|$ **then**
7:      $\overline{T} := (\alpha_p \circ Im_{deq} \circ \gamma_p)(\overline{R}_k)$ $\triangleright$ ***partial* best abstract transformer**
8:      **if** $\overline{T} \subseteq \overline{R}_k$ **then**
9:        **return** "safe for any queue bound"

The key of the algorithm is reflected in Lines 6–9 and is based on the following idea (all claims are proved as part of Theorem 4 below). If the computation of $\overline{R}_k$ reveals no new abstract states in round k (Line 6; by monotonicity, "same size" implies "same sets"), we apply the *best abstract transformer* [9, 27] $\overline{Im} := \alpha_p \circ Im_\rightarrow \circ \gamma_p$ to $\overline{R}_k$: if the result is contained in $\overline{R}_k$, the abstract reachability sequence has converged. However, we can do better: we can restrict the successor function $Im_\rightarrow$ of the CQS to *dequeue* actions, denoted Im_{deq} in Line 7. The ultimate reason is that firing a local or transmit action on two α_p-equivalent states r and s results again in α_p-equivalent states r' and s'. This fact does *not* hold for dequeue actions: the successors r' and s' of dequeues depend on the abstracted parts of r and s, resp., which may differ and become "visible" during the dequeue (e.g. the event behind the queue head moves into the head position). Our main result therefore is: if $\overline{R}_k = \overline{R}_{k-1}$ and dequeue actions do not create new abstract states (Lines 7 and 8), sequence $(\overline{R}_k)_{k=0}^\infty$ has converged:

Theorem 4. *If $\overline{R}_k = \overline{R}_{k-1}$ and $\overline{T} \subseteq \overline{R}_k$, then for any $K \geq k$, $\overline{R}_K = \overline{R}_k$.*

If the sequence of reachable abstract states has converged, then **all** reachable concrete states (any k) belong to $\gamma_p(\overline{R}_k)$ (for the current k). Since the abstraction function α_p respects property Φ, we know that if any reachable concrete state violated Φ, so would any other concrete state that maps to the same abstraction. However, for each abstract state in $\overline{R}_k$, Line 4 has examined at least one state r in its concretization; a violation was not found. We conclude:

Corollary 5. *Line 9 of Algorithm 1 correctly asserts that no reachable concrete state of the given CQS violates Φ.*

The corollary (along with the earlier statement about Lines 4–5) confirms the partial correctness of Algorithm 1. The procedure is, however, necessarily incomplete: if no error is detected and the convergence condition in Line 8 never holds, the **for** loop will run forever.

We conclude this part with two comments. First, note that we do not compute the sets $\overline{R}_k$ as reachability fixpoints in the abstract domain (i.e. the domain of α_p). Instead, we compute the *concrete* reachability sets first, and then obtain the $\overline{R}_k$ via projection (Line 1). The reason is that the projection gives us the *exact* set of abstractions of reachable concrete states, while an abstract fixpoint likely overapproximates (for instance, the best abstract transformer from Line 7 does) and loses precision. Note that a primary motivation for computing abstract fixpoints, namely that the concrete fixpoint may not be computable, does not apply here: the concrete domains are finite, for each k.

Second, we observe that this projection technique comes with a cost: sequence $(\overline{R}_k)_{k=0}^\infty$ may *stutter* at intermediate moments: $\overline{R}_k \subsetneq \overline{R}_{k+1} = \overline{R}_{k+2} \subsetneq \overline{R}_{k+3}$. The reason is that $\overline{R}_{k+3}$ is not obtained as a functional image of $\overline{R}_{k+2}$, but by projection from R_{k+3}. As a consequence, we cannot short-cut the convergence detection by just "waiting" for $(\overline{R}_k)_{k=0}^\infty$ to stabilize, despite the finite domain.

4.3   Computing Partial Best Abstract Transformers

Recall that in Line 7 we compute

$$\overline{T} = \overline{Im}_{deq}(\overline{R}_k) = (\alpha_p \circ Im_{deq} \circ \gamma_p)(\overline{R}_k) . \tag{5}$$

The line applies the best abstract transformer, restricted to dequeue actions, to $\overline{R}_k$. This result cannot be computed as defined in (5), since $\gamma_p(\overline{R}_k)$ is typically infinite. However, $\overline{R}_k$ is finite, so we can iterative over $\bar{r} \in \overline{R}_k$, and little information is actually needed to determine the abstract successors of $\bar{r}$. The "infinite fragment" of $\bar{r}$ remains unchanged, which makes the action implementable.

Formally, let $\bar{r} = (\ell, \overline{\mathcal{Q}})$ with $\overline{\mathcal{Q}} = e_0 e_1 \dots e_{p-1} \mid e_p e_{p+1} \dots e_{z-1}$. To apply a dequeue action to $\bar{r}$, we first perform local-state updates on ℓ as required by the action, resulting in ℓ'. Now consider $\overline{\mathcal{Q}}$. The first suffix event, e_p, moves into the prefix due to the dequeue. We do not know whether there are later occurrences of e_p before or after the first suffix occurrences of $e_{p+1} \dots e_{z-1}$. This information determines the possible abstract queues resulting from the dequeue. To compute the exact best abstract transformer, we enumerate these possibilities:

$$
\overline{Im}_{deq}(\{(\ell, \overline{\mathcal{Q}})\}) \;\; = \;\; \left\{ (\ell', \overline{\mathcal{Q}}') \; : \; \overline{\mathcal{Q}}' \in \left\{ \begin{array}{l} e_1 \dots e_p \mid e_{p+1} e_{p+2} \dots e_{z-1} \\ e_1 \dots e_p \mid \boxed{e_p}\, e_{p+1} e_{p+2} \dots e_{z-1} \\ e_1 \dots e_p \mid e_{p+1} \boxed{e_p}\, e_{p+2} \dots e_{z-1} \\ \vdots \\ e_1 \dots e_p \mid e_{p+1} e_{p+2} \dots e_{z-1} \boxed{e_p} \end{array} \right\} \right\}
$$

The first case for $\overline{\mathcal{Q}}'$ applies if there are no occurrences of e_p in the suffix after the dequeue. The remaining cases enumerate possible positions of the *first* occurrence of e_p (boxed, for readability) in the suffix after the dequeue. The cost of this enumeration is linear in the length of the suffix of the abstract queue.

Since our list abstraction maintains the first occurrence of each event, the semantics of **defer** (see the *Discussion* in Sect. 4.1) can be implemented abstractly without loss of information (not shown above, for simplicity).

5　Abstract Queue Invariant Checking

The abstract transformer function in Sect. 4 is used to decide whether sequence $(\overline{R}_k)_{k=0}^{\infty}$ has converged. Being an overapproximation, the function may generate *spurious* states: they are not reachable, i.e. no concretization of them is. Unfortunate for us, spurious abstract states always prevent convergence.

A key empirical observation is that concretizations of spurious abstract states often violate simple machine invariants, which can be proved from the perspective of a single machine, while collapsing all other machines into a nondeterministically behaving environment. Consider our example from Sect. 2 for $p = 0$. It fails to converge since Line 7 generates an abstract state $\bar{s}$ that features a DONE event followed by a PRIME event in the Receiver's queue. A light-weight static analysis proves that the Sender's machine permits no path from the send DONE to the send PRIME statement. Since **every** concretization of $\bar{s}$ features a DONE followed by a PRIME event, the abstract state $\bar{s}$ is spurious and can be eliminated.

Our tool assists users in *discovering* candidate machine invariants, by facilitating the inspection of states in $\overline{T} \setminus \overline{R}_k$ (which foil the test in Line 8). We *discharge* such invariants separately, via a simple sequential model-check or static analysis. In the section we focus on the more interesting question of how to *use* them. Formally, suppose the P program comes with a *queue invariant I*, i.e. an invariant property of *concrete* queues. The *abstract invariant checking problem* is to decide, for a given abstract queue $\overline{\mathcal{Q}}$, whether *every* concretization of $\overline{\mathcal{Q}}$ violates I; in this case, and this case only, an abstract state containing $\overline{\mathcal{Q}}$ can be eliminated. In the following we define a language QuTL for specifying concrete queue invariants (5.1), and then show how checking an abstract queue against a QuTL invariant can be efficiently solved as a model checking problem (5.2).

5.1 Queue Temporal Logic (QuTL)

Our logic to express invariant properties of queues is a form of first-order linear-time temporal logic. This choice is motivated by the logic's ability to constrain the order (via temporal operators) and multiplicity of queue events, the latter via relational operators that express conditions on the number of event occurrences.

Queue Relational Expressions (QuRelE). These are of the form $\#e \triangleright c$, where $e \in \Sigma$ (queue alphabet), $\triangleright \in \{<, \leq, =, \geq, >\}$, and $c \in \mathbb{N}$ is a literal natural number. The *value* of a QuRelE is defined as the Boolean

$$V(\#e \triangleright c) \quad = \quad |\{i \in \mathbb{N} : 0 \leq i < |\mathcal{Q}| \wedge \mathcal{Q}[i] = e\}| \ \triangleright \ c \qquad (6)$$

where $|\cdot|$ denotes set cardinality and $\triangleright$ is interpreted as the standard integer arithmetic relational operator. In the following we write $\mathcal{Q}[i \rightarrow]$ (read: "$\mathcal{Q}$ from i") for the queue obtained from queue $\mathcal{Q}$ by dropping the first i events.

Definition 6 (Syntax of QuTL). *The following are QuTL formulas:*

- *false and true.*
- *e, for $e \in \Sigma$.*
- *E, for a queue relational expression E.*
- *$X\phi$, $F\phi$, $G\phi$, for a QuTL formula ϕ.*

The set QuTL is the Boolean closure of the above set of formulas.

Definition 7 (Concrete semantics of QuTL). *Concrete queue $\mathcal{Q}$ **satisfies** QuTL formula ϕ, written $\mathcal{Q} \models \phi$, depending on the form of ϕ as follows.*

- *$\mathcal{Q} \models true$.*
- *for $e \in \Sigma$, $\mathcal{Q} \models e$ iff $|\mathcal{Q}| > 0$ and $\mathcal{Q}[0] = e$.*
- *for a queue relational expression E, $\mathcal{Q} \models E$ iff $V(E) = true$.*
- *$\mathcal{Q} \models X\phi$ iff $|\mathcal{Q}| > 0$ and $\mathcal{Q}[1 \rightarrow] \models \phi$.*
- *$\mathcal{Q} \models F\phi$ iff there exists $i \in \mathbb{N}$ such that $0 \leq i < |\mathcal{Q}|$ and $\mathcal{Q}[i \rightarrow] \models \phi$.*
- *$\mathcal{Q} \models G\phi$ iff for all $i \in \mathbb{N}$ such that $0 \leq i < |\mathcal{Q}|$, $\mathcal{Q}[i \rightarrow] \models \phi$.*

Satisfaction of Boolean combinations is defined as usual, e.g. $\mathcal{Q} \models \neg\phi$ iff $\mathcal{Q} \not\models \phi$. No other pair $(\mathcal{Q}, \phi)$ satisfies $\mathcal{Q} \models \phi$.

For instance, formula $\#e \leq 3$ is true exactly for queues containing at most 3 e's, and formula $\mathsf{G}(\#e \geq 1)$ is true of $\mathcal{Q}$ iff $\mathcal{Q}$ is empty or its final event (!) is e. See App. B of [23] for more examples.

Algorithmically checking whether a concrete queue $\mathcal{Q}$ satisfies a QuTL formula ϕ is straightforward, since $\mathcal{Q}$ is of fixed size and straight-line. The situation is different with abstract queues. Our motivation here is to declare that an abstract queue $\overline{\mathcal{Q}}$ *violates* a formula ϕ if *all its concretizations* (Definition 3) do: under this condition, if ϕ is an invariant, we know $\overline{\mathcal{Q}}$ is not reachable. Equivalently:

Definition 8 (Abstract semantics of QuTL). *Abstract queue $\overline{\mathcal{Q}}$ **satisfies** QuTL formula ϕ, written $\overline{\mathcal{Q}} \models_p \phi$, if some concretization of $\overline{\mathcal{Q}}$ satisfies ϕ:*

$$\overline{\mathcal{Q}} \models_p \phi \ := \ \exists \mathcal{Q} \in \gamma_p(\overline{\mathcal{Q}}) : \mathcal{Q} \models \phi. \tag{7}$$

For example, we have $bb \,|\, ba \models_2 \mathsf{G}(a \Rightarrow \mathsf{G}\,\neg b)$ since for instance $bbba \in \gamma_2(bb\,|\,ba)$ satisfies the formula. See App. B of [23] for more examples.

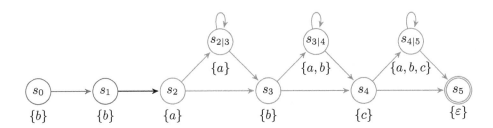

Fig. 2. LTS for $\overline{\mathcal{Q}} = bb \,|\, abc$ $(p = 2)$, with label sets written below each state. The blue and red parts encode the concretizations of the prefix and suffix of $\overline{\mathcal{Q}}$, resp. (Color figure online)

5.2   Abstract QuTL Model Checking

A QuTL *constraint* is a QuTL formula without Boolean connectives. We first describe how to model check against QuTL constraints, and come back to Boolean connectives at the end of Sect. 5.2.

Model checking an abstract queue $\overline{\mathcal{Q}}$ against a QuTL constraint ϕ, i.e. checking whether some concretization of $\overline{\mathcal{Q}}$ satisfies ϕ, can be reduced to a standard model checking problem over a labeled transition system (LTS) $M = (S, T, L)$ with states S, transitions T, and a labeling function $L : S \to 2^\Sigma \cup \{\varepsilon\}$. The LTS *characterizes* the concretization $\gamma_p(\overline{\mathcal{Q}})$ of $\overline{\mathcal{Q}}$, as illustrated in Fig. 2 using an example: the concretizations of $\overline{\mathcal{Q}}$ are formed from the regular-expression traces generated by paths of $\overline{\mathcal{Q}}$'s LTS that end in the double-circled green state.

The straightforward construction of the LTS M is formalized in App. A.2 of [23]. Its size is linear in $|\overline{\mathcal{Q}}|$: $|S| = p+2 \times (|\overline{\mathcal{Q}}|-p)+1$ and $|T| = p+4 \times (|\overline{\mathcal{Q}}|-p)$.

We call a path through M *complete* if it ends in the right-most state s_z of M (green in Fig. 2). The labeling function extends to paths via $L(s_i \to \ldots \to s_j) = L(s_i) \cdot \ldots \cdot L(s_j)$. This gives rise to the following characterization of $\gamma_p(\overline{\mathcal{Q}})$:

Lemma 9. *Given abstract queue $\overline{\mathcal{Q}}$ over alphabet Σ, let $M = (S, T, L)$ be its LTS.*

$$\gamma_p(\overline{\mathcal{Q}}) \;=\; \bigcup \{\mathcal{L}(L(\pi)) \in 2^{\Sigma^*} \mid \pi \text{ is a complete path from } s_0 \text{ in } M\}. \qquad (8)$$

We say path π *satisfies* ϕ, written $\pi \models_p \phi$, if there exists $\mathcal{Q} \in \mathcal{L}(L(\pi))$ s.t. $\mathcal{Q} \models \phi$.

Corollary 10. *Let $\overline{\mathcal{Q}}$ and M as in Lemma 9, and ϕ a QuTL constraint. Then the following are equivalent.*

1. *$\overline{\mathcal{Q}} \models_p \phi$.*
2. *There exists a complete path π from s_0 in M such that $\pi \models_p \phi$.*

Proof. immediate from Definition 8 and Lemma 9. $\qquad\qquad\qquad\qquad\qquad$ □

Given an abstract queue $\overline{\mathcal{Q}}$, its LTS M, and a QuTL constraint ϕ, our abstract queue model checking algorithm is based on Corollary 10: we need to find a complete path from s_0 in M that satisfies ϕ. This is similar to standard model checking against existential temporal logics like ECTL, with two particularities:

First, paths must be complete. This poses no difficulty, as completeness is suffix-closed: a path ends in s_z iff any suffix does. This implies that temporal reductions on QuTL constraints work like in standard temporal logics. For example: there exists a complete path π from s_0 in M such that $\pi \models_p \mathsf{X} \phi$ iff there exists a complete path π' from some successor s_1 of s_0 such that $\pi' \models_p \phi$.

Second, we have domain-specific atomic (non-temporal) propositions. These are accommodated as follows, for an arbitrary start state $s \in S$:

$\exists \pi :\; \pi$ **from s complete and** $\pi \models_p e$ **(for $e \in \Sigma$):**
this is true iff $e \in L(s)$, as is immediate from the $\mathcal{Q} \models e$ case in Definition 7.
$\exists \pi :\; \pi$ **from s complete and** $\pi \models_p \#e > c$ **(for $e \in \Sigma, c \in \mathbb{N}$):** this is true iff
   − the number of states reachable from s labeled e is greater than c,   **or**
   − there exists a state reachable from s labeled with e that has a self-loop.
The other relational expressions $\#e \triangleright c$ are checked similarly. $\qquad\qquad$ □

Boolean Connectives. Let now ϕ be a full-fledged QuTL formula. We first bring it into negation normal form, by pushing negations inside, exploiting the usual dualities $\neg \mathsf{X} = \mathsf{X} \neg$, $\neg \mathsf{F} = \mathsf{G} \neg$, and $\neg \mathsf{G} = \mathsf{F} \neg$. The subset $\triangleright \in \{<, \leq, \geq, >\}$ of the queue relational expressions is semantically closed under negation; "$\neg=$" is replaced by "$> \vee <$". A path π from s satisfies $\neg e$ (for $e \in \Sigma$) iff $L(s) \neq \{e\}$: this condition states that either $L(s) = \varepsilon$, or there exists some label other than e in $L(s)$, so the *existential* property $\neg e$ holds.

  Disjunctions are handled by distributing $\models_p$ over them: $\overline{\mathcal{Q}} \models_p \phi_1 \vee \phi_2$ iff $\overline{\mathcal{Q}} \models_p \phi_1 \vee \overline{\mathcal{Q}} \models_p \phi_2$. What remains are conjunctions. The existential flavor of $\models_p$ implies that $\models_p$ does *not* distribute over them; see Ex. 13 in App. B.1 of [23]. Suppose we ignore this and replace a check of the form $\overline{\mathcal{Q}} \models_p \phi_1 \wedge \phi_2$ by the **weaker** check $\overline{\mathcal{Q}} \models_p \phi_1 \wedge \overline{\mathcal{Q}} \models_p \phi_2$, which may produce false positives. Now consider how we use these results: if $\overline{\mathcal{Q}} \models_p \phi$ holds, we decide to *keep* the state containing the abstract queue. False positives during abstract model checks therefore may create extra work, but do not introduce unsoundness. In summary, our abstract model checking algorithm soundly approximates conjunctions, but remains exact for the purely disjunctive fragment of QuTL.

Table 1. Results: $\#M$: $\#$P machines; *Loc*: $\#$lines of code; *Safe?* = ✓: property holds; p: *minimum* unabstracted prefix for required convergence; $k_{\max}$: point of convergence or exposed bugs (– means divergence); *Time*: runtime (sec); *Mem.*: memory usage (Mb.).

ID/Program	Program Features			PAT				ID/Program	Program Features			PAT			
	$\#M$	*Loc*	*Safe?*	p	$k_{\max}$	*Time*	*Mem.*		$\#M$	*Loc*	*Safe?*	p	$k_{\max}$	*Time*	*Mem.*
1/GERMAN-1	3	242	✓	4	–	TO	–	8/FAILOVER	4	132	✓	0	2	2.91	8.56
2/GERMAN-2	4	244	✓	4	–	TO	–	9/MAXINSTANCES	4	79	✓	0	3	0.14	0.56
3/TOKENRING-BUGGY	6	164	✗	0	2	241.44	35.96	10/PINGPONG	2	76	✓	0	2	0.06	0.43
4/TOKENRING-FIXED	6	164	✓	0	4	1849.25	130.87	11/BOUNDEDASYNC	4	96	✓	0	5	203.39	29.32
5/FAILUREDETECTOR	6	229	✓	0	4	183.99	12.38	12/PINGFLOOD	2	52	✓	4	5	0.11	0.43
6/OSR	5	378	✓	0	5	77.92	44.86	13/ELEVATOR-BUGGY	4	270	✗	0	1	1.29	5.23
7/OPENWSN	6	294	✓	2	5	2574.25	376.29	14/ELEVATOR-FIXED	4	271	✓	0	4	49.23	45.36

6 Empirical Evaluation

We implemented the proposed approaches in C# atop the bounded model checker PTester [11], an analysis tool for P programs. PTester employs a bounded exploration strategy similar to Zing [4]. We denote by PAT the implementation of Algorithm 1, and by PAT+I the version with queue invariants ("PAT+ Invariants"). A detailed introduction to tool design and implementation is available online [22].

Experimental Goals. We evaluate the approaches against the following questions:

Q1. Is PAT effective: does it converge for many programs? for what values of k?
Q2. What is the impact of the QuTL invariant checking?

Experimental Setup. We collected a set of P programs (available online [22]); most have been used in previous publications:

1–5: protocols implemented in P: the German Cache Coherence protocol with different number of clients (**1–2**) [11], a buggy version of a token ring protocol [11], and a fixed version (**3–4**), and a failure detector protocol from [25] (**5**).

6–7: two device drivers where OSR is used for testing USB devices [10].

8–14: miscellaneous: **8–10** [25], **11** [15], **12** is the example from Sect. 2, **13–14** are the buggy and fixed versions of an Elevator controller [11].

We conduct two types of experiments: (i) we run PAT on each benchmark to empirically answer **Q1**; (ii) we run PAT+I on the examples which fail to verify in (i) to answer **Q2**. All experiments are performed on a 2.80 GHz Intel(R) Core(TM) i7-7600 machine with 8 GB memory, running 64-bit Windows 10. The timeout is set to 3600 s (1h); the memory limit to 4 GB.

Results. Table 1 shows that PAT converges on *almost all* safe examples (and successfully exposes the bugs for unsafe ones). Second, in most cases, the k_{max} where convergence was detected is small, 5 or less. This is what enables the use of this technique in practice: the exploration space grows fast with k, so early convergence is critical. Note that k_{max} is guaranteed to be the smallest value for which the respective example converges. If convergent, the verification succeeded fully automatically: the queue abstraction prefix parameter p is incremented in a loop whenever the current value of p caused a spurious abstract state.

The GERMAN protocol does not converge in reasonable time. In this case, we request minimal manual assistance from the designer. Our tool inspects spurious abstract states, compares them to actually reached abstract states, and suggests candidate invariants to exclude them. We describe the process of invariant discovery, and why and how they are easy to prove, in [22].

The following table shows the invariants that make the GERMAN protocol converge, and the resulting times and memory consumption.

Program	p	k_{max}	$Time$	$Mem.$	Invariant
GERMAN-1	0	4	15.65	45.65	**Server:** $\#req\_excl \leq 1 \wedge \#req\_share \leq 1$
GERMAN-2	0	4	629.43	284.75	**Client:** $\#ask\_excl \leq 1 \wedge \#ask\_share \leq 1$

The invariant states that there is always at most one exclusive request and at most one shared request in the **Server** or **Client** machine's queue.

Performance Evaluation. We finally consider the following question: *To perform full verification, how much overhead does PAT incur compared to PTester?* We iteratively run PTester with a queue bound from 1 up to k_{max} (from Table 1).

The figure on the right compares the running times of PAT and PTester. We observe that the difference is small, in all cases, suggesting that turning PTester into a full verifier comes with little

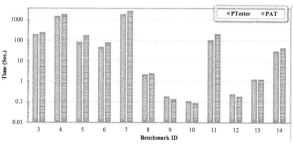

extra cost. Therefore, as for improving PAT's scalability, the focus should be on the efficiency of the R_k computation (Line 3 in Algorithm 1). Techniques that lend themselves here are *partial order reduction* [2,28] or *symmetry reduction* [29]. Note that our proposed approach is orthogonal to how these sets are computed.

7   Related Work

Automatic verification for asynchronous event-driven programs communicating via unbounded FIFO queues is undecidable [8], even when the agents are finite-state machines. To sidestep the undecidability, various remedies are proposed. One is to underapproximate program behaviors using various bounding techniques; examples include depth- [17] and context-bounded analysis [19,20,26], delay-bounding [13], bounded asynchrony [15], preemption-bounding [24], and phase-bounded analysis [3,6]. It has been shown that most of these bounding techniques admit a decidable model checking problem [19,20,26] and thus have been successfully used in practice for finding bugs.

Gall et al. proposed an abstract interpretation of FIFO queues in terms of regular languages [16]. While our works share some basic insights about taming queues, the differences are fundamental: our abstract domain is *finite*, guaranteeing convergence of our sequence. In [16] the abstract domain is infinite; they propose a widening operator for fixpoint computation. More critically, we use the abstract domain *only* for convergence detection; the set of reachable states returned is in the end exact. As a result, we can prove and refute properties but may not terminate; [16] is inexact and cannot refute but always returns.

Several partial verification approaches for asynchronous message-passing programs have been presented recently [5,7,10]. In [5], Bakst et al. propose *canonical sequentialization*, which avoids exploring all interleavings by sequentializing concurrent programs. Desai et al. [10] propose an alternative way, namely by prioritizing receive actions over send actions. The approach is complete in the sense that it is able to construct *almost-synchronous invariants* that cover all reachable local states and hence suffice to prove local assertions. Similarly, Bouajjani et al. [7] propose an iterative analysis that bounds send actions in each interaction phase. It approaches the completeness by checking a program's synchronizability under the bounds. Similar to our work, the above three works are sound but incomplete. An experimental comparison against the techniques reported in [7,10] fails due to the unavailability of a tool that implements them. While tools implementing these techniques are not available [7,10], a comparison based on what is reported in the papers suggests that our approach is competitive in both performance and precision.

Our approach can be categorized as a *cutoff* detection technique [1,12,14,28]. Cutoffs are, however, typically determined statically, often leaving them too large for practical verification. Aiming at minimal cutoffs, our work is closer in nature to earlier *dynamic* strategies [18,21], which targeted different forms of concurrent programs. The *generator* technique proposed in [21] is unlikely to work for P programs, due to the large local state space of machines.

8   Conclusion

We have presented a method to verify safety properties of asynchronous event-driven programs of agents communicating via unbounded queues. Our approach is sound but incomplete: it can both prove (or, by encountering bugs, disprove) such properties but may not terminate. We empirically evaluate our method on a collection of P programs. Our experimental results showcase our method can successfully prove the correctness of programs; such proof is achieved with little extra resource costs compared to plain state exploration. Future work includes an extension to P programs with other sources of unboundedness than the queue length (e.g. messages with integer *payloads*).

Acknowledgments. We thank Dr. Vijay D'Silva (Google, Inc.), for enlightening discussions about partial abstract transformers.

References

1. Abdulla, A.P., Haziza, F., Holík, L.: All for the price of few (parameterized verification through view abstraction). In: VMCAI, pp. 476–495 (2013)
2. Abdulla, P., Aronis, S., Jonsson, B., Sagonas, K.: Optimal dynamic partial order reduction. In: POPL, pp. 373–384 (2014)
3. Abdulla, P.A., Atig, M.F., Cederberg, J.: Analysis of message passing programs using SMT-solvers. In: Van Hung, D., Ogawa, M. (eds.) ATVA 2013. LNCS, vol. 8172, pp. 272–286. Springer, Cham (2013). https://doi.org/10.1007/978-3-319-02444-8_20
4. Andrews, T., Qadeer, S., Rajamani, S.K., Rehof, J., Xie, Y.: Zing: a model checker for concurrent software. In: Alur, R., Peled, D.A. (eds.) CAV 2004. LNCS, vol. 3114, pp. 484–487. Springer, Heidelberg (2004). https://doi.org/10.1007/978-3-540-27813-9_42
5. Bakst, A., Gleissenthall, K.v., Kici, R.G., Jhala, R.: Verifying distributed programs via canonical sequentialization. PACMPL 1(OOPSLA), 110:1–110:27 (2017)
6. Bouajjani, A., Emmi, M.: Bounded phase analysis of message-passing programs. Int. J. Softw. Tools Technol. Transf. **16**(2), 127–146 (2014)
7. Bouajjani, A., Enea, C., Ji, K., Qadeer, S.: On the completeness of verifying message passing programs under bounded asynchrony. In: Chockler, H., Weissenbacher, G. (eds.) CAV 2018. LNCS, vol. 10982, pp. 372–391. Springer, Cham (2018). https://doi.org/10.1007/978-3-319-96142-2_23
8. Brand, D., Zafiropulo, P.: On communicating finite-state machines. J. ACM **30**(2), 323–342 (1983)
9. Cousot, P., Cousot, R.: Systematic design of program analysis frameworks. In: POPL, pp. 269–282 (1979)
10. Desai, A., Garg, P., Madhusudan, P.: Natural proofs for asynchronous programs using almost-synchronous reductions. In: OOPSLA, pp. 709–725 (2014)
11. Desai, A., Gupta, V., Jackson, E., Qadeer, S., Rajamani, S., Zufferey, D.: P: safe asynchronous event-driven programming. In: PLDI, pp. 321–332 (2013)
12. Emerson, E.A., Kahlon, V.: Reducing model checking of the many to the few. In: McAllester, D. (ed.) CADE 2000. LNCS (LNAI), vol. 1831, pp. 236–254. Springer, Heidelberg (2000). https://doi.org/10.1007/10721959_19

13. Emmi, M., Qadeer, S., Rakamarić, Z.: Delay-bounded scheduling. In: POPL, pp. 411–422 (2011)
14. Farzan, A., Kincaid, Z., Podelski, A.: Proof spaces for unbounded parallelism. In: POPL, pp. 407–420 (2015)
15. Fisher, J., Henzinger, T.A., Mateescu, M., Piterman, N.: Bounded asynchrony: concurrency for modeling cell-cell interactions. In: Fisher, J. (ed.) FMSB 2008. LNCS, vol. 5054, pp. 17–32. Springer, Heidelberg (2008). https://doi.org/10.1007/978-3-540-68413-8_2
16. Le Gall, T., Jeannet, B., Jéron, T.: Verification of communication protocols using abstract interpretation of FIFO queues. In: Johnson, M., Vene, V. (eds.) AMAST 2006. LNCS, vol. 4019, pp. 204–219. Springer, Heidelberg (2006). https://doi.org/10.1007/11784180_17
17. Godefroid, P.: Model checking for programming languages using VeriSoft. In: POPL, pp. 174–186 (1997)
18. Kaiser, A., Kroening, D., Wahl, T.: Dynamic cutoff detection in parameterized concurrent programs. In: Touili, T., Cook, B., Jackson, P. (eds.) CAV 2010. LNCS, vol. 6174, pp. 645–659. Springer, Heidelberg (2010). https://doi.org/10.1007/978-3-642-14295-6_55
19. La Torre, S., Parthasarathy, M., Parlato, G.: Analyzing recursive programs using a fixed-point calculus. In: PLDI, pp. 211–222 (2009)
20. Lal, A., Reps, T.: Reducing concurrent analysis under a context bound to sequential analysis. Form. Methods Syst. Des. **35**(1), 73–97 (2009)
21. Liu, P., Wahl, T.: CUBA: interprocedural context-unbounded analysis of concurrent programs. In: PLDI, pp. 105–119 (2018)
22. Liu, P., Wahl, T., Lal, A.: (2019). www.khoury.northeastern.edu/home/lpzun/quba
23. Liu, P., Wahl, T., Lal, A.: Verifying asynchronous event-driven programs using partial abstract transformers (extended manuscript). CoRR abs/1905.09996 (2019)
24. Musuvathi, M., Qadeer, S.: Iterative context bounding for systematic testing of multithreaded programs. In: PLDI, pp. 446–455 (2007)
25. P-GitHub: The P programming langugage (2019). https://github.com/p-org/P
26. Qadeer, S., Rehof, J.: Context-bounded model checking of concurrent software. In: Halbwachs, N., Zuck, L.D. (eds.) TACAS 2005. LNCS, vol. 3440, pp. 93–107. Springer, Heidelberg (2005). https://doi.org/10.1007/978-3-540-31980-1_7
27. Reps, T., Sagiv, M., Yorsh, G.: Symbolic implementation of the best transformer. In: Steffen, B., Levi, G. (eds.) VMCAI 2004. LNCS, vol. 2937, pp. 252–266. Springer, Heidelberg (2004). https://doi.org/10.1007/978-3-540-24622-0_21
28. Sousa, M., Rodríguez, C., D'Silva, V., Kroening, D.: Abstract interpretation with unfoldings. In: Majumdar, R., Kunčak, V. (eds.) CAV 2017. LNCS, vol. 10427, pp. 197–216. Springer, Cham (2017). https://doi.org/10.1007/978-3-319-63390-9_11
29. Wahl, T., Donaldson, A.: Replication and abstraction: symmetry in automated formal verification. Symmetry **2**(2), 799–847 (2010)

6

AliveInLean: A Verified LLVM Peephole Optimization Verifier

Juneyoung Lee[1(✉)], Chung-Kil Hur[1], and Nuno P. Lopes[2]

[1] Seoul National University,
Seoul, Republic of Korea
juneyoung.lee@sf.snu.ac.kr
[2] Microsoft Research, Cambridge, UK

Abstract. Ensuring that compiler optimizations are correct is important for the reliability of the entire software ecosystem, since all software is compiled. Alive [12] is a tool for verifying LLVM's peephole optimizations. Since Alive was released, it has helped compiler developers proactively find dozens of bugs in LLVM, avoiding potentially hazardous miscompilations. Despite having verified many LLVM optimizations so far, Alive is itself not verified, which has led to at least once declaring an optimization correct when it was not.

We introduce AliveInLean, a formally verified peephole optimization verifier for LLVM. As the name suggests, AliveInLean is a reengineered version of Alive developed in the Lean theorem prover [14]. Assuming that the proof obligations are correctly discharged by an SMT solver, AliveInLean gives the same level of correctness guarantees as state-of-the-art formal frameworks such as CompCert [11], Peek [15], and Vellvm [26], while inheriting the advantages of Alive (significantly more automation and easy adoption by compiler developers).

Keywords: Compiler verification · Peephole optimization · LLVM · Lean · Alive

1 Introduction

Verifying compiler optimizations is important to ensure reliability of the software ecosystem. Various frameworks have been proposed to verify optimizations of industrial compilers. Among them, Alive [12] is a tool for verifying peephole optimizations of LLVM that has been successfully adopted by compiler developers. Since it was released, Alive has helped developers find dozens of bugs.

Figure 1 shows the structure of Alive. An optimization pattern of interest written in a domain-specific language is given as input. Alive parses the input, and encodes the behavior of the source and target programs into logic formulas in the theory of quantified bit-vectors and arrays. Finally, several proof obligations are created from the encoded behavior, and then checked by an SMT solver.

Alive relies on the following three-fold trust base. Firstly, the semantics of LLVM's intermediate representation and SMT expressions. Secondly, Alive's verification condition generator. Finally, the SMT solver used to discharge proof

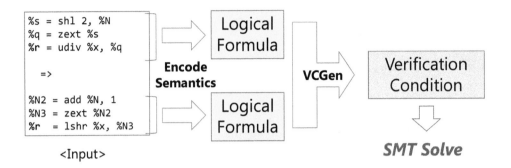

Fig. 1. The structure of Alive and AliveInLean

obligations. None of these are formally verified, and thus an error in any of these may result in an incorrect answer.

To address this problem, we introduce AliveInLean, a formally verified peephole optimization verifier for LLVM. AliveInLean is written in Lean [14], an interactive theorem proving language. Its semantics of LLVM IR (Intermediate Representation) and SMT expressions are rigorously tested using Lean's metaprogramming language [5] and system library. AliveInLean's verification condition generator is formally verified in Lean.

Using AliveInLean requires less human effort than directly proving the optimizations on formal frameworks thanks to automation given by SMT solvers. For example, verifying the correctness of a peephole optimization on a formal framework requires more than a hundred lines of proofs [15]. However, the correctness of AliveInLean relies on the correctness of the used SMT solver. To counteract the dependency on SMT solvers, proof obligations can be cross-checked with multiple SMT solvers. Moreover, there is substantial work towards making SMT solvers generate proof certificates [2,3,6,7].

AliveInLean is a proof of concept. It currently does not support all operations that Alive does like, e.g., memory-related operations. However, AliveInLean supports all integer peephole optimizations, which is already useful in practice as most bugs found by Alive were in integer optimizations [12].

2 Overview

We give an overview of AliveInLean's features from a user's perspective.

Verifying Optimizations. AliveInLean reads optimization(s) from a file and checks their correctness. A user writes an optimization of interest in a DSL with similar syntax to that of LLVM IR:

```
Name: AddSub:1309
%lhs = and i4 %a, %b
%rhs = or i4 %a, %b
%r = add i4 %lhs, %rhs
  =>
%r = add i4 %a, %b
```

This example transformation corresponds to rewriting (%a & %b) + (%a | %b) to %a + %b, given 4-bits integers %a and %b. The last variable %r, or *root* variable, is assumed to be the return value of the programs. AliveInLean encodes the behavior of each program and generates verification conditions (VCs). Finally, AliveInLean calls Z3 to discharge the VCs.

Proving Useful Properties. AliveInLean can be used as a formal framework to prove lemmas using interactive theorem proving. This is helpful when a user wants to show a property of a program which is hard to represent as a transformation.

For example, one may want to prove that the divisor of udiv (unsigned division) is never poison[1] if it did not raise undefined behavior (UB). The lemma below states this in Lean. This lemma says that the divisor val is never poison if the state st' after executing the udiv instruction (step) has no UB.

```
lemma never_poison:
  forall .. (HSTEP: some st' = step st (udiv isz name op1 op2))
            (HNOUB: not (has_ub st'))
            (HVAL:  some val = get_value st op2 (ty.int isz)),
    not (is_poison val)
```

Testing Specifications. AliveInLean supports random testing of AliveInLean's specifications (for which no verification is possible). For example, the step function in the above example implements a specification of the LLVM IR, and it can be tested with respect to the behavior of the LLVM compiler. Another trust-base is the specification of SMT expressions, which defines a relation between expressions (with no free variable) and their corresponding concrete values.

These tests help build confidence in the validity of VC generation. Running tests is helpful when a user wants to use a different version of LLVM or modify AliveInLean's specifications (e.g., adding a new instruction to IR).

3   Verifying Optimizations

In this section we introduce the different components of AliveInLean that work together to verify an optimization.

---

[1] poison is a special value of LLVM representing a result of an erroneous computation.

3.1 Semantics Encoder

Given a program and an initial state, the semantics encoder produces the final state of the program as a set of SMT expressions. The IR interpreter is similar, but works over concrete values rather than symbolic ones. The semantics encoder and the IR interpreter share the same codebase (essentially the LLVM IR semantics). The code is parametric on the type of the program state. For example, the type of undefined behavior can be either initialized as the `bool` type of Lean or the `Bool` SMT expression type. Given the type, Lean can automatically resolve which operations to use to update the state using typeclass resolution.

3.2 Refinement Encoder

Given a source program, a transformed program, and an initial state, the refinement encoder emits an SMT expression that encodes the refinement check between the final states of the two programs. To obtain the final states, the semantics encoder is used.

The refinement check proves that (1) the transformed program only triggers UB when the original program does (i.e., UB can only be removed), (2) the root variable of the transformed program is only `poison` when it is also `poison` in the original program, and (3) variables' values in the final states of the two programs are the same when no UB is triggered and the original value is not `poison`.

3.3 Parser and Z3 Backend

The parser for Alive's DSL is implemented using Lean's parser monad and file I/O library. SMT expressions are processed with Z3 using Lean's SMT interface.

4 Correctness of AliveInLean

We describe how the correctness of AliveInLean is proved. First, we explain the correctness proof of the semantics encoder and the refinement encoder. We show that if the SMT expression encoded by refinement encoder is valid, the optimization is indeed correct. Next, we explain how the trust-base is tested.

4.1 Semantics Encoding

Given an IR interpreter `run`, a semantics encoder `encoder` is correct with respect to `run` if for any IR program and input state, the final program state generated by `run` and the symbolic state encoded by `encoder` are equivalent.

To formally define its correctness, an equivalence relation between SMT expressions and concrete values is defined. We say that an SMT expression e and a Lean value ν are equivalent, or $e \sim \nu$, if e has no free variables and it evaluates to ν. The equivalence relation is inductively defined with respect to the structure of an SMT expression. To deal with free variables, an environment η is defined, which is a set of pairs (x, ν) where x is a variable and ν is a concrete value. $\eta[\![e]\!]$ is an expression with all free variables x replaced with ν if $(x, \nu) \in \eta$.

Next, we define a program state. A state s is defined as (u, r) where u is an undefined behavior flag and r is a register file. r is a list of (x, v) where x is a variable and v is a value. v is defined as (sz, i, p) where sz is its size in bits, i is an integer value, and p is a poison flag.

There are two kinds of states: a symbolic state, and a concrete state. A symbolic state s_s is a state whose u, i, p are SMT expressions. A concrete state s_c is a state whose all attributes are concrete values. We say that s_s and s_c are equivalent, or $s_s \sim s_c$, if s_s has no free variable in its attributes and they are equivalent. $\eta[\![s_s]\!]$ is a symbolic state with the environment η applied to u, i, p.

Now, the correctness of `encoder` with respect to `run` is defined as follows. It states that the result of `encoder` is equivalent to the result of `run`.

Theorem 1. *For all initial states s_s, s_c, program p, and environment η s.t. $\eta[\![s_s]\!] \sim s_c$, we have that $\eta[\![\texttt{encoder}(p, s_s)]\!] \sim \texttt{run}(p, s_c)$.*

4.2   Refinement Encoding

Function $\texttt{check}(p_{src}, p_{tgt}, s_s)$ generates an SMT expression that encodes refinement between the source and target programs, respectively, p_{src} and p_{tgt}.

We first define refinement between two concrete states. As Alive does, AliveInLean only checks the value of the root variable of a program. Given a root variable r, a concrete state s_c' refines s_c, or $s_c' \sqsubseteq s_c$, if (1) s_c has undefined behavior, or (2) both s_c and s_c' have values assigned to r, say v and v', and $v = \texttt{poison} \lor v' = v$. A target program p_{tgt} refines program p_{src} if $\texttt{run}(p_{tgt}, s_c) \sqsubseteq \texttt{run}(p_{src}, s_c)$ holds for any initial concrete state s_c.

The correctness of `check` is stated as follows.

Theorem 2. *Given an initial symbolic state s_s, if $\eta_0[\![\texttt{check}(p_{src}, p_{tgt}, s_s)]\!] \sim$ true for any η_0, then for any environment η and initial state s_c s.t. $\eta[\![s_s]\!] \sim s_c$, we have that $\texttt{run}(p_{tgt}, s_c) \sqsubseteq \texttt{run}(p_{src}, s_c)$.*

This theorem says that if the returned expression of `check` evaluates to true in any environment, program p_{tgt} refines program p_{src}.

4.3   Validity of Trust-Base

Testing Specification of SMT Expressions. Specifications of SMT expressions are traversed using Lean's metaprogramming language and tested. The testing we have done is different from QuickChick [4] because QuickChick evaluates expressions in Coq. The approach cannot be used here because SMT expressions need to be evaluated in an SMT solver (e.g., Z3). Example spec:

```
forall {sz : size} (s1 s2 : sbitvec sz) (b1 b2 : bitvector sz),
  bv_equiv s1 b1 -> bv_equiv s2 b2 ->
    bv_equiv (sbitvec.add s1 s2) (bitvector.add b1 b2)
```

This spec says that if SMT expressions s1, s2 of a bit-vector type (sbitvec) are equivalent to two concrete bit-vector values b1, b2 in Lean (bitvector), an add expression of s1, s2 is equivalent to the result of adding b1 and b2. Function bitvector.add must be called in Lean, so its operands (b1, b2) are assigned random values in Lean. sbitvec.add is translated to SMT's bvadd expression, and s1 and s2 are initialized as BitVec variables in an SMT solver. The testing function generates an SMT expression with random inputs like the following:

```
(assert (forall ((s1 (_ BitVec 4))) (forall ((s2 (_ BitVec 4)))
  (=> (= s1 #xA) (=> (= s2 #x2) (= (bvadd s1 s2) #xC))))))
```

The size of bitvector (sz) is initialized to 4, and b1, b2 were randomly initialized to 10 (#xA) and 2 (#x2). A specification is incorrect if the generated SMT expression is not valid.

Testing Specification of LLVM IR. Specification of LLVM IR is tested using randomly generated IR programs. IR programs of 5–10 randomly chosen instructions are generated, compiled with LLVM, and ran. The result of the execution of the program is compared with the result of AliveInLean's IR interpreter.

5 Evaluation

For the evaluation, we used a computer with an Intel Core i5-6600 CPU and 8 GB of RAM, and Z3 [13] for SMT solving. To test whether AliveInLean and Alive give the same result, we used all of the 150 integer optimizations from Alive's test suite that are supported by AliveInLean. No mismatches were observed.

To test the SMT specification, we randomly generated 10,000 tests for each of the operations (18 bit-vector and 15 boolean). This test took 3 CPU hours.

The LLVM IR specification was tested by running 1,000,000 random IR programs in our interpreter and comparing the output with that of LLVM. This comparison needs to take into account that some programs may trigger UB or yield a poison value, which gives freedom to LLVM to produce a variety of results. These tests took 10 CPU hours overall. Four admitted arithmetic lemmas were tested as well. As a side-effect of the testing, we found several miscompilation bugs in LLVM.[2]

AliveInLean[3] consists of 11.9K lines of code. The optimization verifier consists of 2.2K LoC, the specification tester is 1.5K, and the proof has 8.1K lines. It took 3 person-months to implement the tool and prove its correctness.

6 Related Work

We introduce previous work on compiler verification and validation and compare it with AliveInLean. Also, we give an overview on previous work on semantics of compiler intermediate representations (IRs).

---

[2] https://llvm.org/PR40657.
[3] https://github.com/Microsoft/AliveInLean.

6.1   Compiler Verification

Proving Correctness on Formal Semantics. The correctness of compilation can be proved on a formal semantics of a language that is written in a theorem proving language such as Coq. Vellvm [26] is a Coq formalization of the semantics of LLVM IR. CompCert [11] is a verified C compiler written in Coq, and its compilation to assembly languages including x86, PowerPC is proved correct.

However, it is hard to apply this approach to existing industrial compilers because proving correctness of optimizations requires non-trivial effort. Peek [15] is a framework for implementing and verifying peephole optimizations for x86 on CompCert. They implemented 28 peephole optimizations which required 3.3k lines of code and 6.6k lines of proofs ($\sim$350 LoC each). Even if this is small compared to the size of CompCert, the burden is non-trivial considering that LLVM has more than 1,000 peephole optimizations [12].

Another problem with this approach is that changing the semantics requires modification of the proof. The semantics of `poison` and `undef` value of LLVM is currently not consistent and thus it triggers miscompilations of some programs [10]. Therefore, compiler developers regularly test various `undef` semantics with existing optimizations, which would be a non-trivial task if correctness proofs had to be manually updated.

Translation Validation and Credible Compilation. In translation validation [18], a pair of an original program and an optimized program is given to a validation tool at compile time to check the correctness of the optimization. Several such tools exist for LLVM [20,22,25]. Translation validation is, however, slow, and it cannot tell whether an optimization is correct in general. Consider this optimization:

```
z = 0 - (x / C)
  =>
z = x / -C
```

If `C` is a constant, `-C` can be computed at compile time. However, this optimization is wrong only if `C` is `INT_MIN`. To show that compilation is fully correct, translation validation would need to be run for every combination of inputs.

Credible compilation [19], or witnessing compiler [16,17], is an approach to improve translation validation by accepting witnesses generated by a compiler. Crellvm [8] is a credible compilation framework for LLVM. It requires modifications to the compiler, which makes it harder to apply and maintain.

6.2   Solver-Aided Programming Languages

Proving correctness of optimizations can be represented as a search problem that finds a counter-example for the optimization. Tools like Z3, CVC4 can be used to solve the search problem. Translation of a high-level search problem to the external solver's input has been considered bug-prone, and frameworks like

Rosette [21] and Smten [23] address this issue by providing higher-level languages for describing the search problem. SpaceSearch [24] helps programmers prove the correctness of the description by supporting Coq and Rosette backends from a single specification. AliveInLean provides a stronger guarantee of correctness because translation to SMT expressions is also written in Lean, leaving Lean as the sole trust-base.

6.3 Semantics of Compiler IR

Correctly encoding semantics of compiler IR is important for the validity of a tool. LLVM IR is an SSA-based intermediate representation which is used to represent a program being compiled. LLVM LangRef [1] has an informal definition of the LLVM IR, but there are a few known problems. [10] shows that the semantics of `poison` and `undef` values are inconsistent. [9] shows that the semantics of pointer↔integer casting is inconsistent. AliveInLean supports `poison` but not `undef`, following the suggestion from [10]. AliveInLean does not support memory-related operations including load, store, and pointer ↔ integer casting.

7 Discussion

AliveInLean has several limitations. As discussed before, AliveInLean does not support memory operations. Correctly encoding the memory model of LLVM IR is challenging because the memory model of LLVM IR is more complex than either a byte array or a set of memory objects [9]. Supporting branch instructions and floating point would help developers prove interesting optimizations. Supporting branches is a challenging job especially when loops are involved.

Maintainability of AliveInLean highly relies on one's proficiency in Lean. Changing the semantics of an IR instruction breaks the proof, and updating it requires proficiency in Lean. However, we believe that only relevant parts in the proof need to be updated as the proof is modularized.

Alive has features that are absent in AliveInLean. Alive supports defining a precondition for an optimization, inferring types of variables if not given, and showing counter-examples if the optimization is wrong. We leave this as future work.

8 Conclusion

AliveInLean is a formally verified compiler optimization verifier. Its verification condition generator is formally verified with a machine-checked proof. Using AliveInLean, developers can easily check the correctness of compiler optimizations with high reliability. Also, they can use AliveInLean as a formal framework like Vellvm to prove properties of interest in limited cases. The extensive random testing did not find problems in the trust base, increasing its trustworthiness. Moreover, as a side-effect of the IR semantics testing, we found several bugs in LLVM.

Acknowledgments. The authors thank Leonardo de Moura and Sebastian Ullrich for their help with Lean. This work was supported in part by the Basic Science Research Program through the National Research Foundation of Korea (NRF) funded by the Ministry of Science and ICT (2017R1A2B2007512). The first author was supported by a Korea Foundation for Advanced Studies scholarship.

References

1. LLVM language reference manual. https://llvm.org/docs/LangRef.html
2. Barbosa, H., Blanchette, J.C., Fontaine, P.: Scalable fine-grained proofs for formula processing. In: de Moura, L. (ed.) CADE 2017. LNCS (LNAI), vol. 10395, pp. 398–412. Springer, Cham (2017). https://doi.org/10.1007/978-3-319-63046-5_25
3. Böhme, S., Fox, A.C.J., Sewell, T., Weber, T.: Reconstruction of Z3's bit-vector proofs in HOL4 and Isabelle/HOL. In: Jouannaud, J.-P., Shao, Z. (eds.) CPP 2011. LNCS, vol. 7086, pp. 183–198. Springer, Heidelberg (2011). https://doi.org/10.1007/978-3-642-25379-9_15
4. Dénès, M., Hriţcu, C., Lampropoulos, L., Paraskevopoulou, Z., Pierce, B.C.: Quickchick : Property-based Testing for Coq (2014)
5. Ebner, G., Ullrich, S., Roesch, J., Avigad, J., de Moura, L.: A metaprogramming framework for formal verification. Proc. ACM Program. Lang. 1(ICFP), 34:1–34:29 (2017). https://doi.org/10.1145/3110278
6. Ekici, B., et al.: SMTCoq: a plug-in for integrating SMT solvers into Coq. In: Computer Aided Verification, pp. 126–133 (2017)
7. Hadarean, L., Barrett, C., Reynolds, A., Tinelli, C., Deters, M.: Fine grained SMT proofs for the theory of fixed-width bit-vectors. In: Davis, M., Fehnker, A., McIver, A., Voronkov, A. (eds.) LPAR 2015. LNCS, vol. 9450, pp. 340–355. Springer, Heidelberg (2015). https://doi.org/10.1007/978-3-662-48899-7_24
8. Kang, J., et al.: Crellvm: verified credible compilation for LLVM. In: Proceedings of the 39th ACM SIGPLAN Conference on Programming Language Design and Implementation, pp. 631–645. ACM (2018). https://doi.org/10.1145/3192366.3192377
9. Lee, J., Hur, C.K., Jung, R., Liu, Z., Regehr, J., Lopes, N.P.: Reconciling high-level optimizations and low-level code in LLVM. Proc. ACM Program. Lang. 2(OOPSLA), 125:1–125:28 (2018). https://doi.org/10.1145/3276495
10. Lee, J., et al.: Taming undefined behavior in LLVM. In: Proceedings of the 38th ACM SIGPLAN Conference on Programming Language Design and Implementation, pp. 633–647. ACM (2017). https://doi.org/10.1145/3062341.3062343
11. Leroy, X.: Formal verification of a realistic compiler. Commun. ACM **52**(7), 107–115 (2009). https://doi.org/10.1145/1538788.1538814
12. Lopes, N.P., Menendez, D., Nagarakatte, S., Regehr, J.: Provably correct peephole optimizations with alive. In: Proceedings of the 36th ACM SIGPLAN Conference on Programming Language Design and Implementation, pp. 22–32. ACM (2015). https://doi.org/10.1145/2737924.2737965
13. de Moura, L., Bjørner, N.: Z3: an efficient SMT solver. In: Ramakrishnan, C.R., Rehof, J. (eds.) TACAS 2008. LNCS, vol. 4963, pp. 337–340. Springer, Heidelberg (2008). https://doi.org/10.1007/978-3-540-78800-3_24
14. de Moura, L., Kong, S., Avigad, J., van Doorn, F., von Raumer, J.: The lean theorem prover (System Description). In: Felty, A.P., Middeldorp, A. (eds.) CADE 2015. LNCS (LNAI), vol. 9195, pp. 378–388. Springer, Cham (2015). https://doi.org/10.1007/978-3-319-21401-6_26

15. Mullen, E., Zuniga, D., Tatlock, Z., Grossman, D.: Verified peephole optimizations for CompCert. In: Proceedings of the 37th ACM SIGPLAN Conference on Programming Language Design and Implementation, pp. 448–461. ACM (2016). https://doi.org/10.1145/2908080.2908109

16. Namjoshi, K.S., Tagliabue, G., Zuck, L.D.: A witnessing compiler: a proof of concept. In: Legay, A., Bensalem, S. (eds.) RV 2013. LNCS, vol. 8174, pp. 340–345. Springer, Heidelberg (2013). https://doi.org/10.1007/978-3-642-40787-1_22

17. Namjoshi, K.S., Zuck, L.D.: Witnessing program transformations. In: Logozzo, F., Fähndrich, M. (eds.) SAS 2013. LNCS, vol. 7935, pp. 304–323. Springer, Heidelberg (2013). https://doi.org/10.1007/978-3-642-38856-9_17

18. Pnueli, A., Siegel, M., Singerman, E.: Translation validation. In: Steffen, B. (ed.) TACAS 1998. LNCS, vol. 1384, pp. 151–166. Springer, Heidelberg (1998). https://doi.org/10.1007/BFb0054170

19. Rinard, M.C., Marinov, D.: Credible compilation with pointers. In: Proceedings of the Workshop on Run-Time Result Verification (1999)

20. Stepp, M., Tate, R., Lerner, S.: Equality-based translation validator for LLVM. In: Gopalakrishnan, G., Qadeer, S. (eds.) CAV 2011. LNCS, vol. 6806, pp. 737–742. Springer, Heidelberg (2011). https://doi.org/10.1007/978-3-642-22110-1_59

21. Torlak, E., Bodik, R.: Growing solver-aided languages with Rosette. In: Proceedings of the 2013 ACM International Symposium on New Ideas, New Paradigms, and Reflections on Programming & Software, pp. 135–152. ACM (2013). https://doi.org/10.1145/2509578.2509586

22. Tristan, J.B., Govereau, P., Morrisett, G.: Evaluating value-graph translation validation for LLVM. In: Proceedings of the 32nd ACM SIGPLAN Conference on Programming Language Design and Implementation, pp. 295–305. ACM (2011). https://doi.org/10.1145/1993498.1993533

23. Uhler, R., Dave, N.: Smten: automatic translation of high-level symbolic computations into SMT queries. In: Sharygina, N., Veith, H. (eds.) CAV 2013. LNCS, vol. 8044, pp. 678–683. Springer, Heidelberg (2013). https://doi.org/10.1007/978-3-642-39799-8_45

24. Weitz, K., Lyubomirsky, S., Heule, S., Torlak, E., Ernst, M.D., Tatlock, Z.: Spacesearch: a library for building and verifying solver-aided tools. Proc. ACM Program. Lang. 1(ICFP), 25:1–25:28 (2017). https://doi.org/10.1145/3110269

25. Zaks, A., Pnueli, A.: CoVaC: compiler validation by program analysis of the cross-product. In: Cuellar, J., Maibaum, T., Sere, K. (eds.) FM 2008. LNCS, vol. 5014, pp. 35–51. Springer, Heidelberg (2008). https://doi.org/10.1007/978-3-540-68237-0_5

26. Zhao, J., Nagarakatte, S., Martin, M.M., Zdancewic, S.: Formalizing the LLVM intermediate representation for verified program transformations. In: Proceedings of the 39th Annual ACM SIGPLAN-SIGACT Symposium on Principles of Programming Languages, pp. 427–440. ACM (2012). https://doi.org/10.1145/2103656.2103709

7

Interpolating Strong Induction

Hari Govind Vediramana Krishnan[1]([⊠]), Yakir Vizel[2], Vijay Ganesh[1],
and Arie Gurfinkel[1]

[1] University of Waterloo, Waterloo, Canada
hgvedira@uwaterloo.ca
[2] The Technion, Haifa, Israel

Abstract. The principle of strong induction, also known as k-induction
is one of the first techniques for unbounded SAT-based Model Checking
(SMC). While elegant and simple to apply, properties as such are rarely
k-inductive and when they can be strengthened, there is no effective
strategy to guess the depth of induction. It has been mostly displaced
by techniques that compute inductive strengthenings based on interpolation and property directed reachability (PDR). In this paper, we present
KAVY, an SMC algorithm that effectively uses k-induction to guide interpolation and PDR-style inductive generalization. Unlike pure k-induction,
KAVY uses PDR-style generalization to compute and strengthen an inductive trace. Unlike pure PDR, KAVY uses relative k-induction to construct
an inductive invariant. The depth of induction is adjusted dynamically
by minimizing a proof of unsatisfiability. We have implemented KAVY
within the AVY Model Checker and evaluated it on HWMCC instances.
Our results show that KAVY is more effective than both AVY and PDR,
and that using k-induction leads to faster running time and solving more
instances. Further, on a class of benchmarks, called *shift*, KAVY is orders
of magnitude faster than AVY, PDR and k-induction.

1 Introduction

The principle of strong induction, also known as k-induction, is a generalization
of (simple) induction that extends the base- and inductive-cases to k steps of a
transition system [27]. A safety property P is k-inductive in a transition system
T iff (a) P is true in the first $(k-1)$ steps of T, and (b) if P is assumed to hold
for $(k-1)$ consecutive steps, then P holds in k steps of T. Simple induction
is equivalent to 1-induction. Unlike induction, strong induction is complete for
safety properties: a property P is safe in a transition system T iff there exists a
natural number k such that P is k-inductive in T (assuming the usual restriction
to simple paths). This makes k-induction a powerful method for unbounded SAT-
based Model Checking (SMC).

Unlike other SMC techniques, strong induction reduces model checking to
pure SAT that does not require any additional features such as solving with
assumptions [12], interpolation [24], resolution proofs [17], Maximal Unsatisfiable Subsets (MUS) [2], etc. It easily integrates with existing SAT-solvers

and immediately benefits from any improvements in heuristics [22,23], pre- and in-processing [18], and parallel solving [1]. The simplicity of applying k-induction made it the go-to technique for SMT-based infinite-state model checking [9,11,19]. In that context, it is particularly effective in combination with invariant synthesis [14,20]. Moreover, for some theories, strong induction is strictly stronger than 1-induction [19]: there are properties that are k-inductive, but have no 1-inductive strengthening.

Notwithstanding all of its advantages, strong induction has been mostly displaced by more recent SMC techniques such as Interpolation [25], Property Directed Reachability [3,7,13,15], and their combinations [29]. In SMC k-induction is equivalent to induction: any k-inductive property P can be strengthened to an inductive property Q [6,16]. Even though in the worst case Q is exponentially larger than P [6], this is rarely observed in practice [26]. Furthermore, the SAT queries get very hard as k increases and usually succeed only for rather small values of k. A recent work [16] shows that strong induction can be integrated in PDR. However, [16] argues that k-induction is hard to control in the context of PDR since choosing a proper value of k is difficult. A wrong choice leads to a form of state enumeration. In [16], k is fixed to 5, and regular induction is used as soon as 5-induction fails.

In this paper, we present KAVY, an SMC algorithm that effectively uses k-induction to guide interpolation and PDR-style inductive generalization. As many state-of-the-art SMC algorithms, KAVY iteratively constructs candidate inductive invariants for a given safety property P. However, the construction of these candidates is driven by k-induction. Whenever P is known to hold up to a bound N, KAVY searches for the smallest $k \leq N+1$, such that either P or some of its strengthening is k-inductive. Once it finds the right k and strengthening, it computes a 1-inductive strengthening.

It is convenient to think of modern SMC algorithms (e.g., PDR and AVY), and k-induction, as two ends of a spectrum. On the one end, modern SMC algorithms fix k to 1 and *search* for a 1-inductive strengthening of P. While on the opposite end, k-induction fixes the strengthening of P to be P itself and *searches* for a k such that P is k-inductive. KAVY *dynamically* explores this spectrum, exploiting the interplay between finding the right k and finding the right strengthening.

As an example, consider a system in Fig. 1 that counts upto 64 and resets. The property, $p : c < 66$, is 2-inductive. IC3, PDR and AVY iteratively guess a 1-inductive strengthening of p. In the worst case, they require at least 64 iterations. On the other hand, KAVY determines that p is 2-inductive after 2 iterations, *computes* a 1-inductive invariant $(c \neq 65) \wedge (c < 66)$, and terminates.

```
reg [7:0] c = 0;
always
  if(c == 64)
    c <= 0;
  else
    c <= c + 1;
end
assert property (c < 66);
```

Fig. 1. An example system.

KAVY builds upon the foundations of AVY [29]. AVY first uses Bounded Model Checking [4] (BMC) to prove that the property P holds up to bound N. Then, it uses a sequence interpolant [28] and PDR-style inductive-generalization [7] to construct 1-inductive strengthening candidate for P. We emphasize that using k-induction to construct 1-inductive candidates allows KAVY to efficiently utilize many principles from PDR and AVY. While maintaining k-inductive candidates might seem attractive (since they may be smaller), they are also much harder to generalize effectively [7].

We implemented KAVY in the AVY Model Checker, and evaluated it on the benchmarks from the Hardware Model Checking Competition (HWMCC). Our experiments show that KAVY significantly improves the performance of AVY and solves more examples than either of PDR and AVY. For a specific family of examples from [21], KAVY exhibits nearly constant time performance, compared to an exponential growth of AVY, PDR, and k-induction (see Fig. 2b in Sect. 5). This further emphasizes the effectiveness of efficiently integrating strong induction into modern SMC.

The rest of the paper is structured as follows. After describing the most relevant related work, we present the necessary background in Sect. 2 and give an overview of SAT-based model checking algorithms in Sect. 3. KAVY is presented in Sect. 4, followed by presentation of results in Sect. 5. Finally, we conclude the paper in Sect. 6.

Related Work. KAVY builds on top of the ideas of IC3 [7] and PDR [13]. The use of interpolation for generating an inductive trace is inspired by AVY [29]. While conceptually, our algorithm is similar to AVY, its proof of correctness is non-trivial and is significantly different from that of AVY. We are not aware of any other work that combines interpolation with strong induction.

There are two prior attempts enhancing PDR-style algorithms with k-induction. PD-KIND [19] is an SMT-based Model Checking algorithm for infinite-state systems inspired by IC3/PDR. It infers k-inductive invariants driven by the property whereas KAVY infers 1-inductive invariants driven by k-induction. PD-KIND uses recursive blocking with interpolation and model-based projection to block bad states, and k-induction to propagate (push) lemmas to next level. While the algorithm is very interesting it is hard to adapt it to SAT-based setting (i.e. SMC), and impossible to compare on HWMCC instances directly.

The closest related work is KIC3 [16]. It modifies the counter example queue management strategy in IC3 to utilize k-induction during blocking. The main limitation is that the value for k must be chosen statically ($k = 5$ is reported for the evaluation). KAVY also utilizes k-induction during blocking but computes the value for k dynamically. Unfortunately, the implementation is not available publicly and we could not compare with it directly.

2   Background

In this section, we present notations and background that is required for the description of our algorithm.

Safety Verification. A symbolic transition system T is a tuple $(\bar{v}, \mathit{Init}, \mathit{Tr}, \mathit{Bad})$, where $\bar{v}$ is a set of Boolean *state* variables. A state of the system is a complete valuation to all variables in $\bar{v}$ (i.e., the set of states is $\{0,1\}^{|\bar{v}|}$). We write $\bar{v}' = \{v' \mid v \in \bar{v}\}$ for the set of *primed* variables, used to represent the next state. *Init* and *Bad* are formulas over $\bar{v}$ denoting the set of initial states and bad states, respectively, and *Tr* is a formula over $\bar{v} \cup \bar{v}'$, denoting the transition relation. With abuse of notation, we use formulas and the sets of states (or transitions) that they represent interchangeably. In addition, we sometimes use a state s to denote the formula (cube) that characterizes it. For a formula φ over $\bar{v}$, we use $\varphi(\bar{v}')$, or φ' in short, to denote the formula in which every occurrence of $v \in \bar{v}$ is replaced by $v' \in \bar{v}'$. For simplicity of presentation, we assume that the property $P = \neg \mathit{Bad}$ is true in the initial state, that is $\mathit{Init} \Rightarrow P$.

Given a formula $\varphi(\bar{v})$, an *M-to-N-unrolling* of T, where φ holds in all intermediate states is defined by the formula:

$$Tr[\varphi]_M^N = \bigwedge_{i=M}^{N-1} \varphi(\bar{v}_i) \wedge Tr(\bar{v}_i, \bar{v}_{i+1}) \tag{1}$$

We write $Tr[\varphi]^N$ when $M = 0$ and Tr_M^N when $\varphi = \top$.

A transition system T is UNSAFE iff there exists a state $s \in \mathit{Bad}$ s.t. s is reachable, and is SAFE otherwise. Equivalently, T is UNSAFE iff there exists a number N such that the following *unrolling* formula is satisfiable:

$$\mathit{Init}(\bar{v}_0) \wedge Tr^N \wedge \mathit{Bad}(\bar{v}_N) \tag{2}$$

T is SAFE if no such N exists. Whenever T is UNSAFE and $s_N \in \mathit{Bad}$ is a reachable state, the path from $s_0 \in \mathit{Init}$ to s_N is called a *counterexample*.

An *inductive invariant* is a formula *Inv* that satisfies:

$$\mathit{Init}(\bar{v}) \Rightarrow \mathit{Inv}(\bar{v}) \qquad\qquad \mathit{Inv}(\bar{v}) \wedge Tr(\bar{v}, \bar{v}') \Rightarrow \mathit{Inv}(\bar{v}') \tag{3}$$

A transition system T is SAFE iff there exists an inductive invariant *Inv* s.t. $\mathit{Inv}(\bar{v}) \Rightarrow P(\bar{v})$. In this case we say that *Inv* is a *safe* inductive invariant.

The *safety* verification problem is to decide whether a transition system T is SAFE or UNSAFE, i.e., whether there exists a safe inductive invariant or a counterexample.

Strong Induction. Strong induction (or k-induction) is a generalization of the notion of an inductive invariant that is similar to how "simple" induction is generalized in mathematics. A formula *Inv* is k-*invariant* in a transition system T if it is true in the first k steps of T. That is, the following formula is valid: $\mathit{Init}(\bar{v}_0) \wedge Tr^k \Rightarrow \left(\bigwedge_{i=0}^{k} \mathit{Inv}(\bar{v}_i) \right)$. A formula *Inv* is a k-*inductive invariant* iff *Inv* is a $(k-1)$-invariant and is inductive after k steps of T, i.e., the following formula is valid: $Tr[\mathit{Inv}]^k \Rightarrow \mathit{Inv}(\bar{v}_k)$. Compared to simple induction, k-induction strengthens the hypothesis in the induction step: *Inv* is assumed to hold between steps 0 to $k-1$ and is established in step k. Whenever $\mathit{Inv} \Rightarrow P$, we say that *Inv* is a safe k-inductive invariant. An inductive invariant is a 1-inductive invariant.

Theorem 1. *Given a transition system T. There exists a safe inductive invariant w.r.t. T iff there exists a safe k-inductive invariant w.r.t. T.*

Theorem 1 states that k-induction principle is as complete as 1-induction. One direction is trivial (since we can take $k = 1$). The other can be strengthened further: for every k-inductive invariant Inv_k there exists a 1-inductive strengthening Inv_1 such that $Inv_1 \Rightarrow Inv_k$. Theoretically Inv_1 might be exponentially bigger than Inv_k [6]. In practice, both invariants tend to be of similar size.

We say that a formula φ is k-*inductive relative* to F if it is a $(k-1)$-invariant and $Tr[\varphi \wedge F]^k \Rightarrow \varphi(\bar{v}_k)$.

Craig Interpolation [10]. We use an extension of Craig Interpolants to sequences, which is common in Model Checking. Let $\boldsymbol{A} = [A_1, \ldots, A_N]$ such that $A_1 \wedge \cdots \wedge A_N$ is unsatisfiable. A *sequence interpolant* $\boldsymbol{I} = \text{SEQITP}(\boldsymbol{A})$ for $\boldsymbol{A}$ is a sequence of formulas $\boldsymbol{I} = [I_2, \ldots, I_N]$ such that (a) $A_1 \Rightarrow I_2$, (b) $\forall 1 < i < N \cdot I_i \wedge A_i \Rightarrow I_{i+1}$, (c) $I_N \wedge A_N \Rightarrow \bot$, and (d) I_i is over variables that are shared between the corresponding prefix and suffix of $\boldsymbol{A}$.

3 SAT-Based Model Checking

In this section, we give a brief overview of SAT-based Model Checking algorithms: IC3/PDR [7,13], and AVY [29]. While these algorithms are well-known, we give a uniform presentation and establish notation necessary for the rest of the paper. We fix a symbolic transition system $T = (\bar{v}, Init, Tr, Bad)$.

The main data-structure of these algorithms is a sequence of candidate invariants, called an *inductive trace*. An *inductive trace*, or simply a trace, is a sequence of formulas $\boldsymbol{F} = [F_0, \ldots, F_N]$ that satisfy the following two properties:

$$Init(\bar{v}) = F_0(\bar{v}) \qquad \forall 0 \le i < N \cdot F_i(\bar{v}) \wedge Tr(\bar{v}, \bar{v}') \Rightarrow F_{i+1}(\bar{v}') \qquad (4)$$

An element F_i of a trace is called a *frame*. The index of a frame is called a *level*. $\boldsymbol{F}$ is *clausal* when all its elements are in CNF. For convenience, we view a frame as a set of clauses, and assume that a trace is padded with $\top$ until the required length. The *size* of $\boldsymbol{F} = [F_0, \ldots, F_N]$ is $|\boldsymbol{F}| = N$. For $k \le N$, we write $\boldsymbol{F}^k = [F_k, \ldots, F_N]$ for the k-suffix of $\boldsymbol{F}$.

A trace $\boldsymbol{F}$ of size N is *stronger* than a trace $\boldsymbol{G}$ of size M iff $\forall 0 \le i \le \min(N, M) \cdot F_i(\bar{v}) \Rightarrow G_i(\bar{v})$. A trace is *safe* if each F_i is safe: $\forall i \cdot F_i \Rightarrow \neg Bad$; *monotone* if $\forall 0 \le i < N \cdot F_i \Rightarrow F_{i+1}$. In a monotone trace, a frame F_i over-approximates the set of states reachable in up to i steps of the Tr. A trace is closed if $\exists 1 \le i \le N \cdot F_i \Rightarrow \left(\bigvee_{j=0}^{i-1} F_j \right)$.

We define an unrolling formula of a k-suffix of a trace $\boldsymbol{F} = [F_0, \ldots, F_N]$ as :

$$Tr[\boldsymbol{F}^k] = \bigwedge_{i=k}^{|F|} F_i(\bar{v}_i) \wedge Tr(\bar{v}_i, \bar{v}_{i+1}) \qquad (5)$$

We write $Tr[\boldsymbol{F}]$ to denote an unrolling of a 0-suffix of $\boldsymbol{F}$ (i.e $\boldsymbol{F}$ itself). Intuitively, $Tr[\boldsymbol{F}^k]$ is satisfiable iff there is a k-step execution of the Tr that is consistent with the k-suffix $\boldsymbol{F}^k$. If a transition system T admits a safe trace $\boldsymbol{F}$ of size $|\boldsymbol{F}| = N$, then T does not admit counterexamples of length less than N. A safe trace $\boldsymbol{F}$, with $|\boldsymbol{F}| = N$ is *extendable* with respect to level $0 \leq i \leq N$ iff there exists a safe trace $\boldsymbol{G}$ stronger than $\boldsymbol{F}$ such that $|\boldsymbol{G}| > N$ and $F_i \wedge Tr \Rightarrow G_{i+1}$. $\boldsymbol{G}$ and the corresponding level i are called an *extension trace* and an *extension level* of $\boldsymbol{F}$, respectively. SAT-based model checking algorithms work by iteratively extending a given safe trace $\boldsymbol{F}$ of size N to a safe trace of size $N + 1$.

An extension trace is not unique, but there is a largest extension level. We denote the set of all extension levels of $\boldsymbol{F}$ by $\mathcal{W}(\boldsymbol{F})$. The existence of an extension level i implies that an unrolling of the i-suffix does not contain any *Bad* states:

Proposition 1. *Let $\boldsymbol{F}$ be a safe trace. Then, i, $0 \leq i \leq N$, is an extension level of $\boldsymbol{F}$ iff the formula $Tr[\boldsymbol{F}^i] \wedge Bad(\bar{v}_{N+1})$ is unsatisfiable.*

Example 1. For Fig. 1, $\boldsymbol{F} = [c = 0, c < 66]$ is a safe trace of size 1. The formula $(c < 66) \wedge Tr \wedge \neg(c' < 66)$ is satisfiable. Therefore, there does not exists an extension trace at level 1. Since $(c = 0) \wedge Tr \wedge (c' < 66) \wedge Tr' \wedge (c'' \geq 66)$ is unsatisfiable, the trace is extendable at level 0. For example, a valid extension trace at level 0 is $\boldsymbol{G} = [c = 0, c < 2, c < 66]$.

Both PDR and AVY iteratively extend a safe trace either until the extension is closed or a counterexample is found. However, they differ in how exactly the trace is extended. In the rest of this section, we present AVY and PDR through the lens of extension level. The goal of this presentation is to make the paper self-contained. We omit many important optimization details, and refer the reader to the original papers [7,13,29].

PDR maintains a monotone, clausal trace $\boldsymbol{F}$ with *Init* as the first frame (F_0). The trace $\boldsymbol{F}$ is extended by recursively computing and blocking (if possible) states that can reach *Bad* (called *bad states*). A bad state is blocked at the largest level possible. Algorithm 1 shows PDRBLOCK, the backward search procedure that identifies and blocks bad states. PDRBLOCK maintains a queue of states and the levels at which they have to be blocked. The smallest level at which blocking occurs is tracked in order to show the construction of the extension trace. For each state s in the queue, it is checked whether s can be blocked by the previous frame F_{d-1} (line 5). If not, a predecessor state t of s that satisfies F_{d-1} is computed and added to the queue (line 7). If a predecessor state is found at level 0, the trace is not extendable and an empty trace is returned. If the state s is blocked at level d, PDRINDGEN, is called to generate a clause that blocks s and possibly others. The clause is then added to all the frames at levels less than or equal to d. PDRINDGEN is a crucial optimization to PDR. However, we do not explain it for the sake of simplicity. The procedure terminates whenever there are no more states to be blocked (or a counterexample was found at line 4). By construction, the output trace $\boldsymbol{G}$ is an extension trace of $\boldsymbol{F}$ at the extension level w. Once PDR extends its trace, PDRPUSH is called to check if the clauses it learnt are also true at higher levels. PDR terminates when the trace is closed.

Algorithm 1. PDRBLOCK.	**Algorithm 2.** AVY.
Input: A transition system $T = (Init, Tr, Bad)$	**Input:** A transition system $T = (Init, Tr, Bad)$
Input: A safe trace F with $|F| = N$	**Output:** SAFE/UNSAFE
Output: An extension trace G or an empty trace	1 $F_0 \leftarrow Init$; $N \leftarrow 0$
	2 **repeat**
1 $w \leftarrow N+1$; $G \leftarrow F$; $Q.push(\langle Bad, N+1\rangle)$	3 **if** ISSAT($Tr[F^0] \wedge Bad(\bar{v}_{N+1})$) **then**
2 **while** $\neg Q.empty()$ **do**	**return** UNSAFE
3 $\langle s, d\rangle \leftarrow Q.pop()$	4 $k \leftarrow \max\{i \mid \neg \text{ISSAT}(Tr[F^i] \wedge Bad(\bar{v}_{N+1}))\}$
4 **if** $d == 0$ **then return** [ ]	5 $I_{k+1}, \dots, I_{N+1} \leftarrow$
5 **if** ISSAT($F_{d-1}(\bar{v}) \wedge Tr(\bar{v}, \bar{v}') \wedge s(\bar{v}')$) **then**	SEQITP($Tr[F^k] \wedge Bad(\bar{v}_{N+1})$)
6 $t \leftarrow predecessor(s)$	6 $\forall 0 \leq i \leq k \cdot G_i \leftarrow F_i$
7 $Q.push(t, d-1)$	7 $\forall k < i \leq (N+1) \cdot G_i \leftarrow F_i \wedge I_i$
8 $Q.push(s, d)$	8 $F \leftarrow$ AVYMKTRACE($[G_0, \dots, G_{N+1}]$)
9 **else**	9 $F \leftarrow$ PDRPUSH(F)
10 $\forall 0 \leq i \leq d \cdot G_i \leftarrow$ $(G_i \wedge \text{PDRINDGEN}(\neg s))$	10 **if** $\exists 1 \leq i \leq N \cdot F_i \Rightarrow \left(\bigvee_{j=0}^{i-1} F_j\right)$ **then**
11 $w \leftarrow min(w, d)$	**return** SAFE
	11 $N \leftarrow N+1$
12 **return** G	12 **until** ∞

AVY, shown in Algorithm 2, is an alternative to PDR that combines interpolation and recursive blocking. AVY starts with a trace F, with $F_0 = Init$, that is extended in every iteration of the main loop. A counterexample is returned whenever F is not extendable (line 3). Otherwise, a sequence interpolant is extracted from the unsatisfiability of $Tr[F^{\max(\mathcal{W})}] \wedge Bad(\bar{v}_{N+1})$. A longer trace $G = [G_0, \dots, G_N, G_{N+1}]$ is constructed using the sequence interpolant (line 7). Observe that G is an extension trace of F. While G is safe, it is neither monotone nor clausal. A helper routine AVYMKTRACE is used to convert G to a proper PDR trace on line 8 (see [29] for the details on AVYMKTRACE). AVY converges when the trace is closed.

4   Interpolating k-Induction

In this section, we present KAVY, an SMC algorithm that uses the principle of strong induction to extend an inductive trace. The section is structured as follows. First, we introduce a concept of extending a trace using relative k-induction. Second, we present KAVY and describe the details of how k-induction is used to compute an extended trace. Third, we describe two techniques for computing maximal parameters to apply strong induction. Unless stated otherwise, we assume that all traces are monotone.

A safe trace F, with $|F| = N$, is *strongly extendable* with respect to (i, k), where $1 \leq k \leq i+1 \leq N+1$, iff there exists a safe inductive trace G stronger than F such that $|G| > N$ and $Tr[F_i]^k \Rightarrow G_{i+1}$. We refer to the pair (i, k) as a *strong extension level (SEL)*, and to the trace G as an (i, k)-*extension trace*, or simply a *strong extension trace (SET)* when (i, k) is not important. Note that for $k = 1$, G is just an extension trace.

Example 2. For Fig. 1, the trace $F = [c = 0, c < 66]$ is strongly extendable at level 1. A valid $(1, 2)$-extension trace is $G = [c = 0, (c \neq 65) \wedge (c < 66), c < 66]$. Note that $(c < 66)$ is 2-inductive relative to F_1, i.e. $Tr[F_1]^2 \Rightarrow (c'' < 66)$.

We write $\mathcal{K}(\boldsymbol{F})$ for the set of all SELs of $\boldsymbol{F}$. We define an order on SELs by: $(i_1, k_1) \preceq (i_2, k_2)$ iff (i) $i_1 < i_2$; or (ii) $i_1 = i_2 \wedge k_1 > k_2$. The maximal SEL is $\max(\mathcal{K}(\boldsymbol{F}))$.

Algorithm 3. KAVY algorithm.

Input: A transition system $T = (Init, Tr, Bad)$
Output: SAFE/UNSAFE

1 $\boldsymbol{F} \leftarrow [Init] \, ; N \leftarrow 0$
2 **repeat**
   // Invariant: $\boldsymbol{F}$ is a monotone, clausal, safe, inductive trace
3     $U \leftarrow Tr[\boldsymbol{F}^0] \wedge Bad(\bar{v}_{N+1})$
4   **if** ISSAT(U) **then return** UNSAFE
5     $(i, k) \leftarrow \max\{(i, k) \mid \neg\text{ISSAT}(Tr[\![\boldsymbol{F}^i]\!]^k \wedge Bad(\bar{v}_{N+1}))\}$
6     $[F_0, \ldots, F_{N+1}] \leftarrow \text{KAVYEXTEND}(\boldsymbol{F}, (i, k))$
7     $[F_0, \ldots, F_{N+1}] \leftarrow \text{PDRPUSH}([F_0, \ldots, F_{N+1}])$
8   **if** $\exists 1 \leq i \leq N \cdot F_i \Rightarrow \left(\bigvee_{j=0}^{i-1} F_j \right)$ **then return** SAFE
9     $N \leftarrow N + 1$
10 **until** ∞

Note that the existence of a SEL (i, k) means that an unrolling of the i-suffix with F_i repeated k times does not contain any bad states. We use $Tr[\![\boldsymbol{F}^i]\!]^k$ to denote this *characteristic formula* for SEL (i, k):

$$Tr[\![\boldsymbol{F}^i]\!]^k = \begin{cases} Tr[F_i]_{i+1-k}^{i+1} \wedge Tr[\boldsymbol{F}^{i+1}] & \text{if } 0 \leq i < N \\ Tr[F_N]_{N+1-k}^{N+1} & \text{if } i = N \end{cases} \tag{6}$$

Proposition 2. *Let $\boldsymbol{F}$ be a safe trace, where $|\boldsymbol{F}| = N$. Then, (i, k), $1 \leq k \leq i+1 \leq N+1$, is an SEL of $\boldsymbol{F}$ iff the formula $Tr[\![\boldsymbol{F}^i]\!]^k \wedge Bad(\bar{v}_{N+1})$ is unsatisfiable.*

The level i in the maximal SEL (i, k) of a given trace $\boldsymbol{F}$ is greater or equal to the maximal extension level of $\boldsymbol{F}$:

Lemma 1. *Let $(i, k) = \max(\mathcal{K}(\boldsymbol{F}))$, then $i \geq \max(\mathcal{W}(\boldsymbol{F}))$.*

Hence, extensions based on maximal SEL are constructed from frames at higher level compared to extensions based on maximal extension level.

Example 3. For Fig. 1, the trace $[c = 0, c < 66]$ has a maximum extension level of 0. Since $(c < 66)$ is 2-inductive, the trace is strongly extendable at level 1 (as was seen in Example 2).

kAvy Algorithm. KAVY is shown in Fig. 3. It starts with an inductive trace $\boldsymbol{F} = [Init]$ and iteratively extends $\boldsymbol{F}$ using SELs. A counterexample is returned if the trace cannot be extended (line 4). Otherwise, KAVY computes the largest extension level (line 5) (described in Sect. 4.2). Then, it constructs a strong extension trace using KAVYEXTEND (line 6) (described in Sect. 4.1). Finally, PDRPUSH is called to check whether the trace is closed. Note that $\boldsymbol{F}$ is a monotone, clausal, safe inductive trace throughout the algorithm.

4.1 Extending a Trace with Strong Induction

In this section, we describe the procedure KAVYEXTEND (shown in Algorithm 4) that given a trace $\boldsymbol{F}$ of size $|\boldsymbol{F}| = N$ and an (i, k) SEL of $\boldsymbol{F}$ constructs an (i, k)-extension trace $\boldsymbol{G}$ of size $|\boldsymbol{G}| = N + 1$. The procedure itself is fairly simple, but its proof of correctness is complex. We first present the theoretical results that connect sequence interpolants with strong extension traces, then the procedure, and then details of its correctness. Through the section, we fix a trace $\boldsymbol{F}$ and its SEL (i, k).

Sequence Interpolation for SEL. Let (i, k) be an SEL of $\boldsymbol{F}$. By Proposition 2, $\Psi = Tr[\![\boldsymbol{F}^i]\!]^k \wedge Bad(\bar{v}_{N+1})$ is unsatisfiable. Let $\mathcal{A} = \{A_{i-k+1}, \ldots, A_{N+1}\}$ be a partitioning of Ψ defined as follows:

$$A_j = \begin{cases} F_i(\bar{v}_j) \wedge Tr(\bar{v}_j, \bar{v}_{j+1}) & \text{if } i - k + 1 \leq j \leq i \\ F_j(\bar{v}_j) \wedge Tr(\bar{v}_j, \bar{v}_{j+1}) & \text{if } i < j \leq N \\ Bad(\bar{v}_{N+1}) & \text{if } j = N + 1 \end{cases}$$

Since $(\wedge \mathcal{A}) = \Psi$, $\mathcal{A}$ is unsatisfiable. Let $\boldsymbol{I} = [I_{i-k+2}, \ldots, I_{N+1}]$ be a sequence interpolant corresponding to $\mathcal{A}$. Then, $\boldsymbol{I}$ satisfies the following properties:

$$F_i \wedge Tr \Rightarrow I'_{i-k+2} \qquad \forall i - k + 2 \leq j \leq i \cdot (F_i \wedge I_j) \wedge Tr \Rightarrow I'_{j+1} \qquad (\heartsuit)$$
$$I_{N+1} \Rightarrow \neg Bad \qquad \forall i < j \leq N \cdot (F_j \wedge I_j) \wedge Tr \Rightarrow I'_{j+1}$$

Note that in $(\heartsuit)$, both i and k are fixed—they are the (i, k)-extension level. Furthermore, in the top row F_i is fixed as well.

The conjunction of the first k interpolants in $\boldsymbol{I}$ is k-inductive relative to the frame F_i:

Lemma 2. *The formula* $F_{i+1} \wedge \left(\bigwedge_{m=i-k+2}^{i+1} I_m \right)$ *is k-inductive relative to F_i.*

Proof. Since F_i and F_{i+1} are consecutive frames of a trace, $F_i \wedge Tr \Rightarrow F'_{i+1}$. Thus, $\forall i - k + 2 \leq j \leq i \cdot Tr[F_i]^j_{i-k+2} \Rightarrow F_{i+1}(\bar{v}_{j+1})$. Moreover, by $(\heartsuit)$, $F_i \wedge Tr \Rightarrow I'_{i-k+2}$ and $\forall i - k + 2 \leq j \leq i + 1 \cdot (F_i \wedge I_j) \wedge Tr \Rightarrow I'_{j+1}$. Equivalently, $\forall i - k + 2 \leq j \leq i + 1 \cdot Tr[F_i]^j_{i-k+2} \Rightarrow I_{j+1}(\bar{v}_{j+1})$. By induction over the difference between $(i+1)$ and $(i-k+2)$, we show that $Tr[F_i]^{i+1}_{i-k+2} \Rightarrow (F_{i+1} \wedge \bigwedge^{i+1}_{m=i-k+2} I_m)(\bar{v}_{i+1})$, which concludes the proof. $\qquad\qquad\square$

We use Lemma 2 to define a strong extension trace $\boldsymbol{G}$:

Lemma 3. *Let* $\boldsymbol{G} = [G_0, \ldots, G_{N+1}]$, *be an inductive trace defined as follows:*

$$G_j = \begin{cases} F_j & \text{if } 0 \leq j < i - k + 2 \\ F_j \wedge \left(\bigwedge_{m=i-k+2}^{j} I_m \right) & \text{if } i - k + 2 \leq j < i + 2 \\ (F_j \wedge I_j) & \text{if } i + 2 \leq j < N + 1 \\ I_{N+1} & \text{if } j = (N+1) \end{cases}$$

Then, G is an (i, k)-extension trace of F (not necessarily monotone).

Proof. By Lemma 2, G_{i+1} is k-inductive relative to F_i. Therefore, it is sufficient to show that G is a safe inductive trace that is stronger than F. By definition, $\forall 0 \le j \le N \cdot G_j \Rightarrow F_j$. By ($\heartsuit$), $F_i \wedge Tr \Rightarrow I'_{i-k+2}$ and $\forall i - k + 2 \le j < i + 2 \cdot (F_i \wedge I_j) \wedge Tr \Rightarrow I'_{j+1}$. By induction over j, $\left((F_i \wedge \bigwedge_{m=i-k+2}^{j} I_m) \wedge Tr \right) \Rightarrow \bigwedge_{m=i-k+2}^{j+1} I'_m$ for all $i - k + 2 \le j < i + 2$. Since F is monotone, $\forall i - k + 2 \le j < i + 2 \cdot \left((F_j \wedge \bigwedge_{m=i-k+2}^{j} I_m) \wedge Tr \right) \Rightarrow \bigwedge_{m=i-k+2}^{j+1} I'_m$.

By ($\heartsuit$), $\forall i < j \le N \cdot (F_j \wedge I_j) \wedge Tr \Rightarrow I'_{j+1}$. Again, since F is a trace, we conclude that $\forall i < j < N \cdot (F_j \wedge I_j) \wedge Tr \Rightarrow (F_{j+1} \wedge I_{j+1})'$. Combining the above, $G_j \wedge Tr \Rightarrow G'_{j+1}$ for $0 \le j \le N$. Since F is safe and $I_{N+1} \Rightarrow \neg Bad$, then G is safe and stronger than F. □

Lemma 3 defines an obvious procedure to construct an (i, k)-extension trace G for F. However, such G is neither monotone nor clausal. In the rest of this section, we describe the procedure KAVYEXTEND that starts with a sequence interpolant (as in Lemma 3), but uses PDRBLOCK to systematically construct a safe monotone clausal extension of F.

The procedure KAVYEXTEND is shown in Algorithm 4. For simplicity of the presentation, we assume that PDRBLOCK does not use inductive generalization. The invariants marked by † rely on this assumption. We stress that the assumption is for presentation only. The correctness of KAVYEXTEND is independent of it.

KAVYEXTEND starts with a sequence interpolant according to the partitioning $\mathcal{A}$. The extension trace G is initialized to F and G_{N+1} is initialized to $\top$ (line 2). The rest proceeds in three phases: *Phase 1* (lines 3–5) computes the prefix $G_{i-k+2}, \ldots, G_{i+1}$ using the first $k - 1$ elements of I; *Phase 2* (line 8) computes G_{i+1} using I_{i+1}; *Phase 3* (lines 9–12) computes the suffix G^{i+2} using the last $(N - i)$ elements of I. During this phase, PDRPUSH (line 12) pushes clauses forward so that they can be used in the next iteration. The correctness of the phases follows from the invariants shown in Algorithm 4. We present each phase in turn.

Recall that PDRBLOCK takes a trace F (that is safe up to the last frame) and a transition system, and returns a safe strengthening of F, while ensuring that the result is monotone and clausal. This guarantee is maintained by Algorithm 4, by requiring that any clause added to any frame G_i of G is implicitly added to all frames below G_i.

Phase 1. By Lemma 2, the first k elements of the sequence interpolant computed at line 1 over-approximate states reachable in $i + 1$ steps of Tr. Phase 1 uses this to strengthen G_{i+1} using the first k elements of I. Note that in that phase, new clauses are always added to frame G_{i+1}, and all frames before it!

Algorithm 4. KAVYEXTEND. The invariants marked † hold only when the PDRBLOCK does no inductive generalization.

Input: a monotone, clausal, safe trace $\boldsymbol{F}$ of size N
Input: A strong extension level (i, k) s.t. $Tr[\![\boldsymbol{F}^i]\!]^k \wedge Bad(\bar{v}_{N+1})$ is unsatisfiable
Output: a monotone, clausal, safe trace $\boldsymbol{G}$ of size $N + 1$

1 $I_{i-k+2}, \ldots, I_{N+1} \leftarrow \text{SEQITP}(Tr[\![\boldsymbol{F}^i]\!]^k \wedge Bad(\bar{v}_{N+1}))$
2 $\boldsymbol{G} \leftarrow [F_0, \ldots, F_N, \top]$
3 **for** $j \leftarrow i - k + 1$ **to** i **do**
4 $\quad P_j \leftarrow (G_j \vee (G_{i+1} \wedge I_{j+1}))$
$\qquad$ // Inv_1: $\boldsymbol{G}$ is monotone and clausal
$\qquad$ // Inv_2: $G_i \wedge Tr \Rightarrow P_j$
$\qquad$ // $\text{Inv}_3^\dagger$: $\forall j < m \leq (i+1) \cdot G_m \equiv F_m \wedge \bigwedge_{\ell=i-k+1}^{j-1} (G_\ell \vee I_{\ell+1})$
$\qquad$ // Inv_3 : $\forall j < m \leq (i+1) \cdot G_m \Rightarrow F_m \wedge \bigwedge_{\ell=i-k+1}^{j-1} (G_\ell \vee I_{\ell+1})$
5 $\quad [\_, \_, G_{i+1}] \leftarrow \text{PDRBLOCK}([Init, G_i, G_{i+1}], (Init, Tr, \neg P_j))$

6 $P_i \leftarrow (G_i \vee (G_{i+1} \wedge I_{j+1}))$
7 **if** $i = 0$ **then** $[\_, \_, G_{i+1}] \leftarrow \text{PDRBLOCK}([Init, G_{i+1}], (Init, Tr, \neg P_i))$
8 **else** $[\_, \_, G_{i+1}] \leftarrow \text{PDRBLOCK}([Init, G_i, G_{i+1}], (Init, Tr, \neg P_i))$
$\quad$ // $\text{Inv}_4^\dagger$: $G_{i+1} \equiv F_{i+1} \wedge \bigwedge_{\ell=i-k+1}^{i} (G_\ell \vee I_{\ell+1})$
$\quad$ // Inv_4: $G_{i+1} \Rightarrow F_{i+1} \wedge \bigwedge_{\ell=i-k+1}^{i} (G_\ell \vee I_{\ell+1})$
9 **for** $j \leftarrow i + 1$ **to** $N + 1$ **do**
10 $\quad P_j \leftarrow G_j \vee (G_{j+1} \wedge I_{j+1})$
$\qquad$ // Inv_6: $G_j \wedge Tr \Rightarrow P_j$
11 $\quad [\_, \_, G_{j+1}] \leftarrow \text{PDRBLOCK}([Init, G_j, G_{j+1}], (Init, Tr, \neg P_j))$
12 $\quad \boldsymbol{G} \leftarrow \text{PDRPUSH}(\boldsymbol{G})$

$\quad$ // $\text{Inv}_7^\dagger$: $\boldsymbol{G}$ is an (i, k)-extension trace of $\boldsymbol{F}$
$\quad$ // Inv_7: $\boldsymbol{G}$ is an extension trace of $\boldsymbol{F}$
13 **return** $\boldsymbol{G}$

Correctness of Phase 1 (line 5) follows from the loop invariant Inv_2. It holds on loop entry since $G_i \wedge Tr \Rightarrow I_{i-k+2}$ (since $G_i = F_i$ and $(\heartsuit)$) and $G_i \wedge Tr \Rightarrow G_{i+1}$ (since $\boldsymbol{G}$ is initially a trace). Let G_i and G_i^* be the ith frame before and after execution of iteration j of the loop, respectively. PDRBLOCK blocks $\neg P_j$ at iteration j of the loop. Assume that Inv_2 holds at the beginning of the loop. Then, $G_i^* \Rightarrow G_i \wedge P_j$ since PDRBLOCK strengthens G_i. Since $G_j \Rightarrow G_i$ and $G_i \Rightarrow G_{i+1}$, this simplifies to $G_i^* \Rightarrow G_j \vee (G_i \wedge I_{j+1})$. Finally, since $\boldsymbol{G}$ is a trace, Inv_2 holds at the end of the iteration.

Inv_2 ensures that the trace given to PDRBLOCK at line 5 *can* be made safe relative to P_j. From the post-condition of PDRBLOCK, it follows that at iteration j, G_{i+1} is strengthened to G_{i+1}^* such that $G_{i+1}^* \Rightarrow P_j$ and $\boldsymbol{G}$ remains a monotone clausal trace. At the end of *Phase 1*, $[G_0, \ldots, G_{i+1}]$ is a clausal monotone trace.

Interestingly, the calls to PDRBLOCK in this phase do not satisfy an expected pre-condition: the frame G_i in $[Init, G_i, G_{i+1}]$ might not be safe for property P_j. However, we can see that $Init \Rightarrow P_j$ and from Inv_2, it is clear that P_j is inductive relative to G_i. This is a sufficient precondition for PDRBLOCK.

Phase 2. This phase strengthens G_{i+1} using the interpolant I_{i+1}. After Phase 2, G_{i+1} is k-inductive relative to F_i.

Phase 3. Unlike *Phase 1*, G_{j+1} is computed at the jth iteration. Because of this, the property P_j in this phase is slightly different than that of Phase 1. Correctness follows from invariant Inv_6 that ensures that at iteration j, G_{j+1} *can* be made safe relative to P_j. From the post-condition of PDRBLOCK, it follows that G_{j+1} is strengthened to G_{j+1}^* such that $G_{j+1}^* \Rightarrow P_j$ and G is a monotone clausal trace. The invariant implies that at the end of the loop $G_{N+1} \Rightarrow G_N \vee I_{N+1}$, making G safe. Thus, at the end of the loop G is a safe monotone clausal trace that is stronger than F. What remains is to show is that G_{i+1} is k-inductive relative to F_i.

Let φ be the formula from Lemma 2. Assuming that PDRBLOCK did no inductive generalization, *Phase 1* maintains $\text{Inv}_3^\dagger$, which states that at iteration j, PDRBLOCK strengthens frames $\{G_m\}$, $j < m \leq (i+1)$. $\text{Inv}_3^\dagger$ holds on loop entry, since initially $G = F$. Let G_m, G_m^* ($j < m \leq (i+1)$) be frame m at the beginning and at the end of the loop iteration, respectively. In the loop, PDRBLOCK adds clauses that block $\neg P_j$. Thus, $G_m^* \equiv G_m \wedge P_j$. Since $G_j \Rightarrow G_m$, this simplifies to $G_m^* \equiv G_m \wedge (G_j \vee I_{j+1})$. Expanding G_m, we get $G_m^* \equiv F_m \wedge \bigwedge_{\ell=i-k+1}^{j} (G_\ell \vee I_{\ell+1})$. Thus, $\text{Inv}_3^\dagger$ holds at the end of the loop.

In particular, after line 8, $G_{i+1} \equiv F_{i+1} \wedge \bigwedge_{\ell=i-k+1}^{i} (G_\ell \vee I_{\ell+1})$. Since $\varphi \Rightarrow G_{i+1}$, G_{i+1} is k-inductive relative to F_i.

Theorem 2. *Given a safe trace F of size N and an SEL (i, k) for F, KAVYEX-TEND returns a clausal monotone extension trace G of size $N+1$. Furthermore, if PDRBLOCK does no inductive generalization then G is an (i, k)-extension trace.*

Of course, assuming that PDRBLOCK does no inductive generalization is not realistic. KAVYEXTEND remains correct without the assumption: it returns a trace G that is a monotone clausal extension of F. However, G might be stronger than any (i, k)-extension of F. The invariants marked with † are then relaxed to their unmarked versions. Overall, inductive generalization improves KAVYEXTEND since it is not restricted to only a k-inductive strengthening.

Importantly, the output of KAVYEXTEND is a regular inductive trace. Thus, KAVYEXTEND is a procedure to strengthen a (relatively) k-inductive certificate to a (relatively) 1-inductive certificate. Hence, after KAVYEXTEND, any strategy for further generalization or trace extension from IC3, PDR, or AVY is applicable.

4.2 Searching for the Maximal SEL

In this section, we describe two algorithms for computing the maximal SEL. Both algorithms can be used to implement line 5 of Algorithm 3. They perform a guided search for group minimal unsatisfiable subsets. They terminate when having fewer clauses would not increase the SEL further. The first, called *top-down*, starts from the largest unrolling of the *Tr* and then reduces the length of the unrolling. The second, called *bottom-up*, finds the largest (regular) extension level first, and then grows it using strong induction.

Algorithm 5. A top down alg. for the maximal SEL.

Input: A transition system
$T = (Init, Tr, Bad)$
Input: An extendable monotone clausal
safe trace F of size N
Output: $\max(\mathcal{K}(F))$

1   $i \leftarrow N$
2   **while** $i > 0$ **do**
3   **if** $\neg\text{ISSAT}(Tr[\![F^i]\!]^{i+1} \wedge Bad(\bar{v}_{N+1}))$
     then break
4     $i \leftarrow (i-1)$

5   $k \leftarrow 1$
6   **while** $k < i+1$ **do**
7   **if** $\neg\text{ISSAT}(Tr[\![F^i]\!]^k \wedge Bad(\bar{v}_{N+1}))$ **then**
     break
8     $k \leftarrow (k+1)$

9   **return** (i,k)

Algorithm 6. A bottom up alg. for the maximal SEL.

Input: A transition system
$T = (Init, Tr, Bad)$
Input: An extendable monotone
clausal safe trace F of size N
Output: $\max(\mathcal{K}(F))$

1   $j \leftarrow N$
2   **while** $j > 0$ **do**
3   **if** $\neg\text{ISSAT}(Tr[\![F^j]\!]^1 \wedge Bad(\bar{v}_{N+1}))$
     then break
4     $j \leftarrow (j-1)$

5   $(i,k) \leftarrow (j,1)\,;\, j \leftarrow (j+1)\,;\, \ell \leftarrow 2$
6   **while** $\ell \leq (j+1) \wedge j \leq N$ **do**
7   **if** $\text{ISSAT}(Tr[\![F^j]\!]^\ell \wedge Bad(\bar{v}_{N+1}))$
     then $\ell \leftarrow (\ell+1)$
8   **else**
9      $(i,k) \leftarrow (j,\ell)$
10      $j \leftarrow (j+1)$

11   **return** (i,k)

Top-Down SEL. A pair (i,k) is the maximal SEL iff

$$i = \max \{j \mid 0 \leq j \leq N \cdot Tr[\![F^j]\!]^{j+1} \wedge Bad(\bar{v}_{N+1}) \Rightarrow \bot\}$$
$$k = \min \{\ell \mid 1 \leq \ell \leq (i+1) \cdot Tr[\![F^i]\!]^\ell \wedge Bad(\bar{v}_{N+1}) \Rightarrow \bot\}$$

Note that k depends on i. For a SEL $(i,k) \in \mathcal{K}(F)$, we refer to the formula $Tr[\![F^i]\!]$ as a *suffix* and to number k as the depth of induction. Thus, the search can be split into two phases: (a) find the smallest suffix while using the maximal depth of induction allowed (for that suffix), and (b) minimizing the depth of induction k for the value of i found in step (a). This is captured in Algorithm 5. The algorithm requires at most $(N+1)$ SAT queries. One downside, however, is that the formulas constructed in the first phase (line 3) are large because the depth of induction is the maximum possible.

Bottom-Up SEL. Algorithm 6 searches for a SEL by first finding a maximal regular extension level (line 2) and then searching for larger SELs (lines 6 to 10). Observe that if $(j,\ell) \notin \mathcal{K}(F)$, then $\forall p > j \cdot (p,\ell) \notin \mathcal{K}(F)$. This is used at line 7 to increase the depth of induction once it is known that $(j,\ell) \notin \mathcal{K}(F)$. On the other hand, if $(j,\ell) \in \mathcal{K}(F)$, there might be a larger SEL $(j+1,\ell)$. Thus, whenever a SEL (j,ℓ) is found, it is stored in (i,k) and the search continues (line 10). The algorithm terminates when there are no more valid SEL candidates and returns the last valid SEL. Note that ℓ is incremented only when there does not exists a larger SEL with the current value of ℓ. Thus, for each valid level j, if there exists SELs with level j, the algorithm is guaranteed to find the largest such SEL. Moreover, the level is increased at every possible opportunity. Hence, at the end $(i,k) = \max \mathcal{K}(F)$.

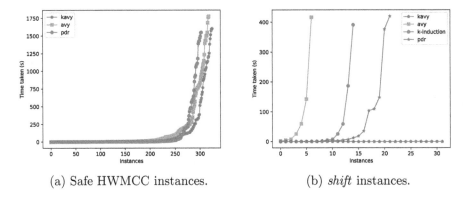

(a) Safe HWMCC instances.   (b) *shift* instances.

Fig. 2. Runtime comparison on SAFE HWMCC instances (a) and *shift* instances (b).

In the worst case, Algorithm 6 makes at most $3N$ SAT queries. However, compared to Algorithm 5, the queries are smaller. Moreover, the computation is incremental and can be aborted with a sub-optimal solution after execution of line 5 or line 9. Note that at line 5, i is a regular extension level (i.e., as in AVY), and every execution of line 9 results in a larger SEL.

5   Evaluation

We implemented KAVY on top of the AVY Model Checker[1]. For line 5 of Algorithm 3 we used Algorithm 5. We evaluated KAVY's performance against a version of AVY [29] from the Hardware Model Checking Competition 2017 [5], and the PDR engine of ABC [13]. We have used the benchmarks from HWMCC'14, '15, and '17. Benchmarks that are not solved by any of the solvers are excluded from the presentation. The experiments were conducted on a cluster running Intel E5-2683 V4 CPUs at 2.1 GHz with 8 GB RAM limit and 30 min time limit.

The results are summarized in Table 1. The HWMCC has a wide variety of benchmarks. We aggregate the results based on the competition, and also benchmark origin (based on the name). Some named categories (e.g., *intel*) include benchmarks that have not been included in any competition. The first column in Table 1 indicates the category. **Total** is the number of all available benchmarks, ignoring duplicates. That is, if a benchmark appeared in multiple categories, it is counted only once. Numbers in brackets indicate the number of instances that are solved uniquely by the solver. For example, KAVY solves 14 instances in *oc8051* that are not solved by any other solver. The VBS column indicates the *Virtual Best Solver*—the result of running all the three solvers in parallel and stopping as soon as one solver terminates successfully.

Overall, KAVY solves more SAFE instances than both AVY and PDR, while taking less time than AVY (we report time for solved instances, ignoring timeouts). The VBS column shows that KAVY is a promising new strategy, significantly improving overall performance. In the rest of this section, we analyze the

---

[1] All code, benchmarks, and results are available at https://arieg.bitbucket.io/avy/.

Table 1. Summary of instances solved by each tool. Timeouts were ignored when computing the time column.

BENCHMARKS	KAVY			AVY			PDR			VBS	
	SAFE	UNSAFE	Time(m)	SAFE	UNSAFE	Time(m)	SAFE	UNSAFE	Time(m)	SAFE	UNSAFE
HWMCC' 17	137 (16)	38	499	128 (3)	38	406	109 (6)	40 (5)	174	150	44
HWMCC' 15	193 (4)	84	412	191 (3)	92 (6)	597	194 (16)	67 (12)	310	218	104
HWMCC' 14	49	27 (1)	124	58 (4)	26	258	55 (6)	19 (2)	172	64	29
intel	32 (1)	9	196	32 (1)	9	218	19	5 (1)	40	33	10
6s	73 (2)	20	157	81 (4)	21 (1)	329	67 (3)	14	51	86	21
nusmv	13	0	5	14	0	29	16 (2)	0	38	16	0
bob	30	5	21	30	6 (1)	30	30 (1)	8 (3)	32	31	9
pdt	45	1	54	45 (1)	1	57	47 (3)	1	62	49	1
oski	26	89 (1)	174	28 (2)	92 (4)	217	20	53	63	28	93
beem	10	1	49	10	2	32	20 (8)	7 (5)	133	20	7
oc8051	34 (14)	0	286	20	0	99	6 (1)	1 (1)	77	35	1
power	4	0	25	3	0	3	8 (4)	0	31	8	0
shift	5 (2)	0	1	1	0	18	3	0	1	5	0
necla	5	0	4	7 (1)	0	1	5 (1)	0	4	8	0
prodcell	0	0	0	0	1	28	0	4 (3)	2	0	4
bc57	0	0	0	0	0	0	0	4 (4)	9	0	4
Total	326 (19)	141 (1)	957	319 (8)	148 (6)	1041	304 (25)	117 (17)	567	370	167

results in more detail, provide detailed run-time comparison between the tools, and isolate the effect of the new k-inductive strategy.

To compare the running time, we present scatter plots comparing KAVY and AVY (Fig. 3a), and KAVY and PDR (Fig. 3b). In both figures, KAVY is at the bottom. Points above the diagonal are better for KAVY. Compared to AVY, whenever an instance is solved by both solvers, KAVY is often faster, sometimes by orders of magnitude. Compared to PDR, KAVY and PDR perform well on very different instances. This is similar to the observation made by the authors of the original paper that presented AVY [29]. Another indicator of performance is the depth of convergence. This is summarized in Fig. 3d and e. KAVY often converges much sooner than AVY. The comparison with PDR is less clear which is consistent with the difference in performance between the two. To get the whole picture, Fig. 2a presents a cactus plot that compares the running times of the algorithms on all these benchmarks.

To isolate the effects of k-induction, we compare KAVY to a version of KAVY with k-induction disabled, which we call VANILLA. Conceptually, VANILLA is similar to AVY since it extends the trace using a 1-inductive extension trace, but its implementation is based on KAVY. The results for the running time and the depth of convergence are shown in Fig. 3c and f, respectively. The results are very clear—using strong extension traces significantly improves performance and has non-negligible affect on depth of convergence.

Finally, we discovered one family of benchmarks, called shift, on which KAVY performs orders of magnitude better than all other techniques. The benchmarks come from encoding bit-vector decision problem into circuits [21,30]. The shift family corresponds to deciding satisfiability of $(x + y) = (x << 1)$ for two

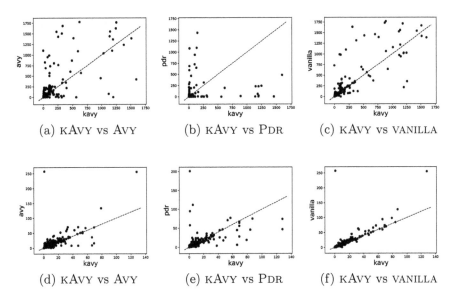

(a) KAVY vs AVY   (b) KAVY vs PDR   (c) KAVY vs VANILLA

(d) KAVY vs AVY   (e) KAVY vs PDR   (f) KAVY vs VANILLA

Fig. 3. Comparing running time ((a), (b), (c)) and depth of convergence ((d), (e), (f)) of AVY, PDR and VANILLA with KAVY. KAVY is shown on the x-axis. Points above the diagonal are better for KAVY. Only those instances that have been solved by both solvers are shown in each plot.

bit-vecors x and y. The family is parameterized by bit-width. The property is k-inductive, where k is the bit-width of x. The results of running AVY, PDR, k-induction[2], and KAVY are shown in Fig. 2b. Except for KAVY, all techniques exhibit exponential behavior in the bit-width, while KAVY remains constant. Deeper analysis indicates that KAVY finds a small inductive invariant while exploring just two steps in the execution of the circuit. At the same time, neither inductive generalization nor k-induction alone are able to consistently find the same invariant quickly.

6 Conclusion

In this paper, we present KAVY—an SMC algorithm that effectively uses k-inductive reasoning to guide interpolation and inductive generalization. KAVY searches both for a good inductive strengthening and for the most effective induction depth k. We have implemented KAVY on top of AVY Model Checker. The experimental results on HWMCC instances show that our approach is effective.

The search for the maximal SEL is an overhead in KAVY. There could be benchmarks in which this overhead outweighs its benefits. However, we have not come across such benchmarks so far. In such cases, KAVY can choose to settle for a sub-optimal SEL as mentioned in Sect. 4.2. Deciding when and how much to settle for remains a challenge.

---

[2] We used the k-induction engine **ind** in ABC [8].

Acknowledgements. We thank the anonymous reviewers and Oded Padon for their thorough review and insightful comments. This research was enabled in part by support provided by Compute Ontario (https://computeontario.ca/), Compute Canada (https://www.computecanada.ca/) and the grants from Natural Sciences and Engineering Research Council Canada.

References

1. Audemard, G., Lagniez, J.-M., Szczepanski, N., Tabary, S.: An adaptive parallel SAT solver. In: Rueher, M. (ed.) CP 2016. LNCS, vol. 9892, pp. 30–48. Springer, Cham (2016). https://doi.org/10.1007/978-3-319-44953-1_3

2. Belov, A., Marques-Silva, J.: MUSer2: an efficient MUS extractor. JSAT **8**(3/4), 123–128 (2012)

3. Berryhill, R., Ivrii, A., Veira, N., Veneris, A.G.: Learning support sets in IC3 and Quip: the good, the bad, and the ugly. In: 2017 Formal Methods in Computer Aided Design, FMCAD 2017, Vienna, Austria, 2–6 October 2017, pp. 140–147 (2017)

4. Biere, A., Cimatti, A., Clarke, E., Zhu, Y.: Symbolic model checking without BDDs. In: Cleaveland, W.R. (ed.) TACAS 1999. LNCS, vol. 1579, pp. 193–207. Springer, Heidelberg (1999). https://doi.org/10.1007/3-540-49059-0_14

5. Biere, A., van Dijk, T., Heljanko, K.: Hardware model checking competition 2017. In: Stewart, D., Weissenbacher, G. (eds.) 2017 Formal Methods in Computer Aided Design, FMCAD 2017, Vienna, Austria, 2–6 October 2017, p. 9. IEEE (2017)

6. Bjørner, N., Gurfinkel, A., McMillan, K., Rybalchenko, A.: Horn clause solvers for program verification. In: Beklemishev, L.D., Blass, A., Dershowitz, N., Finkbeiner, B., Schulte, W. (eds.) Fields of Logic and Computation II. LNCS, vol. 9300, pp. 24–51. Springer, Cham (2015). https://doi.org/10.1007/978-3-319-23534-9_2

7. Bradley, A.R.: SAT-based model checking without unrolling. In: Jhala, R., Schmidt, D. (eds.) VMCAI 2011. LNCS, vol. 6538, pp. 70–87. Springer, Heidelberg (2011). https://doi.org/10.1007/978-3-642-18275-4_7

8. Brayton, R., Mishchenko, A.: ABC: an academic industrial-strength verification tool. In: Touili, T., Cook, B., Jackson, P. (eds.) CAV 2010. LNCS, vol. 6174, pp. 24–40. Springer, Heidelberg (2010). https://doi.org/10.1007/978-3-642-14295-6_5

9. Champion, A., Mebsout, A., Sticksel, C., Tinelli, C.: The KIND 2 model checker. In: Chaudhuri, S., Farzan, A. (eds.) CAV 2016. LNCS, vol. 9780, pp. 510–517. Springer, Cham (2016). https://doi.org/10.1007/978-3-319-41540-6_29

10. Craig, W.: Three uses of the Herbrand-Gentzen theorem in relating model theory and proof theory. J. Symb. Log. **22**(3), 269–285 (1957)

11. de Moura, L., et al.: SAL 2. In: Alur, R., Peled, D.A. (eds.) CAV 2004. LNCS, vol. 3114, pp. 496–500. Springer, Heidelberg (2004). https://doi.org/10.1007/978-3-540-27813-9_45

12. Eén, N., Mishchenko, A., Amla, N.: A single-instance incremental SAT formulation of proof- and counterexample-based abstraction. In: Proceedings of 10th International Conference on Formal Methods in Computer-Aided Design, FMCAD 2010, Lugano, Switzerland, 20–23 October, pp. 181–188 (2010)

13. Eén, N., Mishchenko, A., Brayton, R.K.: Efficient implementation of property directed reachability. In: International Conference on Formal Methods in Computer-Aided Design, FMCAD 2011, Austin, TX, USA, October 30–02 November 2011, pp. 125–134 (2011)

14. Garoche, P.-L., Kahsai, T., Tinelli, C.: Incremental invariant generation using logic-based automatic abstract transformers. In: Brat, G., Rungta, N., Venet, A. (eds.) NFM 2013. LNCS, vol. 7871, pp. 139–154. Springer, Heidelberg (2013). https://doi.org/10.1007/978-3-642-38088-4_10

15. Gurfinkel, A., Ivrii, A.: Pushing to the top. In: Formal Methods in Computer-Aided Design, FMCAD 2015, Austin, Texas, USA, 27–30 September 2015, pp. 65–72 (2015)

16. Gurfinkel, A., Ivrii, A.: K-induction without unrolling. In: 2017 Formal Methods in Computer Aided Design, FMCAD 2017, Vienna, Austria, 2–6 October 2017, pp. 148–155 (2017)

17. Heule, M., Hunt Jr., W.A., Wetzler, N.: Trimming while checking clausal proofs. In: Formal Methods in Computer-Aided Design, FMCAD 2013, Portland, OR, USA, 20–23 October 2013, pp. 181–188 (2013)

18. Järvisalo, M., Heule, M.J.H., Biere, A.: Inprocessing rules. In: Gramlich, B., Miller, D., Sattler, U. (eds.) IJCAR 2012. LNCS (LNAI), vol. 7364, pp. 355–370. Springer, Heidelberg (2012). https://doi.org/10.1007/978-3-642-31365-3_28

19. Jovanovic, D., Dutertre, B.: Property-directed k-induction. In: 2016 Formal Methods in Computer-Aided Design, FMCAD 2016, Mountain View, CA, USA, 3–6 October 2016, pp. 85–92 (2016)

20. Kahsai, T., Ge, Y., Tinelli, C.: Instantiation-based invariant discovery. In: Bobaru, M., Havelund, K., Holzmann, G.J., Joshi, R. (eds.) NFM 2011. LNCS, vol. 6617, pp. 192–206. Springer, Heidelberg (2011). https://doi.org/10.1007/978-3-642-20398-5_15

21. Kovásznai, G., Fröhlich, A., Biere, A.: Complexity of fixed-size bit-vector logics. Theory Comput. Syst. **59**(2), 323–376 (2016)

22. Liang, J.H., Ganesh, V., Poupart, P., Czarnecki, K.: Learning rate based branching heuristic for SAT solvers. In: Creignou, N., Le Berre, D. (eds.) SAT 2016. LNCS, vol. 9710, pp. 123–140. Springer, Cham (2016). https://doi.org/10.1007/978-3-319-40970-2_9

23. Liang, J.H., Oh, C., Mathew, M., Thomas, C., Li, C., Ganesh, V.: Machine learning-based restart policy for CDCL SAT solvers. In: Beyersdorff, O., Wintersteiger, C.M. (eds.) SAT 2018. LNCS, vol. 10929, pp. 94–110. Springer, Cham (2018). https://doi.org/10.1007/978-3-319-94144-8_6

24. McMillan, K.L.: Interpolation and SAT-based model checking. In: Hunt, W.A., Somenzi, F. (eds.) CAV 2003. LNCS, vol. 2725, pp. 1–13. Springer, Heidelberg (2003). https://doi.org/10.1007/978-3-540-45069-6_1

25. McMillan, K.L.: Interpolation and model checking. In: Clarke, E., Henzinger, T., Veith, H., Bloem, R. (eds.) Handbook of Model Checking, pp. 421–446. Springer, Cham (2018)

26. Mebsout, A., Tinelli, C.: Proof certificates for SMT-based model checkers for infinite-state systems. In: 2016 Formal Methods in Computer-Aided Design, FMCAD 2016, Mountain View, CA, USA, 3–6 October 2016, pp. 117–124 (2016)

27. Sheeran, M., Singh, S., Stålmarck, G.: Checking safety properties using induction and a SAT-solver. In: Hunt, W.A., Johnson, S.D. (eds.) FMCAD 2000. LNCS, vol. 1954, pp. 127–144. Springer, Heidelberg (2000). https://doi.org/10.1007/3-540-40922-X_8

28. Vizel, Y., Grumberg, O.: Interpolation-sequence based model checking. In: Proceedings of 9th International Conference on Formal Methods in Computer-Aided Design, FMCAD 2009, 15–18 November 2009, Austin, Texas, USA, pp. 1–8 (2009)

29. Vizel, Y., Gurfinkel, A.: Interpolating property directed reachability. In: Biere, A., Bloem, R. (eds.) CAV 2014. LNCS, vol. 8559, pp. 260–276. Springer, Cham (2014). https://doi.org/10.1007/978-3-319-08867-9_17
30. Vizel, Y., Nadel, A., Malik, S.: Solving linear arithmetic with SAT-based model checking. In: 2017 Formal Methods in Computer Aided Design, FMCAD 2017, Vienna, Austria, 2–6 October 2017, pp. 47–54 (2017)

8

Termination of Triangular Integer Loops is Decidable

Florian Frohn[1]🆔 and Jürgen Giesl[2]([✉])🆔

[1] Max Planck Institute for Informatics, Saarbrücken, Germany
florian.frohn@mpi-inf.mpg.de
[2] LuFG Informatik 2, RWTH Aachen University, Aachen, Germany
giesl@informatik.rwth-aachen.de

Abstract. We consider the problem whether termination of affine integer loops is decidable. Since Tiwari conjectured decidability in 2004 [15], only special cases have been solved [3,4,14]. We complement this work by proving decidability for the case that the update matrix is triangular.

1 Introduction

We consider affine integer loops of the form

$$\textbf{while } \varphi \textbf{ do } \overline{x} \leftarrow A\,\overline{x} + \overline{a}. \qquad (1)$$

Here, $A \in \mathbb{Z}^{d \times d}$ for some dimension $d \geq 1$, $\overline{x}$ is a column vector of pairwise different variables $x_1, \ldots, x_d$, $\overline{a} \in \mathbb{Z}^d$, and φ is a conjunction of inequalities of the form $\alpha > 0$ where $\alpha \in \mathbb{Af}[\overline{x}]$ is an affine expression with rational coefficients[1] over $\overline{x}$ (i.e., $\mathbb{Af}[\overline{x}] = \{\overline{c}^T\,\overline{x} + c \mid \overline{c} \in \mathbb{Q}^d, c \in \mathbb{Q}\}$). So φ has the form $B\,\overline{x} + \overline{b} > \overline{0}$ where $\overline{0}$ is the vector containing k zeros, $B \in \mathbb{Q}^{k \times d}$, and $\overline{b} \in \mathbb{Q}^k$ for some $k \in \mathbb{N}$. Definition 1 formalizes the intuitive notion of termination for such loops.

Definition 1 (Termination). *Let* $f : \mathbb{Z}^d \to \mathbb{Z}^d$ *with* $f(\overline{x}) = A\,\overline{x} + \overline{a}$. *If*

$$\exists \overline{c} \in \mathbb{Z}^d. \ \forall n \in \mathbb{N}. \ \varphi[\overline{x}/f^n(\overline{c})],$$

then (1) is non-terminating *and* $\overline{c}$ *is a* witness *for non-termination. Otherwise, (1)* terminates.

Here, f^n denotes the n-fold application of f, i.e., we have $f^0(\overline{c}) = \overline{c}$ and $f^{n+1}(\overline{c}) = f(f^n(\overline{c}))$. We call f the *update* of (1). Moreover, for any entity s, $s[x/t]$ denotes the entity that results from s by replacing all occurrences of x by t. Similarly, if $\overline{x} = \begin{bmatrix} x_1 \\ \vdots \\ x_m \end{bmatrix}$ and $\overline{t} = \begin{bmatrix} t_1 \\ \vdots \\ t_m \end{bmatrix}$, then $s[\overline{x}/\overline{t}]$ denotes the entity resulting from s by replacing all occurrences of x_i by t_i for each $1 \leq i \leq m$.

---

[1] Note that multiplying with the least common multiple of all denominators yields an equivalent constraint with integer coefficients, i.e., allowing rational instead of integer coefficients does not extend the considered class of loops.

Example 2. *Consider the loop*

$$\textbf{while } y + z > 0 \textbf{ do } \begin{bmatrix} w \\ x \\ y \\ z \end{bmatrix} \leftarrow \begin{bmatrix} 2 \\ x + 1 \\ -w - 2 \cdot y \\ x \end{bmatrix}$$

where the update of all variables is executed simultaneously. This program belongs to our class of affine loops, because it can be written equivalently as follows.

$$\textbf{while } y + z > 0 \textbf{ do } \begin{bmatrix} w \\ x \\ y \\ z \end{bmatrix} \leftarrow \begin{bmatrix} 0 & 0 & 0 & 0 \\ 0 & 1 & 0 & 0 \\ -1 & 0 & -2 & 0 \\ 0 & 1 & 0 & 0 \end{bmatrix} \begin{bmatrix} w \\ x \\ y \\ z \end{bmatrix} + \begin{bmatrix} 2 \\ 1 \\ 0 \\ 0 \end{bmatrix}$$

While termination of affine loops is known to be decidable if the variables range over the real [15] or the rational numbers [4], the integer case is a well-known open problem [2–4,14,15].[2] However, certain special cases have been solved: Braverman [4] showed that termination of *linear* loops is decidable (i.e., loops of the form (1) where $\bar{a}$ is $\bar{0}$ and φ is of the form $B\bar{x} > \bar{0}$). Bozga et al. [3] showed decidability for the case that the update matrix A in (1) has the *finite monoid property*, i.e., if there is an $n > 0$ such that A^n is diagonalizable and all eigenvalues of A^n are in $\{0, 1\}$. Ouaknine et al. [14] proved decidability for the case $d \leq 4$ and for the case that A is diagonalizable.

Ben-Amram et al. [2] showed undecidability of termination for certain extensions of affine integer loops, e.g., for loops where the body is of the form **if** $x > 0$ **then** $\bar{x} \leftarrow A\bar{x}$ **else** $\bar{x} \leftarrow A'\bar{x}$ where $A, A' \in \mathbb{Z}^{d \times d}$ and $x \in \bar{x}$.

In this paper, we present another substantial step towards the solution of the open problem whether termination of affine integer loops is decidable. We show that termination is decidable for *triangular* loops (1) where A is a triangular matrix (i.e., all entries of A below or above the main diagonal are zero). Clearly, the order of the variables is irrelevant, i.e., our results also cover the case that A can be transformed into a triangular matrix by reordering A, $\bar{x}$, and $\bar{a}$ accordingly.[3] So essentially, triangularity means that the program variables $x_1, \ldots, x_d$ can be ordered such that in each loop iteration, the new value of x_i only depends on the previous values of $x_1, \ldots, x_{i-1}, x_i$. Hence, this excludes programs with "cyclic dependencies" of variables (e.g., where the new values of x and y both depend on the old values of both x and y). While triangular loops are a very restricted subclass of general integer programs, integer programs often contain such loops. Hence, tools for termination analysis of such programs (e.g., [5–8,11–13]) could

---

[2] The proofs for real or rational numbers do not carry over to the integers since [15] uses Brouwer's Fixed Point Theorem which is not applicable if the variables range over $\mathbb{Z}$ and [4] relies on the density of $\mathbb{Q}$ in $\mathbb{R}$.

[3] Similarly, one could of course also use other termination-preserving pre-processings and try to transform a given program into a triangular loop.

benefit from integrating our decision procedure and applying it whenever a sub-program is an affine triangular loop.

Note that triangularity and diagonalizability of matrices do not imply each other. As we consider loops with arbitrary dimension, this means that the class of loops considered in this paper is not covered by [3,14]. Since we consider affine instead of linear loops, it is also orthogonal to [4].

To see the difference between our and previous results, note that a triangular matrix A where $c_1, \ldots, c_k$ are the *distinct* entries on the diagonal is diagonalizable iff $(A - c_1 I) \ldots (A - c_k I)$ is the zero matrix.[4] Here, I is the identity matrix. So an easy example for a triangular loop where the update matrix is not diagonalizable is the following well-known program (see, e.g., [2]):

$$\textbf{while } x > 0 \textbf{ do } x \leftarrow x + y; \ y \leftarrow y - 1$$

It terminates as y eventually becomes negative and then x decreases in each iteration. In matrix notation, the loop body is $\begin{bmatrix} x \\ y \end{bmatrix} \leftarrow \begin{bmatrix} 1 & 1 \\ 0 & 1 \end{bmatrix} \begin{bmatrix} x \\ y \end{bmatrix} + \begin{bmatrix} 0 \\ -1 \end{bmatrix}$, i.e., the update matrix is triangular. Thus, this program is in our class of programs where we show that termination is decidable. However, the only entry on the diagonal of the update matrix A is $c = 1$ and $A - cI = \begin{bmatrix} 0 & 1 \\ 0 & 0 \end{bmatrix}$ is not the zero matrix. So A (and in fact each A^n where $n \in \mathbb{N}$) is not diagonalizable. Hence, extensions of this example to a dimension greater than 4 where the loop is still triangular are not covered by any of the previous results.[5]

Our proof that termination is decidable for triangular loops proceeds in three steps. We first prove that termination of triangular loops is decidable iff termination of *non-negative triangular* loops (*nnt-loops*) is decidable, cf. Sect. 2. A loop is non-negative if the diagonal of A does not contain negative entries. Second, we show how to compute *closed forms* for nnt-loops, i.e., vectors $\overline{q}$ of d expressions over the variables $\overline{x}$ and n such that $\overline{q}[n/c] = f^c(\overline{x})$ for all $c \geq 0$, see Sect. 3. Here, triangularity of the matrix A allows us to treat the variables step by step. So for any $1 \leq i \leq d$, we already know the closed forms for $x_1, \ldots, x_{i-1}$ when computing the closed form for x_i. The idea of computing closed forms for the repeated updates of loops was inspired by our previous work on inferring lower bounds on the runtime of integer programs [10]. But in contrast to [10], here the computation of the closed form always succeeds due to the restricted shape of the programs. Finally, we explain how to decide termination of nnt-loops by reasoning about their closed forms in Sect. 4. While our technique does not yield witnesses for non-termination, we show that it yields witnesses for *eventual* non-termination, i.e., vectors $\overline{c}$ such that $f^n(\overline{c})$ witnesses non-termination for some $n \in \mathbb{N}$. Detailed proofs for all lemmas and theorems can be found in [9].

---

[4] The reason is that in this case, $(x - c_1) \ldots (x - c_k)$ is the minimal polynomial of A and diagonalizability is equivalent to the fact that the minimal polynomial is a product of distinct linear factors.

[5] For instance, consider $\textbf{while } x > 0 \textbf{ do } x \leftarrow x + y + z_1 + z_2 + z_3; \ y \leftarrow y - 1$.

2   From Triangular to Non-Negative Triangular Loops

To transform triangular loops into nnt-loops, we define how to *chain* loops. Intuitively, chaining yields a new loop where a single iteration is equivalent to two iterations of the original loop. Then we show that chaining a triangular loop always yields an nnt-loop and that chaining is equivalent w.r.t. termination.

Definition 3 (Chaining). Chaining *the loop (1) yields:*

$$\textbf{while } \varphi \wedge \varphi[\overline{x}/A\,\overline{x} + \overline{a}] \textbf{ do } \overline{x} \leftarrow A^2\,\overline{x} + A\,\overline{a} + \overline{a} \tag{2}$$

Example 4. *Chaining Example 2 yields*

$$\textbf{while } y + z > 0 \wedge -w - 2 \cdot y + x > 0 \textbf{ do}$$

$$\begin{bmatrix} w \\ x \\ y \\ z \end{bmatrix} \leftarrow \begin{bmatrix} 0 & 0 & 0 & 0 \\ 0 & 1 & 0 & 0 \\ -1 & 0 & -2 & 0 \\ 0 & 1 & 0 & 0 \end{bmatrix}^2 \begin{bmatrix} w \\ x \\ y \\ z \end{bmatrix} + \begin{bmatrix} 0 & 0 & 0 & 0 \\ 0 & 1 & 0 & 0 \\ -1 & 0 & -2 & 0 \\ 0 & 1 & 0 & 0 \end{bmatrix} \begin{bmatrix} 2 \\ 1 \\ 0 \\ 0 \end{bmatrix} + \begin{bmatrix} 2 \\ 1 \\ 0 \\ 0 \end{bmatrix}$$

which simplifies to the following nnt-loop:

$$\textbf{while } y + z > 0 \wedge -w - 2 \cdot y + x > 0 \textbf{ do } \begin{bmatrix} w \\ x \\ y \\ z \end{bmatrix} \leftarrow \begin{bmatrix} 0 & 0 & 0 & 0 \\ 0 & 1 & 0 & 0 \\ 2 & 0 & 4 & 0 \\ 0 & 1 & 0 & 0 \end{bmatrix} \begin{bmatrix} w \\ x \\ y \\ z \end{bmatrix} + \begin{bmatrix} 2 \\ 2 \\ -2 \\ 1 \end{bmatrix}$$

Lemma 5 is needed to prove that (2) is an nnt-loop if (1) is triangular.

Lemma 5 (Squares of Triangular Matrices). *For every triangular matrix A, A^2 is a triangular matrix whose diagonal entries are non-negative.*

Corollary 6 (Chaining Loops). *If (1) is triangular, then (2) is an nnt-loop.*

Proof. Immediate consequence of Definition 3 and Lemma 5.   □

Lemma 7 (Equivalence of Chaining). *(1) terminates $\Longleftrightarrow$ (2) terminates.*

Proof. By Definition 1, (1) does not terminate iff

$$\exists \overline{c} \in \mathbb{Z}^d.\ \forall n \in \mathbb{N}.\ \varphi[\overline{x}/f^n(\overline{c})]$$
$$\Longleftrightarrow \exists \overline{c} \in \mathbb{Z}^d.\ \forall n \in \mathbb{N}.\ \varphi[\overline{x}/f^{2 \cdot n}(\overline{c})] \wedge \varphi[\overline{x}/f^{2 \cdot n + 1}(\overline{c})]$$
$$\Longleftrightarrow \exists \overline{c} \in \mathbb{Z}^d.\ \forall n \in \mathbb{N}.\ \varphi[\overline{x}/f^{2 \cdot n}(\overline{c})] \wedge \varphi[\overline{x}/A\,f^{2 \cdot n}(\overline{c}) + \overline{a}] \text{ (by Definition of } f),$$

i.e., iff (2) does not terminate as $f^2(\overline{x}) = A^2\,\overline{x} + A\,\overline{a} + \overline{a}$ is the update of (2). □

Theorem 8 (Reducing Termination to nnt-Loops). *Termination of triangular loops is decidable iff termination of nnt-loops is decidable.*

Proof. Immediate consequence of Corollary 6 and Lemma 7.   □

Thus, from now on we restrict our attention to nnt-loops.

3 Computing Closed Forms

The next step towards our decidability proof is to show that $f^n(\overline{x})$ is equivalent to a vector of *poly-exponential expressions* for each nnt-loop, i.e., the closed form of each nnt-loop can be represented by such expressions. Here, *equivalence* means that two expressions evaluate to the same result for all variable assignments.

Poly-exponential expressions are sums of arithmetic terms where it is always clear which addend determines the asymptotic growth of the whole expression when increasing a designated variable n. This is crucial for our decidability proof in Sect. 4. Let $\mathbb{N}_{\geq 1} = \{b \in \mathbb{N} \mid b \geq 1\}$ (and $\mathbb{Q}_{>0}$, $\mathbb{N}_{>1}$, etc. are defined analogously). Moreover, $\mathrm{Af}[\overline{x}]$ is again the set of all affine expressions over $\overline{x}$.

Definition 9 (Poly-Exponential Expressions). *Let $\mathcal{C}$ be the set of all finite conjunctions over the literals $n = c, n \neq c$ where n is a designated variable and $c \in \mathbb{N}$. Moreover for each formula ψ over n, let $[\![\psi]\!]$ be the characteristic function of ψ, i.e., $[\![\psi]\!](c) = 1$ if $\psi[n/c]$ is valid and $[\![\psi]\!](c) = 0$, otherwise. The set of all poly-exponential expressions over $\overline{x}$ is*

$$\mathbb{PE}[\overline{x}] = \left\{ \sum_{j=1}^{\ell} [\![\psi_j]\!] \cdot \alpha_j \cdot n^{a_j} \cdot b_j^n \;\middle|\; \ell, a_j \in \mathbb{N}, \; \psi_j \in \mathcal{C}, \; \alpha_j \in \mathrm{Af}[\overline{x}], \; b_j \in \mathbb{N}_{\geq 1} \right\}.$$

As n ranges over $\mathbb{N}$, we use $[\![n > c]\!]$ as syntactic sugar for $[\![\bigwedge_{i=0}^{c} n \neq i]\!]$. So an example for a poly-exponential expression is

$$[\![n > 2]\!] \cdot (2 \cdot x + 3 \cdot y - 1) \cdot n^3 \cdot 3^n \; + \; [\![n = 2]\!] \cdot (x - y).$$

Moreover, note that if ψ contains a *positive* literal (i.e., a literal of the form "$n = c$" for some number $c \in \mathbb{N}$), then $[\![\psi]\!]$ is equivalent to either 0 or $[\![n = c]\!]$.

The crux of the proof that poly-exponential expressions can represent closed forms is to show that certain sums over products of exponential and poly-exponential expressions can be represented by poly-exponential expressions, cf. Lemma 12. To construct these expressions, we use a variant of [1, Lemma 3.5]. As usual, $\mathbb{Q}[\overline{x}]$ is the set of all polynomials over $\overline{x}$ with rational coefficients.

Lemma 10 (Expressing Polynomials by Differences [1]). *If $q \in \mathbb{Q}[n]$ and $c \in \mathbb{Q}$, then there is an $r \in \mathbb{Q}[n]$ such that $q = r - c \cdot r[n/n - 1]$ for all $n \in \mathbb{N}$.*

So Lemma 10 expresses a polynomial q via the difference of another polynomial r at the positions n and $n - 1$, where the additional factor c can be chosen freely. The proof of Lemma 10 is by induction on the degree of q and its structure resembles the structure of the following algorithm to compute r. Using the Binomial Theorem, one can verify that $q - s + c \cdot s[n/n - 1]$ has a smaller degree than q, which is crucial for the proof of Lemma 10 and termination of Algorithm 1.

Algorithm 1. compute_r

> **Input:** $q = \sum_{i=0}^{d} c_i \cdot n^i \in \mathbb{Q}[n], \ c \in \mathbb{Q}$
> **Result:** $r \in \mathbb{Q}[n]$ such that $q = r - c \cdot r[n/n - 1]$
> **if** $d = 0$ **then**
> > **if** $c = 1$ **then return** $c_0 \cdot n$ **else return** $\frac{c_0}{1-c}$
> **else**
> > **if** $c = 1$ **then** $s \leftarrow \frac{c_d \cdot n^{d+1}}{d+1}$ **else** $s \leftarrow \frac{c_d \cdot n^d}{1-c}$
> > **return** $s + \text{compute\_r}(q - s + c \cdot s[n/n - 1], \ c)$

Example 11. *As an example, consider $q = 1$ (i.e., $c_0 = 1$) and $c = 4$. Then we search for an r such that $q = r - c \cdot r[n/n - 1]$, i.e., $1 = r - 4 \cdot r[n/n - 1]$. According to Algorithm 1, the solution is $r = \frac{c_0}{1-c} = -\frac{1}{3}$.*

Lemma 12 (Closure of $\mathbb{PE}$ under Sums of Products and Exponentials).
If $m \in \mathbb{N}$ and $p \in \mathbb{PE}[\overline{x}]$, then one can compute a $q \in \mathbb{PE}[\overline{x}]$ which is equivalent to $\sum_{i=1}^{n} m^{n-i} \cdot p[n/i - 1]$.

Proof. Let $p = \sum_{j=1}^{\ell} [\![\psi_j]\!] \cdot \alpha_j \cdot n^{a_j} \cdot b_j^n$. We have:

$$\sum_{i=1}^{n} m^{n-i} \cdot p[n/i - 1] = \sum_{j=1}^{\ell} \sum_{i=1}^{n} [\![\psi_j]\!] (i-1) \cdot m^{n-i} \cdot \alpha_j \cdot (i-1)^{a_j} \cdot b_j^{i-1} \quad (3)$$

As $\mathbb{PE}[\overline{x}]$ is closed under addition, it suffices to show that we can compute an equivalent poly-exponential expression for any expression of the form

$$\sum_{i=1}^{n} [\![\psi]\!] (i-1) \cdot m^{n-i} \cdot \alpha \cdot (i-1)^a \cdot b^{i-1}. \quad (4)$$

We first regard the case $m = 0$. Here, the expression (4) can be simplified to

$$[\![n \neq 0]\!] \cdot [\![\psi[n/n-1]]\!] \cdot \alpha \cdot (n-1)^a \cdot b^{n-1}. \quad (5)$$

Clearly, there is a $\psi' \in \mathcal{C}$ such that $[\![\psi']\!]$ is equivalent to $[\![n \neq 0]\!] \cdot [\![\psi[n/n-1]]\!]$. Moreover, $\alpha \cdot b^{n-1} = \frac{\alpha}{b} \cdot b^n$ where $\frac{\alpha}{b} \in \mathrm{Af}[\overline{x}]$. Hence, due to the Binomial Theorem

$$[\![n \neq 0]\!] \cdot [\![\psi[n/n-1]]\!] \cdot \alpha \cdot (n-1)^a \cdot b^{n-1} = \sum_{i=0}^{a} [\![\psi']\!] \cdot \frac{\alpha}{b} \cdot \binom{a}{i} \cdot (-1)^i \cdot n^{a-i} \cdot b^n \quad (6)$$

which is a poly-exponential expression as $\frac{\alpha}{b} \cdot \binom{a}{i} \cdot (-1)^i \in \mathrm{Af}[\overline{x}]$.

From now on, let $m \geq 1$. If ψ contains a positive literal $n = c$, then we get

$$\left. \begin{array}{l} \quad \sum_{i=1}^{n} [\![\psi]\!] (i-1) \cdot m^{n-i} \cdot \alpha \cdot (i-1)^a \cdot b^{i-1} \\ = \sum_{i=1}^{n} [\![n > i-1]\!] \cdot [\![\psi]\!] (i-1) \cdot m^{n-i} \cdot \alpha \cdot (i-1)^a \cdot b^{i-1} \quad (\dagger) \\ = [\![n > c]\!] \cdot [\![\psi]\!] (c) \cdot m^{n-c-1} \cdot \alpha \cdot c^a \cdot b^c \quad (\dagger\dagger) \\ = \begin{cases} 0, & \text{if } [\![\psi]\!] (c) = 0 \\ [\![n > c]\!] \cdot \frac{1}{m^{c+1}} \cdot \alpha \cdot c^a \cdot b^c \cdot m^n, & \text{if } [\![\psi]\!] (c) = 1 \end{cases} \\ \in \mathbb{PE}[\overline{x}] \quad (\text{since } \frac{1}{m^{c+1}} \cdot \alpha \cdot c^a \cdot b^c \in \mathrm{Af}[\overline{x}]). \end{array} \right\} \quad (7)$$

The step marked with (†) holds as we have $[\![n > i - 1]\!] = 1$ for all $i \in \{1, \ldots, n\}$ and the step marked with (††) holds since $i \neq c + 1$ implies $[\![\psi]\!] (i - 1) = 0$. If ψ does not contain a positive literal, then let c be the maximal constant that occurs in ψ or -1 if ψ is empty. We get:

$$\left.\begin{aligned}
&\sum_{i=1}^{n} [\![\psi]\!] (i - 1) \cdot m^{n-i} \cdot \alpha \cdot (i - 1)^a \cdot b^{i-1} \\
&= \sum_{i=1}^{n} [\![n > i - 1]\!] \cdot [\![\psi]\!] (i - 1) \cdot m^{n-i} \cdot \alpha \cdot (i - 1)^a \cdot b^{i-1} \quad (\dagger) \\
&= \sum_{i=1}^{c+1} [\![n > i - 1]\!] \cdot [\![\psi]\!] (i - 1) \cdot m^{n-i} \cdot \alpha \cdot (i - 1)^a \cdot b^{i-1} \\
&\quad + \sum_{i=c+2}^{n} m^{n-i} \cdot \alpha \cdot (i - 1)^a \cdot b^{i-1}
\end{aligned}\right\} \quad (8)$$

Again, the step marked with (†) holds since we have $[\![n > i - 1]\!] = 1$ for all $i \in \{1, \ldots, n\}$. The last step holds as $i \geq c + 2$ implies $[\![\psi]\!] (i - 1) = 1$. Similar to the case where ψ contains a positive literal, we can compute a poly-exponential expression which is equivalent to the first addend. We have

$$\begin{aligned}
&\sum_{i=1}^{c+1} [\![n > i - 1]\!] \cdot [\![\psi]\!] (i - 1) \cdot m^{n-i} \cdot \alpha \cdot (i - 1)^a \cdot b^{i-1} \\
&= \sum_{\substack{1 \leq i \leq c+1 \\ [\![\psi]\!](i-1)=1}} [\![n > i - 1]\!] \cdot \tfrac{1}{m^i} \cdot \alpha \cdot (i - 1)^a \cdot b^{i-1} \cdot m^n
\end{aligned} \quad (9)$$

which is a poly-exponential expression as $\frac{1}{m^i} \cdot \alpha \cdot (i - 1)^a \cdot b^{i-1} \in \mathrm{Af}[\overline{x}]$. For the second addend, we have:

$$\left.\begin{aligned}
&\sum_{i=c+2}^{n} m^{n-i} \cdot \alpha \cdot (i - 1)^a \cdot b^{i-1} \\
&= \tfrac{\alpha}{b} \cdot m^n \cdot \sum_{i=c+2}^{n} (i - 1)^a \cdot \left(\tfrac{b}{m}\right)^i \\
&= \tfrac{\alpha}{b} \cdot m^n \cdot \sum_{i=c+2}^{n} \left(r[n/i] - \tfrac{m}{b} \cdot r[n/i - 1]\right) \cdot \left(\tfrac{b}{m}\right)^i \quad (\text{Lemma 10 with } c = \tfrac{m}{b}) \\
&= \tfrac{\alpha}{b} \cdot m^n \cdot \left(\sum_{i=c+2}^{n} r[n/i] \cdot \left(\tfrac{b}{m}\right)^i - \sum_{i=c+2}^{n} \tfrac{m}{b} \cdot r[n/i - 1] \cdot \left(\tfrac{b}{m}\right)^i\right) \\
&= \tfrac{\alpha}{b} \cdot m^n \cdot \left(\sum_{i=c+2}^{n} r[n/i] \cdot \left(\tfrac{b}{m}\right)^i - \sum_{i=c+1}^{n-1} r[n/i] \cdot \left(\tfrac{b}{m}\right)^i\right) \\
&= \tfrac{\alpha}{b} \cdot m^n \cdot [\![n > c + 1]\!] \cdot \left(r \cdot \left(\tfrac{b}{m}\right)^n - r[n/c + 1] \cdot \left(\tfrac{b}{m}\right)^{c+1}\right) \\
&= [\![n > c + 1]\!] \cdot \tfrac{\alpha}{b} \cdot r \cdot b^n - [\![n > c + 1]\!] \cdot r[n/c + 1] \cdot \left(\tfrac{b}{m}\right)^{c+1} \cdot \tfrac{\alpha}{b} \cdot m^n
\end{aligned}\right\} \quad (10)$$

Lemma 10 ensures $r \in \mathbb{Q}[n]$, i.e., we have $r = \sum_{i=0}^{d_r} m_i \cdot n^i$ for some $d_r \in \mathbb{N}$ and $m_i \in \mathbb{Q}$. Thus, $r[n/c+1] \cdot \left(\tfrac{b}{m}\right)^{c+1} \cdot \tfrac{\alpha}{b} \in \mathrm{Af}[\overline{x}]$ which implies $[\![n > c + 1]\!] \cdot r[n/c+1] \cdot \left(\tfrac{b}{m}\right)^{c+1} \cdot \tfrac{\alpha}{b} \cdot m^n \in \mathbb{PE}[\overline{x}]$. It remains to show that the addend $[\![n > c + 1]\!] \cdot \tfrac{\alpha}{b} \cdot r \cdot b^n$ is equivalent to a poly-exponential expression. As $\tfrac{\alpha}{b} \cdot m_i \in \mathrm{Af}[\overline{x}]$, we have

$$[\![n > c + 1]\!] \cdot \tfrac{\alpha}{b} \cdot r \cdot b^n = \sum_{i=0}^{d_r} [\![n > c + 1]\!] \cdot \tfrac{\alpha}{b} \cdot m_i \cdot n^i \cdot b^n \in \mathbb{PE}[\overline{x}]. \quad (11)$$

$\square$

The proof of Lemma 12 gives rise to a corresponding algorithm.

Algorithm 2. symbolic_sum

Input: $m \in \mathbb{N}$, $p \in \mathbb{PE}[\overline{x}]$

Result: $q \in \mathbb{PE}[\overline{x}]$ which is equivalent to $\sum_{i=1}^{n} m^{n-i} \cdot p[n/i-1]$

rearrange $\sum_{i=1}^{n} m^{n-i} \cdot p[n/i-1]$ to $\sum_{j=1}^{\ell} p_j$ as in (3)

foreach $p_j \in \{p_1, \ldots, p_\ell\}$ **do**

    if $m = 0$ **then** compute q_j as in (5) and (6)

    else if $p_j = [\![\ldots \wedge n = c \wedge \ldots]\!] \cdot \ldots$ **then** compute q_j as in (7)

    else

        • split p_j into two sums $p_{j,1}$ and $p_{j,2}$ as in (8)

        • compute $q_{j,1}$ from $p_{j,1}$ as in (9)

        • compute $q_{j,2}$ from $p_{j,2}$ as in (10) and (11) using Algorithm 1

        • $q_j \leftarrow q_{j,1} + q_{j,2}$

return $\sum_{j=1}^{\ell} q_j$

Example 13. *We compute an equivalent poly-exponential expression for*

$$\sum_{i=1}^{n} 4^{n-i} \cdot ([\![n = 0]\!] \cdot 2 \cdot w + [\![n \neq 0]\!] \cdot 4 - 2)\,[n/i-1] \tag{12}$$

where w is a variable. (It will later on be needed to compute a closed form for Example 4, see Example 18.) According to Algorithm 2 and (3), we get

$$
\begin{aligned}
&\sum_{i=1}^{n} 4^{n-i} \cdot ([\![n = 0]\!] \cdot 2 \cdot w + [\![n \neq 0]\!] \cdot 4 - 2)\,[n/i-1]\\
={}& \sum_{i=1}^{n} 4^{n-i} \cdot ([\![i-1 = 0]\!] \cdot 2 \cdot w + [\![i-1 \neq 0]\!] \cdot 4 - 2)\\
={}& p_1 + p_2 + p_3
\end{aligned}
$$

with $p_1 = \sum_{i=1}^{n} [\![i-1 = 0]\!] \cdot 4^{n-i} \cdot 2 \cdot w$, $p_2 = \sum_{i=1}^{n} [\![i-1 \neq 0]\!] \cdot 4^{n-i} \cdot 4$, and $p_3 = \sum_{i=1}^{n} 4^{n-i} \cdot (-2)$. We search for $q_1, q_2, q_3 \in \mathbb{PE}[w]$ that are equivalent to p_1, p_2, p_3, i.e., $q_1 + q_2 + q_3$ is equivalent to (12). We only show how to compute q_2 (and omit the computation of $q_1 = [\![n \neq 0]\!] \cdot \frac{1}{2} \cdot w \cdot 4^n$ and $q_3 = \frac{2}{3} - \frac{2}{3} \cdot 4^n$). Analogously to (8), we get:

$$
\begin{aligned}
&\sum_{i=1}^{n} [\![i-1 \neq 0]\!] \cdot 4^{n-i} \cdot 4\\
={}& \sum_{i=1}^{n} [\![n > i-1]\!] \cdot [\![i-1 \neq 0]\!] \cdot 4^{n-i} \cdot 4\\
={}& \sum_{i=1}^{1} [\![n > i-1]\!] \cdot [\![i-1 \neq 0]\!] \cdot 4^{n-1} \cdot 4 \quad + \quad \sum_{i=2}^{n} 4^{n-i} \cdot 4
\end{aligned}
$$

The next step is to rearrange the first sum as in (9). In our example, it directly simplifies to 0 and hence we obtain

$$\sum_{i=1}^{1} [\![n > i-1]\!] \cdot [\![i-1 \neq 0]\!] \cdot 4^{n-1} \cdot 4 + \sum_{i=2}^{n} 4^{n-i} \cdot 4 = \sum_{i=2}^{n} 4^{n-i} \cdot 4.$$

Finally, by applying the steps from (10) we get:

$$
\begin{aligned}
&\sum_{i=2}^{n} 4^{n-i} \cdot 4 \\
&= 4 \cdot 4^{n} \cdot \sum_{i=2}^{n} \left(\tfrac{1}{4}\right)^{i} \\
&= 4 \cdot 4^{n} \cdot \sum_{i=2}^{n} \left(-\tfrac{1}{3} - 4 \cdot \left(-\tfrac{1}{3}\right)\right) \cdot \left(\tfrac{1}{4}\right)^{i} &\text{(†)}\\
&= 4 \cdot 4^{n} \cdot \left(\sum_{i=2}^{n} \left(-\tfrac{1}{3}\right) \cdot \left(\tfrac{1}{4}\right)^{i} - \sum_{i=2}^{n} 4 \cdot \left(-\tfrac{1}{3}\right) \cdot \left(\tfrac{1}{4}\right)^{i}\right) \\
&= 4 \cdot 4^{n} \cdot \left(\sum_{i=2}^{n} \left(-\tfrac{1}{3}\right) \cdot \left(\tfrac{1}{4}\right)^{i} - \sum_{i=1}^{n-1} \left(-\tfrac{1}{3}\right) \cdot \left(\tfrac{1}{4}\right)^{i}\right) \\
&= 4 \cdot 4^{n} \cdot [\![n > 1]\!] \cdot \left(\left(-\tfrac{1}{3}\right) \cdot \left(\tfrac{1}{4}\right)^{n} - \left(-\tfrac{1}{3}\right) \cdot \tfrac{1}{4}\right) \\
&= [\![n > 1]\!] \cdot \left(-\tfrac{4}{3}\right) + [\![n > 1]\!] \cdot \tfrac{1}{3} \cdot 4^{n} \\
&= q_2
\end{aligned}
$$

The step marked with (†) holds by Lemma 10 with $q = 1$ and $c = 4$. Thus, we have $r = -\tfrac{1}{3}$, cf. Example 11.

Recall that our goal is to compute closed forms for loops. As a first step, instead of the n-fold update function $h(n, \overline{x}) = f^{n}(\overline{x})$ of (1) where f is the update of (1), we consider a recursive update function for a single variable $x \in \overline{x}$:

$$
g(0, \overline{x}) = x \quad \text{and} \quad g(n, \overline{x}) = m \cdot g(n - 1, \overline{x}) + p[n/n - 1] \quad \text{for all } n > 0
$$

Here, $m \in \mathbb{N}$ and $p \in \mathbb{PE}[\overline{x}]$. Using Lemma 12, it is easy to show that g can be represented by a poly-exponential expression.

Lemma 14 (Closed Form for Single Variables). *If $x \in \overline{x}$, $m \in \mathbb{N}$, and $p \in \mathbb{PE}[\overline{x}]$, then one can compute a $q \in \mathbb{PE}[\overline{x}]$ which satisfies*

$$
q[n/0] = x \quad \text{and} \quad q = (m \cdot q + p)[n/n - 1] \quad \text{for all } n > 0.
$$

Proof. It suffices to find a $q \in \mathbb{PE}[\overline{x}]$ that satisfies

$$
q = m^{n} \cdot x + \sum_{i=1}^{n} m^{n-i} \cdot p[n/i - 1]. \tag{13}
$$

To see why (13) is sufficient, note that (13) implies

$$
q[n/0] \quad = \quad m^{0} \cdot x + \sum_{i=1}^{0} m^{0-i} \cdot p[n/i - 1] \quad = \quad x
$$

and for $n > 0$, (13) implies

$$
\begin{aligned}
q &= m^{n} \cdot x + \sum_{i=1}^{n} m^{n-i} \cdot p[n/i - 1] \\
&= m^{n} \cdot x + \left(\sum_{i=1}^{n-1} m^{n-i} \cdot p[n/i - 1]\right) + p[n/n - 1] \\
&= m \cdot \left(m^{n-1} \cdot x + \sum_{i=1}^{n-1} m^{n-i-1} \cdot p[n/i - 1]\right) + p[n/n - 1] \\
&= m \cdot q[n/n - 1] + p[n/n - 1] \\
&= (m \cdot q + p)[n/n - 1].
\end{aligned}
$$

By Lemma 12, we can compute a $q' \in \mathbb{PE}[\overline{x}]$ such that

$$
m^{n} \cdot x + \sum_{i=1}^{n} m^{n-i} \cdot p[n/i - 1] \quad = \quad m^{n} \cdot x + q'.
$$

Moreover,

$$\text{if } m = 0, \text{ then } m^n \cdot x = [\![n = 0]\!] \cdot x \in \mathbb{PE}[\overline{x}] \text{ and} \tag{14}$$

$$\text{if } m > 0, \text{ then } m^n \cdot x \in \mathbb{PE}[\overline{x}]. \tag{15}$$

So both addends are equivalent to poly-exponential expressions.   □

Example 15. *We show how to compute the closed forms for the variables w and x from Example 4. We first consider the assignment $w \leftarrow 2$, i.e., we want to compute a $q_w \in \mathbb{PE}[w, x, y, z]$ with $q_w[n/0] = w$ and $q_w = (m_w \cdot q_w + p_w)[n/n-1]$ for $n > 0$, where $m_w = 0$ and $p_w = 2$. According to (13) and (14), q_w is*

$$m_w^n \cdot w + \sum_{i=1}^{n} m_w^{n-i} \cdot p_w[n/i-1] = 0^n \cdot w + \sum_{i=1}^{n} 0^{n-i} \cdot 2 = [\![n = 0]\!] \cdot w + [\![n \neq 0]\!] \cdot 2.$$

For the assignment $x \leftarrow x + 2$, we search for a q_x such that $q_x[n/0] = x$ and $q_x = (m_x \cdot q_x + p_x)[n/n-1]$ for $n > 0$, where $m_x = 1$ and $p_x = 2$. By (13), q_x is

$$m_x^n \cdot x + \sum_{i=1}^{n} m_x^{n-i} \cdot p_x[n/i-1] = 1^n \cdot x + \sum_{i=1}^{n} 1^{n-i} \cdot 2 = x + 2 \cdot n.$$

The restriction to triangular matrices now allows us to generalize Lemma 14 to vectors of variables. The reason is that due to triangularity, the update of each program variable x_i only depends on the previous values of $x_1, \ldots, x_i$. So when regarding x_i, we can assume that we already know the closed forms for $x_1, \ldots, x_{i-1}$. This allows us to find closed forms for one variable after the other by applying Lemma 14 repeatedly. In other words, it allows us to find a vector $\overline{q}$ of poly-exponential expressions that satisfies

$$\overline{q}[n/0] = \overline{x} \quad \text{and} \quad \overline{q} = A\,\overline{q}[n/n-1] + \overline{a} \quad \text{for all } n > 0.$$

To prove this claim, we show the more general Lemma 16. For all $i_1, \ldots, i_k \in \{1, \ldots, m\}$, we define $[z_1, \ldots, z_m]_{i_1, \ldots, i_k} = [z_{i_1}, \ldots, z_{i_k}]$ (and the notation $\overline{y}_{i_1, \ldots, i_k}$ for column vectors is defined analogously). Moreover, for a matrix A, A_i is A's i^{th} row and $A_{i_1, \ldots, i_n; j_1, \ldots, j_k}$ is the matrix with rows $(A_{i_1})_{j_1, \ldots, j_k}, \ldots, (A_{i_n})_{j_1, \ldots, j_k}$.

So for $A = \begin{bmatrix} a_{1,1} & a_{1,2} & a_{1,3} \\ a_{2,1} & a_{2,2} & a_{2,3} \\ a_{3,1} & a_{3,2} & a_{3,3} \end{bmatrix}$, we have $A_{1,2;1,3} = \begin{bmatrix} a_{1,1} & a_{1,3} \\ a_{2,1} & a_{2,3} \end{bmatrix}$.

Lemma 16. (Closed Forms for Vectors of Variables). *If $\overline{x}$ is a vector of at least $d \geq 1$ pairwise different variables, $A \in \mathbb{Z}^{d \times d}$ is triangular with $A_{i;i} \geq 0$ for all $1 \leq i \leq d$, and $\overline{p} \in \mathbb{PE}[\overline{x}]^d$, then one can compute $\overline{q} \in \mathbb{PE}[\overline{x}]^d$ such that:*

$$\overline{q}[n/0] = \overline{x}_{1, \ldots, d} \quad and \tag{16}$$

$$\overline{q} = (A\,\overline{q} + \overline{p})[n/n-1] \quad for \text{ all } n > 0 \tag{17}$$

Proof. Assume that A is lower triangular (the case that A is upper triangular works analogously). We use induction on d. For any $d \geq 1$ we have:

$$
\begin{aligned}
&\overline{q} = (A\,\overline{q} + \overline{p})\,[n/n-1] \\
\Longleftrightarrow\ &\overline{q}_j = (A_j \cdot \overline{q} + \overline{p}_j)\,[n/n-1] && \text{for all } 1 \leq j \leq d \\
\Longleftrightarrow\ &\overline{q}_j = (A_{j;2,\ldots,d} \cdot \overline{q}_{2,\ldots,d} + A_{j;1} \cdot \overline{q}_1 + \overline{p}_j)\,[n/n-1] && \text{for all } 1 \leq j \leq d \\
\Longleftrightarrow\ &\overline{q}_1 = (A_{1;2,\ldots,d} \cdot \overline{q}_{2,\ldots,d} + A_{1;1} \cdot \overline{q}_1 + \overline{p}_1)\,[n/n-1]\ \wedge \\
&\overline{q}_j = (A_{j;2,\ldots,d} \cdot \overline{q}_{2,\ldots,d} + A_{j;1} \cdot \overline{q}_1 + \overline{p}_j)\,[n/n-1] && \text{for all } 1 < j \leq d \\
\Longleftrightarrow\ &\overline{q}_1 = (A_{1;1} \cdot \overline{q}_1 + \overline{p}_1)\,[n/n-1] && \wedge \\
&\overline{q}_j = (A_{j;2,\ldots,d} \cdot \overline{q}_{2,\ldots,d} + A_{j;1} \cdot \overline{q}_1 + \overline{p}_j)\,[n/n-1] && \text{for all } 1 < j \leq d
\end{aligned}
$$

The last step holds as A is lower triangular. By Lemma 14, we can compute a $\overline{q}_1 \in \mathbb{PE}[\overline{x}]$ that satisfies

$$
\overline{q}_1[n/0] = \overline{x}_1 \quad \text{and} \quad \overline{q}_1 = (A_{1;1} \cdot \overline{q}_1 + \overline{p}_1)\,[n/n-1] \quad \text{for all } n > 0.
$$

In the induction base $(d = 1)$, there is no j with $1 < j \leq d$. In the induction step $(d > 1)$, it remains to show that we can compute $\overline{q}_{2,\ldots,d}$ such that

$$
\overline{q}_j[n/0] = \overline{x}_j \quad \text{and} \quad \overline{q}_j = (A_{j;2,\ldots,d} \cdot \overline{q}_{2,\ldots,d} + A_{j;1} \cdot \overline{q}_1 + \overline{p}_j)\,[n/n-1]
$$

for all $n > 0$ and all $1 < j \leq d$, which is equivalent to

$$
\begin{aligned}
&\overline{q}_{2,\ldots,d}[n/0] = \overline{x}_{2,\ldots,d} \quad \text{and} \\
&\overline{q}_{2,\ldots,d} = \left(A_{2,\ldots,d;2,\ldots,d} \cdot \overline{q}_{2,\ldots,d} + \begin{bmatrix} A_{2;1} \\ \vdots \\ A_{d;1} \end{bmatrix} \cdot \overline{q}_1 + \overline{p}_{2,\ldots,d}\right)[n/n-1]
\end{aligned}
$$

for all $n > 0$. As $A_{j;1} \cdot \overline{q}_1 + \overline{p}_j \in \mathbb{PE}[\overline{x}]$ for each $2 \leq j \leq d$, the claim follows from the induction hypothesis. $\qquad\square$

Together, Lemmas 14 and 16 and their proofs give rise to the following algorithm to compute a solution for (16) and (17). It computes a closed form $\overline{q}_1$ for $\overline{x}_1$ as in the proof of Lemma 14, constructs the argument $\overline{p}$ for the recursive call based on A, $\overline{q}_1$, and the current value of $\overline{p}$ as in the proof of Lemma 16, and then determines the closed form for $\overline{x}_{2,\ldots,d}$ recursively.

Algorithm 3. closed_form

Input: $\overline{x}_{1,\ldots,d}$, $A \in \mathbb{Z}^{d \times d}$ where $A_{i;i} \geq 0$ for all $1 \leq i \leq d$, $\overline{p} \in \mathbb{PE}[\overline{x}]^d$
Result: $\overline{q} \in \mathbb{PE}[\overline{x}]^d$ which satisfies (16) & (17) for the given $\overline{x}$, A, and $\overline{p}$
$q \leftarrow$ symbolic_sum$(A_{1;1}, \overline{p}_1)$ (cf. Algorithm 2)
if $A_{1;1} = 0$ **then** $\overline{q}_1 \leftarrow [\![n = 0]\!] \cdot \overline{x}_1 + q$ **else** $\overline{q}_1 \leftarrow A_{1;1}^n \cdot \overline{x}_1 + q$ (cf. (13–15))
if $d > 1$ **then**
$\quad \overline{q}_{2,\ldots,d} \leftarrow$ closed_form$\left(\overline{x}_{2,\ldots,d},\ A_{2,\ldots,d;2,\ldots,d},\ \begin{bmatrix} A_{2;1} \\ \vdots \\ A_{d;1} \end{bmatrix} \cdot \overline{q}_1 + \overline{p}_{2,\ldots,d}\right)$
return $\overline{q}$

We can now prove the main theorem of this section.

Theorem 17 (Closed Forms for nnt-Loops). *One can compute a closed form for every nnt-loop. In other words, if $f : \mathbb{Z}^d \to \mathbb{Z}^d$ is the update function of an nnt-loop with the variables $\overline{x}$, then one can compute a $\overline{q} \in \mathbb{PE}[\overline{x}]^d$ such that $\overline{q}[n/c] = f^c(\overline{x})$ for all $c \in \mathbb{N}$.*

Proof. Consider an nnt-loop of the form (1). By Lemma 16, we can compute a $\overline{q} \subseteq \mathbb{PE}[\overline{x}]^d$ that satisfies

$$\overline{q}[n/0] = \overline{x} \quad \text{and} \quad \overline{q} = (A\,\overline{q} + \overline{a})\,[n/n-1] \quad \text{for all } n > 0.$$

We prove $f^c(\overline{x}) = \overline{q}[n/c]$ by induction on $c \in \mathbb{N}$. If $c = 0$, we get

$$f^c(\overline{x}) = f^0(\overline{x}) = \overline{x} = \overline{q}[n/0] = \overline{q}[n/c].$$

If $c > 0$, we get: $\begin{aligned} f^c(\overline{x}) &= A\,f^{c-1}(\overline{x}) + \overline{a} && \text{by definition of } f \\ &= A\,\overline{q}[n/c-1] + \overline{a} && \text{by the induction hypothesis} \\ &= (A\,\overline{q} + \overline{a})\,[n/c-1] \text{ as } \overline{a} \in \mathbb{Z}^d \text{ does not contain } n \\ &= \overline{q}[n/c] \end{aligned}$

$\square$

So invoking Algorithm 3 on $\overline{x}$, A, and $\overline{a}$ yields the closed form of an nnt-loop (1).

Example 18. *We show how to compute the closed form for Example 4. For*

$$y \leftarrow 2 \cdot w + 4 \cdot y - 2,$$

we obtain

$$\begin{aligned} q_y &= (4 \cdot q_y + 2 \cdot q_w - 2)\,[n/n-1] \\ &= 4^n \cdot y + \textstyle\sum_{i=1}^{n} 4^{n-i} \cdot (2 \cdot q_w - 2)\,[n/i-1] && \text{(by (13))} \\ &= y \cdot 4^n + \textstyle\sum_{i=1}^{n} 4^{n-i} \cdot ([\![n=0]\!] \cdot 2 \cdot w + [\![n \neq 0]\!] \cdot 4 - 2)\,[n/i-1] && \text{(see Example 15)} \\ &= q_0 + q_1 + q_2 + q_3 && \text{(see Example 13)} \end{aligned}$$

where $q_0 = y \cdot 4^n$. For $z \leftarrow x + 1$, we get

$$\begin{aligned} q_z &= (q_x + 1)\,[n/n-1] \\ &= 0^n \cdot z + \textstyle\sum_{i=1}^{n} 0^{n-i} \cdot (q_x + 1)\,[n/i-1] && \text{(by (13))} \\ &= [\![n=0]\!] \cdot z + [\![n \neq 0]\!] \cdot (q_x[n/n-1] + 1) \\ &= [\![n=0]\!] \cdot z + [\![n \neq 0]\!] \cdot ((x + 2 \cdot n)\,[n/n-1] + 1) && \text{(see Example 15)} \\ &= [\![n=0]\!] \cdot z + [\![n \neq 0]\!] \cdot (x - 1) + [\![n \neq 0]\!] \cdot 2 \cdot n. \end{aligned}$$

So the closed form of Example 4 for the values of the variables after n iterations is:

$$\begin{bmatrix} q_w \\ q_x \\ q_y \\ q_z \end{bmatrix} = \begin{bmatrix} [\![n=0]\!] \cdot w + [\![n \neq 0]\!] \cdot 2 \\ x + 2 \cdot n \\ q_0 + q_1 + q_2 + q_3 \\ [\![n=0]\!] \cdot z + [\![n \neq 0]\!] \cdot (x - 1) + [\![n \neq 0]\!] \cdot 2 \cdot n \end{bmatrix}$$

4 Deciding Non-Termination of nnt-Loops

Our proof uses the notion of *eventual non-termination* [4,14]. Here, the idea is to disregard the condition of the loop during a finite prefix of the program run.

Definition 19 (Eventual Non-Termination). *A vector $\overline{c} \in \mathbb{Z}^d$ witnesses eventual non-termination of (1) if*

$$\exists n_0 \in \mathbb{N}. \; \forall n \in \mathbb{N}_{>n_0}. \; \varphi[\overline{x}/f^n(\overline{c})].$$

If there is such a witness, then (1) is eventually non-terminating.

Clearly, (1) is non-terminating iff (1) is eventually non-terminating [14]. Now Theorem 17 gives rise to an alternative characterization of eventual non-termination in terms of the closed form $\overline{q}$ instead of $f^n(\overline{c})$.

Corollary 20 (Expressing Non-Termination with $\mathbb{PE}$). *If $\overline{q}$ is the closed form of (1), then $\overline{c} \in \mathbb{Z}^d$ witnesses eventual non-termination iff*

$$\exists n_0 \in \mathbb{N}. \; \forall n \in \mathbb{N}_{>n_0}. \; \varphi[\overline{x}/\overline{q}][\overline{x}/\overline{c}]. \tag{18}$$

Proof. Immediate, as $\overline{q}$ is equivalent to $f^n(\overline{x})$. $\qquad\square$

So to prove that termination of nnt-loops is decidable, we will use Corollary 20 to show that the existence of a witness for eventual non-termination is decidable. To do so, we first eliminate the factors $[\![\psi]\!]$ from the closed form $\overline{q}$. Assume that $\overline{q}$ has at least one factor $[\![\psi]\!]$ where ψ is non-empty (otherwise, all factors $[\![\psi]\!]$ are equivalent to 1) and let c be the maximal constant that occurs in such a factor. Then all addends $[\![\psi]\!] \cdot \alpha \cdot n^a \cdot b^n$ where ψ contains a positive literal become 0 and all other addends become $\alpha \cdot n^a \cdot b^n$ if $n > c$. Thus, as we can assume $n_0 > c$ in (18) without loss of generality, all factors $[\![\psi]\!]$ can be eliminated when checking eventual non-termination.

Corollary 21 Removing $[\![\psi]\!]$ from $\mathbb{PE}$s). *Let $\overline{q}$ be the closed form of an nnt-loop (1). Let $\overline{q}_{norm}$ result from $\overline{q}$ by removing all addends $[\![\psi]\!] \cdot \alpha \cdot n^a \cdot b^n$ where ψ contains a positive literal and by replacing all addends $[\![\psi]\!] \cdot \alpha \cdot n^a \cdot b^n$ where ψ does not contain a positive literal by $\alpha \cdot n^a \cdot b^n$. Then $\overline{c} \in \mathbb{Z}^d$ is a witness for eventual non-termination iff*

$$\exists n_0 \in \mathbb{N}. \; \forall n \in \mathbb{N}_{>n_0}. \; \varphi[\overline{x}/\overline{q}_{norm}][\overline{x}/\overline{c}]. \tag{19}$$

By removing the factors $[\![\psi]\!]$ from the closed form $\overline{q}$ of an nnt-loop, we obtain *normalized* poly-exponential expressions.

Definition 22 (Normalized $\mathbb{PE}$s). *We call $p \in \mathbb{PE}[\overline{x}]$ normalized if it is in*

$$\mathbb{NPE}[\overline{x}] = \left\{ \sum_{j=1}^{\ell} \alpha_j \cdot n^{a_j} \cdot b_j^n \; \middle| \; \ell, a_j \in \mathbb{N}, \; \alpha_j \in \mathbb{Af}[\overline{x}], \; b_j \in \mathbb{N}_{\geq 1} \right\}.$$

W.l.o.g., we always assume $(b_i, a_i) \neq (b_j, a_j)$ for all $i,j \in \{1,\ldots,\ell\}$ with $i \neq j$. We define $\mathbb{NPE} = \mathbb{NPE}[\varnothing]$, i.e., we have $p \in \mathbb{NPE}$ if $\alpha_j \in \mathbb{Q}$ for all $1 \leq j \leq \ell$.

Example 23. *We continue Example 18. By omitting the factors $[\![\psi]\!]$,*

$$q_w = [\![n = 0]\!] \cdot w + [\![n \neq 0]\!] \cdot 2 \qquad\qquad\qquad \text{becomes } 2,$$
$$q_z = [\![n = 0]\!] \cdot z + [\![n \neq 0]\!] \cdot (x - 1) + [\![n \neq 0]\!] \cdot 2 \cdot n \quad \text{becomes } x - 1 + 2 \cdot n,$$

and $q_x = x + 2 \cdot n$, $q_0 = y \cdot 4^n$, and $q_3 = \frac{2}{3} - \frac{2}{3} \cdot 4^n$ remain unchanged. Moreover,

$$q_1 = [\![n \neq 0]\!] \cdot \tfrac{1}{2} \cdot w \cdot 4^n \qquad\qquad \text{becomes } \tfrac{1}{2} \cdot w \cdot 4^n \qquad \text{and}$$
$$q_2 = [\![n > 1]\!] \cdot \left(-\tfrac{4}{3}\right) + [\![n > 1]\!] \cdot \tfrac{1}{3} \cdot 4^n \text{ becomes } \left(-\tfrac{4}{3}\right) + \tfrac{1}{3} \cdot 4^n.$$

Thus, $q_y = q_0 + q_1 + q_2 + q_3$ becomes

$$y \cdot 4^n + \tfrac{1}{2} \cdot w \cdot 4^n - \tfrac{4}{3} + \tfrac{1}{3} \cdot 4^n + \tfrac{2}{3} - \tfrac{2}{3} \cdot 4^n = 4^n \cdot \left(y - \tfrac{1}{3} + \tfrac{1}{2} \cdot w\right) - \tfrac{2}{3}.$$

Let $\sigma = \left[w/2, \, x/x + 2 \cdot n, \, y/4^n \cdot \left(y - \tfrac{1}{3} + \tfrac{1}{2} \cdot w\right) - \tfrac{2}{3}, \, z/x - 1 + 2 \cdot n\right]$. Then we get that Example 2 is non-terminating iff there are $w, x, y, z \in \mathbb{Z}, n_0 \in \mathbb{N}$ such that

$$(y + z)\,\sigma > 0 \wedge (-w - 2 \cdot y + x)\,\sigma > 0 \qquad\qquad \Longleftrightarrow$$
$$4^n \cdot \left(y - \tfrac{1}{3} + \tfrac{1}{2} \cdot w\right) - \tfrac{2}{3} + x - 1 + 2 \cdot n > 0 \qquad \wedge$$
$$-2 - 2 \cdot \left(4^n \cdot \left(y - \tfrac{1}{3} + \tfrac{1}{2} \cdot w\right) - \tfrac{2}{3}\right) + x + 2 \cdot n > 0 \Longleftrightarrow$$
$$p_1^\varphi > 0 \wedge p_2^\varphi > 0$$

holds for all $n > n_0$ where

$$p_1^\varphi = 4^n \cdot \left(y - \tfrac{1}{3} + \tfrac{1}{2} \cdot w\right) + 2 \cdot n + x - \tfrac{5}{3} \text{ and}$$
$$p_2^\varphi = 4^n \cdot \left(\tfrac{2}{3} - 2 \cdot y - w\right) + 2 \cdot n + x - \tfrac{2}{3}.$$

Recall that the loop condition φ is a conjunction of inequalities of the form $\alpha > 0$ where $\alpha \in \mathbb{Af}[\overline{x}]$. Thus, $\varphi[\overline{x}/\overline{q}_{norm}]$ is a conjunction of inequalities $p > 0$ where $p \in \mathbb{NPE}[\overline{x}]$ and we need to decide if there is an instantiation of these inequalities that is valid "for large enough n". To do so, we order the coefficients α_j of the addends $\alpha_j \cdot n^{a_j} \cdot b_j^n$ of normalized poly-exponential expressions according to the addend's asymptotic growth when increasing n. Lemma 24 shows that $\alpha_2 \cdot n^{a_2} \cdot b_2^n$ grows faster than $\alpha_1 \cdot n^{a_1} \cdot b_1^n$ iff $b_2 > b_1$ or both $b_2 = b_1$ and $a_2 > a_1$.

Lemma 24 (Asymptotic Growth). *Let $b_1, b_2 \in \mathbb{N}_{\geq 1}$ and $a_1, a_2 \in \mathbb{N}$. If $(b_2, a_2) >_{lex} (b_1, a_1)$, then $\mathcal{O}(n^{a_1} \cdot b_1^n) \subsetneq \mathcal{O}(n^{a_2} \cdot b_2^n)$. Here, $>_{lex}$ is the lexicographic order, i.e., $(b_2, a_2) >_{lex} (b_1, a_1)$ iff $b_2 > b_1$ or $b_2 = b_1 \wedge a_2 > a_1$.*

Proof. By considering the cases $b_2 > b_1$ and $b_2 = b_1$ separately, the claim can easily be deduced from the definition of $\mathcal{O}$. $\qquad\qquad\qquad\qquad\qquad \square$

Definition 25 (Ordering Coefficients). *Marked coefficients are of the form $\alpha^{(b,a)}$ where $\alpha \in \mathbb{Af}[\overline{x}], b \in \mathbb{N}_{\geq 1}$, and $a \in \mathbb{N}$. We define $\text{unmark}(\alpha^{(b,a)}) = \alpha$ and $\alpha_2^{(b_2,a_2)} \succ \alpha_1^{(b_1,a_1)}$ if $(b_2, a_2) >_{lex} (b_1, a_1)$. Let*

$$p = \sum_{j=1}^{\ell} \alpha_j \cdot n^{a_j} \cdot b_j^n \in \mathbb{NPE}[\overline{x}],$$

where $\alpha_j \neq 0$ *for all* $1 \leq j \leq \ell$. *The marked coefficients of* p *are*

$$\text{coeffs}(p) = \begin{cases} \left\{ 0^{(1,0)} \right\}, & \text{if } \ell = 0 \\ \left\{ \alpha_j^{(b_j,a_j)} \;\middle|\; 0 \leq j \leq \ell \right\}, & \text{otherwise.} \end{cases}$$

Example 26. *In Example 23 we saw that the loop from Example 2 is non-terminating iff there are* $w, x, y, z \in \mathbb{Z}, n_0 \in \mathbb{N}$ *such that* $p_1^{\varphi} > 0 \wedge p_2^{\varphi} > 0$ *for all* $n > n_0$. *We get:*

$$\text{coeffs}\left(p_1^{\varphi}\right) = \left\{ \left(y - \tfrac{1}{3} + \tfrac{1}{2} \cdot w\right)^{(4,0)}, 2^{(1,1)}, \left(x - \tfrac{5}{3}\right)^{(1,0)} \right\}$$

$$\text{coeffs}\left(p_2^{\varphi}\right) = \left\{ \left(\tfrac{2}{3} - 2 \cdot y - w\right)^{(4,0)}, 2^{(1,1)}, \left(x - \tfrac{2}{3}\right)^{(1,0)} \right\}$$

Now it is easy to see that the asymptotic growth of a normalized poly-exponential expression is solely determined by its $\succ$-maximal addend.

Corollary 27 (Maximal Addend Determines Asymptotic Growth). *Let* $p \in \text{NPE}$ *and let* $\max_{\succ}(\text{coeffs}(p)) = c^{(b,a)}$. *Then* $\mathcal{O}(p) = \mathcal{O}(c \cdot n^a \cdot b^n)$.

Proof. Clear, as $c \cdot n^a \cdot b^n$ is the asymptotically dominating addend of p. □

Note that Corollary 27 would be incorrect for the case $c = 0$ if we replaced $\mathcal{O}(p) = \mathcal{O}(c \cdot n^a \cdot b^n)$ with $\mathcal{O}(p) = \mathcal{O}(n^a \cdot b^n)$ as $\mathcal{O}(0) \neq \mathcal{O}(1)$. Building upon Corollary 27, we now show that, for large n, the sign of a normalized poly-exponential expression is solely determined by its $\succ$-maximal coefficient. Here, we define $\text{sign}(c) = -1$ if $c \in \mathbb{Q}_{<0} \cup \{-\infty\}$, $\text{sign}(0) = 0$, and $\text{sign}(c) = 1$ if $c \in \mathbb{Q}_{>0} \cup \{\infty\}$.

Lemma 28 (Sign of NPEs). *Let* $p \in \text{NPE}$. *Then* $\lim_{n \mapsto \infty} p \in \mathbb{Q}$ *iff* $p \in \mathbb{Q}$ *and otherwise,* $\lim_{n \mapsto \infty} p \in \{\infty, -\infty\}$. *Moreover, we have*

$$\text{sign}\left(\lim_{n \mapsto \infty} p\right) = \text{sign}(\text{unmark}(\max_{\succ}(\text{coeffs}(p)))).$$

Proof. If $p \notin \mathbb{Q}$, then the limit of each addend of p is in $\{-\infty, \infty\}$ by definition of NPE. As the asymptotically dominating addend determines $\lim_{n \mapsto \infty} p$ and $\text{unmark}(\max_{\succ}(\text{coeffs}(p)))$ determines the sign of the asymptotically dominating addend, the claim follows. □

Lemma 29 shows the connection between the limit of a normalized poly-exponential expression p and the question whether p is positive for large enough n. The latter corresponds to the existence of a witness for eventual non-termination by Corollary 21 as $\varphi[\overline{x}/\overline{q}_{norm}]$ is a conjunction of inequalities $p > 0$ where $p \in \text{NPE}[\overline{x}]$.

Lemma 29 (Limits and Positivity of NPEs). *Let* $p \in \text{NPE}$. *Then*

$$\exists n_0 \in \mathbb{N}. \; \forall n \in \mathbb{N}_{>n_0}. \; p > 0 \iff \lim_{n \mapsto \infty} p > 0.$$

Proof. By case analysis over $\lim_{n \mapsto \infty} p$.   □

Now we show that Corollary 21 allows us to decide eventual non-termination by examining the coefficients of normalized poly-exponential expressions. As these coefficients are in $\mathrm{Af}[\overline{x}]$, the required reasoning is decidable.

Lemma 30 (Deciding Eventual Positiveness of NPEs). *Validity of*

$$\exists \overline{c} \in \mathbb{Z}^d, n_0 \in \mathbb{N}. \; \forall n \in \mathbb{N}_{>n_0}. \; \bigwedge_{i=1}^{k} p_i[\overline{x}/\overline{c}] > 0 \tag{20}$$

where $p_1, \ldots, p_k \in \mathrm{NPE}[\overline{x}]$ *is decidable.*

Proof. For any p_i with $1 \leq i \leq k$ and any $\overline{c} \in \mathbb{Z}^d$, we have $p_i[\overline{x}/\overline{c}] \in \mathrm{NPE}$. Hence:

$$\begin{aligned}
&\exists n_0 \in \mathbb{N}. \; \forall n \in \mathbb{N}_{>n_0}. \; \bigwedge_{i=1}^{k} p_i[\overline{x}/\overline{c}] > 0 \\
\Longleftrightarrow \;&\bigwedge_{i=1}^{k} \exists n_0 \in \mathbb{N}. \; \forall n \in \mathbb{N}_{>n_0}. \; p_i[\overline{x}/\overline{c}] > 0 \\
\Longleftrightarrow \;&\bigwedge_{i=1}^{k} \lim_{n \mapsto \infty} p_i[\overline{x}/\overline{c}] > 0 &&\text{(by Lemma 29)} \\
\Longleftrightarrow \;&\bigwedge_{i=1}^{k} \mathrm{unmark}(\max_{\succ}(\mathrm{coeffs}(p_i[\overline{x}/\overline{c}]))) > 0 &&\text{(by Lemma 28)}
\end{aligned}$$

Let $p \in \mathrm{NPE}[\overline{x}]$ with $\mathrm{coeffs}(p) = \left\{ \alpha_1^{(b_1, a_1)}, \ldots, \alpha_\ell^{(b_\ell, a_\ell)} \right\}$ where $\alpha_i^{(b_i, a_i)} \succ \alpha_j^{(b_j, a_j)}$ for all $1 \leq i < j \leq \ell$. If $p[\overline{x}/\overline{c}] = 0$ holds, then $\mathrm{coeffs}(p[\overline{x}/\overline{c}]) = \{0^{(1,0)}\}$ and thus $\mathrm{unmark}(\max_{\succ}(\mathrm{coeffs}(p[\overline{x}/\overline{c}]))) = 0$. Otherwise, there is an $1 \leq j \leq \ell$ with $\mathrm{unmark}(\max_{\succ}(\mathrm{coeffs}(p[\overline{x}/\overline{c}]))) = \alpha_j[\overline{x}/\overline{c}] \neq 0$ and we have $\alpha_i[\overline{x}/\overline{c}] = 0$ for all $1 \leq i \leq j - 1$. Hence, $\mathrm{unmark}(\max_{\succ}(\mathrm{coeffs}(p[\overline{x}/\overline{c}]))) > 0$ holds iff $\bigvee_{j=1}^{\ell} \left(\alpha_j[\overline{x}/\overline{c}] > 0 \wedge \bigwedge_{i=0}^{j-1} \alpha_i[\overline{x}/\overline{c}] = 0 \right)$ holds, i.e., iff $[\overline{x}/\overline{c}]$ is a model for

$$\mathrm{max\_coeff\_pos}(p) = \bigvee_{j=1}^{\ell} \left(\alpha_j > 0 \wedge \bigwedge_{i=0}^{j-1} \alpha_i = 0 \right). \tag{21}$$

Hence by the considerations above, (20) is valid iff

$$\exists \overline{c} \in \mathbb{Z}^d. \; \bigwedge_{i=1}^{k} \mathrm{max\_coeff\_pos}(p_i)[\overline{x}/\overline{c}] \tag{22}$$

is valid. By multiplying each (in-)equality in (22) with the least common multiple of all denominators, one obtains a first-order formula over the theory of linear integer arithmetic. It is well known that validity of such formulas is decidable. □

Note that (22) is valid iff $\bigwedge_{i=1}^{k} \mathrm{max\_coeff\_pos}(p_i)$ is satisfiable. So to implement our decision procedure, one can use integer programming or SMT solvers to check satisfiability of $\bigwedge_{i=1}^{k} \mathrm{max\_coeff\_pos}(p_i)$. Lemma 30 allows us to prove our main theorem.

Theorem 31. *Termination of triangular loops is decidable.*

Proof. By Theorem 8, termination of triangular loops is decidable iff termination of nnt-loops is decidable. For an nnt-loop (1) we obtain a $\overline{q}_{norm} \in \mathrm{NPE}[\overline{x}]^d$ (see Theorem 17 and Corollary 21) such that (1) is non-terminating iff

$$\exists \overline{c} \in \mathbb{Z}^d, n_0 \in \mathbb{N}. \; \forall n \in \mathbb{N}_{>n_0}. \; \varphi[\overline{x}/\overline{q}_{norm}][\overline{x}/\overline{c}], \tag{20}$$

where φ is a conjunction of inequalities of the form $\alpha > 0$, $\alpha \in \mathbb{Af}[\overline{x}]$. Hence,

$$\varphi[\overline{x}/\overline{q}_{norm}][\overline{x}/\overline{c}] \;=\; \bigwedge_{i=1}^{k} p_i[\overline{x}/\overline{c}] > 0$$

where $p_1, \ldots, p_k \in \mathbb{NPE}[\overline{x}]$. Thus, by Lemma 30, validity of (20) is decidable. $\square$

The following algorithm summarizes our decision procedure.

Algorithm 4. Deciding Termination of Triangular Loops

Input: a triangular loop (1)
Result: $\top$ if (1) terminates, $\bot$ otherwise
- apply Definition 3 to (1), i.e.,
  $$\varphi \leftarrow \varphi \wedge \varphi[\overline{x}/A\,\overline{x} + \overline{a}]$$
  $$A \leftarrow A^2$$
  $$\overline{a} \leftarrow A\,\overline{a} + \overline{a}$$
- $\overline{q} \leftarrow$ closed_form$(\overline{x}, A, \overline{a})$ (cf. Algorithm 3)
- compute $\overline{q}_{norm}$ as in Corollary 21
- compute $\varphi[\overline{x}/\overline{q}_{norm}] = \bigwedge_{i=1}^{k} p_i > 0$
- compute $\phi = \bigwedge_{i=1}^{k} \text{max\_coeff\_pos}(p_i)$ (cf. (21))
- **if** ϕ *is satisfiable* **then return** $\bot$ **else return** $\top$

Example 32. *In Example 26 we showed that Example 2 is non-terminating iff*

$$\exists w, x, y, z \in \mathbb{Z}, \; n_0 \in \mathbb{N}. \; \forall n \in \mathbb{N}_{>n_0}. \; p_1^{\varphi} > 0 \wedge p_2^{\varphi} > 0$$

is valid. This is the case iff $\text{max\_coeff\_pos}(p_1) \wedge \text{max\_coeff\_pos}(p_2)$, *i.e.,*

$$y - \tfrac{1}{3} + \tfrac{1}{2}{\cdot}w > 0 \vee 2 > 0 \wedge y - \tfrac{1}{3} + \tfrac{1}{2}{\cdot}w = 0 \vee x - \tfrac{5}{3} > 0 \wedge 2 = 0 \wedge y - \tfrac{1}{3} + \tfrac{1}{2}{\cdot}w = 0$$
$$\wedge$$
$$\tfrac{2}{3} - 2{\cdot}y - w > 0 \vee 2 > 0 \wedge \tfrac{2}{3} - 2{\cdot}y - w = 0 \vee x - \tfrac{2}{3} > 0 \wedge 2 = 0 \wedge \tfrac{2}{3} - 2{\cdot}y - w = 0$$

is satisfiable. This formula is equivalent to $6 \cdot y - 2 + 3 \cdot w = 0$ *which does not have any integer solutions. Hence, the loop of Example 2 terminates.*

Example 33 shows that our technique does not yield witnesses for non-termination, but it only proves the existence of a witness for *eventual* non-termination. While such a witness can be transformed into a witness for non-termination by applying the loop several times, it is unclear how often the loop needs to be applied.

Example 33. *Consider the following non-terminating loop:*

$$\textbf{while } x > 0 \textbf{ do } \begin{bmatrix} x \\ y \end{bmatrix} \leftarrow \begin{bmatrix} x + y \\ 1 \end{bmatrix} \tag{23}$$

The closed form of x is $q = [\![n = 0]\!] \cdot x + [\![n \neq 0]\!] \cdot (x + y + n - 1)$. Replacing x with q_{norm} in $x > 0$ yields $x + y + n - 1 > 0$. The maximal marked coefficient of $x + y + n - 1$ is $1^{(1,1)}$. So by Algorithm 4, (23) does not terminate if $\exists x, y \in \mathbb{Z}. \, 1 > 0$ is valid. While $1 > 0$ is a tautology, (23) terminates if $x \leq 0$ or $x \leq -y$.

However, the final formula constructed by Algorithm 4 precisely describes all witnesses for eventual non-termination.

Lemma 34 (Witnessing Eventual Non-Termination). *Let (1) be a triangular loop, let $\overline{q}_{norm}$ be the normalized closed form of (2), and let*

$$(\varphi \wedge \varphi[\overline{x}/A\,\overline{x} + \overline{a}])\,[\overline{x}/\overline{q}_{norm}] = \bigwedge_{i=1}^{k} p_i > 0.$$

Then $\overline{c} \in \mathbb{Z}^d$ witnesses eventual non-termination of (1) iff $[\overline{x}/\overline{c}]$ is a model for

$$\bigwedge_{i=1}^{k} \mathrm{max\_coeff\_pos}(p_i).$$

5   Conclusion

We presented a decision procedure for termination of affine integer loops with triangular update matrices. In this way, we contribute to the ongoing challenge of proving the 15 years old conjecture by Tiwari [15] that termination of affine integer loops is decidable. After linear loops [4], loops with at most 4 variables [14], and loops with diagonalizable update matrices [3,14], triangular loops are the fourth important special case where decidability could be proven.

The key idea of our decision procedure is to compute *closed forms* for the values of the program variables after a symbolic number of iterations n. While these closed forms are rather complex, it turns out that reasoning about first-order formulas over the theory of linear integer arithmetic suffices to analyze their behavior for large n. This allows us to reduce (non-)termination of triangular loops to integer programming. In future work, we plan to investigate generalizations of our approach to other classes of integer loops.

References

1. Bagnara, R., Zaccagnini, A., Zolo, T.: The Automatic Solution of Recurrence Relations. I. Linear Recurrences of Finite Order with Constant Coefficients. Technical report. Quaderno 334. Dipartimento di Matematica, Università di Parma, Italy (2003). http://www.cs.unipr.it/Publications/
2. Ben-Amram, A.M., Genaim, S., Masud, A.N.: On the termination of integer loops. ACM Trans. Programm. Lang. Syst. **34**(4), 16:1–16:24 (2012). https://doi.org/10.1145/2400676.2400679
3. Bozga, M., Iosif, R., Konecný, F.: Deciding conditional termination. Logical Methods Comput. Sci. **10**(3) (2014). https://doi.org/10.2168/LMCS-10(3:8)2014
4. Braverman, M.: Termination of integer linear programs. In: Ball, T., Jones, R.B. (eds.) CAV 2006. LNCS, vol. 4144, pp. 372–385. Springer, Heidelberg (2006). https://doi.org/10.1007/11817963_34
5. Brockschmidt, M., Cook, B., Ishtiaq, S., Khlaaf, H., Piterman, N.: T2: temporal property verification. In: Chechik, M., Raskin, J.-F. (eds.) TACAS 2016. LNCS, vol. 9636, pp. 387–393. Springer, Heidelberg (2016). https://doi.org/10.1007/978-3-662-49674-9_22

6. Chen, Y.-F., et al.: Advanced automata-based algorithms for program termination checking. In: Foster, J.S., Grossman, D. (eds.) PLDI 2018, pp. 135–150 (2018). https://doi.org/10.1145/3192366.3192405

7. Chen, H.-Y., David, C., Kroening, D., Schrammel, P., Wachter, B.: Bit-precise procedure-modular termination analysis. ACM Trans. Programm. Lang. Syst. **40**(1), 1:1–1:38 (2018). https://doi.org/10.1145/3121136

8. D'Silva, V., Urban, C.: Conflict-driven conditional termination. In: Kroening, D., Păsăreanu, C.S. (eds.) CAV 2015. LNCS, vol. 9207, pp. 271–286. Springer, Cham (2015). https://doi.org/10.1007/978-3-319-21668-3_16

9. Frohn, F., Giesl, J.: Termination of triangular integer loops is decidable. In: CoRR abs/1905.08664 (2019). https://arxiv.org/abs/1905.08664

10. Frohn, F., Naaf, M., Hensel, J., Brockschmidt, M., Giesl, J.: Lower runtime bounds for integer programs. In: Olivetti, N., Tiwari, A. (eds.) IJCAR 2016. LNCS (LNAI), vol. 9706, pp. 550–567. Springer, Cham (2016). https://doi.org/10.1007/978-3-319-40229-1_37

11. Giesl, J., et al.: Analyzing program termination and complexity automatically with AProVE. J. Autom. Reasoning **58**(1), 3–31 (2017). https://doi.org/10.1007/s10817-016-9388-y

12. Larraz, D., Oliveras, A., Rodríguez-Carbonell, E., Rubio, A.: Proving termination of imperative programs using Max-SMT. In: Jobstmann, B., Ray, S. (eds.) FMCAD 2013, pp. 218–225 (2013). https://doi.org/10.1109/FMCAD.2013.6679413

13. Le, T.C., Qin, S., Chin, W.-N.: Termination and non-termination specification inference. In: Grove, D., Blackburn, S. (eds.) PLDI 2015, pp. 489–498 (2015). https://doi.org/10.1145/2737924.2737993

14. Ouaknine, J., Pinto, J.S., Worrell, J.: On termination of integer linear loops. In: Indyk, P. (ed.) SODA 2015, pp. 957–969 (2015). https://doi.org/10.1137/1.9781611973730.65

15. Tiwari, A.: Termination of linear programs. In: Alur, R., Peled, D.A. (eds.) CAV 2004. LNCS, vol. 3114, pp. 70–82. Springer, Heidelberg (2004). https://doi.org/10.1007/978-3-540-27813-9_6

9

Violat: Generating Tests of Observational Refinement for Concurrent Objects

Michael Emmi[1]([✉]) and Constantin Enea[2]

[1] SRI International, New York, NY, USA
michael.emmi@sri.com
[2] Université de Paris, IRIF, CNRS,
75013 Paris, France
cenea@irif.fr

Abstract. High-performance multithreaded software often relies on optimized implementations of common abstract data types (ADTs) like counters, key-value stores, and queues, i.e., *concurrent objects*. By using fine-grained and non-blocking mechanisms for efficient inter-thread synchronization, these implementations are vulnerable to violations of ADT-consistency which are difficult to detect: bugs can depend on specific combinations of method invocations and argument values, as well as rarely-occurring thread interleavings. Even given a bug-triggering interleaving, detection generally requires unintuitive test assertions to capture inconsistent combinations of invocation return values.

In this work we describe the Violat tool for generating tests that witness violations to atomicity, or weaker consistency properties. Violat generates self-contained and efficient programs that test *observational refinement*, i.e., substitutability of a given ADT with a given implementation. Our approach is both sound and complete in the limit: for every consistency violation there is a failed execution of some test program, and every failed test signals an actual consistency violation. In practice we compromise soundness for efficiency via random exploration of test programs, yielding probabilistic soundness instead. Violat's tests reliably expose ADT-consistency violations using off-the-shelf approaches to concurrent test validation, including stress testing and explicit-state model checking.

1 Introduction

Many mainstream software platforms including Java and .NET support multithreading to enable parallelism and reactivity. Programming multithreaded code effectively is notoriously hard, and prone to data races on shared memory accesses, or deadlocks on the synchronization used to protect accesses. Rather than confronting these difficulties, programmers generally prefer to leverage libraries providing *concurrent objects* [19,29], i.e., optimized thread-safe implementations of common abstract data types (ADTs) like counters, key-value stores, and queues. For instance, Java's concurrent collections include implementations which eschew the synchronization bottlenecks associated with lock-based mutual exclusion, opting instead for non-blocking mechanisms [28] provided by hardware operations like *atomic compare and exchange*.

Concurrent object implementations are themselves vulnerable to elusive bugs: even with effective techniques for exploring the space of thread interleavings, like stress testing or model checking [7,30,47], bugs often depend on specific combinations of method invocations and argument values. Furthermore, even recognizing whether a given execution is *correct* is non-trivial, since recognition generally requires unintuitive test assertions to identify inconsistent combinations of return values. Technically, correctness amounts to *observational refinement* [18,21,32], which captures the substitutability of an ADT with an implementation [23]: any combination of values admitted by a given implementation is also admitted by the given ADT specification.

In this work we describe an approach to generating tests of observational refinement for concurrent objects, as implemented by the Violat tool, which we use to discover violations to atomicity (and weaker consistency properties) in widely-used concurrent objects [9,10,12]. Unlike previous approaches based on *linearizability* [4,20,46], Violat generates self-contained test programs which do not require enumerating linearizations dynamically *per execution*, instead statically precomputing the ADT-admitted return-value outcomes *per test program*, once, prior to testing. Despite this optimization, the approach is both sound and complete, i.e., in the limit: for every consistency violation there is a failed execution of some test program, and every failed test witnesses an actual consistency violation. In practice, we compromise soundness for efficiency via random exploration of test programs, achieving probabilistic soundness instead.

Besides improving the efficiency of test execution, Violat's self-contained tests can be validated by both stress testers and model checkers, and double as regression and conformance tests. Our previous works [9,10,12] demonstrate that Violat's tests reliably expose ADT-consistency violations in Java implementations using the Java Concurrency Stress testing tool [42]. In particular, Violat has uncovered atomicity violations in over 50 methods from Java's concurrent collections; many of these violations seem to correspond with their documentations' mention of *weakly-consistent* behavior, while others indicate confirmed implementation bugs, which we have reported.

Previous work used Violat in empirical studies, without artifact evaluation [9,10,12]. This article is the first to consider Violat itself for evaluation, the first to describe its implementation and usage, and includes several novel extensions. For instance, in addition to stress testing, Violat now includes an integration with Java Pathfinder [47]; besides enabling complete systematic coverage of a given test program, this integration enables the output of the execution traces leading to consistency violations, thus facilitating diagnosis and repair. Furthermore, Violat is now capable of generating tests of any user-provided implementation, in addition to those distributed with Java.

2 Overview of Test Generation with Violat

Violat generates self-contained programs to test the observational refinement of a given concurrent object implementation with respect to its abstract data type (ADT), according to Fig. 1. While its methodology is fairly platform agnostic, Violat currently integrates with the Java platform. Accordingly, its input includes the fully-qualified name of a single Java class, which is assumed to be available either on the system classpath, or in a user-provided Java archive (JAR); its output is a sequence of Java classes which can be tested with off-the-shelf back-end analysis engines, including the Java Concurrency Stress testing tool [42] and Java Pathfinder [47]. Our current implementation integrates directly with both back-ends, and thus reports test results directly, signaling any discovered consistency violations.

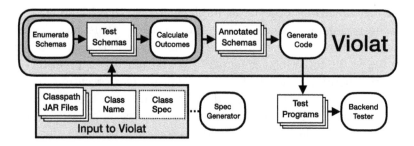

Fig. 1. Violat generates tests by enumerating program schemas invoking a given concurrent object, annotating those schemas with the expected outcomes of invocations according to ADT specifications, and translating annotated schemas to executable tests.

Violat generates tests according to a three-step pipeline. The first step, described in Sect. 3, enumerates test program *schemas*, i.e., concise descriptions of programs as parallel sequences of invocations of the given concurrent object's methods. For example, Fig. 2 lists several test schemas for Java's ConcurrentHashMap. The second step, described in Sect. 4, annotates each schema with a set of expected *outcomes*, i.e., the combinations of return values among the given schema's invocations which are admitted according to the given object's ADT specification. The final step, described in Sect. 5, translates each schema into a self-contained[1] Java class.

Technically, to guide the enumeration of schemas and calculation of outcomes, Violat requires a specification of the given concurrent object, describing constructor and method signatures. While this could be generated automatically from the object's bytecode, our current implementation asks the user to input this specification in JSON format. By additionally indicating whether methods are read-only or weakly-consistent, the user can provide additional hints to

---

[1] The generated class imports only a given concurrent object, and a few basic `java.util` classes.

improve schema enumeration and outcome calculation. For instance, excessive generation of programs with only read-only methods is unlikely to uncover consistency violations, and weakly-consistent ADT methods generally allow additional outcomes – see Emmi and Enea [12]. Furthermore, Violat attempts to focus the blame for discovered violations by constructing tests with a small number of specified *untrusted* methods, e.g., just one.

3   Test Enumeration

To enumerate test programs effectively, Violat considers a simple representation of program *schemas*, as depicted in Fig. 2. We write schemas with a familiar notation, as parallel compositions $\{\ldots\}||\{\ldots\}$ of method-invocation sequences. Intuitively, schemas capture parallel threads invoking sequences of methods of a given concurrent object. Besides the parallelism, these schemas include only trivial control and data flow. For instance, we exclude conditional statements and loops, as well as passing return values as arguments, in favor of straight-line code with literal argument values. Nevertheless, this simple notion is expressive enough to capture any possible *outcome*, i.e., combination of invocation return values, of programs with arbitrarily complex control flow, data flow, and synchronization. To see this, consider any outcome y admitted by some execution of a program with arbitrarily-complex control and data flow in which methods are invoked with argument values x, collectively. The schema in which each thread invokes the same methods of a thread of the original program with literal values x, collectively, is guaranteed to admit the same outcome y.

java.util.ConcurrentHashMap	
Schema / **Method**	Outcome
{ put(0,0); put(1,1); put(1,1)} || { put(0,1); **clear()** }	N,N,N,N,()
{ put(0,0); remove(1) } || { put(1,0); **contains**(0) }	N,0,N,F
{ get(1); **containsValue**(1) } || { put(1,1); put(0,1); put(1,0) }	1,F,N,N,1
{ put(0,1); put(1,0) } || { **elements()** }	N,N,[0]
{ put(0,1); put(1,0) } || { **entrySet()** }	N,N,[1=0]
{ put(1,1) } || { put(1,2); **isEmpty()** }	N,1,T
{ put(0,1); put(1,1) } || { **keySet()** }	N,N,[1]
{ **keys()** } || { put(0,1); put(1,1) }	[1],N,N
{ put(1,0); put(1,1); **mappingCount()** } || { remove(1) }	N,N,2,0
{ put(1,0); put(1,1); **size()** } || { remove(1) }	N,N,2,0
{ put(0,1); put(1,1) } || { **toString()** }	N,N,1=1
{ put(0,1); put(1,0) } || { **values()** }	N,N,[0]

Fig. 2. Program schemas generated by Violat for Java's ConcurrentHashMap class, along with outcomes which are observed in testing, yet not predicated by Violat.

For a given concurrent object, Violat enumerates schemas according to a few configurable parameters, including bounds on the number of threads, invocations, and (primitive) values. By default, Violat generates schemas with exactly 2 threads, between 3 and 6 invocations, and exactly 2 values. While our initial implementation enumerated schemas systematically according to a well-defined order, empirically we found that this strategy spends too much time in neighborhoods of uninteresting schemas, i.e., which do not expose violations. Ultimately we adopted a pseudorandom enumeration which constructs each schema independently by randomly choosing the number of threads, invocations, and values, within the given parameter bounds, and randomly populating threads with invocations. Methods are selected according to a weighted random choice, in which the weights of read-only and untrusted methods is 1; trusted mutator methods have weight 3. The read-only and trusted designations are provided by class specifications – see Sect. 2. Integer argument values are chosen randomly between 0 and 1, according to the default value bound; generic-typed arguments are assumed to be integers. Collection and map values are constructed from randomly-chosen integer values, up to size 2. In principle, all of these bounds are configurable, but we have found these defaults to work reasonably well.

Note that while the manifestation of a given concurrency bug can, in principle, rely on large bounds on threads, invocations, and values, recent studies demonstrate that the majority (96%) can be reproduced with just 2 threads [25]. Furthermore, while our current implementation adheres to the simple notion of schema in which all threads are execute in parallel, Violat can easily be extended to handle a more complex notion of schema in which threads are partially ordered, thus capturing arbitrary program synchronization. Nevertheless, this simple notion seems effective at exposing violations without requiring additional synchronization – see Emmi and Enea [12, Section 5.2].

4   Computing Expected Outcomes

To capture violations to observational refinement, Violat computes the set of *expected outcomes*, i.e., those admitted by a given concurrent object's abstract data type (ADT), for each program schema. Violat essentially follows the approach of Line-Up [4] by computing expected outcomes from sequential executions of the given implementation. While this approach assumes that the sequential behavior of a given implementation does adhere to its implicit ADT specification – and that the outcomes of concurrent executions are also outcomes of sequential executions – there is typically no practical alternative, since behavioral ADT specifications are rarely provided.

Violat computes the expected outcomes of a given schema once, by enumerating all possible shuffles of threads' invocations, and recording the return values of each shuffle when executed by the given implementation. For instance, there are 10 ways to shuffle the threads of the schema

```
{ get(1); containsValue(1) } || { put(1,1); put(0,1); put(1,0) }
```

from Fig. 2, including the sequence

```
get(1); put(1,1); put(0,1); put(1,0); containsValue(1).
```

Executing Java's ConcurrentHashMap on this shuffle yields the values null, null, null, 1, and true, respectively. To construct the generated outcome, Violat reorders the return values according to the textual order of their corresponding invocations in the given schema; since containsValue is second in this order, after get, the generated outcome is null, true, null, null, 1. Among the 10 possible shuffles of this schema, there are only four unique outcomes – shown later in Figs. 3 and 4.

```
public class Test {
  public static class StringResult5 {
    @sun.misc.Contended public String r1;
    @sun.misc.Contended public String r2;
    ...
    public String toString() {
      return r1 + ", " + ... + ", " + r5;
    }
  }

  static StringResult5 results;
  static HashSet<String> expected;
  static ConcurrentHashMap obj;
  static {
    obj = new ConcurrentHashMap();
    results = new StringResult5();
    expected = new HashSet<String>();
    expected.add("0, true, null, null, 1");
    expected.add("1, true, null, null, 1");
    expected.add("null, true, null, null, 1");
    expected.add("null, false, null, null, 1");
  }
```

```
// ...continued from the column to the left

  static String stringify(Object object) { ... }

  public static void main(String[] args) {
    Thread thread1 = new Thread(() -> {
      results.r1 = stringify(obj.get(1));
      results.r2 = stringify(obj.containsValue(1));
    });

    Thread thread2 = new Thread(() -> {
      results.r3 = stringify(obj.put(1, 1));
      results.r4 = stringify(obj.put(0, 1));
      results.r5 = stringify(obj.put(1, 0));
    });

    thread1.start(); thread2.start();
    thread1.join(); thread2.join();

    assert expected.contains(results.toString());
  }
}
```

Fig. 3. Code generated for the containsValue schema of Fig. 2 for Java Pathfinder. Code generation for jcstress similar, but conforms to the tool's idiomatic test format using decorators, and built-in thread and outcome management.

Note that in contrast to existing approaches based on *linearizability* [20], including Line-Up [4], which enumerate linearizations *per execution* of a given program, Violat only enumerates linearizations once *per schema*. This is made possible for two reasons. First, by considering simple test programs in which all invocations are known *statically*, we know the precise set of invocations (including argument values) to linearize even before executing the program. Second, according to sequential happens-before consistency [12], we consider the recording of real-time ordering among invocations infeasible on modern platforms like Java and C++11, which provide only weak ordering guarantees according to a platform-defined happens-before relation. This enables the static prediction of ordering constraints among invocations. While this static enumeration is also exponential in the number of invocations, it becomes an additive rather than multiplicative factor, amounting to significant performance gains in testing.

ConcurrentHashMap: containsValue { get(1); containsValue(1) } || { put(1,1); put(0,1); put(1,0) }			
outcome	atomic?	paths (JPF)	frequency (jcstress)
0, true, null, null, 1	✓	3	13,287
1, false, null, null, 1	✗	3	2
1, true, null, null, 1	✓	3	16,417
null, false, null, null, 1	✓	6	3,638,600
null, true, null, null, 1	✓	3	9,504

Fig. 4. Observed outcomes for the size method, recorded by Java Pathfinder and jcstress. Outcomes list return values in program-text order, e.g., get's return value is listed first.

5   Code Generation and Back-End Integrations

Once schemas are annotated with expected outcomes, the translation to actual test programs is fairly straightforward. Note that until this point, Violat is mainly agnostic to the underlying platform for which tests are being generated. The only exception is in computing the expected outcomes for schema linearizations, which executes the given concurrent object implementation as a stand-in oracle for its implicit ADT specification.

Figure 3 lists a simplification of the code generated for the containsValue schema of Fig. 2. The test program initializes a concurrent-object instance and a hash table of expected outcomes, then runs the schema's threads in parallel, recording the results of each invocation, and checks, after threads complete, whether the recorded outcome is expected. To avoid added inter-thread interference and the masking of potential weak-memory effects, each recorded result is isolated to a distinct cache line via Java's *contended* decorator. The actual generated code also includes exception handling, elided here for brevity.

Our current implementation of Violat integrates with two analysis back-ends: the Java Concurrency Stress testing tool [42] (jcstress) and Java Pathfinder [47]. Figure 4 demonstrates the results of each tool on the code generated from the containsValue schema of Fig. 2. Each tool observes executions with the 4 expected outcomes, as well as executions yielding an outcome that Violat does not predict, thus signaling a violation to observational refinement (and atomicity). Java Pathfinder explores 18 program paths in a few seconds – achieving exhaustiveness via partial-order reduction [16] – while jcstress explores nearly 4 million executions in 1 s, observing the unpredicted outcome only twice. Aside from this example, Violat has uncovered consistency violations in over 50 methods of Java's concurrent collections [9, 10, 12].

6 Usage

Violat is implemented as a Node.js command-line application, available from GitHub and npm.[2] Its basic functionality is provided by the command:

```
$ violat-validator ConcurrentHashMap.json
...
violation discovered
---
{ put(0,1); size(); contains(1) } || { put(0,0); put(1,1) }
---
outcome                 OK  frequency
---------------------   --  ---------
0, 0, true, null, null   X  7
0, 1, true, null, null   ✓  703
0, 2, true, null, null   ✓  94,636
null, 1, false, 1, null  ✓  2,263
null, 1, true, 1, null   ✓  59,917
null, 2, true, 1, null   ✓  4
...
```

reporting violations among 100 generated programs. User-provided classes, individual schemas, program limits, and particular back-ends can also be specified:

```
$ violat-validator MyConcurrentHashMap.json \
--jar MyCollections.jar \
--schema "{get(1); containsValue(1)} || {put(1,1); put(0,1); put(1,0)}" \
--max-programs 1000 \
--tester "Java Pathfinder"
```

A full selection of parameters is available from the usage instructions:

```
$ violat-validator --help
```

7 Related Work

Terragni and Pezzà survey several works on test generation for concurrent objects [45]. Like Violat, Ballerina [31] and ConTeGe [33] enumerate tests randomly, while ConSuite [43], AutoConTest [44], and CovCon [6] exploit static analysis to compute potential shared-memory access conflicts to reduce redundancy among generated tests. Similarly, Omen [35–38], Narada [40], Intruder [39], and Minion [41] reduce redundancy by anticipating potential concurrency faults during sequential execution. Ballerina [31] and ConTeGe [33] compute linearizations, but only identify generic faults like data races, deadlocks, and exceptions, being neither sound nor complete for testing observational refinement: fault-free executions with un-admitted return-value combinations are false negatives, while faulting executions with admitted return-value combinations are generally false positives – many non-blocking concurrent objects exhibit

---

[2] https://github.com/michael-emmi/violat.

data races by design. We consider the key innovations of these works, i.e., redundancy elimination, orthogonal and complementary to ours. While Pradel and Gross do consider subclass substitutability [34], they only consider programs with two concurrent invocations, and require exhaustive enumeration of the superclass's thread interleavings to calculate admitted outcomes. In contrast, Violat computes expected outcomes without interleaving method implementations, i.e., considering them atomic.

Others generate tests for memory consistency. TSOtool [17] generates random tests against the total-store order (TSO) model, while LCHECK [5] employs genetic algorithms. Mador-Haim et al. [26,27] generate litmus tests to distinguish several memory models, including TSO, partial-store order (PSO), relaxed-memory order (RMO), and sequential consistency (SC). CppMem [2] considers the C++ memory model, while Herd [1] considers release-acquire (RA) and Power in addition to the aforementioned models. McVerSi [8] employs genetic algorithms to enhance test coverage, while Wickerson et al. [48] leverage the Alloy model finder [22]. In some sense, these works generate tests of observational refinement for platforms implementing memory-system ADTs, i.e., with read and write operations, whereas Violat targets arbitrary ADTs, including collections with arbitrarily-rich sets of operations.

Violat more closely follows work on *linearizability* checking. Herlihy and Wing [20] established the soundness of linearizability for observational refinement, and Filipovic et al. [14] established completeness. Wing and Gong [49] developed a linearizability-checking algorithm, which was later adopted by Line-Up [4] and optimized by Lowe [24]; while Violat pays the exponential cost of enumerating linearizations once *per program*, these approaches pay that cost *per execution* – an exponential quantity itself. Gibbons and Korach [15] established NP-hardness of per-execution linearizability checking for arbitrary objects, while Emmi and Enea [11] demonstrate tractability for collections. Bouajjani et al. [3] propose polynomial-time approximations, and Emmi et al. [13] demonstrate efficient symbolic algorithms. Finally, Emmi and Enea [9,10,12] apply Violat to checking atomicity and weak-consistency of Java concurrent objects.

Acknowledgement. This work is supported in part by the European Research Council (ERC) under the European Union's Horizon 2020 research and innovation programme (grant No. 678177).

References

1. Alglave, J., Maranget, L., Tautschnig, M.: Herding cats: modelling, simulation, testing, and data mining for weak memory. ACM Trans. Program. Lang. Syst. **36**(2), 7:1–7:74 (2014). https://doi.org/10.1145/2627752
2. Batty, M., Owens, S., Sarkar, S., Sewell, P., Weber, T.: Mathematizing C++ concurrency. In: Ball, T., Sagiv, M. (eds.) Proceedings of the 38th ACM SIGPLAN-SIGACT Symposium on Principles of Programming Languages, POPL 2011, Austin, TX, USA, 26–28 January 2011, pp. 55–66. ACM (2011). https://doi.org/10.1145/1926385.1926394

3. Bouajjani, A., Emmi, M., Enea, C., Hamza, J.: Tractable refinement checking for concurrent objects. In: Rajamani, S.K., Walker, D. (eds.) Proceedings of the 42nd Annual ACM SIGPLAN-SIGACT Symposium on Principles of Programming Languages, POPL 2015, Mumbai, India, 15–17 January 2015, pp. 651–662. ACM (2015). https://doi.org/10.1145/2676726.2677002

4. Burckhardt, S., Dern, C., Musuvathi, M., Tan, R.: Line-up: a complete and automatic linearizability checker. In: Zorn, B.G., Aiken, A. (eds.) Proceedings of the 2010 ACM SIGPLAN Conference on Programming Language Design and Implementation, PLDI 2010, Toronto, Ontario, Canada, 5–10 June 2010, pp. 330–340. ACM (2010). https://doi.org/10.1145/1806596.1806634

5. Chen, Y., et al.: Fast complete memory consistency verification. In: 15th International Conference on High-Performance Computer Architecture (HPCA-15 2009), 14–18 February 2009, Raleigh, North Carolina, USA, pp. 381–392. IEEE Computer Society (2009). https://doi.org/10.1109/HPCA.2009.4798276

6. Choudhary, A., Lu, S., Pradel, M.: Efficient detection of thread safety violations via coverage-guided generation of concurrent tests. In: Uchitel, S., Orso, A., Robillard, M.P. (eds.) Proceedings of the 39th International Conference on Software Engineering, ICSE 2017, Buenos Aires, Argentina, 20–28 May 2017, pp. 266–277. IEEE/ACM (2017). https://doi.org/10.1109/ICSE.2017.32

7. Clarke, E.M., Grumberg, O., Peled, D.A.: Model Checking. MIT Press (2001). http://books.google.de/books?id=Nmc4wEaLXFEC

8. Elver, M., Nagarajan, V.: McVerSi: a test generation framework for fast memory consistency verification in simulation. In: 2016 IEEE International Symposium on High Performance Computer Architecture, HPCA 2016, Barcelona, Spain, 12–16 March 2016, pp. 618–630. IEEE Computer Society (2016). https://doi.org/10.1109/HPCA.2016.7446099

9. Emmi, M., Enea, C.: Exposing non-atomic methods of concurrent objects. CoRR abs/1706.09305 (2017). http://arxiv.org/abs/1706.09305

10. Emmi, M., Enea, C.: Monitoring weak consistency. In: Chockler, H., Weissenbacher, G. (eds.) CAV 2018. LNCS, vol. 10981, pp. 487–506. Springer, Cham (2018). https://doi.org/10.1007/978-3-319-96145-3_26

11. Emmi, M., Enea, C.: Sound, complete, and tractable linearizability monitoring for concurrent collections. PACMPL 2(POPL), 25:1–25:27 (2018). https://doi.org/10.1145/3158113

12. Emmi, M., Enea, C.: Weak-consistency specification via visibility relaxation. PACMPL 3(POPL), 60:1–60:28 (2019). https://dl.acm.org/citation.cfm?id=3290373

13. Emmi, M., Enea, C., Hamza, J.: Monitoring refinement via symbolic reasoning. In: Grove, D., Blackburn, S. (eds.) Proceedings of the 36th ACM SIGPLAN Conference on Programming Language Design and Implementation, Portland, OR, USA, 15–17 June 2015, pp. 260–269. ACM (2015). https://doi.org/10.1145/2737924.2737983

14. Filipovic, I., O'Hearn, P.W., Rinetzky, N., Yang, H.: Abstraction for concurrent objects. Theor. Comput. Sci. 411(51–52), 4379–4398 (2010). https://doi.org/10.1016/j.tcs.2010.09.021

15. Gibbons, P.B., Korach, E.: Testing shared memories. SIAM J. Comput. 26(4), 1208–1244 (1997). https://doi.org/10.1137/S0097539794279614

16. Godefroid, P. (ed.): Partial-Order Methods for the Verification of Concurrent Systems. LNCS, vol. 1032. Springer, Heidelberg (1996). https://doi.org/10.1007/3-540-60761-7

17. Hangal, S., Vahia, D., Manovit, C., Lu, J.J., Narayanan, S.: TSOtool: a program for verifying memory systems using the memory consistency model. In: 31st International Symposium on Computer Architecture (ISCA 2004), 19–23 June 2004, Munich, Germany, pp. 114–123. IEEE Computer Society (2004). https://doi.org/10.1109/ISCA.2004.1310768

18. He, J., Hoare, C.A.R., Sanders, J.W.: Data refinement refined resume. In: Robinet, B., Wilhelm, R. (eds.) ESOP 1986. LNCS, vol. 213, pp. 187–196. Springer, Heidelberg (1986). https://doi.org/10.1007/3-540-16442-1_14

19. Herlihy, M., Shavit, N.: The Art of Multiprocessor Programming. Morgan Kaufmann, San Mateo (2008)

20. Herlihy, M., Wing, J.M.: Linearizability: a correctness condition for concurrent objects. ACM Trans. Program. Lang. Syst. **12**(3), 463–492 (1990). https://doi.org/10.1145/78969.78972

21. Hoare, C.A.R., He, J., Sanders, J.W.: Prespecification in data refinement. Inf. Process. Lett. **25**(2), 71–76 (1987). https://doi.org/10.1016/0020-0190(87)90224-9

22. Jackson, D.: Alloy: a lightweight object modelling notation. ACM Trans. Softw. Eng. Methodol. **11**(2), 256–290 (2002). https://doi.org/10.1145/505145.505149

23. Liskov, B., Wing, J.M.: A behavioral notion of subtyping. ACM Trans. Program. Lang. Syst. **16**(6), 1811–1841 (1994). https://doi.org/10.1145/197320.197383

24. Lowe, G.: Testing for linearizability. Concurrency Comput. Pract. Exp. **29**(4) (2017). https://doi.org/10.1002/cpe.3928

25. Lu, S., Park, S., Seo, E., Zhou, Y.: Learning from mistakes: a comprehensive study on real world concurrency bug characteristics. In: Eggers, S.J., Larus, J.R. (eds.) Proceedings of the 13th International Conference on Architectural Support for Programming Languages and Operating Systems, ASPLOS 2008, Seattle, WA, USA, 1–5 March 2008, pp. 329–339. ACM (2008). https://doi.org/10.1145/1346281.1346323

26. Mador-Haim, S., Alur, R., Martin, M.M.K.: Generating litmus tests for contrasting memory consistency models. In: Touili, T., Cook, B., Jackson, P. (eds.) CAV 2010. LNCS, vol. 6174, pp. 273–287. Springer, Heidelberg (2010). https://doi.org/10.1007/978-3-642-14295-6_26

27. Mador-Haim, S., Alur, R., Martin, M.M.K.: Litmus tests for comparing memory consistency models: how long do they need to be? In: Stok, L., Dutt, N.D., Hassoun, S. (eds.) Proceedings of the 48th Design Automation Conference, DAC 2011, San Diego, California, USA, 5–10 June 2011, pp. 504–509. ACM (2011). https://doi.org/10.1145/2024724.2024842

28. Michael, M.M., Scott, M.L.: Simple, fast, and practical non-blocking and blocking concurrent queue algorithms. In: Burns, J.E., Moses, Y. (eds.) Proceedings of the Fifteenth Annual ACM Symposium on Principles of Distributed Computing, Philadelphia, Pennsylvania, USA, 23–26 May 1996, pp. 267–275. ACM (1996). https://doi.org/10.1145/248052.248106

29. Moir, M., Shavit, N.: Concurrent data structures. In: Mehta, D.P., Sahni, S. (eds.) Handbook of Data Structures and Applications. Chapman and Hall/CRC (2004). https://doi.org/10.1201/9781420035179.ch47

30. Musuvathi, M., Qadeer, S.: CHESS: systematic stress testing of concurrent software. In: Puebla, G. (ed.) LOPSTR 2006. LNCS, vol. 4407, pp. 15–16. Springer, Heidelberg (2007). https://doi.org/10.1007/978-3-540-71410-1_2

31. Nistor, A., Luo, Q., Pradel, M., Gross, T.R., Marinov, D.: Ballerina: automatic generation and clustering of efficient random unit tests for multithreaded code. In: Glinz, M., Murphy, G.C., Pezzè, M. (eds.) 34th International Conference on Software Engineering, ICSE 2012, 2–9 June 2012, Zurich, Switzerland, pp. 727–737. IEEE Computer Society (2012). https://doi.org/10.1109/ICSE.2012.6227145

32. Plotkin, G.D.: LCF considered as a programming language. Theor. Comput. Sci. **5**(3), 223–255 (1977). https://doi.org/10.1016/0304-3975(77)90044-5

33. Pradel, M., Gross, T.R.: Fully automatic and precise detection of thread safety violations. In: Vitek, J., Lin, H., Tip, F. (eds.) ACM SIGPLAN Conference on Programming Language Design and Implementation, PLDI 2012, Beijing, China, 11–16 June 2012, pp. 521–530. ACM (2012). https://doi.org/10.1145/2254064.2254126

34. Pradel, M., Gross, T.R.: Automatic testing of sequential and concurrent substitutability. In: Notkin, D., Cheng, B.H.C., Pohl, K. (eds.) 35th International Conference on Software Engineering, ICSE 2013, San Francisco, CA, USA, 18–26 May 2013, pp. 282–291. IEEE Computer Society (2013). https://doi.org/10.1109/ICSE.2013.6606574

35. Samak, M., Ramanathan, M.K.: Multithreaded test synthesis for deadlock detection. In: Black, A.P., Millstein, T.D. (eds.) Proceedings of the 2014 ACM International Conference on Object Oriented Programming Systems Languages & Applications, OOPSLA 2014, Part of SPLASH 2014, Portland, OR, USA, 20–24 October 2014, pp. 473–489. ACM (2014). https://doi.org/10.1145/2660193.2660238

36. Samak, M., Ramanathan, M.K.: Omen+: a precise dynamic deadlock detector for multithreaded java libraries. In: Cheung, S., Orso, A., Storey, M.D. (eds.) Proceedings of the 22nd ACM SIGSOFT International Symposium on Foundations of Software Engineering, (FS-22), Hong Kong, China, 16–22 November 2014, pp. 735–738. ACM (2014). https://doi.org/10.1145/2635868.2661670

37. Samak, M., Ramanathan, M.K.: Omen: a tool for synthesizing tests for deadlock detection. In: Black, A.P. (ed.) Conference on Systems, Programming, and Applications: Software for Humanity, SPLASH 2014, Portland, OR, USA, 20–24 October 2014, Companion Volume, pp. 37–38. ACM (2014). https://doi.org/10.1145/2660252.2664663

38. Samak, M., Ramanathan, M.K.: Trace driven dynamic deadlock detection and reproduction. In: Moreira, J.E., Larus, J.R. (eds.) ACM SIGPLAN Symposium on Principles and Practice of Parallel Programming, PPoPP 2014, Orlando, FL, USA, 15–19 February 2014, pp. 29–42. ACM (2014). https://doi.org/10.1145/2555243.2555262

39. Samak, M., Ramanathan, M.K.: Synthesizing tests for detecting atomicity violations. In: Nitto, E.D., Harman, M., Heymans, P. (eds.) Proceedings of the 2015 10th Joint Meeting on Foundations of Software Engineering, ESEC/FSE 2015, Bergamo, Italy, 30 August–4 September 2015, pp. 131–142. ACM (2015). https://doi.org/10.1145/2786805.2786874

40. Samak, M., Ramanathan, M.K., Jagannathan, S.: Synthesizing racy tests. In: Grove, D., Blackburn, S. (eds.) Proceedings of the 36th ACM SIGPLAN Conference on Programming Language Design and Implementation, Portland, OR, USA, 15–17 June 2015, pp. 175–185. ACM (2015). https://doi.org/10.1145/2737924.2737998

41. Samak, M., Tripp, O., Ramanathan, M.K.: Directed synthesis of failing concurrent executions. In: Visser, E., Smaragdakis, Y. (eds.) Proceedings of the 2016 ACM SIGPLAN International Conference on Object-Oriented Programming, Systems, Languages, and Applications, OOPSLA 2016, Part of SPLASH 2016, Ams-

terdam, The Netherlands, 30 October–4 November 2016, pp. 430–446. ACM (2016). https://doi.org/10.1145/2983990.2984040

42. Shipilev, A.: The java concurrency stress tests (2018). https://wiki.openjdk.java. net/display/CodeTools/jcstress

43. Steenbuck, S., Fraser, G.: Generating unit tests for concurrent classes. In: Sixth IEEE International Conference on Software Testing, Verification and Validation, ICST 2013, Luxembourg, Luxembourg, 18–22 March 2013, pp. 144–153. IEEE Computer Society (2013). https://doi.org/10.1109/ICST.2013.33

44. Terragni, V., Cheung, S.: Coverage-driven test code generation for concurrent classes. In: Dillon, L.K., Visser, W., Williams, L. (eds.) Proceedings of the 38th International Conference on Software Engineering, ICSE 2016, Austin, TX, USA, 14–22 May 2016, pp. 1121–1132. ACM (2016). https://doi.org/10.1145/2884781. 2884876

45. Terragni, V., Pezzè, M.: Effectiveness and challenges in generating concurrent tests for thread-safe classes. In: Huchard, M., Kästner, C., Fraser, G. (eds.) Proceedings of the 33rd ACM/IEEE International Conference on Automated Software Engineering, ASE 2018, Montpellier, France, 3–7 September 2018, pp. 64–75. ACM (2018). https://doi.org/10.1145/3238147.3238224

46. Vafeiadis, V.: Automatically proving linearizability. In: Touili, T., Cook, B., Jackson, P. (eds.) CAV 2010. LNCS, vol. 6174, pp. 450–464. Springer, Heidelberg (2010). https://doi.org/10.1007/978-3-642-14295-6_40

47. Visser, W., Pasareanu, C.S., Khurshid, S.: Test input generation with java pathfinder. In: Avrunin, G.S., Rothermel, G. (eds.) Proceedings of the ACM/SIGSOFT International Symposium on Software Testing and Analysis, ISSTA 2004, Boston, Massachusetts, USA, 11–14 July 2004, pp. 97–107. ACM (2004). https:// doi.org/10.1145/1007512.1007526

48. Wickerson, J., Batty, M., Sorensen, T., Constantinides, G.A.: Automatically comparing memory consistency models. In: Castagna, G., Gordon, A.D. (eds.) Proceedings of the 44th ACM SIGPLAN Symposium on Principles of Programming Languages, POPL 2017, Paris, France, 18–20 January 2017, pp. 190–204. ACM (2017). http://dl.acm.org/citation.cfm?id=3009838

49. Wing, J.M., Gong, C.: Testing and verifying concurrent objects. J. Parallel Distrib. Comput. **17**(1–2), 164–182 (1993). https://doi.org/10.1006/jpdc.1993.1015

10

Automated Parameterized Verification of CRDTs

Kartik Nagar$^{(\boxtimes)}$ and Suresh Jagannathan

Purdue University, West Lafayette, USA
{nagark,suresh}@cs.purdue.edu

Abstract. Maintaining multiple replicas of data is crucial to achieving scalability, availability and low latency in distributed applications. *Conflict-free Replicated Data Types* (CRDTs) are important building blocks in this domain because they are designed to operate correctly under the myriad behaviors possible in a weakly-consistent distributed setting. Because of the possibility of concurrent updates to the same object at different replicas, and the absence of any ordering guarantees on these updates, *convergence* is an important correctness criterion for CRDTs. This property asserts that two replicas which receive the same set of updates (in any order) must nonetheless converge to the same state. One way to prove that operations on a CRDT converge is to show that they commute since commutative actions by definition behave the same regardless of the order in which they execute. In this paper, we present a framework for automatically verifying convergence of CRDTs under different weak-consistency policies. Surprisingly, depending upon the consistency policy supported by the underlying system, we show that not all operations of a CRDT need to commute to achieve convergence. We develop a proof rule parameterized by a consistency specification based on the concepts of *commutativity modulo consistency policy* and *non-interference to commutativity*. We describe the design and implementation of a verification engine equipped with this rule and show how it can be used to provide the first automated convergence proofs for a number of challenging CRDTs, including sets, lists, and graphs.

1 Introduction

For distributed applications, keeping a single copy of data at one location or multiple fully-synchronized copies (i.e. state-machine replication) at different locations, makes the application susceptible to loss of availability due to network and machine failures. On the other hand, having multiple un-synchronized replicas of the data results in high availability, fault tolerance and uniform low latency, albeit at the expense of consistency. In the latter case, an update issued at one replica can be asynchronously transmitted to other replicas, allowing the system to operate continuously even in the presence of network or node failures [8]. However, mechanisms must now be provided to ensure replicas are kept consistent with each other in the face of concurrent updates and arbitrary re-ordering of such updates by the underlying network.

Over the last few years, *Conflict-free Replicated Datatypes* (CRDTs) [19–21] have emerged as a popular solution to this problem. In op-based CRDTs, when an operation on a CRDT instance is issued at a replica, an *effector* (basically an update function) is generated locally, which is then asynchronously transmitted (and applied) at all other replicas.[1] Over the years, a number of CRDTs have been developed for common datatypes such as maps, sets, lists, graphs, etc.

The primary correctness criterion for a CRDT implementation is *convergence* (sometimes called *strong eventual consistency* [9,20] (SEC)): two replicas which have received the same set of effectors must converge to the same CRDT state. Because of the weak default guarantees assumed to be provided by the underlying network, however, we must consider the possibility that effectors can be applied in arbitrary order on different replicas, complicating correctness arguments. This complexity is further exacerbated because CRDTs impose no limitations on how often they are invoked, and may assume additional properties on network behaviour [14] that must be taken into account when formulating correctness arguments.

Given these complexities, verifying convergence of operations in a replicated setting has proven to be challenging and error-prone [9]. In response, several recent efforts have used mechanized proof assistants to yield formal machine-checked proofs of correctness [9,24]. While mechanization clearly offers stronger assurance guarantees than handwritten proofs, it still demands substantial manual proof engineering effort to be successful. In particular, correctness arguments are typically given in terms of constraints on CRDT states that must be satisfied by the underlying network model responsible for delivering updates performed by other replicas. Relating the state of a CRDT at one replica with the visibility properties allowed by the underlying network has typically involved constructing an intricate simulation argument or crafting a suitably precise invariant to establish convergence. This level of sophisticated reasoning is required for every CRDT and consistency model under consideration. There is a notable lack of techniques capable of reasoning about CRDT correctness under different weak consistency policies, even though such techniques exist for other correctness criteria such as preservation of state invariants [10,11] or serializability [4,16] under weak consistency.

To overcome these challenges, we propose a novel *automated* verification strategy that does not require complex proof-engineering of handcrafted simulation arguments or invariants. Instead, our methodology allows us to directly connect constraints on events imposed by the consistency model with constraints on states required to prove convergence. Consistency model constraints are extracted from an axiomatization of network behavior, while state constraints are generated using reasoning principles that determine the *commutativity* and *non-interference* of sequences of effectors, subject to these consistency constraints. Both sets of constraints can be solved using off-the-shelf theorem

---

[1] In this work, we focus on the op-based CRDT model; however, our technique naturally extends to state-based CRDTs since they can be emulated by an op-based model [20].

provers. Because an important advantage of our approach is that it is parametric on weak consistency schemes, we are able to analyze the problem of CRDT convergence under widely different consistency policies (e.g., eventual consistency, causal consistency, parallel snapshot isolation (PSI) [23], among others), and for the first time verify CRDT convergence under such stronger models (efficient implementations of which are supported by real-world data stores). A further pleasant by-product of our approach is a pathway to take advantage of such stronger models to simplify existing CRDT designs and allow composition of CRDTs to yield new instantiations for more complex datatypes.

The paper makes the following contributions:

1. We present a proof methodology for verifying the correctness of CRDTs amenable to automated reasoning.
2. We allow the proof strategy to be parameterized on a weak consistency specification that allows us to state correctness arguments for a CRDT based on constraints imposed by these specifications.
3. We experimentally demonstrate the effectiveness of our proposed verification strategy on a number of challenging CRDT implementations across multiple consistency schemes.

Collectively, these contributions yield (to the best of our knowledge) the first automated and parameterized proof methodology for CRDT verification.

The remainder of the paper is organized as follows. In the next section, we provide further motivation and intuition for our approach. Section 3 formalizes the problem definition, providing an operational semantics and axiomatizations of well-known consistency specifications. Section 4 describes our proof strategy for determining CRDT convergence that is amenable to automated verification. Section 5 provides details about our implementation and experimental results justifying the effectiveness of our framework. Section 6 presents related work and conclusions.

2 Illustrative Example

$$S \in \mathbb{P}(E)$$
$$\texttt{Add(a):S} \quad \lambda S'.S' \cup \{a\}$$
$$\texttt{Remove(a):S} \quad \lambda S'.S' \setminus \{a\}$$
$$\texttt{Lookup(a):S} \quad a \in S$$

Fig. 1. A simple Set CRDT definition.

We illustrate our approach using a Set CRDT specification as a running example. A CRDT $(\Sigma, O, \sigma_{\text{init}})$ is characterized by a set of states Σ, a set of operations O and an initial state $\sigma_{\text{init}} \in \Sigma$, where each operation $o \in O$ is a function with signature $\Sigma \to (\Sigma \to \Sigma)$. The state of a CRDT is replicated, and when operation o is issued at a replica with state σ, the effector $o(\sigma)$ is generated, which is immediately applied at the local replica (which we also call the *source* replica) and transmitted to all other replicas, where it is subsequently applied upon receipt.

Additional constraints on the order in which effectors can be received and applied at different replicas are specified by a consistency policy, discussed below. In the absence of any such additional constraints, however, we assume the underlying network only offers *eventually consistent* guarantees - all replicas eventually receive all effectors generated by all other replicas, with no constraints on the order in which these effectors are received.

Consider the simple **Set** CRDT definition shown in Fig. 1. Let E be an arbitrary set of elements. The state space Σ is $\mathbb{P}(E)$. `Add(a):S` denotes the operation `Add(a)` applied on a replica with state `S`, which generates an effector which simply adds `a` to the state of all other replicas it is applied to. Similarly, `Remove(a):S` generates an effector that removes `a` on all replicas to which it is applied. `Lookup(a):S` is a query operation which checks whether the queried element is present in the source replica `S`.

A CRDT is *convergent* if during any execution, any two replicas which have received the same set of effectors have the same state. Our strategy to prove convergence is to show that any two effectors of the CRDT pairwise commute with each other modulo a consistency policy, i.e. for two effectors e_1 and e_2, $e_1 \circ e_2 = e_2 \circ e_1$. Our simple **Set** CRDT clearly does not converge when executed on an eventually consistent data store since the effectors $e_1 = \texttt{Add(a)}:S_1$ and $e_2 = \texttt{Remove(a)}:S_2$ do not commute, and the semantics of eventual consistency imposes no additional constraints on the visibility or ordering of these operations that could be used to guarantee convergence. For example, if e_1 is applied to the state at some replica followed by the application of e_2, the resulting state does not include the element `a`; conversely, applying e_2 to a state at some replica followed by e_1 leads to a state that does contain the element `a`.

However, while commutativity is a sufficient property to show convergence, it is not always a necessary one. In particular, different consistency models impose different constraints on the visibility and ordering of effectors that can obviate the need to reason about their commutativity. For example, if the consistency model enforces `Add(a)` and `Remove(a)` effectors to be applied in the same order at all replicas, then the **Set** CRDT will converge. As we will demonstrate later, the PSI consistency model

```
S ∈ ℙ(E × I)
Add(a,i):S
    λS'.S'∪{(a,i)}
Remove(a):S
    λS'.S'\{(a,i):(a,i)∈S}
Lookup(a):S
    ∃(a,i)∈A
```

Fig. 2. A definition of an ORSet CRDT.

exactly matches this requirement. To further illustrate this, consider the definition of the **ORSet** CRDT shown in Fig. 2. Here, every element is tagged with a unique identifier (coming from the set I). `Add(a,i):S` simply adds the element `a` tagged with `i`[2], while `Remove(a):S` returns an effector that when applied to a replica state will remove all tagged versions of `a` that were present in `S`, the source replica.

---

[2] Assume that every call to **Add** uses a unique identifier, which can be easily arranged, for example by keeping a local counter at every replica which is incremented at every operation invocation, and using the id of the replica and the value of the counter as a unique identifier.

Suppose e_1 =Add(a,i):S_1 and e_2 =Remove(a):S_2. If it is the case that S_2 does not contain (a,i), then these two effectors are guaranteed to commute because e_2 is unaware of (a,i) and thus behaves as a no-op with respect to effector e_1 when it is applied to any replica state. Suppose, however, that e_1's effect was visible to e_2; in other words, e_1 is applied to S_2 before e_2 is generated. There are two possible scenarios that must be considered. (1) Another replica (call it S') has e_2 applied before e_1. Its final state reflects the effect of the Add operation, while S_2's final state reflects the effect of applying the Remove; clearly, convergence is violated in this case. (2) All replicas apply e_1 and e_2 in the same order; the interesting case here is when the effect of e_1 is always applied before e_2 on every replica. The constraint that induces an effector order between e_1 and e_2 on every replica as a consequence of e_1's visibility to e_2 on S_2 is supported by a causally consistent distributed storage model. Under causal consistency, whenever e_2 is applied to a replica state, we are guaranteed that e_1's effect, which adds (a,i) to the state, would have occurred. Thus, even though e_1 and e_2 do not commute when applied to an arbitrary state, their execution under causal consistency nonetheless allows us to show that all replica states converge. The essence of our proof methodology is therefore to reason about *commutativity modulo consistency* - it is only for those CRDT operations unaffected by the constraints imposed by the consistency model that proving commutativity is required. Consistency properties that affect the visibility of effectors are instead used to guide and simplify our analysis. Applying this notion to pairs of effectors in arbitrarily long executions requires incorporating commutativity properties under a more general induction principle to allow us to generalize the commutativity of effectors in bounded executions to the unbounded case. This generalization forms the heart of our automated verification strategy.

```
S∈ ℙ(E × I) × ℙ(E × I)
Add(a,i):(A,R)
   λ(A',R').(A'∪{(a,i)},R')

Remove(a):(A,R)
   λ(A',R').(A',R'∪{(a,i):(a,i)∈A}

Lookup(a):(A,R)
   ∃(a,i)∈A∧(a,i)∉R
```

Fig. 3. A variant of the ORSet using tombstones.

Figure 3 defines an ORSet with "tombstone" markers used to keep track of deleted elements in a separate set. Our proof methodology is sufficient to automatically show that this CRDT converges under EC.

3 Problem Definition

In this section, we formalize the problem of determining convergence in CRDTs parametric to a weak consistency policy. First, we define a general operational semantics to describe all valid executions of a CRDT under any given weak consistency policy. As stated earlier, a CRDT program $\mathcal{P}$ is specified by the tuple $(\Sigma, O, \sigma_{init})$. Here, we find it to convenient to define an operation $o \in O$ as a function $(\Sigma \times (\Sigma \to \Sigma)^*) \to (\Sigma \to \Sigma)$. Instead of directly taking as input a generating state, operations are now defined to take as input a start state and a sequence of effectors. The intended semantics is that the sequence of effectors would be applied to the start state to obtain the generating state. Using this syntax allows us simplify the presentation of the proof methodology in the next section, since we can abstract a history of effectors into an equivalent start state.

Formally, if $\hat{o} : \Sigma \to (\Sigma \to \Sigma)$ was the original op-based definition, then we define the operation $o : (\Sigma \times (\Sigma \to \Sigma)^*) \to (\Sigma \to \Sigma)$ as follows:

$$\forall \sigma. \quad o(\sigma, \epsilon) = \hat{o}(\sigma)$$
$$\forall \sigma, \pi, f. \ \ o(\sigma, \pi f) = o(f(\sigma), \pi)$$

Note that ϵ indicates the empty sequence. Hence, for all states σ and sequence of functions π, we have $o(\sigma, \pi) = \hat{o}(\pi(\sigma))$.

To define the operational semantics, we abstract away from the concept of replicas, and instead maintain a global pool of effectors. A new CRDT operation is executed against a CRDT state obtained by first selecting a subset of effectors from the global pool and then applying the elements in that set in some non-deterministically chosen permutation to the initial CRDT state. The choice of effectors and their permutation must obey the weak consistency policy specification. Given a CRDT $\mathcal{P} = (\Sigma, O, \sigma_{\text{init}})$ and a weak consistency policy Ψ, we define a **labeled transition system** $\mathcal{S}_{\mathcal{P}, \Psi} = (\mathcal{C}, \to)$, where $\mathcal{C}$ is a set of configurations and $\to$ is the transition relation. A **configuration** $c = (\Delta, \text{vis}, \text{eo})$ consists of three components: Δ is a set of events, $\text{vis} \subseteq \Delta \times \Delta$ is a *visibility* relation, and $\text{eo} \subseteq \Delta \times \Delta$ is a global *effector order* relation (constrained to be anti-symmetric). An **event** $\eta \in \Delta$ is a tuple $(\text{eid}, o, \sigma_s, \Delta_r, \text{eo})$ where eid is a unique event id, $o \in O$ is a CRDT operation, $\sigma_s \in \Sigma$ is the start CRDT state, Δ_r is the set of events visible to η (also called the history of η), and eo is a total order on the events in Δ_r (also called the local effector order relation). We assume projection functions for each component of an event (for example $\sigma_s(\eta)$ projects the start state of the event η).

Given an event $\eta = (\text{eid}, o, \sigma_s, \Delta_r, \text{eo})$, we define η^e to be the **effector** associated with the event. This effector is obtained by executing the CRDT operation o against the start CRDT state σ_s and the sequence of effectors obtained from the events in Δ_r arranged in the reverse order of eo. Formally,

$$\eta^e = \begin{cases} o(\sigma_s, \epsilon) & \text{if } \Delta_r = \phi \\ o(\sigma_s, \prod_{i=1}^{k} \eta^e_{P(i)}) & \text{if } \Delta_r = \{\eta_1, \ldots, \eta_k\} \text{ where } P : \{1, \ldots, k\} \to \{1, \ldots, k\} \\ & \forall i, j.i < j \Rightarrow (\eta_{P(j)}, \eta_{P(i)}) \in \text{eo} \end{cases}$$

$$(1)$$

In the above definition, when Δ_r is non-empty, we define a permutation P of the events in Δ_r such that the permutation order is the inverse of the effector order eo. This ensures that if $(\eta_i, \eta_j) \in \text{eo}$, then η^e_j occurs before η^e_i in the sequence passed to the CRDT operation o, effectively applying η^e_i before η^e_j to obtain the generating state for o.

The following rule describes the transitions allowed in $\mathcal{S}_{\mathcal{P},\Psi}$:

$$\frac{\begin{array}{c} \Delta_r \subseteq \Delta \quad o \in O \quad \sigma_s \in \Sigma \quad \mathsf{eo}_r \text{ is a total order on } \Delta_r \\ \mathsf{eo} \subseteq \mathsf{eo}_r \quad \text{fresh id} \quad \eta = (\mathsf{id}, o, \sigma_s, \Delta_r, \mathsf{eo}) \\ \Delta' = \Delta \cup \{\eta\} \quad \mathsf{vis}' = \mathsf{vis} \cup \{(\eta', \eta) \mid \eta' \in \Delta_r\} \quad \Psi(\Delta', \mathsf{vis}', \mathsf{eo}') \end{array}}{(\Delta, \mathsf{vis}, \mathsf{eo}) \xrightarrow{\eta} (\Delta', \mathsf{vis}', \mathsf{eo}')}$$

The rule describes the effect of executing a new operation o, which begins by first selecting a subset of already completed events (Δ_r) and a total order eo_r on these events which obeys the global effector order eo. This mimics applying the operation o on an arbitrary replica on which the events of Δ_r have been applied in the order eo_r. A new event (η) corresponding to the issued operation o is computed, which is used to label the transition and is also added to the current configuration. All the events in Δ_r are visible to the new event η, which is reflected in the new visibility relation vis'. The system moves to the new configuration $(\Delta', \mathsf{vis}', \mathsf{eo}')$ which must satisfy the consistency policy Ψ. Note that even though the general transition rule allows the event to pick any arbitrary start state σ_s, we restrict the start state of all events in a **well-formed execution** to be the initial CRDT state σ_{init}, i.e. the state in which all replicas begin their execution. A trace of $\mathcal{S}_{\mathcal{P},\Psi}$ is a sequence of transitions. Let $[\![\mathcal{S}_{\mathcal{P},\Psi}]\!]$ be the set of all finite traces. Given a trace τ, $L(\tau)$ denotes all events (i.e. labels) in τ.

Definition 1 (Well-formed Execution). *A trace* $\tau \in [\![\mathcal{S}_{\mathcal{P},\Psi}]\!]$ *is a well-formed execution if it begins from the empty configuration* $C_{\mathsf{init}} = (\{\}, \{\}, \{\})$ *and* $\forall \eta \in L(\tau), \ \sigma_s(\eta) = \sigma_{\mathsf{init}}$.

Let $\mathcal{WF}(\mathcal{S}_{\mathcal{P},\Psi})$ denote all well-formed executions of $\mathcal{S}_{\mathcal{P},\Psi}$. The **consistency policy** $\Psi(\Delta, \mathsf{vis}, \mathsf{eo})$ is a formula constraining the events in Δ and relations vis and eo defined over these events. Below, we illustrate how to express certain well-known consistency policies in our framework:

Consistency scheme	$\Psi(\Delta, \mathsf{vis}, \mathsf{eo})$
Eventual Consistency [3]	$\forall \eta, \eta' \in \Delta.\neg\mathsf{eo}(\eta, \eta')$
Causal Consistency [14]	$\forall \eta, \eta' \in \Delta.\mathsf{vis}(\eta, \eta') \Leftrightarrow \mathsf{eo}(\eta, \eta')$
	$\wedge \forall \eta, \eta', \eta'' \in \Delta.\mathsf{vis}(\eta, \eta') \wedge \mathsf{vis}(\eta', \eta'') \Rightarrow \mathsf{vis}(\eta, \eta'')$
RedBlue Consistency (O_r) [13]	$\forall \eta, \eta' \in \Delta.o(\eta) \in O_r \wedge o(\eta') \in O_r \wedge \mathsf{vis}(\eta, \eta') \Leftrightarrow \mathsf{eo}(\eta, \eta')$
	$\wedge \forall \eta, \eta' \in \Delta.o(\eta) \in O_r \wedge o(\eta') \in O_r \Rightarrow \mathsf{vis}(\eta, \eta') \vee \mathsf{vis}(\eta', \eta)$
Parallel Snapshot Isolation [23]	$\forall \eta, \eta' \in \Delta.(\mathsf{Wr}(\eta^e) \cap \mathsf{Wr}(\eta'^e) \neq \phi \wedge \mathsf{vis}(\eta, \eta')) \Leftrightarrow \mathsf{eo}(\eta, \eta')$
	$\wedge \forall \eta, \eta' \in \Delta.\mathsf{Wr}(\eta^e) \cap \mathsf{Wr}(\eta'^e) \neq \phi \Rightarrow \mathsf{vis}(\eta, \eta') \vee \mathsf{vis}(\eta', \eta)$
Strong Consistency	$\forall \eta, \eta' \in \Delta.\mathsf{vis}(\eta, \eta') \Leftrightarrow \mathsf{eo}(\eta, \eta')$
	$\wedge \forall \eta, \eta' \in \Delta.\mathsf{vis}(\eta, \eta') \vee \mathsf{vis}(\eta', \eta)$

For Eventual Consistency (EC) [3], we do not place any constraints on the visibility order and require the global effector order to be empty. This reflects the fact that in EC, any number of events can occur concurrently at different replicas, and hence a replica can witness any arbitrary subset of events which may be applied in any order. In Causal Consistency (CC) [14], an event is applied at a replica only if all causally dependent events have already been applied. An event η_1 is causally dependent on η_2 if η_1 was generated at a replica where either η_2 or any other event causally dependent on η_2 had already been applied. The visibility relation vis captures causal dependency, and by making vis transitive, we ensure that all causal dependencies of events in Δ_r are also present in Δ_r (this is because in the transition rule, Ψ is checked on the updated visibility relation which relates events in Δ_r with the newly generated event). Further, causally dependent events must be applied in the same order at all replicas, which we capture by asserting that vis implies eo. In RedBlue Consistency (RB) [13], a subset of CRDT operations ($O_r \subseteq O$) are synchronized, so that they must occur in the same order at all replicas. We express RB in our framework by requiring the visibility relation to be total among events whose operations are in O_r. In Parallel Snapshot Isolation (PSI) [23], two events which conflict with each other (because they write to a common variable) are not allowed to be executed concurrently, but are synchronized across all replicas to be executed in the same order. Similar to [10], we assume that when a CRDT is used under PSI, its state space Σ is a map from variables to values, and every operation generates an effector which simply writes to certain variables. We assume that $\mathsf{Wr}(\eta^e)$ returns the set of variables written by the effector η^e, and express PSI in our framework by requiring that events which write a common variable are applied in the same order (determined by their visibility relation) across all replicas; furthermore, the policy requires that the visibility operation among such events is total. Finally, in Strong Consistency, the visibility relation is total and all effectors are applied in the same order at all replicas.

Given an execution $\tau \in [\![\mathcal{S}_{\mathcal{P},\Psi}]\!]$ and a transition $C \xrightarrow{\eta} C'$ in τ, we associate a set of replica states Σ_η that the event can potentially witness, by considering all permutations of the effectors visible to η which obey the global effector order, when applied to the start state $\sigma_s(\eta)$. Formally, this is defined as follows, assuming $\eta = (\mathsf{eid}, o, \sigma_s, \{\eta_1, \ldots, \eta_k\}, \mathsf{eo}_r)$ and $C = (\Delta, \mathsf{vis}, \mathsf{eo})$:

$$\Sigma_\eta = \{\eta^e_{P(1)} \circ \eta^e_{P(2)} \circ \ldots \circ \eta^e_{P(k)}(\sigma_s) \mid P : \{1, \ldots, k\} \to \{1, \ldots, k\},$$
$$\mathsf{eo}_P \text{ is a total order }, i < j \Rightarrow (\eta_{P(j)}, \eta_{P(i)}) \in \mathsf{eo}_P, \mathsf{eo} \subseteq \mathsf{eo}_P\}$$

In the above definition, for all valid local effector orders eo_P, we compute the CRDT states obtained on applying those effectors on the start CRDT state, which constitute Σ_η. The original event η presumably would have witnessed one of these states.

Definition 2 (Convergent Event). *Given an execution $\tau \in [\![\mathcal{S}_{\mathcal{P},\Psi}]\!]$ and an event $\eta \in L(\tau)$, η is convergent if Σ_η is singleton.*

Definition 3 (Strong Eventual Consistency). *A CRDT* $(\Sigma, O, \sigma_{\text{init}})$ *achieves strong eventual consistency* (SEC)*under a weak consistency specification* Ψ *if for all well-formed executions* $\tau \in \mathcal{WF}(\mathcal{S}_{\mathcal{P},\Psi})$ *and for all events* $\eta \in L(\tau)$, η *is convergent.*

An event is convergent if all valid permutations of visible events according to the specification Ψ lead to the same state. This corresponds to the requirement that if two replicas have witnessed the same set of operations, they must be in the same state. A CRDT achieves SEC if all events in all executions are convergent.

4 Automated Verification

In order to show that a CRDT achieves SEC under a consistency specification, we need to show that all events in any execution are convergent, which in turn requires us to show that any valid permutation of valid subsets of events in an execution leads to the same state. This is a hard problem because we have to reason about executions of unbounded length, involving unbounded sets of effectors and reconcile the declarative event-based specifications of weak consistency with states generated during execution. To make the problem tractable, we use a two-fold strategy. First, we show that if any pair of effectors generated during any execution either commute with each other or are forced to be applied in the same order by the consistency policy, then the CRDT achieves SEC. Second, we develop an inductive proof rule to show that *all* pairs of effectors generated during any (potentially unbounded) execution obey the above mentioned property. To ensure soundness of the proof rule, we place some reasonable assumptions on the consistency policy that (intuitively) requires behaviorally equivalent events to be treated the same by the policy, regardless of context (i.e., the length of the execution history at the time the event is applied). We then extract a simple sufficient condition which we call as *non-interference to commutativity* that captures the heart of the inductive argument. Notably, this condition can be automatically checked for different CRDTs under different consistency policies using off-the-shelf theorem provers, thus providing a pathway to performing automated parametrized verification of CRDTs.

Given a transition $(\Delta, \text{vis}, \text{eo}) \xrightarrow{\eta} C$, we denote the global effector order in the starting configuration of η, i.e. eo as eo_η. We first show that a sufficient condition to prove that a CRDT is convergent is to show that any two events in its history either commute or are related by the global effector order.

Lemma 1. *Given an execution* $\tau \in [\![\mathcal{S}_{\mathcal{P},\Psi}]\!]$, *and an event* $\eta = (\text{id}, o, \sigma_s, \Delta_r, \text{eo}_r) \in L(\tau)$, *if for all* $\eta_1, \eta_2 \in \Delta_r$ *such that* $\eta_1 \neq \eta_2$, *either* $\eta_1^e \circ \eta_2^e = \eta_2^e \circ \eta_1^e$ *or* $\text{eo}_\eta(\eta_1, \eta_2)$ *or* $\text{eo}_\eta(\eta_2, \eta_1)$, *then* η *is convergent*[3].

---

[3] All proofs can be found in the extended version [15] of the paper.

We now present a property that consistency policies must obey for our verification methodology to be soundly applied. First, we define the notion of behavioral equivalence of events:

Definition 4 (Behavioral Equivalence).
Two events $\eta_1 = (\mathsf{id}_1, o_1, \sigma_1, \Delta_1, \mathsf{eo}_1)$ and $\eta_2 = (\mathsf{id}_2, o_2, \sigma_2, \Delta_2, \mathsf{eo}_2)$ are behaviorally equivalent if $\eta_1^e = \eta_2^e$ and $o_1 = o_2$.

That is, behaviorally equivalent events produce the same effectors. We use the notation $\eta_1 \equiv \eta_2$ to indicate that they are behaviorally equivalent.

Definition 5 (Behaviorally Stable Consistency Policy). *A consistency policy Ψ is behaviorally stable if $\forall \Delta, \mathsf{vis}, \mathsf{eo}, \Delta', \mathsf{vis}', \mathsf{eo}', \eta_1, \eta_2 \in \Delta, \eta_1', \eta_2' \in \Delta'$ the following holds:*

$$(\Psi(\Delta, \mathsf{vis}, \mathsf{eo}) \wedge \Psi(\Delta', \mathsf{vis}', \mathsf{eo}') \wedge \eta_1 \equiv \eta_1' \wedge \eta_2 \equiv \eta_2' \wedge \mathsf{vis}(\eta_1, \eta_2) \Leftrightarrow \mathsf{vis}'(\eta_1', \eta_2'))$$
$$\Rightarrow \mathsf{eo}(\eta_1, \eta_2) \Leftrightarrow \mathsf{eo}'(\eta_1', \eta_2') \tag{2}$$

Behaviorally stable consistency policies treat behaviorally equivalent events which have the same visibility relation among them in the same manner by enforcing the same effector order. All consistency policies that we discussed in the previous section (representing the most well-known in the literature) are behaviorally stable:

Lemma 2. EC, CC, PSI, RB *and* SC *are behaviorally stable.*

EC does not enforce any effector ordering and hence is trivially stable behaviorally. CC forces causally dependent events to be in the same order, and hence behaviorally equivalent events which have the same visibility order will be forced to be in the same effector order. RB forces events whose operations belong to a specific subset to be in the same order, but since behaviorally equivalent events perform the same operation, they would be enforced in the same effector ordering. Similarly, PSI forces events writing to a common variable to be in the same order, but since behaviorally equivalent events generate the same effector, they would also write to the same variables and hence would be forced in the same effector order. SC forces all events to be in the same order which is equal to the visibility order, and hence is trivially stable behaviorally. In general, behaviorally stable consistency policies do not consider the context in which events occur, but instead rely only on observable behavior of the events to constrain their ordering. A simple example of a consistency policy which is not behaviorally stable is a policy which maintains bounded concurrency [12] by limiting the number of concurrent operations across all replicas to a fixed bound. Such a policy would synchronize two events only if they occur in a context where keeping them concurrent would violate the bound, but behaviorally equivalent events in a different context may not be synchronized.

For executions under a behaviorally stable consistency policy, the global effector order between events only grows in an execution, so that if two events η_1 and

η_2 are in the history of some event η are related by eo_η, then if they later occur in the history of any other event, they would be related in the same effector order. Hence, we can now define a common global effector order for an execution. Given an execution $\tau \in [\![\mathcal{S}_{\mathcal{P},\Psi}]\!]$, the effector order $\text{eo}_\tau \subseteq L(\tau) \times L(\tau)$ is an anti-symmetric relation defined as follows:

$$\text{eo}_\tau = \{(\eta_1, \eta_2) \mid \exists \eta \in L(\tau).\ (\eta_1, \eta_2) \in \text{eo}_\eta\}$$

Similarly, we also define vis_τ to be the common visibility relation for an execution τ, which is nothing but the vis relation in the final configuration of τ.

Definition 6 (Commutative modulo Consistency Policy). *Given a CRDT $\mathcal{P}$, a behaviorally stable weak consistency specification Ψ and an execution $\tau \in [\![\mathcal{S}_{\mathcal{P},\Psi}]\!]$, two events $\eta_1, \eta_2 \in L(\tau)$ such that $\eta_1 \neq \eta_2$ commute modulo the consistency policy Ψ if either $\eta_1^e \circ \eta_2^e = \eta_2^e \circ \eta_1^e$ or $\text{eo}_\tau(\eta_1, \eta_2)$ or $\text{eo}_\tau(\eta_2, \eta_1)$.*

The following lemma is a direct consequence of Lemma 1:

Lemma 3. *Given a CRDT $\mathcal{P}$ and a behaviorally stable consistency specification Ψ, if for all $\tau \in \mathcal{WF}(\mathcal{S}_{\mathcal{P},\Psi})$, for all $\eta_1, \eta_2 \in L(\tau)$ such that $\eta_1 \neq \eta_2$, η_1 and η_2 commute modulo the consistency policy Ψ, then $\mathcal{P}$ achieves SEC under Ψ.*

Our goal is to use Lemma 3 to show that all events in any execution commute modulo the consistency policy. However, executions can be arbitrarily long and have an unbounded number of events. Hence, for events occurring in such large executions, we will instead consider behaviorally equivalent events in a smaller execution and show that they commute modulo the consistency policy, which by stability of the consistency policy directly translates to their commutativity in the larger context. Recall that the effector generated by an operation depends on its start state and the sequence of other effectors applied to that state. To generate behaviorally equivalent events with arbitrarily long histories in short executions, we summarize these long histories into the start state of events, and use commutativity itself as an inductive property of these start states. That is, we ask if two events with arbitrary start states and empty histories commute modulo Ψ, whether the addition of another event to their histories would continue to allow them to commute modulo Ψ.

Definition 7 (Non-interference to Commutativity). (Non-Interf) *A CRDT $\mathcal{P} = (\Sigma, O, \sigma_{init})$ satisfies non-interference to commutativity under a consistency policy Ψ if and only if the following conditions hold:*

1. *For all executions $C_{init} \xrightarrow{\eta_1} C_1 \xrightarrow{\eta_2} C_2$ in $\mathcal{WF}(\mathcal{S}_{\mathcal{P},\Psi})$, η_1 and η_2 commute modulo Ψ.*
2. *For all $\sigma_1, \sigma_2, \sigma_3 \in \Sigma$, if for execution $\tau \equiv C_{init} \xrightarrow{\eta_1} C_1 \xrightarrow{\eta_2} C_2$ in $[\![\mathcal{S}_{\mathcal{P},\Psi}]\!]$ where $\sigma_s(\eta_1) = \sigma_1$, $\sigma_s(\eta_2) = \sigma_2$, η_1 and η_2 commute modulo Ψ, then for all executions $\tau' \equiv C_{init} \xrightarrow{\eta_3} C_1' \xrightarrow{\eta_1'} C_2' \xrightarrow{\eta_2'} C_3'$ such that $\sigma_s(\eta_1') = \sigma_1$, $o(\eta_1') = o(\eta_1)$, $\sigma_s(\eta_2') = \sigma_2$, $o(\eta_2') = o(\eta_2)$, $\sigma_s(\eta_3) = \sigma_3$, and $\text{vis}_\tau(\eta_1, \eta_2) \Leftrightarrow \text{vis}_{\tau'}(\eta_1', \eta_2')$, η_1' and η_2' commute modulo Ψ.*

Condition (1) corresponds to the base case of our inductive argument and requires that in well-formed executions with 2 events, both the events commute modulo Ψ. For condition (2), our intention is to consider two events η_a and η_b with any arbitrary histories which can occur in any well-formed execution and, assuming that they commute modulo Ψ, show that even after the addition of another event to their histories, they continue to commute. We use CRDT states σ_1, σ_2 to summarize the histories of the two events, and construct behaviorally equivalent events ($\eta_1 \equiv \eta_a$ and $\eta_2 \equiv \eta_b$) which would take σ_1, σ_2 as their start states. That is, if η_a produced the effector $o(\sigma_{\text{init}}, \pi)^4$, where o is the CRDT operation corresponding to η_a and π is the sequence of effectors in its history, we leverage the observation that $o(\sigma_{\text{init}}, \pi) = o(\pi(\sigma_{\text{init}}), \epsilon)$, and assuming $\sigma_1 = \pi(\sigma_{\text{init}})$, we obtain the behaviorally equivalent event η_1, i.e. $\eta_1^e \equiv \eta_a^e$. Similar analysis establishes that $\eta_2^e \equiv \eta_b^e$. However, since we have no way of characterizing states σ_1 and σ_2 which are obtained by applying arbitrary sequences of effectors, we use commutativity itself as an identifying characteristic, focusing on only those σ_1 and σ_2 for which the events η_1 and η_2 commute modulo Ψ.

The interfering event is also summarized by another CRDT state σ_3, and we require that after suffering interference from this new event, the original two events would continue to commute modulo Ψ. This would essentially establish that any two events with any history would commute modulo Ψ in these small executions, which by the behavioral stability of Ψ would translate to their commutativity in any execution.

Theorem 1. *Given a CRDT $\mathcal{P}$ and a behaviorally stable consistency policy Ψ, if $\mathcal{P}$ satisfies non-interference to commutativity under Ψ, then $\mathcal{P}$ achieves SEC under Ψ.*

Example: Let us apply the proposed verification strategy to the ORSet CRDT shown in Fig. 2. Under EC, condition (1) of Non-Interf fails, because in the execution $C_{\text{init}} \xrightarrow{\eta_1} C_1 \xrightarrow{\eta_2} C_2$ where $o(\eta_1) =$ Add(a,i) and $o(\eta_2) =$ Remove(a) and vis(η_1, η_2), η_1 and η_2 don't commute modulo EC, since (a,i) would be present in the source replica of Remove(a). However, η_1 and η_2 would commute modulo CC, since they would be related by the effector order. Now, moving to condition (2) of Non-interf, we limit ourselves to source replica states σ_1 and σ_2 where Add(a,i) and Remove(a) do commute modulo CC. If $\text{vis}_\tau(\eta_1, \eta_2)$, then after interference, in execution τ', $\text{vis}_{\tau'}(\eta_1', \eta_2')$, in which case η_1' and η_2' trivially commute modulo CC (because they would be related by the effector order). On the other hand, if $\neg\text{vis}_\tau(\eta_1, \eta_2)$, then for η_1 and η_2 to commute modulo CC, we must have that the effectors η_1^e and η_2^e themselves commute, which implies that (a,i) $\notin \sigma_2$. Now, consider any execution τ' with an interfering operation η_3. If η_3 is another Add(a,i') operation, then i' $\neq$ i, so that even if it is visible to η_2', $\eta_2'^e$ will not remove (a,i), so that η_1' and η_2' would commute. Similarly, if η_3 is another Remove(a) operation, it can only remove tagged versions of a from the source replicas of η_2', so that the effector $\eta_2'^e$ would not remove (a,i).

---

[4] Note that in a well-formed execution, the start state is always σ_{init}.

5   Experimental Results

In this section, we present the results of applying our verification methodology to a number of CRDTs under different consistency models. We collected CRDT implementations from a number of sources [1,19,20] and since all of the existing implementations assume a very weak consistency model (primarily CC), we additionally implemented a few CRDTs on our own intended to only work under stronger consistency schemes but which are better in terms of time/space complexity and ease of development. Our implementations are not written in any specific language but instead are specified abstractly akin to the definitions given in Figs. 1 and 2. To specify CRDT states and operations, we fix an abstract language that contains uninterpreted datatypes (used for specifying elements of sets, lists, etc.), a set datatype with support for various set operations (add, delete, union, intersection, projection, lookup), a tuple datatype (along with operations to create tuples and project components) and a special uninterpreted datatype equipped with a total order for identifiers. Note that the set datatype used in our abstract language is different from the Set CRDT, as it is only intended to perform set operations locally at a replica. All existing CRDT definitions can be naturally expressed in this framework.

Here, we revert back to the op-based specification of CRDTs. For a given CRDT $\mathcal{P} = (\Sigma, O, \sigma_{\text{init}})$, we convert all its operations into FOL formulas relating the source, input and output replica states. That is, for a CRDT operation $o : \Sigma \to \Sigma \to \Sigma$, we create a predicate $o : \Sigma \times \Sigma \times \Sigma \to \mathbb{B}$ such that $o(\sigma_s, \sigma_i, \sigma_o)$ is true if and only if $o(\sigma_s)(\sigma_i) = \sigma_o$. Since CRDT states are typically expressed as sets, we axiomatize set operations to express their semantics in FOL.

In order to specify a consistency model, we introduce a sort for events and binary predicates vis and eo over this sort. Here, we can take advantage of the declarative specification of consistency models and directly encode them in FOL. Given an encoding of CRDT operations and a consistency model, our verification strategy is to determine whether the Non-Interf property holds. Since both conditions of this property only involve executions of finite length (at most 3), we can directly encode them as UNSAT queries by asking for executions which break the conditions. For condition (1), we query for the existence of two events η_1 and η_2 along with vis and eo predicates which satisfy the consistency specification Ψ such that these events are not related by eo and their effectors do not commute. For condition (2), we query for the existence of events η_1, η_2, η_3 and their respective start states $\sigma_1, \sigma_2, \sigma_3$, such that η_1 and η_2 commute modulo Ψ but after interference from η_3, they are not related by eo and do not commute. Both these queries are encoded in EPR [18], a decidable fragment of FOL, so if the CRDT operations and the consistency policy can also be encoded in a decidable fragment of FOL (which is the case in all our experiments), then our verification strategy is also decidable. We write Non-Interf-1 and Non-Interf-2 for the two conditions of Non-Interf.

Figure 4 shows the results of applying the proposed methodology on different CRDTs. We used Z3 to discharge our satisfiability queries. For every combination of a CRDT and a consistency policy, we write ✗ to indicate that verification of

CRDT	EC	CC	PSI+RB	PSI	Verif. Time (s)
Set					
Simple-Set	✗	✗	✓	✓	0.23
ORSet [20]	✗	✓	✓	✓	0.6
ORSet with Tombstones	✓	✓	✓	✓	0.04
USet[20]	✗	✗	✗	✓	0.1
List					
RGA[1]	✗	✓	✓	✓	5.3
RGA-No-Tomb	✗	✗	✓	✓	3
Graph					
2P2P-Graph[20]	✗	✓	✓	✓	3.5
Graph-with-ORSet	✗	✗	✓	✓	46.3

Fig. 4. Convergence of CRDTs under different consistency policies.

Non-Interf failed, while ✓ indicates that it was satisfied. We also report the verification time taken by Z3 for every CRDT across all consistency policies executing on a standard desktop machine. We have picked the three collection datatypes for which CRDTs have been proposed i.e. Set, List and Graph, and for each such datatype, we consider multiple variants that provide a tradeoff between consistency requirements and implementation complexity. Apart from EC, CC and PSI, we also use a combination of PSI and RB, which only enforce PSI between selected pairs of operations (in contrast to simple RB which would enforce SC between all selected pairs). Note that when verifying a CRDT under PSI, we assume that the set operations are implemented as Boolean assignments, and the write set Wr consists of elements added/removed. We are unaware of any prior effort that has been successful in automatically verifying *any* CRDT, let alone those that exhibit the complexity of the ones considered here.

Set: The Simple-Set CRDT in Fig. 1 does not converge under EC or CC, but achieves convergence under PSI+RB which only synchronizes Add and Remove operations to the same elements, while all other operations continue to run under EC, since they do commute with each other. As explained earlier, ORSet does not converge under EC and violates Non-Interf-1. ORSet with tombstones converges under EC as well since it uses a different set (called a tombstone) to keep track of removed elements. USet is another implementation of the Set CRDT which converges under the assumptions that an element is only added once, and removes only work if the element is already present in the source replica. USet converges only under PSI, because under any weaker consistency model, NON-INTERF-2 breaks, since Add(a) interferes and breaks the commutativity of Add(a) and Remove(a). Notice that as the consistency level weakens, implementations need to keep more and more information to maintain convergence–compute unique ids, tag elements with them or keep track of deleted elements. If the underlying replicated store supports stronger consistency levels such as PSI, simpler definitions are sufficient.

List: The List CRDT maintains a total ordering between its elements. It supports two operations: `AddRight(e,a)` adds new element `a` to the right of existing element `e`, while `Remove(e)` removes `e` from the list. We use the implementation in [1] (called RGA) which uses time-stamped insertion trees. To maintain integrity of the tree structure, the immediate predecessor of every list element must be present in the list, due to which operations `AddRight(a,b)` and `AddRight(b,c)` do not commute. Hence RGA does not converge under EC because Non-Interf-1 is violated, but converges under CC.

To make adds and removes involving the same list element commute, RGA maintains a tombstone set for all deleted list elements. This can be expensive as deleted elements may potentially need to be tracked forever, even with garbage collection. We consider a slight modification of RGA called RGA-No-Tomb which does not keep track of deleted elements. This CRDT now has a convergence violation under CC (because of Non-Interf-1), but achieves convergence under PSI+RB where we enforce PSI only for pairs of `AddRight` and `Remove` operations.

Graph: The Graph CRDT maintains sets of vertices and edges and supports operations to add and remove vertices and edges. The 2P2P-Graph specification uses separate 2P-Sets for both vertices and edges, where a 2P-Set itself maintains two sets for addition and removal of elements. While 2P sets themselves converge under EC, the 2P2P-Graph has convergence violations (to Non-Interf-1) involving `AddVertex(v)` and `RemoveVertex(v)` (similarly for edges) since it removes a vertex from a replica only if it is already present. We verify that it converges under CC. Graphs require an integrity constraint that edges in the edge-set must always be incident on vertices in the vertex-set. Since concurrent `RemoveVertex(v)` and `AddEdge(v,v')` can violate this constraint, the 2P2P-Graph uses the internal structure of the 2P-Set which keeps track of deleted elements and considers an edge to be in the edge set only if its vertices are not in the vertex tombstone set (leading to a remove-wins strategy).

Building a graph CRDT can be viewed as an exercise in composing CRDTs by using two ORSet CRDTs, keeping the internal implementation of the ORSet opaque, using only its interface. The Graph-with-ORSet implementation uses separate ORSets for vertices and edges and explicitly maintains the graph integrity constraint. We find convergence violations (to Non-Interf-1) between `RemoveVertex(v)` and `AddEdge(v,v')`, and `RemoveVertex(v)` and `RemoveEdge(v,v')` under both EC and CC. Under PSI+RB (enforcing RB on the above two pairs of operations), we were able to show convergence.

When a CRDT passes Non-Interf under a consistency policy, we can guarantee that it achieves SEC under that policy. However, if it fails Non-Interf, it may or may not converge. In particular, if it fails Non-Interf-1 it will definitely not converge (because Non-Interf-1 constructs a well-formed execution), but if it passes Non-Interf-1 and fails Non-Interf-2, it may still converge because of the imprecision of Non-Interf-2. There are two sources of imprecision, both concerning the start states of the events picked in the condition: (1) we only use commutativity as a distinguishing property of the start states, but this may not be a sufficiently strong inductive invariant, (2) we place no constraints on the start state of the interfering operation. In practice, we have found that for all cases except U-Set, convergence violations manifest via failure of Non-Interf-1. If Non-Interf-2 breaks, we can search for well-formed executions of higher length upto a bound. For U-Set, we were successful in adopting this approach, and were able to find a non-convergent well-formed execution of length 3.

6 Related Work and Conclusions

Reconciling concurrent updates in a replicated system is a important well-studied problem in distributed applications, having been first studied in the context of collaborative editing systems [17]. Incorrect implementation of replicated sets in Amazon's Dynamo system [7] motivated the design of CRDTs as a principled approach to implementing replicated data types. Devising correct implementations has proven to be challenging, however, as evidenced by the myriad pre-conditions specified in the various CRDT implementations [20].

Burckhardt *et al.* [6] present an abstract event-based framework to describe executions of CRDTs under different network conditions; they also propose a rigorous correctness criterion in the form of abstract specifications. Their proof strategy, which is neither automated nor parametric on consistency policies, verifies CRDT implementations against these specifications by providing a simulation invariant between CRDT states and event structures. Zeller *et al.* [24] also require simulation invariants to verify convergence, although they only target state-based CRDTs. Gomes *et al.* [9] provide mechanized proofs of convergence for ORSet and RGA CRDTs under causal consistency, but their approach is neither automated nor parametric.

A number of earlier efforts [2,10–12,22] have looked at the problem of verifying state-based invariants in distributed applications. These techniques typically target applications built using CRDTs, and assume their underlying correctness. Because they target correctness specifications in the form of state-based invariants, it is unclear if their approaches can be applied directly to the convergence problem we consider here. Other approaches [4,5,16] have also looked at the verification problem of transactional programs running on replicated systems under weak consistency, but these proposals typically use serializability as the correctness criterion, adopting a "last-writer wins" semantics, rather than convergence, to deal with concurrent updates.

This paper demonstrates the automated verification of CRDTs under different weak consistency policies. We rigorously define the relationship between commutativity and convergence, formulating the notion of commutativity modulo consistency policy as a sufficient condition for convergence. While we require a non-trivial inductive argument to show that non-interference to commutativity is sufficient for convergence, the condition itself is designed to be simple and amenable to automated verification using off-the-shelf theorem-provers. We have successfully applied the proposed verification strategy for all major CRDTs, additionally motivating the need for parameterization in consistency policies by showing variants of existing CRDTs which are simpler in terms of implementation complexity but converge under different weak consistency models.

Acknowledgments. We thank the anonymous reviewers for their insightful comments. This material is based upon work supported by the National Science Foundation under Grant No. CCF-SHF 1717741 and the Air Force Research Lab under Grant No. FA8750-17-1-0006.

References

1. Attiya, H., Burckhardt, S., Gotsman, A., Morrison, A., Yang, H., Zawirski, M.: Specification and complexity of collaborative text editing. In: Proceedings of the 2016 ACM Symposium on Principles of Distributed Computing, PODC 2016, Chicago, IL, USA, 25–28 July 2016, pp. 259–268 (2016). https://doi.org/10.1145/2933057.2933090
2. Bailis, P., Fekete, A., Franklin, M.J., Ghodsi, A., Hellerstein, J.M., Stoica, I.: Coordination avoidance in database systems. PVLDB **8**(3), 185–196 (2014). https://doi.org/10.14778/2735508.2735509. http://www.vldb.org/pvldb/vol8/p185-bailis.pdf
3. Bailis, P., Ghodsi, A.: Eventual consistency today: limitations, extensions, and beyond. Commun. ACM **56**(5), 55–63 (2013). https://doi.org/10.1145/2447976.2447992
4. Bernardi, G., Gotsman, A.: Robustness against consistency models with atomic visibility. In: 27th International Conference on Concurrency Theory, CONCUR 2016, 23–26 August 2016, Québec City, Canada, pp. 7:1–7:15 (2016). https://doi.org/10.4230/LIPIcs.CONCUR.2016.7
5. Brutschy, L., Dimitrov, D., Müller, P., Vechev, M.T.: Static serializability analysis for causal consistency. In: Proceedings of the 39th ACM SIGPLAN Conference on Programming Language Design and Implementation, PLDI 2018, Philadelphia, PA, USA, 18–22 June 2018, pp. 90–104 (2018). https://doi.org/10.1145/3192366.3192415
6. Burckhardt, S., Gotsman, A., Yang, H., Zawirski, M.: Replicated data types: specification, verification, optimality. In: The 41st Annual ACM SIGPLAN-SIGACT Symposium on Principles of Programming Languages, POPL 2014, San Diego, CA, USA, 20–21 January 2014, pp. 271–284 (2014). https://doi.org/10.1145/2535838.2535848
7. DeCandia, G., et al.: Dynamo: amazon's highly available key-value store. In: Proceedings of the 21st ACM Symposium on Operating Systems Principles 2007, SOSP 2007, Stevenson, Washington, USA, 14–17 October 2007, pp. 205–220 (2007). https://doi.org/10.1145/1294261.1294281
8. Gilbert, S., Lynch, N.A.: Brewer's conjecture and the feasibility of consistent, available, partition-tolerant web services. SIGACT News **33**(2), 51–59 (2002). https://doi.org/10.1145/564585.564601. http://doi.acm.org/10.1145/564585.564601
9. Gomes, V.B.F., Kleppmann, M., Mulligan, D.P., Beresford, A.R.: Verifying strong eventual consistency in distributed systems. PACMPL **1**(OOPSLA), 109:1–109:28 (2017). https://doi.org/10.1145/3133933

10. Gotsman, A., Yang, H., Ferreira, C., Najafzadeh, M., Shapiro, M.: 'Cause i'm strong enough: reasoning about consistency choices in distributed systems. In: Proceedings of the 43rd Annual ACM SIGPLAN-SIGACT Symposium on Principles of Programming Languages, POPL 2016, St. Petersburg, FL, USA, 20–22 January 2016, pp. 371–384 (2016). https://doi.org/10.1145/2837614.2837625, http://doi.acm.org/10.1145/2837614.2837625

11. Houshmand, F., Lesani, M.: Hamsaz: replication coordination analysis and synthesis. PACMPL **3**(POPL), 74:1–74:32 (2019). https://dl.acm.org/citation.cfm?id=3290387

12. Kaki, G., Earanky, K., Sivaramakrishnan, K.C., Jagannathan, S.: Safe replication through bounded concurrency verification. PACMPL **2**(OOPSLA), 164:1–164:27 (2018). https://doi.org/10.1145/3276534

13. Li, C., Porto, D., Clement, A., Gehrke, J., Preguiça, N.M., Rodrigues, R.: Making geo-replicated systems fast as possible, consistent when necessary. In: 10th USENIX Symposium on Operating Systems Design and Implementation, OSDI 2012, Hollywood, CA, USA, 8–10 October 2012, pp. 265–278 (2012). https://www.usenix.org/conference/osdi12/technical-sessions/presentation/li

14. Lloyd, W., Freedman, M.J., Kaminsky, M., Andersen, D.G.: Don't settle for eventual: scalable causal consistency for wide-area storage with COPS. In: Proceedings of the 23rd ACM Symposium on Operating Systems Principles 2011, SOSP 2011, Cascais, Portugal, 23–26 October 2011, pp. 401–416 (2011). https://doi.org/10.1145/2043556.2043593, http://doi.acm.org/10.1145/2043556.2043593

15. Nagar, K., Jagannathan, S.: Automated Parameterized Verification of CRDTs (Extended Version). https://arxiv.org/abs/1905.05684

16. Nagar, K., Jagannathan, S.: Automated detection of serializability violations under weak consistency. In: 29th International Conference on Concurrency Theory, CONCUR 2018, 4–7 September 2018, Beijing, China, pp. 41:1–41:18 (2018). https://doi.org/10.4230/LIPIcs.CONCUR.2018.41

17. Nichols, D.A., Curtis, P., Dixon, M., Lamping, J.: High-latency, low-bandwidth windowing in the jupiter collaboration system. In: Proceedings of the 8th Annual ACM Symposium on User Interface Software and Technology, UIST 1995, Pittsburgh, PA, USA, 14–17 November 1995, pp. 111–120 (1995). https://doi.org/10.1145/215585.215706

18. Piskac, R., de Moura, L.M., Bjørner, N.: Deciding effectively propositional logic using DPLL and substitution sets. J. Autom. Reasoning **44**(4), 401–424 (2010). https://doi.org/10.1007/s10817-009-9161-6

19. Preguiça, N.M., Baquero, C., Shapiro, M.: Conflict-free replicated data types (CRDTs). CoRR abs/1805.06358 (2018). http://arxiv.org/abs/1805.06358

20. Shapiro, M., Preguiça, N., Baquero, C., Zawirski, M.: A comprehensive study of Convergent and Commutative Replicated Data Types. Technical report RR-7506, INRIA, Inria - Centre Paris-Rocquencourt (2011)

21. Shapiro, M., Preguiça, N., Baquero, C., Zawirski, M.: Conflict-free replicated data types. In: Défago, X., Petit, F., Villain, V. (eds.) SSS 2011. LNCS, vol. 6976, pp. 386–400. Springer, Heidelberg (2011). https://doi.org/10.1007/978-3-642-24550-3_29

22. Sivaramakrishnan, K.C., Kaki, G., Jagannathan, S.: Declarative programming over eventually consistent data stores. In: Proceedings of the 36th ACM SIGPLAN Conference on Programming Language Design and Implementation, Portland, OR, USA, 15–17 June 2015, pp. 413–424 (2015). https://doi.org/10.1145/2737924.2737981

23. Sovran, Y., Power, R., Aguilera, M.K., Li, J.: Transactional storage for geo-replicated systems. In: Proceedings of the 23rd ACM Symposium on Operating Systems Principles 2011, SOSP 2011, Cascais, Portugal, 23–26 October 2011, pp. 385–400 (2011). https://doi.org/10.1145/2043556.2043592, http://doi.acm.org/10.1145/2043556.2043592
24. Zeller, P., Bieniusa, A., Poetzsch-Heffter, A.: Formal specification and verification of CRDTs. In: Ábrahám, E., Palamidessi, C. (eds.) FORTE 2014. LNCS, vol. 8461, pp. 33–48. Springer, Heidelberg (2014). https://doi.org/10.1007/978-3-662-43613-4_3

11

Rely-Guarantee Reasoning About Concurrent Memory Management in Zephyr RTOS

Yongwang Zhao[1,2](✉) and David Sanán[3]

[1] School of Computer Science and Engineering, Beihang University, Beijing, China
zhaoyw@buaa.edu.cn
[2] Beijing Advanced Innovation Center for Big Data and Brain Computing,
Beihang University, Beijing, China
[3] School of Computer Science and Engineering, Nanyang Technological University,
Singapore, Singapore

Abstract. Formal verification of concurrent operating systems (OSs) is challenging, and in particular the verification of the dynamic memory management due to its complex data structures and allocation algorithm. Up to our knowledge, this paper presents the first formal specification and mechanized proof of a concurrent buddy memory allocation for a real-world OS. We develop a fine-grained formal specification of the buddy memory management in Zephyr RTOS. To ease validation of the specification and the source code, the provided specification closely follows the C code. Then, we use the rely-guarantee technique to conduct the compositional verification of functional correctness and invariant preservation. During the formal verification, we found three bugs in the C code of Zephyr.

1 Introduction

The operating system (OS) is a fundamental component of critical systems. Thus, correctness and reliability of systems highly depend on the system's underlying OS. As a key functionality of OSs, the memory management provides ways to dynamically allocate portions of memory to programs at their request, and to free them for reuse when no longer needed. Since program variables and data are stored in the allocated memory, an incorrect specification and implementation of the memory management may lead to system crashes or exploitable attacks on the whole system. RTOS are frequently deployed on critical systems, making formal verification of RTOS necessary to ensure their reliability. One of the state of the art RTOS is Zephyr RTOS [1], a Linux Foundation project. Zephyr is an open source RTOS for connected, resource-constrained devices, and built with security and safety design in mind. Zephyr uses a buddy memory allocation algorithm optimized for RTOS, and that allows multiple threads to concurrently manipulate shared memory pools with fine-grained locking.

Formal verification of the concurrent memory management in Zephyr is a challenging work. (1) To achieve high performance, data structures and algorithms in Zephyr are laid out in a complex manner. The buddy memory allocation can split large blocks into smaller ones, allowing blocks of different sizes to be allocated and released efficiently while limiting memory fragmentation concerns. Seeking performance, Zephyr uses a multi-level structure where each level has a bitmap and a linked list of free memory blocks. The levels of bitmaps actually form a forest of quad trees of bits. Memory addresses are used as a reference to memory blocks, so the algorithm has to deal with address alignment and computation concerning the block size at each level, increasing the complexity of its verification. (2) A complex algorithm and data structures imply as well complex invariants that the formal model must preserve. These invariants have to guarantee the well-shaped bitmaps and their consistency to free lists. To prevent memory leaks and block overlapping, a precise reasoning shall keep track of both numerical and shape properties. (3) Thread preemption and fine-grained locking make the kernel execution of memory services to be concurrent.

In this paper, we apply the rely-guarantee reasoning technique to the concurrent buddy memory management in Zephyr. This work uses π-Core, a rely-guarantee framework for the specification and verification of concurrent reactive systems. π-Core introduces a concurrent imperative system specification language driven by "events" that supports reactive semantics of interrupt handlers (e.g. kernel services, scheduler) in OSs, and thus makes the formal specification of Zephyr simpler. The language embeds Isabelle/HOL data types and functions, therefore it is as rich as the own Isabelle/HOL. π-Core concurrent constructs allow the specification of Zephyr multi-thread interleaving, fine-grained locking, and thread preemption. Compositionality of rely-guarantee makes feasible to prove the functional correctness of Zephyr and invariants over its data structures. The formal specification and proofs are developed in Isabelle/HOL. They are available at https://lvpgroup.github.io/picore/.

We first analyze the structural properties of memory pools in Zephyr (Sect. 3). The properties clarify the constraints and consistency of quad trees, free block lists, memory pool configuration, and waiting threads. All of them are defined as invariants for which its preservation under the execution of services is formally verified. From the well-shaped properties of quad trees, we can derive a critical property to prevent memory leaks, i.e., memory blocks cover the whole memory address of the pool, but not overlap each other.

Together with the formal verification of Zephyr, we aim at the highest evaluation assurance level (EAL 7) of Common Criteria (CC) [2], which was declared this year as the candidate standard for security certification by the Zephyr project. Therefore, we develop a fine-grained low level formal specification of a buddy memory management (Sect. 4). The specification has a line-to-line correspondence with the Zephyr C code, and thus is able to do the *code-to-spec* review required by the EAL 7 evaluation, covering all the data structures and imperative statements present in the implementation.

We enforce the formal verification of functional correctness and invariant preservation by using a rely-guarantee proof system (Sect. 5), which supports total correctness for loops where fairness does not need to be considered. The formal verification revealed three bugs in the C code: an incorrect block split, an incorrect return from the kernel services, and non-termination of a loop (Sect. 6). Two of them are critical and have been repaired in the latest release of Zephyr. The third bug causes nontermination of the allocation service when trying to allocate a block of a larger size than the maximum allowed.

Related Work. (1) Memory models [17] provide the necessary abstraction to separate the behaviour of a program from the behaviour of the memory it reads and writes. There are many formalizations of memory models in the literature, e.g., [10,14,15,19,21], where some of them only create an abstract specification of the services for memory allocation and release [10,15,21]. (2) Formal verification of OS memory management has been studied in CertiKOS [11,20], seL4 [12,13], Verisoft [3], and in the hypervisors from [4,5], where only the works in [4,11] consider concurrency. Comparing to buddy memory allocation, the data structures and algorithms verified in [11] are relatively simpler, without block split/coalescence and multiple levels of free lists and bitmaps. [4] only considers virtual mapping but not allocation or deallocation of memory areas. (3) Algorithms and implementations of dynamic memory allocation have been formally specified and verified in an extensive number of works [7–9,16,18,23]. However, the buddy memory allocation is only studied in [9], which does not consider concrete data structures (e.g. bitmaps) and concurrency. To the best of our knowledge, this paper presents the first formal specification and mechanized proof for a concurrent buddy memory allocation of a realistic operating system.

2 Concurrent Memory Management in Zephyr RTOS

In Zephyr, a memory pool is a kernel object that allows memory blocks to be dynamically allocated, from a designated memory region, and released back into the pool. Its definition in the C code is shown as follows. A memory pool's buffer ($*buf$) is an n_max-size array of blocks of max_sz bytes at level 0, with no wasted space between them. The size of the buffer is thus $n\_max \times max\_sz$ bytes long. Zephyr tries to accomplish a memory request by splitting available blocks into smaller ones fitting as best as possible the requested size. Each "level 0" block is a quad-block that can be split into four smaller "level 1" blocks of equal size. Likewise, each level 1 block is itself a quad-block that can be split again. At each level, the four smaller blocks become *buddies* or *partners* to each other. The block size at level l is thus $max\_sz/4^l$.

```
struct k_mem_block_id {          struct k_mem_block {
  u32_t pool  : 8;                 void *data;
  u32_t level : 4;                 struct k_mem_block_id id;
  u32_t block : 20;              };
};                               struct k_mem_pool {
struct k_mem_pool_lvl {            void *buf;
  union {                          size_t max_sz;
    u32_t *bits_p;                 u16_t n_max;
    u32_t bits;                    u8_t n_levels;
  };                               u8_t max_inline_level;
  sys_dlist_t free_list;           struct k_mem_pool_lvl *levels;
};                                 _wait_q_t wait_q;
                                 };
```

The pool is initially configured with the parameters n_max and max_sz, together with a third parameter min_sz. min_sz defines the minimum size for an allocated block and must be at least $4 \times X$ ($X > 0$) bytes long. Memory pool blocks are recursively split into quarters until blocks of the minimum size are obtained, at which point no further split can occur. The depth at which min_sz blocks are allocated is n_levels and satisfies that $n\_max = min\_sz \times 4^{n\_levels}$.

Every memory block is composed of a *level*; a *block* index within the level, ranging from 0 to $(n\_max \times 4^{level}) - 1$; and the *data* representing the block start address, which is equal to $buf + (max\_sz/4^{level}) \times block$. We use a tuple $(level, block)$ to uniquely represent a block within a pool p.

A memory pool keeps track of how its buffer space has been split using a linked list *free_list* with the start address of the free blocks in each level. To improve the performance of coalescing partner blocks, memory pools maintain a bitmap at each level to indicate the allocation status of each block in the level. This structure is represented by a C union of an integer *bits* and an array *bits_p*. The implementation can allocate the bitmaps at levels smaller than $max\_inlinle\_levels$ using only an integer *bits*. However, the number of blocks in levels higher than $max\_inlinle\_levels$ make necessary to allocate the bitmap information using the array *bits_map*. In such a design, the levels of bitmaps actually form a forest of complete quad trees. The bit i in the bitmap of level j is set to 1 for the block (i, j) iff it is a free block, i.e. it is in the free list at level i. Otherwise the bitmap for such block is set to 0.

Zephyr provides two kernel services $k\_mem\_pool\_alloc$ and $k\_mem\_pool\_free$, for memory allocation and release respectively. The main part of the C code of $k\_mem\_pool\_alloc$ is shown in Fig. 1. When an application requests for a memory block, Zephyr first computes $alloc\_l$ and $free\_l$. $alloc\_l$ is the level with the size of the smallest block that will satisfy the request, and $free\_l$, with $free\_l \leqslant alloc\_l$, is the lowest level where there are free memory blocks. Since the services are concurrent, when the service tries to allocate a free block blk from level $free\_l$ (Line 8), blocks at that level may be allocated or merged into a bigger block by other concurrent threads. In such case the service will back out (Line 9) and tell the main function $k\_mem\_pool\_alloc$ to retry. If blk is successfully locked for allocation, then it is broken down to level $alloc\_l$ (Lines 11–14). The allocation service $k\_mem\_pool\_alloc$ supports a *timeout* parameter to allow threads waiting for that pool for a period of time when the call does not succeed. If the allocation

```
1   static int pool_alloc(struct k_mem_pool *p,struct k_mem_block *block,size_t size)
2   {
3     ..... //calcuate lsizes[], alloc_l and free_l
4     if (alloc_l < 0 || free_l < 0) {
5       block->data = NULL;
6       return -ENOMEM;
7     }
8     blk = alloc_block(p, free_l, lsizes[free_l]);
9     if (!blk) { return -EAGAIN; }
10    /* Iteratively break the smallest enclosing block... */
11    for (from_l = free_l; level_empty(p, alloc_l) && from_l < alloc_l;
12            from_l++) {
13      blk = break_block(p, blk, from_l, lsizes);
14    }
15    block->id.level = alloc_l; //assign block level to the variable *block.
16    ...... //assign other block info to the variable *block
17    return 0;
18  }
19
20  int k_mem_pool_alloc(struct k_mem_pool *p, struct k_mem_block *block, size_t size,
          s32_t timeout)
21  {
22    ...... // initialize local vars, calculate the end time for timeout.
23    while (1) {
24      ret = pool_alloc(p, block, size);
25      if (ret == 0 || timeout == K_NO_WAIT ||
26          ret == -EAGAIN || (ret && ret != -ENOMEM)) {
27        return ret;
28      }
29      key = irq_lock();
30      _pend_current_thread(&p->wait_q, timeout);
31      _Swap(key);
32      ...... //if timeout > 0, break the loop if time out
33    }
34    return -EAGAIN;
35  }
```

Fig. 1. The C source code of memory allocation in Zephyr v1.8.0

fails (Line 24) and the timeout is not *K_NO_WAIT*, the thread is suspended (Line 30) in a linked list *wait_q* and the context is switched to another thread (Line 31).

Interruptions are always enabled in both services with the exception of the code for the functions *alloc_block* and *break_block*, which invoke *irq_lock* and *irq_unlock* to respectively enable and disable interruptions. Similar to *k_mem_pool_alloc*, the execution of *k_mem_pool_free* is interruptable too.

3   Defining Structures and Properties of Buddy Memory Pools

As a specification at design level, we use abstract data types to represent the complete structure of memory pools. We use an abstract reference *ref* in Isabelle to define pointers to memory pools. Starting addresses of memory blocks, memory pools, and unsigned integers in the implementation are defined as *natural* numbers (*nat*). Linked lists used in the implementation for the elements *levels* and *free_list*, together with the bitmaps used in *bits* and *bits_p*, are defined as a *list* type. C *structs* are modelled in Isabelle as *records* of the same name as the implementation and comprising the same data. There are two exceptions to this: (1) $k\_mem\_block\_id$ and k_mem_block are merged in one single record, (2) the union in the struct $k\_mem\_pool\_lvl$ is replaced by a single list representing the bitmap, and thus max_inline_level is removed.

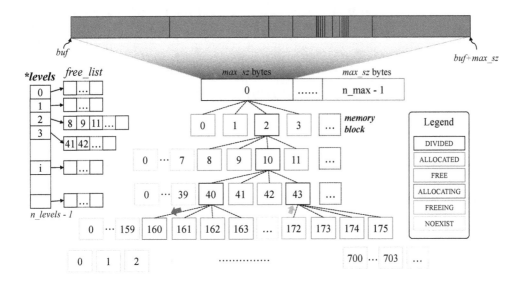

Fig. 2. Structure of memory pools

The Zephyr implementation makes use of a bitmap to represent the state of a memory block. The bit j of the bitmap for level a i is set to 1 iff the memory address of the memory block (i, j) is in the free list at level i. A bit j at a level i is set to 0 under the following conditions: (1) its corresponding memory block is allocated ($ALLOCATED$), (2) the memory block has been split ($DIVIDED$), (3) the memory block is being split in the allocation service ($ALLOCATING$) (Line 13 in Fig. 1), (4) the memory block is being coalesced in the release service ($FREEING$), and (5) the memory block does not exist ($NOEXIST$). Instead of only using a binary representation, our formal specification models the bitmap using a datatype $BlockState$ that is composed of these cases together with $FREE$. The reason of this decision is to simplify proving that the bitmap shape is well-formed. In particular, this representation makes less complex to verify the case in which the descendant of a free block is a non-free block. This is the case where the last free block has not been split and therefore lower levels do not exist. We illustrate a structure of a memory pool in Fig. 2. The top of the figure shows the real memory of the first block at level 0.

The structural properties clarify the constraints on and consistency of quad trees, free block lists, the memory pool configuration, and waiting threads. All of them are thought of as invariants on the kernel state and have been formally verified on the formal specification in Isabelle/HOL.

Well-Shaped Bitmaps. We say that the logical memory block j at a level i physically exists iff the bitmap j for the level i is *ALLOCATED*, *FREE*, *ALLO-CATING*, or *FREEING*, represented by the predicate *is_memblock*. We do not consider blocks marked as *DIVIDED* as physical blocks since it is only a logical block containing other blocks. Threads may split and coalesce memory blocks. A valid forest is defined by the following rules: (1) the parent bit of an existing memory block is *DIVIDED* and its child bits are *NOEXIST*, denoted by the predicate *noexist_bits* that checks for a given bitmap b and a position j that nodes $b!j$ to $b!(j+3)$ are set as *NOEXIST*; (2) the parent bit of a *DIVIDED* block is also *DIVIDED*; and (3) the child bits of a *NOEXIST* bit are also *NOEX-IST* and its parent can not be a *DIVIDED* block. The property is defined as the predicate **inv-bitmap**(s), where s is the state.

There are two additional properties on bitmaps. First, the address space of any memory pool cannot be empty, i.e., the bits at level 0 have to be different to *NOEXIST*. Second, the allocation algorithm may split a memory block into smaller ones, but not the those blocks at the lowest level (i.e. level $n\_levels - 1$), therefore the bits at the lowest level cannot not be *DIVIDED*. The first property is defined as **inv-bitmap0**(s) and the second as **inv-bitmapn**(s).

Consistency of the Memory Configuration. The configuration of a memory pool is set when it is initialized. Since the minimum block size is aligned to 4 bytes, there must exists an $n > 0$ such that the maximum size of a pool is equal to $4 \times n \times 4^{n\_levels}$, relating the number of levels of a level 0 block with its maximum size. Moreover, the number of blocks at level 0 and the number of levels have to be greater than zero, since the memory pool cannot be empty. The number of levels is equal to the length of the pool *levels* list. Finally, the length of the bitmap at level i should be $n\_max \times 4^i$. This property is defined as **inv-mempool-info**(s).

Memory Partition Property. Memory blocks partition the pool they belong to, and then not overlapping blocks and the absence of memory leaks are critical properties. For a memory block of index j at level i, its address space is the interval $[j \times (max\_sz/4^i), (j+1) \times (max\_sz/4^i))$. For any relative memory address $addr$ in the memory domain of a memory pool, and hence $addr < n\_max * max\_sz$, there is one and only one memory block whose address space contains $addr$. Here, we use relative address for $addr$. The property is defined as **mem-part**(s).

From the invariants of the bitmap, we derive the general property for the memory partition.

Theorem 1 (Memory Partition). *For any kernel state s, If the memory pools in s are consistent in their configuration, and their bitmaps are well-shaped, the memory pools satisfy the partition property in s:*

$$inv\_mempool\_info(s) \land inv\_bitmap(s) \land inv\_bitmap0(s) \land inv\_bitmapn(s) \implies mem\_part(s)$$

Together with the memory partition property, pools must also satisfy the following:

No Partner Fragmentation. The memory release algorithm in Zephyr coalesces free partner memory blocks into blocks as large as possible for all the descendants from the root level, without including it. Thus, a memory pool does not contain four *FREE* partner bits.

Validity of Free Block Lists. The free list at one level keeps the starting address of free memory blocks. The memory management ensures that the addresses in the list are valid, i.e., they are different from each other and aligned to the *block size*, which at a level i is given by $(max\_sz/4^i)$. Moreover, a memory block is in the free list iff the corresponding bit of the bitmap is *FREE*.

Non-overlapping of Memory Pools. The memory spaces of the set of pools defined in a system must be disjoint, so the memory addresses of a pool does not belong to the memory space of any other pool.

Other Properties. The state of a suspended thread in *wait_q* has to be consistent with the threads waiting for a memory pool. Threads can only be blocked once, and those threads waiting for available memory blocks have to be in a *BLOCKED* state. During allocation and free of a memory block, blocks of the tree may temporally be manipulated during the coalesce and division process. A block can be only manipulated by a thread at a time, and the state bit of a block being temporally manipulate has to be *FREEING* or *ALLOCATING*.

4 Formalizing Zephyr Memory Management

For the purpose of formal verification of event-driven systems such as OSs, we have developed π-Core, a framework for rely-guarantee reasoning of components running in parallel invoking events. π-Core has support for concurrent OSs features like modelling shared-variable concurrency of multiple threads, interruptable execution of handlers, self-suspending threads, and rescheduling. In this section, we first introduce the modelling language in π-Core and an execution model of Zephyr using this language. Then we discuss in detail the low-level design specification for the kernel services that the memory management provides. Since this work focuses on the memory management, we only provide very abstract models for other kernel functionalities such as the kernel scheduling and thread control.

4.1 Event-Based Execution Model of Zephyr

The Language in π-Core. Interrupt handlers in π-Core are considered as reaction services which are represented as *events*:

EVENT $\mathcal{E}$ $[p_1, ..., p_n]@\kappa$ **WHEN** g **THEN** P **END**

In this representation, an event is a parametrized imperative program P with a name $\mathcal{E}$, a list of service input parameters $p_1, ..., p_n$, and a guard condition g to determine the conditions triggering the event. In addition to the input parameters, an event has a special parameter κ which indicates the execution context, e.g. the scheduler and the thread invoking the event. The imperative commands of an event body P in π-Core are standard sequential constructs such as conditional execution, loop, and sequential composition of programs. It also includes a synchronization construct for concurrent processes represented by **AWAIT** b **THEN** P **END**. The body P is executed atomically if and only if the boolean condition b holds, not progressing otherwise. **ATOM** P **END** denotes an *Await* statement for which its guard is *True*.

Threads and kernel processes have their own execution context and local states. Each of them is modelled in π-Core as a set of events called *event systems* and denoted as **ESYS** $\mathcal{S} \equiv \{\mathcal{E}_0, ..., \mathcal{E}_n\}$. The operational semantics of an event system is the *sequential composition* of the execution of the events composing it. It consists in the continuous evaluation of the guards of the system events. From the set of events for which the associated guard g holds in the current state, one event $\mathcal{E}$ is non-deterministically selected to be triggered, and its body P executed. After P finishes, the evaluation of the guards starts again looking for the next event to be executed. Finally, π-Core has a construct for parallel composition of event systems $esys_0 \parallel ... \parallel esys_n$ which interleaves the execution of the events composing each event system $esys_i$ for $0 \le i \le n$.

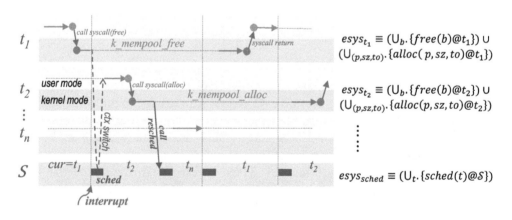

Fig. 3. An execution model of Zephyr memory management

Execution Model of Zephyr. If we do not consider its initialization, an OS kernel can be consider as a reactive system that is in an *idle* loop until it receives an interruption which is handled by an interruption handler. Whilst interrupt handlers execution is atomic in sequential kernels, it can be interrupted in concurrent kernels [6,22] allowing services invoked by threads to be interrupted and resumed later. In the execution model of Zephyr, we consider a scheduler $\mathcal{S}$ and a set of threads $t_1, ..., t_n$. In this model, the execution of the scheduler is atomic since kernel services can not interrupt it. But kernel services can be interrupted via the scheduler, i.e., the execution of a memory service invoked by a thread t_i may be interrupted by the kernel scheduler to execute a thread t_j. Figure 3 illustrates Zephyr execution model, where solid lines represent execution steps of the threads/kernel services and dotted lines mean the suspension of the thread/code. For instance, the execution of $k\_mempool\_free$ in thread t_1 is interrupted by the scheduler, and the context is switched to thread t_2 which invokes $k\_mempool\_alloc$. During the execution of t_2, the kernel service may suspend the thread and switch to another thread t_n by calling *rescheduling*. Later, the execution is switched back to t_1 and continues the execution of $k\_mempool\_free$ in a different state from when it was interrupted.

The event systems of Zephyr are illustrated in the right part of Fig. 3. A user thread t_i invoke allocation/release services, thus the event system for t_i is $esys_{t_i}$, a set composed of the events *alloc* and *free*. The input parameters for these events correspond with the arguments of the service implementation, that are constrained by the guard for each service. Together with system users we model the event service for the scheduler $esys_{sched}$ consisting on a unique event *sched* whose argument is a thread t to be scheduled when t is in the $READY$ state. The formal specification of the memory management is the parallel composition of the event system for the threads and the scheduler $esys_{t_1} \parallel ... \parallel esys_{t_n} \parallel esys_{sched}$

Thread Context and Preemption. Events are parametrized by a thread identifier used to access to the execution context of the thread invoking it. As shown in Fig. 3, the execution of an event executed by a thread can be stopped by the scheduler to be resumed later. This behaviour is modelled using a global variable cur that indicates the thread being currently has been scheduled and is being executed, and conditioning the execution of parametrized events in t only when t is scheduled. This is achieved by using the expression t ▶ p ≡ **AWAIT** $cur = t$ **THEN** p **END**, so an event invoked by a thread t only progresses when t is scheduled. This scheme allows to use rely-guarantee for concurrent execution of threads on mono-core architectures, where only the scheduled thread is able to modify the memory.

4.2   Formal Specification of Memory Management Services

This section discusses the formal specification of the memory management services. These services deal with the initialization of pools, and memory allocation and release.

System State. The system state includes the memory model introduced in Sect. 4, together with the thread under execution in variable cur and local variables to the memory services used to keep temporal changes to the structure, guards in conditional and loop statements, and index accesses. The memory model is represented as a set mem_pools storing the references of all memory pools and a mapping mem_pool_info to query a pool by a pool reference. Local variables are modelled as total functions from threads to variable values, representing that the event is accessing the thread context. In the formal model of the events we represent access to a state component c using $'c$ and the value of a local component c for the thread t is represented as $'c\ t$. Local variables *allocating_node* and *freeing_node* are relevant for the memory services, storing the temporal blocks being split/coalesced in alloc/release services respectively.

Memory Pool Initialization. Zephyr defines and initializes memory pools at compile time by constructing a static variable of type **struct** *k_mem_pool*. The implementation initializes each pool with *n_max* level 0 blocks with size *max_sz* bytes. Bitmaps of level 0 are set to 1 and free list contains all level 0 blocks. Bitmaps and free lists of other level are initialized to 0 and to the empty list respectively. In the formal model, we specify a state corresponding to the implementation initial state and we show that it belongs to the set of states satisfying the invariant.

```
1   WHILE 'free-block-r t DO
2      t ▶ 'lsz := 'lsz (t := 'lsizes t ! ('lvl t));;
3      t ▶ 'blk := 'blk (t := block-ptr ('mem-pool-info (pool b)) ('lsz t) ('bn t));;
4      t ▶ ATOM
5         'mem-pool-info := set-bit-free 'mem-pool-info (pool b) ('lvl t) ('bn t);;
6         'freeing-node := 'freeing-node (t := None);;
7         IF 'lvl t > 0 ∧ partner-bits ('mem-pool-info (pool b)) ('lvl t) ('bn t) THEN
8            FOR 'i := 'i(t := 0); 'i t < 4; 'i := 'i(t := 'i t + 1) DO
9               'bb := 'bb (t := ('bn t div 4) * 4 + 'i t);;
10              'mem-pool-info := set-bit-noexist 'mem-pool-info (pool b) ('lvl t) ('bb t);;
11              'block-pt := 'block-pt (t := block-ptr ('mem-pool-info (pool b)) ('lsz t) ('bb t));;
12              IF 'bn t ≠ 'bb t ∧ block-fits ('mem-pool-info (pool b)) ('block-pt t) ('lsz t) THEN
13                 'mem-pool-info := 'mem-pool-info ((pool b) :=
14                    remove-free-list ('mem-pool-info (pool b)) ('lvl t) ('block-pt t))
15              FI
16           ROF;;
17           'lvl := 'lvl (t := 'lvl t − 1);;
18           'bn := 'bn (t := 'bn t div 4);;
19           'mem-pool-info := set-bit-freeing 'mem-pool-info (pool b) ('lvl t) ('bn t);;
20           'freeing-node := 'freeing-node (t := Some (|pool = (pool b), level = ('lvl t),
21              block = ('bn t), data = block-ptr ('mem-pool-info (pool b))
22                 ((((ALIGN4 (max-sz ('mem-pool-info (pool b)))) div (4 ^ ('lvl t)))) ('bn t) |))
23        ELSE
24           IF block-fits ('mem-pool-info (pool b)) ('blk t) ('lsz t) THEN
25              'mem-pool-info := 'mem-pool-info ((pool b) :=
26                 append-free-list ('mem-pool-info (pool b)) ('lvl t) ('blk t) )
27           FI;;
28           'free-block-r := 'free-block-r (t := False)
29        FI
30     END
31  OD
```

Fig. 4. The π-Core specification of *free_block*

Memory Allocation/Release Services. The C code of Zephyr uses the recursive function *free_block* to coalesce free partner blocks and the *break* statement to stop the execution of a loop statements, which are not supported by the imperative language in π-Core. The formal specification overcomes this by transforming the recursion into a loop controlled by the recursion condition, and using a control variable to exit loops with breaks when the condition to execute the loop break is satisfied. Additionally, the memory management services use the atomic body *irq_lock(); P; irq_unlock();* to keep interruption handlers *reentrant* by disabling interruptions. We simplify this behaviour in the specification using an **ATOM** statement, avoiding that the service is interrupted at that point. The rest of the formal specification closely follows the implementation, where variables are modified using higher order functions changing the state as the code does it. The reason of using Isabelle/HOL functions is that π-Core does not provide a semantic for expressions, using instead state transformer relying on high order functions to change the state.

Figure 4 illustrates the π-Core specification of the *free_block* function invoked by *k_mem_pool_free* when releasing a memory block. The code accesses the following variables: *lsz*, *lsize*, and *lvl* to keep information about the current level; *blk*, *bn*, and *bb* to represent the address and number of the block currently being accessed; *freeing_node* to represent the node being freeing; and *i* to iterate blocks. Additionally, the model includes the component *free_block_r* to model the recursion condition. To simplify the representation the model uses predicates and functions to access and modify the state. Due to space constrains, we are unable to provide detailed explanation of these functions. However the name of the functions can help the reader to better understand their functionality. We refer readers to the Isabelle/HOL sources for the complete specification of the formal model.

In the C code, *free_block* is a recursive function with two conditions: (1) the block being released belongs to a level higher than zero, since blocks at level zero cannot be merged; and (2) the partners bits of the block being released are *FREE* so they can be merged into a bigger block. We represent (1) with the predicate *'lvl t > 0* and (2) with the predicate *partner_bit_free*. The formal specification follows the same structure translating the recursive function into a loop that is controlled by a variable mimicking the recursion.

The formal specification for *free_block* first releases an allocated memory block *bn* setting it to *FREEING*. Then, the loop statement sets *free_block* to *FREE* (Line 5), and also checks that the iteration/recursive condition holds in Line 7. If the condition holds, the partner bits are set to *NOEXIST*, and remove their addresses from the free list for this level (Lines 12–14). Then, it sets the parent block bit to *FREEING* (Lines 17–22), and updates the variables controlling the current block and level numbers, before going back to the beginning of the loop again. If the iteration condition is not true it sets the bit to *FREE* and add the block to the free list (Lines 24–28) and sets the loop condition to false to end the procedure. This function is illustrated in Fig. 2. The block 172 is released by a thread and since its partner blocks (block 173–175) are free, Zephyr coalesces the four blocks and sets their parent block 43 as *FREEING*. The coalescence continues iteratively if the partners of block 43 are all free.

5   Correctness and Rely-Guarantee Proof

We have proven correctness of the buddy memory management in Zephyr using the rely-guarantee proof system of π-Core. We ensure functional correctness of each kernel service w.r.t. the defined pre/post conditions, invariant preservation, termination of loop statements in the kernel services, the preservation of the memory configuration during small steps of kernel services, and the separation of local variables of threads. In this section, we introduce the rely-guarantee proof system of π-Core and how these properties are specified and verified using it.

5.1   Rely-Guarantee Proof Rules and Verification

A rely-guarantee specification for a system is a quadruple $RGCond = \langle pre, R, G, pst \rangle$, where pre is the pre-condition, R is the rely condition, G is the guarantee condition, and pst is the post-condition. The intuitive meaning of a valid rely-guarantee specification for a parallel component P, denoted by $\models P$ **sat** $\langle pre, R, G, pst \rangle$, is that if P is executed from an initial state $s \in pre$ and any environment transition belongs to the rely relation R, then the state transitions carried out by P belong to the guarantee relation G and the final states belong to pst.

We have defined a rely-guarantee axiomatic proof system for the π-Core specification language to prove validity of rely-guarantee specifications, and proven in Isabelle/HOL its soundness with regards to the definition of validity. Some of the rules composing the axiomatic reasoning system are shown in Fig. 5.

[AWAIT]
$\vdash P$ **sat** $\langle pre \cap b \cap \{V\}, Id, UNIV, \{s \mid (V, s) \in G\} \cap pst \rangle$
$stable(pre, R)$ $stable(pst, R)$

$\overline{\qquad \vdash (\textbf{Await } b\ P) \textbf{ sat } \langle pre, R, G, pst \rangle \qquad}$

[BASICEVT]
$\vdash body(\alpha)$ **sat** $\langle pre \cap guard(\alpha), R, G, pst \rangle$
$stable(pre, R)$ $\forall s.\ (s, s) \in G$

$\overline{\qquad \vdash \textbf{Event } \alpha \textbf{ sat } \langle pre, R, G, pst \rangle \qquad}$

[WHILE]
$\vdash P$ **sat** $\langle loopinv \cap b, R, G, loopinv \rangle$
$loopinv \cap -b \subseteq pst$ $\forall s.\ (s, s) \in G$
$stable(loopinv, R)$ $stable(pst, R)$

$\overline{\qquad \vdash (\textbf{While } b\ P) \textbf{ sat } \langle loopinv, R, G, pst \rangle \qquad}$

[PAR]
$(1) \forall \kappa. \vdash \mathcal{PS}(\kappa)$ **sat** $\langle pres_\kappa, Rs_\kappa, Gs_\kappa, psts_\kappa \rangle$
$(2) \forall \kappa.\ pre \subseteq pres_\kappa$ $(3) \forall \kappa.\ psts_\kappa \subseteq pst$ $(4) \forall \kappa.\ Gs_\kappa \subseteq G$
$(5) \forall \kappa.\ R \subseteq Rs_\kappa$ $(6) \forall \kappa, \kappa'.\ \kappa \neq \kappa' \longrightarrow Gs_\kappa \subseteq Rs_{\kappa'}$

$\overline{\qquad \vdash \mathcal{PS} \textbf{ sat } \langle pre, R, G, pst \rangle \qquad}$

Fig. 5. Typical rely-guarantee proof rules in π-Core

A predicate P is stable w.r.t. a relation R, represented as $stable(P, R)$, when for any pair of states (s, t) such that $s \in P$ and $(s, t) \in R$ then $t \in P$. The intuitive meaning is that an environment represented by R does not affect the satisfiability of P. The parallel rule in Fig. 5 establishes compositionality of the proof system, where verification of the parallel specification can be reduced to the verification of individual event systems first and then to the verification of individual events. It is necessary that each event system $\mathcal{PS}(\kappa)$ satisfies its specification $\langle pres_\kappa, Rs_\kappa, Gs_\kappa, psts_\kappa \rangle$ (Premise 1); the pre-condition for the parallel composition implies all the event system's pre-conditions (Premise 2); the overall post-condition must be a logical consequence of all post-conditions of event systems (Premise 3); since an action transition of the concurrent system is performed by one of its event system, the guarantee condition Gs_κ of each event system must be a subset of the overall guarantee condition G (Premise 4); an environment transition Rs_κ for the event system κ corresponds to a transition from the overall environment R (Premise 5); and an action transition of an event system κ should be defined in the rely condition of another event system κ', where $\kappa \neq \kappa'$ (Premise 6).

To prove loop termination, loop invariants are parametrized with a logical variable α. It suffices to show total correctness of a loop statement by the following proposition where $loopinv(\alpha)$ is the parametrize invariant, in which the logical variable is used to find a convergent relation to show that the number of iterations of the loop is finite.

$$\vdash P \text{ sat } \langle loopinv(\alpha) \cap \{\!| \alpha > 0 \,|\!\}, R, G, \exists \beta < \alpha. \; loopinv(\beta) \rangle \wedge loopinv(\alpha) \cap \{\!| \alpha > 0 \,|\!\} \subseteq \{\!| b \,|\!\}$$

$$\wedge \; loopinv(0) \subseteq \{\!| \neg b \,|\!\} \wedge \forall s \in loopinv(\alpha). \; (s,t) \in R \longrightarrow \exists \beta \leqslant \alpha. \; t \in loopinv(\beta)$$

5.2 Correctness Specification

Using the compositional reasoning of π-Core, correctness of Zephyr memory management can be specified and verified with the rely-guarantee specification of each event. The functional correctness of a kernel service is specified by its pre/post-conditions. Invariant preservation, memory configuration, and separation of local variables is specified in the guarantee condition of each service.

The guarantee condition for both memory services is defined as:

$$\textbf{Mem-pool-alloc-guar } t \equiv \overbrace{Id}^{(1)} \cup (\overbrace{gvars\_conf\_stable}^{(2)} \cap$$

$$\{(s,r). \; (\overbrace{cur \; s \neq Some \; t}^{(3.1)} \longrightarrow gvars\text{-}nochange \; s \; r \wedge lvars\text{-}nochange \; t \; s \; r \;)$$

$$\wedge \; (\overbrace{cur \; s = Some \; t}^{(3.2)} \longrightarrow inv \; s \longrightarrow inv \; r \;) \wedge (\overbrace{\forall t'. \; t' \neq t}^{(4)} \longrightarrow lvars\text{-}nochange \; t' \; s \; r \;) \})$$

This relation states that *alloc* and *free* services may not change the state (1), e.g., a blocked await or selecting branch on a conditional statement. If it changes the state then: (2) the static configuration of memory pools in the model do not change; (3.1) if the scheduled thread is not the thread invoking the event then variables for that thread do not change (since it is blocked in an *Await* as explained in Sect. 3); (3.2) if it is, then the relation preserves the memory invariant, and consequently each step of the event needs to preserve the invariant; (4) a thread does not change the local variables of other threads.

Using the π-Core proof rules we verify that the invariant introduced in Sect. 4 is preserved by all the events. Additionally, we prove that when starting in a valid memory configuration given by the invariant, then if the service does not returns an error code then it returns a valid memory block with size bigger or equal than the requested capacity. The property is specified by the following postcondition:

Mem-pool-alloc-pre $t \equiv \{s.\ invs \wedge allocating\text{-}nodes\ t = None \wedge freeing\text{-}nodes\ t = None\}$
Mem-pool-alloc-post $t\ p\ sz\ timeout \equiv$
$\{s.\ inv\ s \wedge allocating\text{-}node\ s\ t = None \wedge freeing\text{-}node\ s\ t = None$
 $\wedge\ (timeout = FOREVER \longrightarrow$
  $(ret\ s\ t = ESIZEERR \wedge mempoolalloc\text{-}ret\ s\ t = None \vee$
  $ret\ s\ t = OK \wedge (\exists\ mblk.\ mempoolalloc\text{-}ret\ s\ t = Some\ mblk \wedge mblk\text{-}valid\ s\ p\ sz$
$mblk)))$
  $\wedge\ (timeout = NOWAIT \longrightarrow$
   $((ret\ s\ t = ENOMEM \vee ret\ s\ t = ESIZEERR) \wedge mempoolalloc\text{-}ret\ s\ t = None) \vee$
   $(ret\ s\ t = OK \wedge (\exists\ mblk.\ mempoolalloc\text{-}ret\ s\ t = Some\ mblk \wedge mblk\text{-}valid\ s\ p\ sz$
$mblk)))$
  $\wedge\ (timeout > 0 \longrightarrow$
   $((ret\ s\ t = ETIMEOUT \vee ret\ s\ t = ESIZEERR) \wedge mempoolalloc\text{-}ret\ s\ t = None) \vee$
   $(ret\ s\ t = OK \wedge (\exists\ mblk.\ mempoolalloc\text{-}ret\ s\ t = Some\ mblk$
         $\wedge\ mblk\text{-}valid\ s\ p\ sz\ mblk)))\}$

If a thread requests a memory block in mode *FOREVER*, it may successfully allocate a valid memory block, or fail (*ESIZEERR*) if the request size is larger than the size of the memory pool. If the thread is requesting a memory pool in mode *NOWAIT*, it may also get the result of *ENOMEM* if there is no available blocks. But if the thread is requesting in mode *TIMEOUT*, it will get the result of *ETIMEOUT* if there is no available blocks in *timeout* milliseconds.

The property is indeed weak since even if the memory has a block able to allocate the requested size before invoking the allocation service, another thread running concurrently may have taken the block first during the execution of the service. For the same reason, the released block may be taken by another concurrent thread before the end of the release services.

5.3 Correctness Proof

In the π-Core system, verification of a rely-guarantee specification proving a property is carried out by inductively applying the proof rules for each system event and discharging the proof obligations the rules generate. Typically, these proof obligations require to prove stability of the pre- and post-condition to check that changes of the environment preserve them, and to show that a statement modifying a state from the precondition gets a state belonging to the postcondition.

To prove termination of the loop statement in *free_block* shown in Fig. 4, we define the loop invariant with the logical variable α as follows.

mp-free-loopinv $t\ b\ \alpha \equiv \{\!\!|\ ... \wedge\ ´inv \wedge level\ b < length\ (´lsizes\ t)$
 $\wedge\ (\forall\ ii < length\ (´lsizes\ t).\ ´lsizes\ t\ !\ ii = (max\text{-}sz\ (´mem\text{-}pool\text{-}info\ (pool\ b)))\ div\ (4 \ ˆ ii))$
 $\wedge\ ´bn\ t < length\ (bits\ (levels\ (´mem\text{-}pool\text{-}info\ (pool\ b))!(´lvl\ t)))$
 $\wedge\ ´bn\ t = (block\ b)\ div\ (4 \ ˆ (level\ b - ´lvl\ t)) \wedge ´lvl\ t \leq level\ b$
 $\wedge\ (´free\text{-}block\text{-}r\ t \longrightarrow (\exists\ blk.\ ´freeing\text{-}node\ t = Some\ blk \wedge pool\ blk = pool\ b$
        $\wedge\ level\ blk = ´lvl\ t \wedge block\ blk = ´bn\ t)$

$$\land \ {}'alloc\text{-}memblk\text{-}data\text{-}valid \ (pool \ b) \ (the \ ({}'freeing\text{-}node \ t)))$$
$$\land \ (\neg \ {}'free\text{-}block\text{-}r \ t \longrightarrow {}'freeing\text{-}node \ t = None) \ \} \cap$$
$$\{\!\!\{ \ \alpha = (if \ {}'freeing\text{-}node \ t \neq None \ then \ {}'lvl \ t + 1 \ else \ 0) \ \}\!\!\}$$

$freeing\_node$ and lvt are local variables respectively storing the node being free and the level that the node belongs to. In the body of the loop, if $lvl \ t > 0$ and $partner\_bit$ is *true*, then $lvl = lvl - 1$ at the end of the body. Otherwise, $freeing\_node \ t = None$. So at the end of the loop body, α decreases or $\alpha = 0$. If $\alpha = 0$, we have $freeing\_node \ t = None$, and thus the negation of the loop condition $\neg free\_block\_r \ t$, concluding termination of $free\_block$.

Due to concurrency, it is necessary to consider fairness to prove termination of the loop statement in $k\_mempool\_alloc$ from Line 23 to 33 in Fig. 1. On the one hand, when a thread requests a memory block in the *FOREVER* mode, it is possible that there will never be available blocks since other threads do not release allocated blocks. On the other hand, even when other threads release blocks, it is possible that the available blocks are always raced by threads.

6   Evaluation and Results

Evaluation. The verification conducted in this work is on Zhephyr v1.8.0, released in 2017. The C code of the buddy memory management is $\approx$400lines, not counting blank lines and comments. Table 1 shows the statistics for the effort and size of the proofs in the Isabelle/HOL theorem prover. In total, the models and mechanized verification consists of $\approx$28,000 lines of specification and proofs, and the total effort is $\approx$12 person-months. The specification and proof of π-Core are reusable for the verification of other systems.

Table 1. Specification and proof statistics

π-Core language		Memory management	
Item	LOS/LOP	Item	LOS/LOP
Language and proof rules	700	Specification	400
Lemmas of language/semantics	3000	Auxiliary lemmas/invariant	1700
Soundness	7100	Proof of allocation	10600
Invariant	100	Proof of free	4950
Total	10,900	Total	17,650

Bugs in Zephyr. During the formal verification, we found 3 bugs in the C code of Zephyr. The first two bugs are critical and have been repaired in the latest release of Zephyr. To avoid the third one, callers to $k\_mem\_pool\_alloc$ have to constrain the argument $t\_size \ size$.

(1) **Incorrect block split:** this bug is located in the loop in Line 11 of the *k_mem_pool_alloc* service, shown in Fig. 1. The *level_empty* function checks if a pool p has blocks in the free list at level *alloc_l*. Concurrent threads may release a memory block at that level making the call to *level_empty(p, alloc_l)* to return *false* and stopping the loop. In such case, it allocates a memory block of a bigger capacity at a level i but it still sets the level number of the block as *alloc_l* at Line 15. The service allocates a larger block to the requesting thread causing an internal fragmentation of $max\_sz/4^i - max\_sz/4^{alloc\_l}$ bytes. When this block is released, it will be inserted into the free list at level *alloc_l*, but not at level i, causing an external fragmentation of $max\_sz/4^i - max\_sz/4^{alloc\_l}$. The bug is fixed by removing the condition *level_empty(p, alloc_l)* in our specification.

(2) **Incorrect return from *k_mem_pool_alloc*:** this bug is found at Line 26 in Fig. 1. When a suitable free block is allocated by another thread, the *pool_alloc* function returns *EAGAIN* at Line 9 to ask the thread to retry the allocation. When a thread invokes *k_mem_pool_alloc* in *FOREVER* mode and this case happens, the service returns *EAGAIN* immediately. However, a thread invoking *k_mem_pool_alloc* in *FOREVER* mode should keep retrying when it does not succeed. We repair the bug by removing the condition $ret == EAGAIN$ at Line 26. As explained in the comments of the C Code, *EAGAIN* should not be returned to threads invoking the service. Moreover, the *return EAGAIN* at Line 34 is actually the case of time out. Thus, we introduce a new return code *ETIMEOUT* in our specification.

(3) **Non-termination of *k_mem_pool_alloc*:** we have discussed that the loop statement at Lines 23–33 in Fig. 1 does not terminate. However, it should terminate in certain cases, which are actually violated in the C code. When a thread requests a memory block in *FOREVER* mode and the requested size is larger than *max_sz*, the maximum size of blocks, the loop at Lines 23–33 in Fig. 1 never finishes since *pool_alloc* always returns *ENOMEM*. The reason is that the *"return ENOMEM"* at Line 6 does not distinguish two cases, $alloc\_l < 0$ and $free\_l < 0$. In the first case, the requested size is larger than *max_sz* and the kernel service should return immediately. In the second case, there are no free blocks larger than the requested size and the service tries forever until some free block available. We repair the bug by splitting the *if* statement at Lines 4–7 into these two cases and introducing a new return code *ESIZEERR* in our specification. Then, we change the condition at Lines 25–26 to check that the returned value is *ESIZEERR* instead of *ENOMEM*.

7   Conclusion and Future Work

In this paper, we have developed a formal specification at low-level design of the concurrent buddy memory management of Zephyr RTOS. Using the rely-guarantee technique in the π-Core framework, we have formally verified a set of critical properties for OS kernels such as invariant preservation, and preservation of memory configuration. Finally, we identified some critical bugs in the C code of Zephyr.

Our work explores the challenges and cost of certifying concurrent OSs for the highest-level assurance. The definition of properties and rely-guarantee relations is complex and the verification task becomes expensive. We used 40 times of LOS/LOP than the C code at low-level design. Next, we are planning to verify other modules of Zephyr, which may be easier due to simpler data structures and algorithms. For the purpose of fully formal verification of OSs at source code level, we will replace the imperative language in π-Core by a more expressive one and add a verification condition generator (VCG) to reduce the cost of the verification.

References

1. The Zephyr Project. https://www.zephyrproject.org/. Accessed Dec 2018
2. Common Criteria for Information Technology Security Evaluation (v3.1, Release 5). https://www.commoncriteriaportal.org/. Accessed Apr 2017
3. Alkassar, E., Schirmer, N., Starostin, A.: Formal pervasive verification of a paging mechanism. In: Ramakrishnan, C.R., Rehof, J. (eds.) TACAS 2008. LNCS, vol. 4963, pp. 109–123. Springer, Heidelberg (2008). https://doi.org/10.1007/978-3-540-78800-3_9
4. Blanchard, A., Kosmatov, N., Lemerre, M., Loulergue, F.: A case study on formal verification of the anaxagoros hypervisor paging system with Frama-C. In: Núñez, M., Güdemann, M. (eds.) FMICS 2015. LNCS, vol. 9128, pp. 15–30. Springer, Cham (2015). https://doi.org/10.1007/978-3-319-19458-5_2
5. Bolignano, P., Jensen, T., Siles, V.: Modeling and abstraction of memory management in a hypervisor. In: Stevens, P., Wąsowski, A. (eds.) FASE 2016. LNCS, vol. 9633, pp. 214–230. Springer, Heidelberg (2016). https://doi.org/10.1007/978-3-662-49665-7_13
6. Chen, H., Wu, X., Shao, Z., Lockerman, J., Gu, R.: Toward compositional verification of interruptible OS kernels and device drivers. In: Proceedings of 37th ACM SIGPLAN Conference on Programming Language Design and Implementation (PLDI), pp. 431–447. ACM (2016)
7. Fang, B., Sighireanu, M.: Hierarchical shape abstraction for analysis of free list memory allocators. In: Hermenegildo, M.V., Lopez-Garcia, P. (eds.) LOPSTR 2016. LNCS, vol. 10184, pp. 151–167. Springer, Cham (2017). https://doi.org/10.1007/978-3-319-63139-4_9
8. Fang, B., Sighireanu, M.: A refinement hierarchy for free list memory allocators. In: Proceedings of ACM SIGPLAN International Symposium on Memory Management, pp. 104–114. ACM (2017)
9. Fang, B., et al.: Formal modelling of list based dynamic memory allocators. Sci. China Inf. Sci. **61**(12), 103–122 (2018)
10. Gallardo, M.D.M., Merino, P., Sanán, D.: Model checking dynamic memory allocation in operating systems. J. Autom. Reasoning **42**(2), 229–264 (2009)
11. Gu, R., et al.: CertiKOS: an extensible architecture for building certified concurrent OS kernels. In: Proceedings of 12th USENIX Symposium on Operating Systems Design and Implementation (OSDI), pp. 653–669. USENIX Association, Savannah, GA (2016)
12. Klein, G., et al.: seL4: formal verification of an OS kernel. In: Proceedings of 22nd ACM SIGOPS Symposium on Operating Systems Principles (SOSP), pp. 207–220. ACM Press (2009)

13. Klein, G., Tuch, H.: Towards verified virtual memory in L4. In: Proceedings of TPHOLs Emerging Trends, p. 16. Park City, Utah, USA, September 2004

14. Leroy, X., Blazy, S.: Formal verification of a C-like memory model and its uses for verifying program transformations. J. Autom. Reasoning **41**(1), 1–31 (2008)

15. Mansky, W., Garbuzov, D., Zdancewic, S.: An axiomatic specification for sequential memory models. In: Kroening, D., Păsăreanu, C.S. (eds.) CAV 2015. LNCS, vol. 9207, pp. 413–428. Springer, Cham (2015). https://doi.org/10.1007/978-3-319-21668-3_24

16. Marti, N., Affeldt, R., Yonezawa, A.: Formal verification of the heap manager of an operating system using separation logic. In: Liu, Z., He, J. (eds.) ICFEM 2006. LNCS, vol. 4260, pp. 400–419. Springer, Heidelberg (2006). https://doi.org/10.1007/11901433_22

17. Saraswat, V.A., Jagadeesan, R., Michael, M., von Praun, C.: A theory of memory models. In: Proceedings of the 12th ACM SIGPLAN Symposium on Principles and Practice of Parallel Programming (PPoPP), pp. 161–172. ACM (2007)

18. Su, W., Abrial, J.R., Pu, G., Fang, B.: Formal development of a real-time operating system memory manager. In: Proceedings of International Conference on Engineering of Complex Computer Systems (ICECCS), pp. 130–139 (2016)

19. Tews, H., Völp, M., Weber, T.: Formal memory models for the verification of low-level operating-system code. J. Autom. Reasoning **42**(2), 189–227 (2009)

20. Vaynberg, A., Shao, Z.: Compositional verification of a baby virtual memory manager. In: Hawblitzel, C., Miller, D. (eds.) CPP 2012. LNCS, vol. 7679, pp. 143–159. Springer, Heidelberg (2012). https://doi.org/10.1007/978-3-642-35308-6_13

21. Ševčík, J., Vafeiadis, V., Nardelli, F.Z., Jagannathan, S., Sewell, P.: CompCertTSO: a verified compiler for relaxed-memory concurrency. J. ACM **60**(3), 22:1–22:50 (2013)

22. Xu, F., Fu, M., Feng, X., Zhang, X., Zhang, H., Li, Z.: A practical verification framework for preemptive OS kernels. In: Chaudhuri, S., Farzan, A. (eds.) CAV 2016. LNCS, vol. 9780, pp. 59–79. Springer, Cham (2016). https://doi.org/10.1007/978-3-319-41540-6_4

23. Yu, D., Hamid, N.A., Shao, Z.: Building certified libraries for PCC: dynamic storage allocation. In: Degano, P. (ed.) ESOP 2003. LNCS, vol. 2618, pp. 363–379. Springer, Heidelberg (2003). https://doi.org/10.1007/3-540-36575-3_25

12

Integrating Formal Schedulability Analysis into a Verified OS Kernel

Xiaojie Guo[1,2], Maxime Lesourd[1,2], Mengqi Liu[3],
Lionel Rieg[1,3(✉)], and Zhong Shao[3]

[1] Univ. Grenoble Alpes, CNRS, Grenoble INP,
VERIMAG, Grenoble, France
[2] Univ. Grenoble Alpes, Inria, CNRS, Grenoble INP,
LIG, Grenoble, France
[3] Yale University, New Haven, CT, USA
`lionel.rieg@univ-grenoble-alpes.fr`

Abstract. Formal verification of real-time systems is attractive because these systems often perform critical operations. Unlike non real-time systems, latency and response time guarantees are of critical importance in this setting, as much as functional correctness. Nevertheless, formal verification of real-time OSes usually stops the scheduling analysis at the policy level: they only prove that the scheduler (or its abstract model) satisfies some scheduling policy. In this paper, we go further and connect together Prosa, a verified schedulability analyzer, and RT-CertiKOS, a verified single-core sequential real-time OS kernel. Thus, we get a more general and extensible schedulability analysis proof for RT-CertiKOS, as well a concrete implementation validating Prosa models. It also showcases that it is realistic to connect two completely independent formal developments in a proof assistant.

Keywords: Formal methods · Proof assistant · Real-time scheduling · OS kernel · Schedulability analysis

1 Introduction

The real-time and OS communities have seen recent effort towards formal proofs, through several techniques such as model checking [16,22] and interactive theorem provers [7,14,17]. This trend is motivated by the high stakes of critical systems and the combinatorial complexity of considering all possible interleavings of states of a system, which makes pen-and-paper reasoning too error-prone.

Real-time OSes used in critical areas such as avionics and automobile applications must ensure not only functional correctness but also timing requirements. Indeed, a missed deadline may have catastrophic consequences. Schedulability analysis aims to guarantee the absence of deadline miss given a scheduling algorithm which decides which task is going to execute.

In the current state of the art, the schedulability analysis is decoupled from the kernel code verification. This is good from a separation of concern perspective as both kernel verification and schedulability analysis are already complex enough without adding in the other. Nevertheless, this gap also means that both communities may lack validation from the other one.

On the one hand, schedulability analysis itself is error-prone, *e.g.,* a flaw was found in the original schedulability analysis [26,27,29] for the Controller Area Network bus, which is widely used in automobile. To tackle this issue, the Prosa library [7] provides mechanized schedulability proofs. This library is developed with a focus on readable specifications in order to ensure wide acceptance by the community. It is currently a reference for mechanized schedulability proofs and was able to verify several existing multicore scheduling policies under a new setting with jitter. However, some of its design decisions, in particular for task models and scheduling policies, are highly unusual and their adequacy to reality has never been justified by connecting them to a concrete OS kernel enforcing a real-time scheduling policy.

On the other hand, OS kernels are very sensitive and bug-prone pieces of code, which inspires a lot of existing work on using formal methods to prove functional correctness and other requirements, such as access control policies [17], scheduling policies [31], timing requirements, etc. One such verified OS kernel is RT-CertiKOS [21], developed by the Yale FLINT group and built on top of the sequential CertiKOS [9,13]. Its verification focuses on extensions beyond pure functional correctness, such as real-time guarantees and isolation between components. However, any major extension such as real-time adds a lot of proof burden.

In this paper, we solve both problems at once by combining the formal schedulability analysis given by Prosa with the functional correctness guarantees of RT-CertiKOS. Thus, we get a formal schedulability proof for this kernel: if it accepts a task set, then formal proofs ensure that there will be no deadline miss during execution. Furthermore, this work also produces a concrete instance of the definitions used in Prosa, ensuring their consistency and adequacy with a real system.

Contributions. In this paper, we make the following contributions:

- Definition of a clear interface for schedulability analysis between a kernel (here, RT-CertiKOS) and a schedulability analyzer (here, Prosa);
- A workaround for the mismatch between the notion of jobs in schedulability analysis (which contains actual execution time) and in OS scheduling through the scheduling trace;
- A way to extend a finite scheduling trace (from RT-CertiKOS) into an infinite one (for Prosa) while still satisfying the fixed priority preemptive (FPP) scheduling policy;
- A formally proven connection between RT-CertiKOS and Prosa, validating Prosa modeling choices and enabling RT-CertiKOS to benefit from the state-of-the-art schedulability results of Prosa.

Outline of the Paper. Section 2 introduces the Prosa library and its description of scheduling. In Sect. 3, we describe RT-CertiKOS, its scheduler, as well as the associated verification technique, abstraction layers. Section 4 then highlights the key differences between the models of Prosa and RT-CertiKOS, and how we resolve them. Finally, Sects. 5, 6, and 7, evaluate our work, present future work and related work before concluding.

2 Prosa

Prosa [7] is a Coq [25] library of models and analyses for real-time systems. The library is aimed towards the real-time community and provides models and analyses found in the literature with a focus on readable specifications.

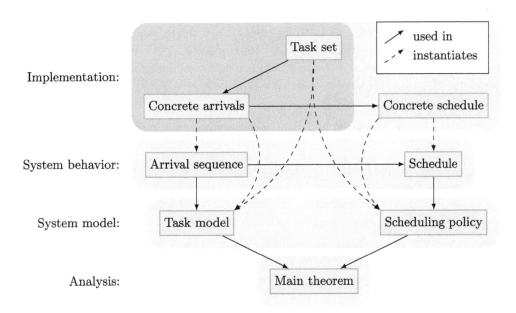

Fig. 1. An overview of Prosa layers

The library contains four basic layers, which are presented in Fig. 1:

System behavior. The base of the library is a model of discrete time traces as infinite sequences of events. We consider two such kinds of sequences: arrival sequences record requests for service called *job* activations and schedules record which job is able to progress.

System model. In order to reason about system behavior, jobs with similar properties are grouped into *tasks*. Based on system behavior, task models (arrival patterns and cost models) and scheduling policies are defined. These models are axiomatic in the sense that they are given as predicates on traces/schedules and not as generating and scheduling functions. In particular, a "FPP scheduler" (see Sect. 2.2) is modeled as "any trace satisfying the FPP policy".

Analysis. The library provides response time and schedulability analyses for these models.

Implementation. Finally, examples of traces and schedulers are implemented to validate the specifications axiomatized in the System model layer and to use the results proven in the Analysis layer. It is this part (more precisely, the top left dark block of Fig. 1) that is meant to connect with RT-CertiKOS.

2.1 System Behavior

The basic definitions in Prosa concern concrete system behavior. The notion of time used in the library corresponds to scheduling ticks: durations are given in number of ticks and instants are given as number of ticks from initialization of the system. For this paper, we focus on single-core systems[1] on which instances of a finite set $TaskSet$ of tasks are scheduled. To each task τ is associated a relative deadline D_τ which corresponds to the delay we want to guarantee between the activation of an instance of a task and its completion. We defer the definition of tasks (Definition 4) until their parameters are relevant and focus first on the modeling of system behavior in Prosa. The instances of tasks which are to be scheduled are called *jobs*.

Definition 1 (Job). *A job $\jmath$ is defined by a task $\tau_\jmath$, a positive cost $\mathbf{c}_\jmath$, and a unique identifier.*

We do not use the identifier directly, it is only used to distinguish jobs of the same task in traces.

These jobs are used to describe the workload to be scheduled. This workload is defined by an *arrival sequence* which is a trace of job activations.

Definition 2 (Arrival sequence). *An* arrival sequence *is a function ρ mapping any time instant t to a finite (possibly empty) set of jobs $\rho(t)$.*
A job can only appear once in an arrival sequence.

Since a job $\jmath$ can appear at most once in an arrival sequence ρ, we can define its *arrival time* $\mathbf{a}_\rho(\jmath)$ in ρ as the instant t such that $\jmath \in \rho(t)$.

We do not model the scheduler as a function, instead we work with *schedules* over an arrival sequence which are traces of scheduled jobs.

Definition 3 (Schedule). *A schedule* over an arrival sequence ρ is a function σ which maps any time instant t to either a job appearing in ρ or $\bot$.

The symbol $\bot$ is used for instants at which no job is scheduled. Given an arrival sequence ρ and a schedule σ over ρ, a job $\jmath \in \rho$ is said to be *scheduled at an instant t* if $\sigma(t) = \jmath$, the *service* received by $\jmath$ up to time t is the number of instants before t at which $\jmath$ is scheduled. A job $\jmath$ is said to be complete at time t if its service received up to time t is equal to its cost $\mathbf{c}_\jmath$ and $\jmath$ is said to be *pending at time t* if it has arrived before time t and is not complete at time t. From now on, we require schedules to only schedule pending jobs. A job $\jmath$ is said to be schedulable if it is complete by its *absolute deadline* $d_\jmath := \mathbf{a}_\rho(\jmath) + D_{\tau_\jmath}$.

---

[1] Multicore systems are handled by Prosa but we do not consider them here.

2.2 System Model

Task Model. In order to specify the behavior of the system we are interested in, Prosa introduces predicates on traces for which the response time analysis provides guarantees.

We now focus on the definitions related to the *sporadic* task model and the *fixed priority preemptive* (FPP) scheduling policy.

Definition 4 (Sporadic FPP task). *A sporadic FPP task τ is defined by a deadline $D_\tau \in \mathbb{N}$, a minimal inter-arrival time $\delta_\tau^- \in \mathbb{N}$, a worst case execution time (WCET) $\mathbf{C}\tau$, and a priority $p_\tau \in \mathbb{N}$. When D_τ is equal to δ_τ^-, the deadline is said* implicit.

Sporadic Task Model. The sporadic task model is specified by a sporadic arrival model and a cost model.

In the sporadic arrival model, consecutive activations of a task τ are separated by a minimum distance δ_τ^-: an arrival sequence ρ is sporadic if for any two distinct jobs $\jmath_1, \jmath_2 \in \rho$ of the same task τ, $|\mathbf{a}_\rho(\jmath_1) - \mathbf{a}_\rho(\jmath_2)| \geq \delta_\tau^-$. Periodic arrivals are a particular case of this model where δ_τ^- is the period and jobs arrives exactly at intervals of δ_τ^-. This is sufficient for us as the schedulability analysis for FPP yields the same bounds for sporadic and periodic activations.

The considered cost model is a constraint on activations: jobs in the arrival sequence must respect the WCET of their task, that is, for any $\jmath \in \rho$, $\mathbf{c}_\jmath \leq \mathbf{C}_{\tau_\jmath}$.

FPP Scheduling Policy. The FPP policy is modeled in Prosa as two constraints on the schedule: it must be *work conserving*, that is, it cannot be idle when there are pending tasks; and it must respect the priorities, that is, a scheduled job always has the highest priority among pending jobs.

2.3 Analysis

Prosa contains a proof of Bertogna and Cirinei's [4] response time analysis for FPP single-core schedules of sporadic tasks, with exact bounds for implicit deadlines. The analysis is based on the following property of the maximum workload for these schedules.

Definition 5 (Maximum Workload). *Given a task $\tau \in TaskSet$ and a duration Δ, the maximum workload of the system w.r.t. τ within that duration is*

$$W_\tau(\Delta) := \sum_{\substack{\tau' \in TaskSet \\ p_{\tau'} \geq p_\tau}} \mathbf{C}_{\tau'} \times \left\lceil \frac{\Delta}{\delta_{\tau'}^-} \right\rceil$$

The maximum workload $W_\tau(\Delta)$ corresponds to the worst case activation pattern in which all tasks are simultaneously activated with maximum cost (WCET of their task) and minimal inter-arrival distance. It is an upper bound on the amount of service required to schedule activations of the tasks with a priority higher than or equal to p_τ in any interval of size Δ. Based on this property, we can derive a response time bound for our system model if we can find a Δ larger than $W_\tau(\Delta)$.

Theorem 1 (Response Time Bound). *Given a sporadic taskset $TaskSet$ and a task $\tau \in TaskSet$ then for any $R > 0$ such that $R \geq W_\tau(R)$, any job $\jmath$ of task τ in an FPP schedule σ over an arrival sequence ρ is completed by $\mathbf{a}_\rho(\jmath) + R$.*

For instance, the smallest response time bound for a task $\tau \in TaskSet$ can be computed by the least positive fixed point of the function W_τ. Using this response time bound, we can derive a *schedulability criterion* by requiring this bound to be smaller than or equal to the deadline of task τ.

2.4 Implementation and Motivation for the Connection with RT-CertiKOS

The Prosa library includes functions to generate periodic traces and the corresponding FPP schedules, together with proofs of these properties and an instantiation of the schedulability criterion for these traces. This implementation was initially provided as a way to check that the modeling of the arrival model and scheduling policy are not contradictory and as such the implementation is as simple as possible. Although this is a good step in order to make the axiomatic definition of scheduling policies more acceptable, there is still room for improvement: these implementations are still rather ad-hoc and there is no connection to an actual system. This is where the link with RT-CertiKOS is beneficial to the Prosa ecosystem: it justifies that the model is indeed suitable for a concrete and independently developed real-time OS scheduler.

3 The RT-CertiKOS OS Kernel

RT-CertiKOS [21], developed by the Yale FLINT group, is a real-time extension of the single-core sequential CertiKOS [9,13],[2] whose functional correctness has been mechanized in the Coq proof assistant [25]. The sequential restriction greatly simplifies the implementation of the OS kernel. However, it does not support multicore, and the lack of kernel preemption can also degrade the responsiveness of the whole system. RT-CertiKOS proves spatial and temporal isolation (including schedulability) between components.

Both CertiKOS and RT-CertiKOS follow the same proof methodology, organized around the notion of abstraction layers that permits decomposition of the kernel into small pieces that are easier to verify.

---

[2] There is a multicore version of CertiKOS [14,15], but RT-CertiKOS is developed on top of the sequential version.

3.1 Abstraction Layers

Abstraction layers [13] are essentially a way to combine code fragments and their interface with simulation proofs. They consist of four elements: *(a)* a piece of code; *(b)* an *underlay*, the interface that the code relies on; *(c)* an *overlay*, the interface that the code provides; *(d)* a *simulation proof* ensuring that the code running on top of the underlay indeed provides the functionalities described in the overlay.

Implementation details of lower layers are encapsulated in higher layers, allowing to reason directly with the specifications rather than the implementation.

Notice that the underlay and overlay are specifications written in Coq and may be expressed using the semantics of several programming languages at once. This explains how CertiKOS (and RT-CertiKOS) manages to encompass both C and assembly code verification into a unified framework. Notice further that this notion of interface not only includes functions but also some *abstract state*, which exposes memory states of lower layers in a clean and structured way, and allows the overlay to access them only by invoking verified functions.

3.2 The Scheduler in RT-CertiKOS

RT-CertiKOS supports user-level fixed-priority preemptive scheduling. Its scheduler is invoked by timer interrupts periodically, dividing CPU time into intervals, which are called *time slots*, *time quanta*, or *time slices*.

Task Model. Each task in RT-CertiKOS is defined by a fixed priority, a period, and a budget (or WCET), the latter two being given in time slot units. Tasks are strictly periodic, with implicit hard deadlines, that is, the deadlines are the start of the next period and no deadline miss is allowed at all. While this is a restricted setting, it is enough to handle closed-loop control, used in control real-time systems. Furthermore, RT-CertiKOS only allows for fixed priorities in order to get maximum predictability, which is of utmost importance in critical systems. Finally, RT-CertiKOS also enforces budgets at the task level: in each period, a task cannot be scheduled for more than its specified budget.

Fixed-Priority Scheduler. The RT-CertiKOS scheduler maintains an integer array to keep track of time quantum usage for each task. Upon invocation, the scheduler first iterates over all tasks, replenishing quotas whenever a new period arrives. It then loops again and finds the highest priority task that has not used up its budget, followed by a decrement on the chosen task's current quota. Its abstraction is a Coq function that iterates over an abstract array of task control blocks, updates them, and returns the highest task identifier available for scheduling.

Yield System Call. Tasks do not always use up their budgets. A task can yield to relinquish any remaining quota, so that lower priority tasks may be scheduled earlier and more time slots may be dedicated to non real-time tasks.

3.3 Proof Methodology

Based on sequential CertiKOS, RT-CertiKOS [21] follows the idea of deep specifications[3] in which the specification should be rich enough to deduce any property of interest: there should never be any need to consider the implementation. In particular, even though its source code is written in both C and assembly, the underlay always abstracts the concrete memory states it operates on into abstract states, and abstracts concrete code into Coq functions that act as executable specification. Subsequent layers relying on this underlay will invoke Coq functions instead of the concrete code, thus hiding implementation details.

In the case of scheduling, there are essentially two functions: the scheduler and the yield system call. The scheduler relies on two concrete data structures: a counter tracking the current time (in time slot units) and an array tracking the current quota for each periodic task. The yield system call simply sets the remaining quota of the current task to zero. Both functions are verified in RT-CertiKOS, that is, formals proofs ensure that their C code implementations indeed simulate the corresponding Coq specifications.

3.4 Motivation for the Connection with Prosa

Upgrading an OS kernel into a real-time one is not an easy task. When one further adds formal proofs about functional correctness, isolation, and timing requirements, the proof burden becomes enormous. In particular, there is still room for future work on RT-CertiKOS, *e.g.,* a WCET analysis of its system calls.

In order to reduce the overall proof burden, it is important to try to delegate as much as possible to specialized libraries and tools. Thus, from the RT-CertiKOS perspective, the benefit of using Prosa is precisely to have state-of-the-art schedulability analyses already mechanized in Coq, without having to prove all these results.

Furthermore, the schedulability check of Prosa is only performed once while verifying the proofs, such that there is no runtime overhead and no loss of performance for RT-CertiKOS.

4   From RT-CertiKOS to Prosa: A Schedule Connection

Prosa definitions cannot apply to RT-CertiKOS directly. Indeed, the perspectives of Prosa and RT-CertiKOS on the real-time aspects of a system are not the same, which is reflected in the differences in their task models, their executions, and the information they need. In this section, we explain how we bridge these gaps to actually perform the connection. Table 1 summarizes the various definitions and proofs and how they relate to each other.

---

[3] https://deepspec.org/.

Table 1. Summary of the range of the various data between RT-CertiKOS and Prosa

RT-CertiKOS	Simplified Model	Interface	Prosa
scheduler quota array			
schedule prefix with batch tasks	schedule prefix		infinite schedule
	valid schedule prefix		valid infinite schedule
	FPP prefix		
			FPP schedulability analysis schedulable execution
schedulable prefix			

4.1 Interface Between RT-CertiKOS and Prosa

We design an interface to link RT-CertiKOS and Prosa, focusing on the precise amount of information that needs to be transmitted between them. The interface is shaped by the information Prosa needs to perform the schedulability analysis: a task set and a schedule, together with some properties.

Key Elements of the Interface. The task model we consider is the one of RT-CertiKOS, as it is more restrictive than the ones supported by Prosa. Tasks are defined by a priority level p, a period T_p and a WCET (more accurately a budget) C_p. Since we only allow one task per priority level, we identify tasks and priority levels and we write C_p, D_p, and T_p instead of C_τ, D_τ, and T_τ. In order for this setting to make sense, we assume the following inequality for each task p: $0 < C_p \leq T_p$. Notice that this is a particular case of Prosa's FPP task model (Definition 4). There is no definition of the jobs of a task as they can be easily defined from a task and a period number.

The second element Prosa needs is an infinite schedule. RT-CertiKOS cannot provide such an infinite schedule, as only a finite prefix can be known, up to the current time. Thus, we keep RT-CertiKOS's finite schedule as is in the interface and it is up to Prosa to extend it into an infinite one, suitable for its analysis.

Finally, Prosa needs two properties about the schedule: *(a)* any task receives no more service than its WCET in any period; *(b)* the schedule indeed follows the FPP policy. We refer to schedules satisfying these properties as *valid schedule prefixes*. Proving these properties falls to RT-CertiKOS.

Handling Service and Job Cost. In RT-CertiKOS, and more generally in any OS, we only assume a bound on the execution time of a task, used as a budget. The exact execution time of each of its jobs is not known beforehand and can be observed only at runtime. On the opposite, Prosa assumes that costs for all jobs of all tasks are part of the problem description and thus are available from the start.

To fix this mismatch, we define a job cost function computed from a schedule prefix: its value is the actual service received if the job has yielded and the WCET of its task otherwise. This definition relies on the computation of service in any period, which we also provide as part of the interface.

4.2   The RT-CertiKOS Side

Adding the Schedule in RT-CertiKOS. RT-CertiKOS only maintains the current state of the system, which the scheduler relies on, such as the current time and quota array. However, the interface requires a schedule trace. We introduce such a ghost variable in RT-CertiKOS, and update a few scheduling-related primitives to extend this trace whenever a task is scheduled.

This introduction adds absolutely no proof overhead, since it does not affect the scheduling decisions, thus existing proofs about the rest of the system still hold. Furthermore, it is a purely logical variable introduced through refinement, meaning that it does not exist in the C code, thus it causes no computation overhead.

Too Much Information in RT-CertiKOS. The full RT-CertiKOS model contains too much information compared to what the interface requires.

Firstly, services in RT-CertiKOS may affect a part of the state that is relevant to practical scheduling, but is of no interest to the scheduling model we want to verify, like batch tasks.

Secondly, due to the nature of *deep specification*, the abstraction of the whole scheduling operation contains more information than what is required for reasoning about real-time properties. For example, saving and restoring registers is essential for the correctness of context switches (thus, of the scheduler), but it is irrelevant to temporal properties.

Thirdly, specifications in RT-CertiKOS enumerate preconditions of the scheduler such as the correct configuration of the paging bit in the control register, the validity of the current stack and so on. These are required for other invariants of the kernel at other abstraction levels, but again they are irrelevant to scheduling.

Simplified Model of RT-CertiKOS. For all these reasons, we define a simplified scheduling model of RT-CertiKOS, with a much simpler abstract state containing only the data structures that are actually used in scheduling, from which the interface data and its properties must be derived. This simplified abstract state contains four fields:

ticks   the current time, that is, the number of past time slots;
quanta   a map giving the remaining quota for each priority;
cid   the identifier of the running process (if it exists);
schedule the schedule prefix remembering past scheduling decisions.

This abstract state is not equivalent to the complete one, because it operates on a totally different abstract data type where all irrelevant fields are removed.

It is also more permissive: more transitions are allowed since it does not perform the sanity checks about preconditions such as being in kernel mode, host mode, etc. Nevertheless, we still have a simulation: any step in the full RT-CertiKOS is also allowed in the simplified version and results in the same scheduling decision and trace. This simulation is enough for our purposes as we are ultimately interested in the behavior of the full RT-CertiKOS.

Proving the Properties Required by Prosa. The interface requires two key properties: *(a)* the service received by each job is at most the WCET of its task; and *(b)* the schedule prefix follows FPP. These properties must be proven on the RT-CertiKOS side for any schedule that might be generated. This way, Prosa can rely on them through the interface.

Since RT-CertiKOS verification is based on state invariants rather than traces, we prove these properties using the following main invariants on the simplified scheduling model:

- the length of the schedule trace is the current time + 1 (the scheduler takes a decision for the *next* time slot);
- if a task has yielded in the current period, its remaining quota is 0;
- the service plus the remaining quota is equal to the job cost;
- the service received in any period is less than the WCET;
- pending jobs have two equivalent definitions (having positive remaining quota or having less service than their job cost);
- the current schedule follows FPP.

To prove that these statements are indeed invariants, we must prove that they are preserved by any step, that is, by the scheduler (triggered by the user-level timer interrupt) and by the yield system call (triggered by the user process), since all other kernel steps do not modify the scheduling data of the simplified scheduling model.

Simulation Between the Simplified Scheduling Model and RT-CertiKOS. To connect the full RT-CertiKOS model and the simplified one, we define a projection function $RData\_proj$ extracting the relevant fields from the full RT-CertiKOS state to build the simplified one.

As shown in Fig. 2, we prove that given a scheduler transition of RT-CertiKOS between the (full) states d and d', there is also a transition from their projections s and s' by invoking the simplified scheduler.[4] If the states d and s satisfy respectively the invariants for RT-CertiKOS and the simplified model, then so do d' and s' (they are invariants). As the states s and s' are projections of d and d', the invariants of s and s' also hold on the corresponding fields in d and d'. This allows us to utilize the invariants proved in the simplified model to establish properties on the full state of RT-CertiKOS. Notice that the schedulability property we study is a safety property (deadlines are never missed) and not a liveness one (everything is eventually scheduled).

---

[4] More precisely, we prove that `certikos_sched`(s) and $RData\_proj(d')$ are *extensionally* equal.

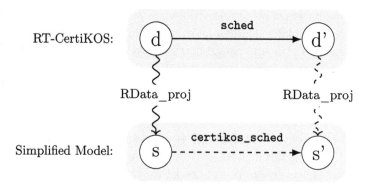

Fig. 2. Simulation between simplified scheduling and RT-CertiKOS

4.3 The Prosa Side

Proven Schedulability Analysis in Prosa. In order to use the response time bound of Sect. 2, we need to relate any finite schedule prefix from the interface to an arrival sequence and a schedule satisfying the model described in Sect. 2. We can then rely on any schedulability criterion (*e.g.*, the one described at the end of Sect. 2.3) to prove that the response time bound holds and deduce that any valid schedule prefix from the interface is indeed schedulable.

Bridging the Gap Between the Interface and Prosa. The interface provides Prosa with a task set, service and job cost functions, and a valid schedule prefix. We first build an arrival sequence from the schedule prefix where the n-th job ($n > 0$) for a given task p arrives at time $(n-1) \times T_p$ with the cost given by the interface. Note that jobs that do not arrive within the prefix cannot have yielded yet so that their costs is the WCET of their tasks: we assume the worst case for the future.

The arrival sequence is then defined by adding all jobs of each task p from $TaskSet$, that is, the arrival sequence at time t contains the $(\lfloor t/T_p \rfloor + 1)$-th job of p iff t is divisible by T_p.

Next, we need to turn the finite schedule prefix into an infinite one. There are two possibilities: either build a full schedule from the arrival sequence using the Prosa implementation of FPP, or start from the schedule prefix of the interface and extend it into an infinite one. The first technique gives for free the fact that the infinite schedule satisfies the FPP model from Prosa. The difficulty lies in proving that the schedule prefix from the interface is indeed a prefix of this infinite schedule. The second technique starts from the schedule prefix and the difficulty is proving that it satisfies the FPP model as specified on the Prosa side.

In this paper, we use the first strategy and prove that the prefix of the schedule built by Prosa is equal to the schedule prefix provided in the interface. To do so, we use the fact that two FPP schedule prefixes with the same arrival sequence and job costs (only known at runtime) are the same, provided we take care to properly remember when jobs yield.

Assuming that the task set is accepted by the schedulability criterion, we know that the Prosa schedule is schedulable and, since this implies that its prefix is also schedulable, we deduce that the valid schedule prefix given by the interface is schedulable.

5 Evaluation and Future Work

5.1 Evaluation

As the C and assembly source code of RT-CertiKOS was not modified at all, this connection does not introduce any overhead to its performance and there is no need for a new performance evaluation. Instead, we focus on the benefits this works brings and on the amount of work involved, described in Table 2.

Benefits for RT-CertiKOS and Prosa. The schedulability analysis already present in RT-CertiKOS was manually proved and took around 8k LoC to handle the precise setting described in this paper. By contrast, interfacing with Prosa requires 50% less proofs, is more flexible and can easily be extended (see Sect. 5.3). The introduction of a simplified scheduling model also reduced by 75% the size of proofs of invariants about the high-level abstract scheduler since we are freed from the unnecessary information described in Sect. 4.2.

On the Prosa side, having a complete formal connection with an actual OS kernel developed independently validates the modeling choices made for describing real-time systems. Indeed, seeing schedulers as predicates over scheduling traces is very general but one can legitimately wonder whether such predicates accurately describe reality.

Proof Effort. Designing a good interface allowed us to cleanly separate the work required on the RT-CertiKOS and Prosa sides.

On the RT-CertiKOS side, the design of the simplified scheduling setting was pretty straightforward, as was the correctness of the translation. Indeed, this translation is essentially a projection, except for batch tasks which are removed. Designing adequate inductive invariants to prove the two properties required by the interface was the most challenging part of this work and unsurprisingly, it took several iterations to find correct definitions.

On the Prosa side, building the arrival sequence and the infinite schedule is quite effortless given a prefix and a job cost function. The subtle thing was to find a good definition of the job cost function, which made the corresponding proofs significantly easier. Proving that the prefix of the built infinite schedule is the same as the interface prefix $w.r.t.$ executions was troublesome for two reasons. First, the interface prefix contains an additional boolean representing whether the scheduled job yielded and which is used for computing job costs, whereas it does not exist in the built schedule. Second, the definition of the FPP property in the interface depends on a schedule prefix, while the one in Prosa depends on an infinite schedule.

Overall, we see the small amount of LoC required to perform this work as a validation of the adequacy of our method to the considered problem.

Table 2. Proof effort

Feature	Changes (LoC)
Adding a schedule field to RT-CertiKOS	15
Interface (with proofs)	380
Simplified scheduling	100
Proving the invariants about the simplified scheduling	950
Translation RT-CertiKOS → simplified scheduling	380
Conversion between ZArith and SSReflect	280
Translation interface → Prosa	1900
Using the schedulability analysis of Prosa	130
Total	4135

5.2   Lessons Learned

Beyond the particular artifact linking RT-CertiKOS with Prosa, what more general lessons can we learn from this connection?

First, using the same proof assistant greatly helps. Indeed, beyond the absence of technical hassle of inter-operability between different formal tools, it also avoids the pitfall of a formalization mismatch between both formal models and permits sharing common definitions.

Second, the creation of an explicit interface between both tools clearly marks the flow of information, stays focused on the essential information, and delimits the "proof responsibility": which side is responsible for proving which fact. It also segregate the proof techniques used on each side so as not to pollute the other one, either on a technical aspect (vanilla Coq for RT-CertiKOS *vs* the SSReflect extension for Prosa) or on the verification methods used (invariant-based properties for RT-CertiKOS *vs* trace-based properties for Prosa). This separation makes it unnecessary to have people be experts in both tools at once: once the interface was clearly defined, experts on each side could work with only a rough description of the other one, even though this interface required a few later changes. In particular, it is interesting to notice that half the authors are experts in RT-CertiKOS whereas the other half are experts in Prosa.

Third, the common part of the models used by both sides must be amenable to agreement: in our case, this means having the same notion of time (scheduling slots, or ticks) and a compatible notion of schedule (finite and infinite).

Finally, we expect the interface we designed to be reusable for other verified kernels wanting to connect to Prosa or for linking RT-CertiKOS to other formal schedulability analysis tools.

5.3   Future Work

Evolving with RT-CertiKOS. The existing implementation of the scheduler in RT-CertiKOS imposes a fixed priority scheduling policy with implicit deadlines. In the future, as RT-CertiKOS evolves and supports more task models, the interface connecting it with Prosa should also extend.

A straightforward extension is to allow *constrained deadlines*, that is, to have the deadline D_p be shorter than the period T_p (but greater than the WCET C_p) as the schedulability result we use from Prosa already supports it. This requires RT-CertiKOS to support an extended task model where a task is also specified by its deadline. Furthermore, RT-CertiKOS would also need to enforce budget at the deadlines, instead of at the beginning of the next period as it is currently the case.

Another extension would be to consider the Earliest Deadline First (EDF) scheduling policy which provides better utilization ratio. In addition to relaxing the current task model by not including priorities, the main proof effort would be to implement and verify this new scheduler in RT-CertiKOS.

Extensions to Prosa. Our experience connecting RT-CertiKOS and Prosa shows that Prosa's assumption of having an infinite schedule is quite impractical when verifying instances of real-time systems. This advocates for building reusable connections between Prosa's system model based on infinite traces and a model similar to the one used in the interface with RT-CertiKOS. Thus, one would prove analyses in the convenient setting of infinite traces and still be able to apply them to lower level models of real-time systems with finite traces.

6   Related Work

Schedulability Analysis. Schedulability analysis as a key theory in the real-time community has been widely studied in the past decades. Liu and Layland's seminal work [20] presents a schedulability analysis technique for a simple system model described as a set of assumptions. Many later work [3,5,11,23,28] aim to capture more *realistic*[5] and complex system models by generalizing those assumptions.

In order to provide formal guarantees to those results, several formal approaches have been used for the formalism of schedulability analyses, such as model checking [8,12,16], temporal logic [32,33], and theorem proving [10,30].

As far as we know, none of the above work has been applied to a formally verified OS kernel.

Verification of Real-Time OS Kernels. There is a lot of work about formal verification of OS kernels, see [18] for a survey. Therefore, we restrict our attention to verification of real-time kernels using proof assistants. We also do

---

[5] In terms of executions and arrival model.

not consider WCET computation, be it of the kernel itself (*e.g.*, [6,24]) or of the task set we consider. This is a complementary but clearly distinct task to get verified time bounds.

The eChronos OS [1,2] is a real-time OS running on single-core embedded systems. It stops its verification at the scheduling policy level, proving that the currently running task always has the highest priority among ready tasks. Xu et al. [31] verify the functional correctness of μC/OS-II [19], a real-time operating system with optimizations such as bitmaps. They also prove some high level properties, such as priority inversion freedom of shared memory IPC.

RT-CertiKOS [21] is a verified single-core real-time OS kernel developed by the Yale FLINT group, based on sequential CertiKOS [9,13]. It proves both temporal and spatial isolation among different components, where temporal isolation entails schedulability, etc. However, as explained in Sect. 5.1, its schedulability proof is longer whereas connecting to an existing schedulability analyzer is easier and more flexible.

7   Conclusion

Formal verification aims at providing stronger guarantees than testing. Real-time systems are a good target because they are often part of critical systems. Both the scheduling and OS communities have developed their own formally verified tools but there is a lack of integration between them. In this paper, we make a first step toward bridging this gap by integrating a formally proven schedulability analysis tool, Prosa, with a verified sequential real-time OS kernel, RT-CertiKOS. This gives two benefits: first, it provides RT-CertiKOS with a modular, extensible, state-of-the-art formal schedulability analysis proof; second, it gives a concrete instance of one of the scheduling theories described in Prosa, thus ensuring that its model is consistent and applicable to actual systems. We believe this connection can be easily adapted for other verified kernels or schedulability analyzers.

It also showcases that it is possible and practical to connect two completely independent medium- to large-scale formal proof developments.

Acknowledgments. This research has been partially supported by the following grants: PEPS INS2I JCJC 2019 Vefose, NSF grants 1521523, 1715154, and 1763399, DARPA grant FA8750-15-C-0082, as well as by the RT-PROOFS project (grant ANR-17-CE25-0016) and the CASERM project through the LabEx PERSYVAL-Lab (grant ANR-11-LABX-0025-01). The U.S. Government is authorized to reproduce and distribute reprints for Governmental purposes notwithstanding any copyright notation thereon. The views and conclusions contained herein are those of the authors and should not be interpreted as necessarily representing the official policies or endorsements, either expressed or implied, of DARPA or the U.S. Government.

References

1. Andronick, J., Lewis, C., Matichuk, D., Morgan, C., Rizkallah, C.: Proof of OS scheduling behavior in the presence of interrupt-induced concurrency. In: Blanchette, J.C., Merz, S. (eds.) ITP 2016. LNCS, vol. 9807, pp. 52–68. Springer, Cham (2016). https://doi.org/10.1007/978-3-319-43144-4_4

2. Andronick, J., Lewis, C., Morgan, C.: Controlled Owicki-Gries concurrency: reasoning about the preemptible eChronos embedded operating system. In: Proceedings Workshop on Models for Formal Analysis of Real Systems, MARS, pp. 10–24 (2015). https://doi.org/10.4204/EPTCS.196.2

3. Baruah, S.: Techniques for multiprocessor global schedulability analysis. In: Proceedings - 28th IEEE International Real-Time Systems Symposium (RTSS), pp. 119–128, December 2007. https://doi.org/10.1109/RTSS.2007.35

4. Bertogna, M., Cirinei, M.: Response-time analysis for globally scheduled symmetric multiprocessor platforms. In: 28th IEEE International Real-Time Systems Symposium (RTSS), pp. 149–160, December 2007. https://doi.org/10.1109/RTSS.2007.31

5. Bini, E., Buttazzo, G.C.: Schedulability analysis of periodic fixed priority systems. IEEE Trans. Comput. **53**(11), 1462–1473 (2004)

6. Blackham, B., Shi, Y., Chattopadhyay, S., Roychoudhury, A., Heiser, G.: Timing analysis of a protected operating system kernel. In: 2011 IEEE 32nd Real-Time Systems Symposium (RTSS), pp. 339–348, November 2011. https://doi.org/10.1109/RTSS.2011.38

7. Cerqueira, F., Stutz, F., Brandenburg, B.B.: PROSA: a case for readable mechanized schedulability analysis. In: 28th Euromicro Conference on Real-Time Systems (ECRTS), pp. 273–284 (2016). https://doi.org/10.1109/ECRTS.2016.28

8. Cordovilla, M., Boniol, F., Noulard, E., Pagetti, C.: Multiprocessor schedulability analyser. In: Proceedings of the 2011 ACM Symposium on Applied Computing, SAC 2011, pp. 735–741 (2011). http://doi.acm.org/10.1145/1982185.1982345

9. Costanzo, D., Shao, Z., Gu, R.: End-to-end verification of information-flow security for C and assembly programs. In: Proceedings of the 37th ACM SIGPLAN Conference on Programming Language Design and Implementation (PLDI), pp. 648–664 (2016). http://doi.acm.org/10.1145/2908080.2908100

10. Dutertre, B.: The priority ceiling protocol: formalization and analysis using PVS. In: Proceedings of the 21st IEEE Conference on Real-Time Systems Symposium (RTSS), pp. 151–160 (1999)

11. Feld, T., Biondi, A., Davis, R.I., Buttazzo, G.C., Slomka, F.: A survey of schedulability analysis techniques for rate-dependent tasks. J. Syst. Softw. **138**, 100–107 (2018). https://doi.org/10.1016/j.jss.2017.12.033

12. Fersman, E., Mokrushin, L., Pettersson, P., Yi, W.: Schedulability analysis of fixed-priority systems using timed automata. Theor. Comput. Sci. **354**(2), 301–317 (2006)

13. Gu, R., et al.: Deep specifications and certified abstraction layers. In: Proceedings of the 42nd Annual ACM SIGPLAN-SIGACT Symposium on Principles of Programming Languages (POPL), pp. 595–608 (2015). http://doi.acm.org/10.1145/2676726.2676975

14. Gu, R., et al.: CertiKOS: an extensible architecture for building certified concurrent OS kernels. In: 12th USENIX Symposium on Operating Systems Design and Implementation (OSDI), pp. 653–669. USENIX Association (2016). https://www.usenix.org/conference/osdi16/technical-sessions/presentation/gu

15. Gu, R., et al.: Certified concurrent abstraction layers. In: Proceedings of the 39th ACM SIGPLAN Conference on Programming Language Design and Implementation (PLDI), pp. 646–661 (2018). http://doi.acm.org/10.1145/3192366.3192381

16. Guan, N., Gu, Z., Deng, Q., Gao, S., Yu, G.: Exact schedulability analysis for static-priority global multiprocessor scheduling using model-checking. In: IFIP International Workshop on Software Technolgies for Embedded and Ubiquitous Systems, pp. 263–272 (2007)

17. Klein, G., et al.: seL4: formal verification of an OS kernel. In: Proceedings of the ACM SIGOPS 22nd Symposium on Operating Systems Principles (SOSP), pp. 207–220 (2009). https://doi.org/10.1145/1629575.1629596

18. Klein, G., Huuck, R., Schlich, B.: Operating system verification. J. Autom. Reasoning **42**(2–4), 123–124 (2009). https://doi.org/10.1007/s10817-009-9126-9

19. Labrosse, J.J.: Microc/OS-II, 2nd edn. R&D Books, Gilroy (1998)

20. Liu, C.L., Layland, J.W.: Scheduling algorithms for multiprogramming in a hard-real-time environment. J. ACM (JACM) **20**(1), 46–61 (1973)

21. Liu, M., et al.: Compositional verification of preemptive OS kernels with temporal and spatial isolation. Technical report, YALEU/DCS/TR-1549. Department of Computer Science, Yale University (2019)

22. Nelson, L., et al.: Hyperkernel: push-button verification of an OS kernel. In: Proceedings of the 26th Symposium on Operating Systems Principles (SOSP), Shanghai, China, 28–31 October 2017, pp. 252–269 (2017). https://doi.org/10.1145/3132747.3132748

23. Palencia, J.C., Harbour, M.G.: Schedulability analysis for tasks with static and dynamic offsets. In: Proceedings 19th IEEE Real-Time Systems Symposium (RTSS), pp. 26–37. IEEE (1998)

24. Sewell, T., Kam, F., Heiser, G.: High-assurance timing analysis for a high-assurance real-time operating system. Real-Time Syst. **53**(5), 812–853 (2017). https://doi.org/10.1007/s11241-017-9286-3

25. The Coq Development Team: The Coq Proof Assistant Reference Manual. INRIA, 8.4pl4 edn. (2014). https://coq.inria.fr/distrib/8.4pl4/files/Reference-Manual.pdf

26. Tindell, K., Burns, A.: Guaranteeing message latencies on controller area network (CAN). In: Proceedings of 1st International CAN Conference, pp. 1–11 (1994)

27. Tindell, K., Burns, A., Wellings, A.: Calculating controller area network (CAN) message response times. Control Eng. Pract. **3**(8), 1163–1169 (1995)

28. Tindell, K., Clark, J.: Holistic schedulability analysis for distributed hard real-time systems. Microprocessing Microprogramming **40**(2–3), 117–134 (1994)

29. Tindell, K., Hanssmon, H., Wellings, A.J.: Analysing real-time communications: controller area network (CAN). In: Proceedings of the 15th IEEE Real-Time Systems Symposium (RTSS), San Juan, Puerto Rico, 7–9 December 1994, pp. 259–263 (1994). https://doi.org/10.1109/REAL.1994.342710

30. Wilding, M.: A machine-checked proof of the optimality of a real-time scheduling policy. In: Proceedings of the 10th International Conference on Computer Aided Verification (CAV), pp. 369–378 (1998)

31. Xu, F., Fu, M., Feng, X., Zhang, X., Zhang, H., Li, Z.: A practical verification framework for preemptive OS kernels. In: Chaudhuri, S., Farzan, A. (eds.) CAV 2016. LNCS, vol. 9780, pp. 59–79. Springer, Cham (2016). https://doi.org/10.1007/978-3-319-41540-6_4
32. Xu, Q., Zhan, N.: Formalising scheduling theories in duration calculus. Nord. J. Comput. **14**(3), 173–201 (2008)
33. Yuhua, Z., Chaochen, Z.: A formal proof of the deadline driven scheduler. In: International Symposium on Formal Techniques in Real-Time and Fault-Tolerant Systems, pp. 756–775 (1994)

13

What's Wrong with On-the-Fly Partial Order Reduction

Stephen F. Siegel$^{(\boxtimes)}$ ⓘ

University of Delaware, Newark, DE, USA
siegel@udel.edu

Abstract. Partial order reduction and on-the-fly model checking are well-known approaches for improving model checking performance. The two optimizations interact in subtle ways, so care must be taken when using them in combination. A standard algorithm combining the two optimizations, published over twenty years ago, has been widely studied and deployed in popular model checking tools. Yet the algorithm is incorrect. Counterexamples were discovered using the Alloy analyzer. A fix for a restricted class of property automata is proposed.

Keywords: Model checking · Partial order reduction · On-the-fly · Spin

1 Introduction

Partial order reduction (POR) refers to a family of model checking techniques used to reduce the size of the state space that must be explored when verifying a property of a program. The techniques vary, but all share the core observation that when two independent operations are enabled in a state, it is often safe to ignore traces that begin with one of them. A large number of POR techniques have been explored, differing in details such as the range of properties to which they apply. This paper focuses on *ample set* POR [4], an approach which applies to stutter-invariant properties and is used in the model checker Spin [8].

In the automata-theoretic view of model checking, the negation of the property to be verified is represented by an ω-automaton. The basic algorithm computes the product of this automaton with the state space of the program. The language of the product is empty if and only if the program cannot violate the property. *On-the-fly* model checking refers to an optimization of this basic algorithm in which the enumeration of the reachable program states, computation of the product, and language emptiness check are interleaved, rather than occurring in sequence.

These two optimizations must be combined with care, because they interact in subtle ways.[1] A standard algorithm for on-the-fly ample set POR is described

---

[1] Previous work, for example, has dealt with problems, distinct from those discussed in this paper, that arise when combining nested depth first search and POR [7,14].

in [12] and in further detail in [13]. I shall refer to this algorithm as the *combined algorithm*. Theorem 4.2 of [13] asserts the soundness of the combined algorithm. A proof of the theorem is also given in [13].

The proof has a gap. This was pointed out in [16, Sect. 5], with details in [15]. The gap was rediscovered in the course of developing mechanized correctness proofs for model checking algorithms; an explicit counterexample to the incorrect proof step was also found ([2, Sect. 8.4.5] and [3, Sect. 5]). The fact that the proof is erroneous, however, does not imply the theorem is wrong. To the best of my knowledge, no one has yet produced a proof or a counterexample for the soundness of the combined algorithm.

In this paper, I show that the combined algorithm is not sound; a counterexample is given in Sect. 3.1. I found this counterexample by modeling the combined algorithm in Alloy and using the Alloy analyzer [11] to check its soundness. Sect. 4 describes this model. Spin's POR is based on the combined algorithm, and in Sect. 5, Spin is seen to return an incorrect result on a Promela model derived from the theoretical counterexample.

There is a small adjustment to the combined algorithm, yielding an algorithm that is arguably more natural and that returns the correct result on the previous counterexample; this is described in Sect. 6. It turns out this one is also unsound, as demonstrated by another Alloy-produced counterexample. However, in Sect. 7, I show that this variation is sound if certain restrictions are placed on the property automaton.

2   Preliminaries

Definition 1. *A* finite state program *is a triple* $P = \langle T, Q, \iota \rangle$, *where Q is a* finite set *of states,* $\iota \in Q$ *is the* initial state, *and T is a finite set of* operations. *Each operation* $\alpha \in T$ *is a function from a set* $\mathrm{en}_\alpha \subseteq Q$ *to Q.*

Fix a finite state program $P = \langle T, Q, \iota \rangle$.

Definition 2. *For $q \in Q$, define* $\mathrm{en}(q) = \{\alpha \in T \mid q \in \mathrm{en}_\alpha\}$.

Definition 3. *An* execution *of P is an infinite sequence of operations $\alpha_1 \alpha_2 \cdots$ that* generates *the sequence of states* $\xi = q_0 q_1 q_2 \cdots$ *such that $q_0 = \iota$ and for $i \geq 0$, $q_i \in \mathrm{en}_{\alpha_{i+1}}$ and $q_{i+1} = \alpha_{i+1}(q_i)$. An* admissible *sequence is any segment of an execution.*

Definition 4. *A* Büchi automaton *is a tuple* $\mathcal{B} = \langle S, \Delta, \Sigma, \delta, F \rangle$, *where S is a finite set of* automaton states, $\Delta \subseteq S$ *is the set of* initial states, Σ *is a finite set called the* alphabet, $\delta \subseteq S \times \Sigma \times S$ *is the* transition relation, *and $F \subseteq S$ is the set of* accepting states. *The* language *of $\mathcal{B}$, denoted $\mathcal{L}(\mathcal{B})$, is the set of all $\xi \in \Sigma^\omega$ generated by infinite paths in $\mathcal{B}$ that pass through an accepting state infinitely often.*

Fix a finite set AP of *atomic propositions* and let $\Sigma = 2^{\mathsf{AP}}$.
Fix an *interpretation mapping* for P, i.e., a function $L : Q \to \Sigma$.

Definition 5. *The* language of P*, denoted* $\mathcal{L}(P)$*, is the set of all infinite words* $L(q_0)L(q_1)\cdots \in \Sigma^\omega$*, where* $q_0 q_1 \cdots$ *is the sequence of states generated by an execution of* P*.*

Definition 6. *A language* $L \subseteq \Sigma^\omega$ *is* stutter-invariant *if, for any* $a_0, a_1, \ldots \in \Sigma$ *and positive integers* $i_0, i_1 \ldots,$ $a_0 a_1 \cdots \in L \Leftrightarrow a_0^{i_0} a_1^{i_1} \cdots \in L$*, where* a^i *denotes the concatenation of* i *copies of* a*.*

Definition 7. *Let* $\mathcal{B} = \langle S, \Delta, \Sigma, \delta, F \rangle$*, be a Büchi automaton with alphabet* Σ*. The* product *of* P *and* $\mathcal{B}$ *is the Büchi automaton*

$$P \otimes \mathcal{B} = \langle Q \times S, \{\iota\} \times \Delta, T \times \Sigma, \delta_\otimes, Q \times F \rangle,$$

where

$$\delta_\otimes = \{(\langle q, s\rangle, \langle \alpha, \sigma\rangle, \langle q', s'\rangle) \mid \sigma = L(q) \wedge \langle s, \sigma, s'\rangle \in \delta \wedge q' = \alpha(q)\}.$$

Note 1. A transition from product state $x = \langle q, s\rangle$ can be viewed as taking place in two steps. First, a transition $s \xrightarrow{L(q)} s'$ in $\mathcal{B}$ executes, leading to an "intermediate state" $x' = \langle q, s'\rangle$. Then a program transition $q \xrightarrow{\alpha} q'$ executes, culminating in $y = \langle q', s'\rangle$. While this is a good mental model, the product automaton does not necessarily contain a transition from x to x' or from x' to y. The intermediate state x' is not even necessarily reachable in the product. The transition in the product goes directly from x to y with label $\langle \alpha, L(q)\rangle$.

It is well-known that

$$\mathcal{L}(P) \cap \mathcal{L}(\mathcal{B}) = \emptyset \Leftrightarrow \mathcal{L}(P \otimes \mathcal{B}) = \emptyset.$$

In the context of model checking, $\mathcal{B}$ is used to represent the negation of a desirable property; the program P satisfies the property if, and only if, no execution of P is accepted by $\mathcal{B}$, i.e., $\mathcal{L}(P) \cap \mathcal{L}(\mathcal{B}) = \emptyset$. The automaton $\mathcal{B}$ may be generated from a (negated) LTL formula, but that assumption is not needed here.

The goal of "offline" (not on-the-fly) partial order reduction is to generate some subspace P' of P with the guarantee that

$$\mathcal{L}(P') \cap \mathcal{L}(\mathcal{B}) = \emptyset \Leftrightarrow \mathcal{L}(P) \cap \mathcal{L}(\mathcal{B}) = \emptyset$$

The emptiness of $\mathcal{L}(P' \otimes \mathcal{B}) = \mathcal{L}(P') \cap \mathcal{L}(\mathcal{B})$ can be decided in various ways, such as a nested depth first search (NDFS) [5].

3   On-the-Fly Partial Order Reduction

In on-the-fly model checking, the state space of the product automaton is enumerated directly, without first enumerating the program states. Adding POR to the mix means that at each state reached in the product automaton, some subset of enabled transitions will be explored. The goal is to ensure that if the language of the full product automaton is nonempty, then the language of the resulting reduced automaton must be nonempty.

To make this precise, fix a finite state program $P = \langle T, Q, \iota \rangle$, a set AP of atomic propositions, an interpretation $L \colon Q \to \Sigma = 2^{\mathsf{AP}}$, and Büchi automaton $\mathcal{B} = \langle S, \Delta, \Sigma, \delta, F \rangle$. Let $\mathcal{A} = P \otimes \mathcal{B}$.

Definition 8. *A function* amp$\colon Q \times S \to 2^T$ *is an* ample selector *if* amp$(q, s) \subseteq$ en(q) *for all* $q \in Q, s \in S$. *Each* amp(q, s) *is an* ample set.

An ample selector determines a subautomaton $\mathcal{A}' = \mathsf{reduced}(\mathcal{A}, \mathsf{amp})$ of $\mathcal{A}$: $\mathcal{A}'$ is defined exactly as in Definition 7, except that the transition relation has the additional restriction that $\alpha \in \mathsf{amp}(q, s')$:

$$\mathcal{A}' = \langle Q \times S, \{\iota\} \times \Delta, T \times \Sigma, \delta', Q \times F \rangle \tag{1}$$

$$\begin{aligned}\delta' = \{(\langle q, s \rangle, \langle \alpha, \sigma \rangle, \langle q', s' \rangle) \in (Q \times S) \times (T \times \Sigma) \times (Q \times S) \mid \\ \sigma = L(q) \wedge \langle s, \sigma, s' \rangle \in \delta \wedge \alpha \in \mathsf{amp}(q, s') \wedge q' = \alpha(q)\}\,.\end{aligned} \tag{2}$$

Definition 9. *An ample selector* amp *is* POR-sound *if the following holds:*

$$\mathcal{L}(\mathsf{reduced}(\mathcal{A}, \mathsf{amp})) = \emptyset \Leftrightarrow \mathcal{L}(P) \cap \mathcal{L}(\mathcal{B}) = \emptyset.$$

The goal is to define some constraints on an ample selector that guarantee it is POR-sound. Before stating the constraints, we need two more concepts:

Definition 10. *An* independence relation *is an irreflexive and symmetric relation* $I \subseteq T \times T$ *satisfying the following: if* $(\alpha, \beta) \in I$ *and* $q \in$ en$_\alpha \cap$ en$_\beta$, *then* $\alpha(q) \in$ en$_\beta$, $\beta(q) \in$ en$_\alpha$, *and* $\alpha(\beta(q)) = \beta(\alpha(q))$.

Fix an independence relation I. We say α and β are *dependent* if $(\alpha, \beta) \notin I$.

Definition 11. *An operation* $\alpha \in T$ *is* invisible *with respect to* L *if, for all* $q \in$ en$_\alpha$, $L(q) = L(\alpha(q))$.

Note 2. The definition in [13] is slightly different. Given an LTL formula ϕ over AP, let AP$'$ be the set of atomic propositions occurring syntactically in ϕ. The definition in [13] says α is *invisible in* ϕ if, for all $p \in$ AP$'$ and $q \in$ en$_\alpha$, $p \in L(q) \Leftrightarrow p \in L(\alpha(q))$. However, there is no loss of generality using Definition 11, since one can define a new interpretation $L' \colon Q \to 2^{\mathsf{AP}'}$ by $L'(q) = L(q) \cap \mathsf{AP}'$. Then α is invisible for ϕ if, and only if, α is invisible with respect to L', and the results of this paper can be applied without modification to P, AP$'$, and L'.

We now define the following constraints on an ample selector amp:[2]

C0 For all $q \in Q$, $s \in S$: en$(q) \neq \emptyset \implies$ amp$(q, s) \neq \emptyset$.

---

[2] I am using the numbering from [4]. In [13], **C2** and **C3** are swapped.

C1 For all $q \in Q$, $s \in S$: in any admissible sequence in P starting from q, no operation in $T \setminus \mathsf{amp}(q, s)$ that is dependent on an operation in $\mathsf{amp}(q, s)$ can occur before some operation in $\mathsf{amp}(q, s)$ occurs.

C2 For all $q \in Q$, $s \in S$: if $\mathsf{amp}(q, s) \neq \mathsf{en}(q)$ then $\forall \alpha \in \mathsf{amp}(q, s)$, α is invisible.

C3 There is a depth-first search of $\mathcal{A}' = \mathsf{reduced}(\mathcal{A}, \mathsf{amp})$ with the following property: whenever there is a transition in $\mathcal{A}'$ from a node $\langle q, s \rangle$ on the top of the stack to a node $\langle q', s' \rangle$ on the stack, $\mathsf{amp}(q, s') = \mathsf{en}(q)$.

Condition **C3** is the interesting one. The combined algorithm of [13] enforces it using a DFS (the outer search of the NDFS) of the reduced space and the following protocol: given a new state $\langle q, s \rangle$ that has just been pushed onto the stack, first iterate over all Büchi transitions $\langle s, L(q), s' \rangle$ departing from s and labeled by $L(q)$. For each of these, a candidate ample set for $\mathsf{amp}(q, s')$ that satisfies the first three conditions is computed; this computation does not depend on s'. If any operation in that candidate set leads back to a state on the search stack (a "back edge"), a different candidate is tried and the process is repeated until a satisfactory one is found. If no such candidate is found, $\mathsf{en}(q)$ is used for the ample set.

Hence the process for choosing the ample set depends on the current state of the search. If $y_1 \neq y_2$, it is not necessarily the case that $\mathsf{amp}(x, y_1) = \mathsf{amp}(x, y_2)$, because it is possible that when $\langle x, y_1 \rangle$ was encountered, a back edge existed for a candidate, but when $\langle x, y_2 \rangle$ was encountered, there was no back edge.

3.1 Counterexample

Theorem 4.2 of [13] can be expressed as follows: if $\mathcal{L}(\mathcal{B})$ is stutter-invariant and the language of an LTL formula, and amp satisfies **C0–C3**, then amp is POR-sound.

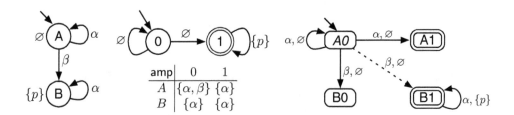

Fig. 1. Counterexample to combined theorem. Left: program and interpretation. Center: property automaton $\mathcal{B}_1$ and ample selector function. Right: the reachable product state space; dashed edges are in the full, but not reduced, space.

A counterexample to this claim is given in Fig. 1. The program consists of two states, A and B, and two operations, α and β. There is a single atomic proposition, p, which is *false* at A and *true* at B. Note that α and β are independent. Also, α is invisible, and β is not.

The property automaton, $\mathcal{B}_1$, is shown in Fig. 1 (center top). It has two states, numbered 0 and 1. State 1 is the sole accepting state. The language consists of all infinite words of the following form: a finite nonempty prefix of $\varnothing$s followed by an infinite sequence of $\{p\}$s. This language is stutter-invariant, and is the language of the LTL formula $(\neg p) \wedge ((\neg p)\,\mathbf{U}\,\mathbf{G}p)$.

The ample selector is specified by the table (center bottom). Notice that $\mathsf{amp}(A, 1) \neq \mathsf{en}(A)$, but the other three ample sets are full. **C0** holds because the ample sets are never empty. **C1** holds because β is independent of α. **C2** holds because α is invisible. The reachable product space is shown in Fig. 1 (right). In any DFS of $\mathsf{reduced}(\mathcal{A}, \mathsf{amp})$, the only back edge is the self-loop on $A0$ labeled $\langle \alpha, \varnothing \rangle$. Since $\mathsf{amp}(A, 0)$ is full, **C3** holds. Yet there is an accepting path in the full space, but not in the reduced space.

4 Alloy Models of POR Schemes

Alloy is a "lightweight formal methods" language and tool. It has been used in a wide variety of contexts, from exploring software designs to studying weak memory-consistency models. An Alloy model specifies *signatures*, each of which defines a type, relations on signatures, and constraints on the signatures and relations. Constraints are expressed in a logic that combines elements of first order logic and relational logic, and includes a transitive closure operator. An *instance* of a model assigns a finite set of *atoms* to each signature, and a finite set of tuples (of the right type) to each relation, in such a way that the constraints are satisfied. The Alloy analyzer can be used to check that an assertion holds on all instances in which the sizes of the signatures are within some specified bounds. The analyzer converts the question of the validity of the assertion into a SAT problem and invokes a SAT solver. Based on the result, it reports either that the assertion holds within the given bounds, or it produces an instance of the model violating the assertion.

I developed an Alloy model to search for counterexamples to various POR claims, such as the one in Sect. 3.1. The model encodes the main concepts of the previous two sections, including program, operations, interpretation, invisibility and independence, property automaton, the product space, ample selectors and the constraints on them, and a language emptiness predicate. The model culminates in an assertion which states that an ample selector satisfying the four constraints is POR-sound.

I was not able to find a way to encode stutter-invariance. In the end, I developed a small set of Büchi automata based on my own intuition of what would make interesting tests. I encoded these in Alloy and used the analyzer to explore all possible programs and ample selectors for each.

The first part of the model is a simple encoding of a finite state automaton. The following is a listing of file `ba.als`:

```
1    module ba   -- module for simple model of Büchi automata
2    sig Sigma {} -- alphabet of BA, valuation on atomic props
3    sig BState {} -- a state in the Büchi Automaton
```

```
4   one sig Binit extends BState {} -- initial state of BA
5   sig AState in BState {} -- accepting states of BA
6   -- a transition has a source state, label, and destination state...
7   sig BTrans { src: one BState, label: one Sigma, dest: one BState }
```

The alphabet is some unconstrained set `Sigma`. The set of states is represented by signature `BState`. There is a single initial state, and any number of accepting states. Each transition has a source and destination state, and label. Relations declared within a signature declaration have that signature as an implicit first argument. So, for example, `src` is a binary relation of type `BTrans × BState`. Furthermore, the relation is many-to-one: each transition has exactly one `BState` atom associated to it by the `src` relation.

The remaining concepts are incorporated into module `por_v0`:

```
1    module por_v0   -- on-the-fly POR variant 0, corresponding to [13]
2    open ba   -- import the Büchi automata module
3    sig Operation {} -- program operation
4    sig PState { -- program state
5      label: one Sigma,   -- the set of propositions which hold in this state
6      enabled: set Operation,   -- the set of all operations enabled at this state
7      nextState: enabled -> one PState,   -- the next-state function
8      ample: BState -> set Operation   -- ample(q,s)
9    }{ all s: BState | ample[s] in enabled } -- ample sets subsets of enabled
10   fun amp[q: PState, s: BState] : set Operation { q.ample[s] }
11   one sig Pinit extends PState {}   -- initial program state
12   fact { -- all program states are reachable from Pinit
13     let r = {q, q': PState | some op: Operation | q.nextState[op]=q'} |
14       PState = Pinit.*r
15   }
16   sig ProdState { -- state in the product of program and property automaton
17     pstate: PState,   -- the program state component
18     bstate: BState,   -- the property state component
19     nextFull: set ProdState,   -- all next states in the full product space
20     nextReduced: set ProdState   -- all next states in the reduced product space
21   }
22   one sig ProdInit extends ProdState {} -- initial product state
23   pred transitionInProduct[q,q': PState, op: Operation, s,s': BState] {
24     q->op->q' in nextState
25     some t : BTrans | t.src = s and t.dest = s' and t.label = q.label
26   }
27   pred nextProd[x: ProdState, op: Operation, x': ProdState] {
28     transitionInProduct[x.pstate, x'.pstate, op, x.bstate, x'.bstate]
29   }
30   pred independent[op1, op2 : Operation] {
31     all q: PState | (op1+op2 in q.enabled) implies (
32       op2 in q.nextState[op1].enabled and
33       op1 in q.nextState[op2].enabled and
34       q.nextState[op1].nextState[op2] = q.nextState[op2].nextState[op1])
35   }
36   pred invisible[op: Operation] {
```

```
37      all q: PState | op in q.enabled => q.nextState[op].label = q.label
38    }
39    fact C0 { all q: PState, s: BState | some q.enabled => some amp[q,s] }
40    fact C1 {
41      all q: PState, s: BState | let A=amp[q,s] |
42        let r = { q1, q2: PState | some op: Operation-A |
43                  q1->op->q2 in nextState } |
44          all q': q.*r, op1: q'.enabled-A, op2: A | independent[op1, op2]
45    }
46    fact C2 {
47      all q: PState, s: BState | let A = amp[q,s] |
48        A != q.enabled implies all op: A | invisible[op]
49    }
50    fact C3' {
51      let r = { x, x' : ProdState | x->x' in nextReduced and
52                  amp[x.pstate, x'.bstate] != x.pstate.enabled } |
53        no x: ProdState | x in x.^r
54    }
55    fact { -- generate all reachable product states, etc.
56      nextFull = {x,y: ProdState | some op: Operation | nextProd[x,op,y]}
57      nextReduced = {x,y: ProdState |
58        some op: amp[x.pstate, y.bstate] | nextProd[x,op,y]}
59      ProdState = ProdInit.*nextFull
60      all x,y: ProdState | (x.pstate=y.pstate && x.bstate=y.bstate) => x=y
61      ProdInit.pstate = Pinit and ProdInit.bstate = Binit
62      all x: ProdState, op: Operation, q': PState, s': BState |
63        transitionInProduct[x.pstate, q', op, x.bstate, s'] implies
64          some y: ProdState | y.pstate = q' and y.bstate = s'
65    }
66    pred nonemptyLang[r: ProdState->ProdState] { -- r reaches accepting cycle
67      some x: ProdInit.*r | (x.bstate in AState and x in x.^r)
68    }
69    assert PORsoundness { -- if full space has a lasso, so does the reduced
70      nonemptyLang[nextFull] => nonemptyLang[nextReduced]
71    }
```

The facts are constraints that any instance must satisfy; some of the facts are given names for readability. A pred declaration defines a (typed) predicate.

Most aspects of this model are self-explanatory; I will comment only on the less obvious features. The relations nextFull and nextReduced represent the next state relations in the full and reduced spaces, respectively. They are declared in ProdState, but specified completely in the final fact on lines 56–58. Strictly speaking, one could remove those predicates and substitute their definitions, but this seemed more convenient. Line 60 asserts that a product state is determined uniquely by its program and property components. Line 61 specifies the initial product state.

Line 59 insists that only states reachable (in the full space) from the initial state will be included in an instance (∗ is the reflexive transitive closure operator). Lines 62–64 specify the converse. Hence in any instance of this model, `ProdState` will consist of exactly the reachable product states in the full space.

The encoding of **C1** is based on the following observation: given $q \in Q$ and a set A of operations enabled at q, define $r \subseteq Q \times Q$ by removing from the program's next-state relation all edges labeled by operations in A. Then "no operation dependent on an operation in A can occur unless an operation in A occurs first" is equivalent to the statement that on any path from q using edges in r, all enabled operations encountered will either be in A or independent of every operation in A.

Condition **C3** is difficult to encode, in that it depends on specifying a depth-first search. I have replaced it with a weaker condition, which is similar to a well-known cycle proviso in the offline theory:

C3′ In any cycle in $\mathsf{reduced}(\mathcal{A}, \mathsf{amp})$, there is a transition from $\langle q, s \rangle$ to $\langle q', s' \rangle$ for which $\mathsf{amp}(q, s') = \mathsf{en}(q)$.

Equivalently: if one removes from the reduced product space all such transitions, then the resulting graph should have no cycles. This is the meaning of lines 50–54 (^ is the strict transitive closure operator).

The next step is to create tests for specific property automata. This example is for the automaton $\mathcal{B}_1$ of Fig. 1:

```
1    module ba1
2    open ba
3    one sig X0, X1 extends Sigma {}
4    one sig B1 extends BState {}
5    one sig T1, T2, T3 extends BTrans {}
6    fact {
7      AState = B1   -- B1 is the sole accepting state
8      T1.src=Binit && T1.label=X0 && T1.dest=Binit
9      T2.src=Binit && T2.label=X0 && T2.dest=B1
10     T3.src=B1 && T3.label=X1 && T3.dest=B1
11   }
```

The final step is a test that combines the modules above:

```
1    open por_v0
2    open ba1
3    checkPORsoundness for exactly 2 Sigma, exactly 2 BState,
4      exactly 3 BTrans, 2 Operation, 2 PState, 4 ProdState
```

It places upper bounds on the numbers of operations, program states, and product states while checking the soundness assertion. Using the Alloy analyzer to check the assertion above results in a counterexample like the one in Fig. 1. The runtime is a fraction of a second. The Alloy instance uses two uninterpreted atoms for the elements of `Sigma`; I have simply substituted the sets $\varnothing$ and $\{p\}$ for them to produce Fig. 1. As we have seen, this counterexample happens to also satisfy the stronger constraint **C3**.

5 Spin

The POR algorithm used by Spin is described in [10] and is similar to the combined algorithm. We can see what Spin actually does by encoding examples in Promela and executing Spin with and without POR.

```
bit p = 0;
active proctype p0() { p=1 }
active proctype p1() { bit x=0; do :: x=0 od }
never {
  B0: do :: !p :: !p -> break od
  accept_B1: do :: p od
}
```

Fig. 2. Promela representation of counterexample using $\mathcal{B}_1$ of Fig. 1

Figure 2 shows an encoding of the example of Fig. 1. Transition α corresponds to the assignment x = 0, where x is a variable local to p1. Transition β corresponds to the assignment p = 1, where p is a shared variable. Applying Spin with the following commands allows one to see the structure of the program graphs for each process, as well as each step in the search of the full space:

spin -a test1.pml; cc -o pan -DCHECK -DNOREDUCE pan.c; ./pan -d; ./pan -a

I did this with Spin version 6.4.9, the latest stable release. The output indicates that 4 states and 5 transitions are explored, and one state is matched—exactly as in Fig. 1 (right). As expected, the output also reports a violation—a path to an accepting cycle that corresponds to the transition from $A0$ to $B1$ followed by the self-loop on $B1$ repeated forever.

Repeat this experiment without the -DNOREDUCE, however, and Spin finds no errors. The output indicates that it misses the transition from $A0$ to $B1$.

6 Ignoring the Intermediate States

An interesting aspect of the combined algorithm is that the ample set is a function of an intermediate state. I.e., given a product state $x = \langle q, s \rangle$, the ample set is determined by the intermediate state $x' = \langle q, s' \rangle$ obtained after executing a property transition. This introduces a difference between the on-the-fly scheme and offline schemes, where there is no notion of intermediate state. It also introduces other complexities. For example, it is possible that x' was reached earlier in the search through some other state $\langle q, s_2 \rangle$, because of a property transition $s_2 \xrightarrow{L(q)} s'$. How does the algorithm guarantee that the ample set selected for x' will be the same as the earlier choice? This issue is not addressed in [13] or [10].

These problems go away if one simply makes the ample set a function of the source product state x. The intermediate states do not have to play a role.

Specifically, given an ample selector amp, define $\mathsf{reduced}_2(\mathcal{A}, \mathsf{amp})$ as in (1) and (2), except replace "$\alpha \in \mathsf{amp}(q, s')$" in (2) with "$\alpha \in \mathsf{amp}(q, s)$". Perform the same substitution in **C3** and call the resulting condition **C3$_1$**. The weaker version of **C3$_1$** is simply:

C3$_1'$ In any cycle in $\mathsf{reduced}_2(\mathcal{A}, \mathsf{amp})$ there is a state $\langle q, s \rangle$ with $\mathsf{amp}(q, s) = \mathsf{en}(q)$.

Conditions **C0**–**C2** are unchanged. I refer to this scheme as V1, and to the original combined algorithm as V0. The Alloy model of V0 in Sect. 4 can be easily modified to represent V1.

Using V1, the example of Fig. 1 is no longer a counterexample. In fact, Alloy reports there are no counterexamples using $\mathcal{B}_1$, at least for small bounds on the program size. Figure 5 gives detailed results for this and other Alloy experiments.

Unfortunately, Alloy does find a counterexample for a slightly more complicated property automaton, $\mathcal{B}_2$, which is shown in Fig. 3.

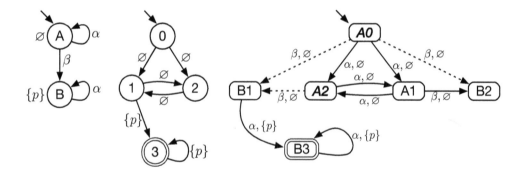

Fig. 3. Counterexample to V1 with $\mathcal{B}_2$ (center). $A0$ and $A2$ have proper ample set $\{\alpha\}$.

The program is the same as the one in Sect. 3.1. Automaton $\mathcal{B}_2$ has four states, with state 3 the sole accepting state. The language is the same as that of $\mathcal{B}_1$: all infinite words formed by concatenating a finite nonempty prefix of $\varnothing$s and an infinite sequence of $\{p\}$s. If the prefix has odd length, the accepting run begins with the transition $0 \to 1$, otherwise it begins with the transition $0 \to 2$.

In the ample selector, only $A0$ and $A2$ are not fully enabled:

amp	0	1	2	3
A	$\{\alpha\}$	$\{\alpha, \beta\}$	$\{\alpha\}$	$\{\alpha, \beta\}$
B	$\{\alpha\}$	$\{\alpha\}$	$\{\alpha\}$	$\{\alpha\}$.

C0–**C2** hold for the reasons given in Sect. 3.1. **C3$_1$** holds for any DFS in which $A2$ is pushed onto the stack before $A1$. In that case, there is no back edge from $A2$; there will be a back edge when $A1$ is pushed, but $A1$ is fully enabled.

7   What's Right

In this section, I show that POR scheme V1 of Sect. 6 is sound if one introduces certain assumptions on the property automaton. The following definition is similar to the notion of *stutter invariant (SI) automaton* in [6] and to that of *closure under stuttering* in [9]. The main differences derive from the use of Muller automata in [6] and *Büchi transition systems* in [9], while we are dealing with ordinary Büchi automata.

Definition 12. *A Büchi automaton* $\mathcal{B} = \langle S, \{s_{init}\}, \Sigma, \delta, F \rangle$, *is in* SI *normal form if it has a single initial state* s_{init} *with no incoming edges, and for each* $s \in S \setminus \{s_{init}\}$, *there is some* $a_s \in \Sigma$ *such that the following all hold:*

1. *Every edge terminating in* s *is labeled* a_s.
2. s *has exactly one outgoing edge with label* a_s.
3. *If* $s \notin F$ *then* $\langle s, a_s, s \rangle \in \delta$.
4. *If* $\langle s, a_s, s \rangle \notin \delta$, *then there exists* $s^\sharp \in S \setminus F$ *such that (i)* $\langle s, a_s, s^\sharp \rangle \in \delta$ *and (ii) for all* $a \in \Sigma$ *and* $s' \in S$, $\langle s, a, s' \rangle \in \delta \Leftrightarrow \langle s^\sharp, a, s' \rangle \in \delta$.

Lemma 1. *Let* $\mathcal{B}$ *be a Büchi automaton in* SI *normal form. Suppose* $a, b \in \Sigma$ *and* $a \neq b$. *Both of the following hold:*

1. *If* $s_1 \xrightarrow{a} s_2 \xrightarrow{b} s_3$ *is a path in* $\mathcal{B}$, *then for some* $s_2' \in S$, $s_1 \xrightarrow{a} s_2 \xrightarrow{a} s_2' \xrightarrow{b} s_3$ *is a path in* $\mathcal{B}$.
2. *If* $s_1 \xrightarrow{a} s_2 \xrightarrow{a} s_3 \xrightarrow{b} s_4$ *is a path in* $\mathcal{B}$, *then* $s_1 \xrightarrow{a} s_2 \xrightarrow{b} s_4$ *is a path in* $\mathcal{B}$. *Moreover, if* s_3 *is accepting, then* s_2 *is accepting.*

Following the approach of [6], one can show that the language of an automaton in SI normal form is stutter-invariant. Moreover, any Büchi automaton with a stutter-invariant language can be transformed into SI normal form without changing the language. The conversion satisfies $|S'| \leq O(|\Sigma||S|)$, where $|S|$ and $|S'|$ are the number of states in the original and new automaton, respectively. For details and proofs, see [17]. An example is given in Fig. 4; the language of $\mathcal{B}_3$ (or $\mathcal{B}_4$) consists of all words with a finite number of $\{p\}$s.

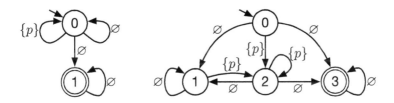

Fig. 4. Property automaton $\mathcal{B}_3$ and result of transformation to SI normal form, $\mathcal{B}_4$.

Theorem 1. *Suppose* $\mathcal{B}$ *is in* SI *normal form and* amp: $Q \times S \to 2^T$ *is an ample selector satisfying* C0–C2 *and* C3$_1'$. *Then* amp *is POR-sound.*

The remainder of this section is devoted to the proof of Theorem 1. The proof is similar to the proof of the offline case in [4].

Let θ be an accepting path in the full space $\mathcal{A}$. An infinite sequence of accepting paths $\pi_0, \pi_1, \dots$ will be constructed, where $\pi_0 = \theta$. For each $i \geq 0$, π_i will be decomposed as $\eta_i \circ \theta_i$, where η_i is a finite path of length i in the *reduced space*, θ_i is an infinite path, η_i is a prefix of η_{i+1}, and $\circ$ denotes concatenation. For $i = 0$, η_0 is empty and $\theta_0 = \theta$.

Assume $i \geq 0$ and we have defined η_j and θ_j for $j \leq i$. Write

$$\theta_i = \langle q_0, s_0 \rangle \xrightarrow{\langle \alpha_1, \sigma_0 \rangle} \langle q_1, s_1 \rangle \xrightarrow{\langle \alpha_2, \sigma_1 \rangle} \cdots \tag{3}$$

where $\sigma_k = L(q_k)$ for $k \geq 0$. Then η_{i+1} and θ_{i+1} are defined as follows. Let $A = \mathsf{amp}(q_0, s_0)$. There are two cases:

Case 1: $\alpha_1 \in A$. Let η_{i+1} be the path obtained by appending the first transition of θ_i to η_i, and θ_{i+1} the path obtained by removing the first transition from θ_i.

Case 2: $\alpha_1 \notin A$. Then there are two sub-cases:

Case 2a: Some operation in A occurs in θ_i. Let n be the index of the first occurrence, so that $\alpha_n \in A$, but $\alpha_j \notin A$ for $1 \leq j < n$. By **C1**, α_j and α_n are independent for $1 \leq j < n$. By repeated application of the independence property, there are paths in P

$$
\begin{array}{ccccccccccc}
q_0 & \xrightarrow{\alpha_1} & q_1 & \xrightarrow{\alpha_2} & q_2 & \xrightarrow{\alpha_3} & \cdots & \xrightarrow{\alpha_{n-2}} & q_{n-2} & \xrightarrow{\alpha_{n-1}} & q_{n-1} \\
\downarrow{\alpha_n} & & \downarrow{\alpha_n} & & \downarrow{\alpha_n} & & & & \downarrow{\alpha_n} & & \downarrow{\alpha_n} \\
q_1' & \xrightarrow{\alpha_1} & q_2' & \xrightarrow{\alpha_2} & q_3' & \xrightarrow{\alpha_3} & \cdots & \xrightarrow{\alpha_{n-2}} & q_{n-1}' & \xrightarrow{\alpha_{n-1}} & q_n & \xrightarrow{\alpha_{n+1}} q_{n+1} \xrightarrow{\alpha_{n+2}} \cdots
\end{array}
$$

By **C2**, α_n is invisible, whence $L(q_{j+1}') = \sigma_j$ for $0 \leq j \leq n - 2$, and $\sigma_{n-1} = \sigma_n$. Hence the admissible sequence

$$q_0 \xrightarrow{\alpha_n} q_1' \xrightarrow{\alpha_1} q_2' \xrightarrow{\alpha_2} q_3' \to \cdots \xrightarrow{\alpha_{n-2}} q_{n-1}' \xrightarrow{\alpha_{n-1}} q_n \xrightarrow{\alpha_{n+1}} q_{n+1} \xrightarrow{\alpha_{n+2}} q_{n+2} \to \cdots \tag{4}$$

generates the word

$$\sigma_0 \sigma_0 \sigma_1 \sigma_2 \cdots \sigma_{n-2} \sigma_n \sigma_{n+1} \sigma_{n+2} \cdots . \tag{5}$$

Now the projection of θ_i onto $\mathcal{B}$ has the form

$$s_0 \xrightarrow{\sigma_0} s_1 \xrightarrow{\sigma_1} s_2 \xrightarrow{\sigma_2} \cdots \xrightarrow{\sigma_{n-2}} s_{n-1} \xrightarrow{\sigma_n} s_n \xrightarrow{\sigma_n} s_{n+1} \xrightarrow{\sigma_{n+1}} s_{n+2} \xrightarrow{\sigma_{n+2}} \cdots$$

since $\sigma_{n-1} = \sigma_n$. By Lemma 1, there is a path in $\mathcal{B}$

$$s_0 \xrightarrow{\sigma_0} s_1 \xrightarrow{\sigma_0} s_1' \xrightarrow{\sigma_1} s_2 \xrightarrow{\sigma_2} \cdots \xrightarrow{\sigma_{n-2}} s_{n-1} \xrightarrow{\sigma_n} s_n \xrightarrow{\sigma_{n+1}} s_{n+2} \xrightarrow{\sigma_{n+2}} \cdots \tag{6}$$

which accepts the word (5). Composing (4) and (6) therefore gives a path through the product space. Removing the first transition (labeled $\langle \alpha_n, \sigma_0 \rangle$) from this path yields θ_{i+1}. Appending that transition to η_i yields η_{i+1}.

Case 2b: No operation in A occurs in θ_i. By **C0**, A is nonempty. Let $\beta \in A$. By **C2**, every operation in θ_i is independent of β. With an argument that is similar to the one for Case 2a, we can see there is a path in the product space for which the projection onto the program component has the form

$$q_0 \xrightarrow{\beta} q_1' \xrightarrow{\alpha_1} q_2' \xrightarrow{\alpha_2} q_3' \rightarrow \cdots$$

and the projection onto the property component has the form

$$s_0 \xrightarrow{\sigma_0} s_1 \xrightarrow{\sigma_0} s_1' \xrightarrow{\sigma_1} s_2 \xrightarrow{\sigma_2} \cdots .$$

Removing the first transition from this path yields θ_{i+1}. Appending that transition to η_i yields η_{i+1}. This completes the definitions of η_{i+1} and θ_{i+1}.

Let η be the limit of the η_i. Clearly η is an infinite path through the reduced product space, starting from the initial state. We must show that it passes through an accepting state infinitely often. To do so, we must examine more closely the sequence of property states through which each θ_i passes.

Let $i \geq 0$, and s_0 the final state of η_i. Say θ_i passes through states $s_0 s_1 s_2 \cdots$. Then the final state of η_{i+1} will be s_1, and the state sequence of θ_{i+1} is determined by the three cases as follows:

> Case 1: $s_1 s_2 \cdots$
> Case 2a: $s_1 s_1' s_2 \cdots s_n s_{n+2} \cdots$ $(s_{n+1} \in F \implies s_n \in F)$ (7)
> Case 2b: $s_1 s_1' s_2 \cdots$

We first claim that for all $i \geq 0$, θ_i passes through an accepting state infinitely often. This holds for θ_0, which is an accepting path by assumption. Assume it holds for θ_i. In each case of (7), we see that the state sequence of θ_{i+1} has a suffix which is a suffix of the state sequence of θ_i, so the claim holds for θ_{i+1}.

Definition 13. *For any path $\xi = s_0 \rightarrow s_1 \rightarrow \cdots$ through $\mathcal{B}$ which passes through an accepting state infinitely often, define the* accepting distance *of ξ, written* $\mathrm{AD}(\xi)$, *to be the minimum $k \geq 1$ for which s_k is accepting.*

Lemma 2. *Let $i \geq 0$ and say the state sequence of θ_i is $s_0 s_1 s_2 \cdots$. If s_1 is not accepting then one of the following holds:*

- *Case 1 holds and $\mathrm{AD}(\theta_{i+1}) < \mathrm{AD}(\theta_i)$, or*
- *Case 2a or 2b holds and $\mathrm{AD}(\theta_{i+1}) \leq \mathrm{AD}(\theta_i)$.*

Proof. If s_1 is not accepting then there is some $k \geq 2$ for which s_k is accepting. The result follows by examining (7). In Case 1, the accepting distance decreases by 1. In Case 2a, the accepting distance is either unchanged (if $k \leq n$) or decreases by 1 (if $k > n$). In Case 2b, the accepting distance is unchanged. $\qquad \square$

Lemma 3. *For an infinite number of $i \geq 0$, Case 1 holds for θ_i.*

Proof. Suppose not. Then there is some $i \geq 0$ such that Case 2 holds for all $j \geq i$. Let α_1 be the first program operation of θ_i. Then α_1 is the first program operation of θ_j, for all $j \geq i$. Furthermore, for all $j \geq i$, α_1 is not in the ample set of the final state of η_j. Since the product space has only a finite number of states, this means there is a cycle in the reduced space for which α_1 is enabled but never in the ample set, contradicting **C3$'_1$**. $\qquad\qquad\square$

We now show that η passes through an accepting state infinitely often. Note that, if $\mathsf{AD}(\theta_i) = 1$, an accepting state is added to η_i to form η_{i+1}. Suppose η does not pass through an accepting state infinitely often. Then there is some $i \geq 0$ such that for all $j \geq i$, $\mathsf{AD}(\theta_j) > 1$. By Lemma 2, $(\mathsf{AD}(\theta_j))_{j \geq i}$ is a nonincreasing sequence of positive integers, and by Lemma 3, this sequence strictly decreases infinitely often, a contradiction. This completes the proof of Theorem 1.

Remark 1. The proof goes through with minor modifications for V0 in place of V1. Let $A = \mathsf{amp}(q_0, s_1)$ instead of $\mathsf{amp}(q_0, s_0)$. In Case 2a (similarly in 2b), note the first transition $s_0 \xrightarrow{\sigma_0} s_1$ in the path in $\mathcal{B}$ remains in the new path (6).

8   Summary of Experimental Results and Conclusion

We have seen that standard ways of combining POR and on-the-fly model checking are unsound. This is not only a theoretical issue—the defect in the algorithm is realized in Spin, which can produce an incorrect result. A modification (V1) seems to help, but is still not enough to guarantee soundness for any Büchi automaton with a stutter-invariant language. However, any such automaton can be transformed into a normal form for which algorithm V1 is sound.

v	BA	Sigma	BState	BTrans	Operation	PState	ProdState	time (s)	Result
V0	$\mathcal{B}_1$	2	2	3	≤ 2	≤ 2	≤ 4	0.3	✗
V1	$\mathcal{B}_1$	2	2	3	≤ 3	≤ 5	≤ 10	42.3	✓
V0	$\mathcal{B}_2$	2	4	6	≤ 2	≤ 2	≤ 6	0.4	✗
V1	$\mathcal{B}_2$	2	4	6	≤ 2	≤ 2	≤ 6	0.3	✗
V0	$\mathcal{B}_3$	2	2	4	≤ 3	≤ 5	≤ 10	256.3	✓
V1	$\mathcal{B}_3$	2	2	4	≤ 3	≤ 5	≤ 10	280.7	✓
V0	$\mathcal{B}_4$	2	4	9	≤ 3	≤ 4	≤ 16	39.5	✓
V1	$\mathcal{B}_4$	2	4	9	≤ 3	≤ 4	≤ 16	37.7	✓
V0	$\mathcal{B}_5$	≤ 3	≤ 4	≤ 6	≤ 3	≤ 4	≤ 16	2264.9	✓
V1	$\mathcal{B}_5$	≤ 3	≤ 4	≤ 6	≤ 3	≤ 4	≤ 16	1653.9	✓

Fig. 5. Bounded verification of soundness of POR schemes V0 and V1 on various Büchi automata using Alloy. $\mathcal{B}_5$ represents all automata in SI normal form within the bounds. Each run resulted in either a counterexample (✗) or not (✓).

Alloy proved useful for reasoning about the algorithms and generating small counterexamples. A summary of the Alloy experiments and results is given in

Fig. 5. These were run on an 8-core 3.7GHz Intel Xeon W-2145 and used the plingeling SAT solver [1].[3] In addition to the experiments already discussed, Alloy found no soundness counterexamples for property automata $\mathcal{B}_3$ or $\mathcal{B}_4$, using V0 or V1. In the case of $\mathcal{B}_4$, this is what Theorem 1 predicts. For further confirmation of Theorem 1, I constructed a general Alloy model of Büchi automata in SI normal form, represented by $\mathcal{B}_5$ in the table. Alloy confirms that both V0 and V1 are sound for all such automata within small bounds on program and automata size.

It is possible that the use of the normal form, while correct, cancels out the benefits of POR. A comprehensive exploration of this issue is beyond the scope of this paper, but I can provide data on one non-trivial example. I encoded an n-process version of Peterson's mutual exclusion algorithm in Promela, and used Spin to verify starvation-freedom for one process in the case $n = 5$. If p is the predicate that holds whenever the process is enabled, a trace violates this property if p holds only a finite number of times in the trace, i.e., if the trace is in $\mathcal{L}(\mathcal{B}_3) = \mathcal{L}(\mathcal{B}_4)$. Figure 6 shows the results of Spin verification using $\mathcal{B}_3$ without POR, and using $\mathcal{B}_3$ and $\mathcal{B}_4$ with POR. The results indicate that POR significantly improves performance on this problem, and that using the normal form $\mathcal{B}_4$ in place of $\mathcal{B}_3$ actually *improves* performance further by a small amount.

BA	POR	states(stored)	transitions	time(s)	Result
$\mathcal{B}_3$	N	18,964,912	116,510,960	25.8	✓
$\mathcal{B}_3$	Y	4,742,982	13,823,705	3.6	✓
$\mathcal{B}_4$	Y	4,719,514	12,503,008	3.4	✓

Fig. 6. Spin verification of starvation-freedom for 5-process Peterson. Using the SI normal form $\mathcal{B}_4$ instead of the smaller $\mathcal{B}_3$ has little impact on performance.

It is likely that V1 is sound for other interesting classes of automata. Observe, for example, that $\mathcal{B}_2$ of Fig. 3 has states u where the language of the automaton with u considered as the initial state is *not* stutter-invariant. If we restrict to automata in which every state has a stutter-invariant language, is V1 sound? I have neither a proof nor a counterexample. (This is certainly not true of V0, as $\mathcal{B}_1$ is a counterexample.) To explore this question, it would help to find a way to encode the stutter-invariant property—or a suitable approximation—in Alloy.

Finally, the proof of Theorem 1 is complicated and might also be flawed. Recent work mechanizing such proofs [3] represents an important advance in raising the level of assurance in model checking algorithms. It would be interesting to see if the proof of this theorem is amenable to such methods. However, constructing such proofs requires far more effort than the Alloy approach described here. One possible approach moving forward is to use tools such as Alloy when prototyping a new algorithm, to get feedback quickly and root out

---

[3] All artifacts needed to reproduce the experiments reported in this paper can be downloaded from http://vsl.cis.udel.edu/cav19.

bugs. Once Alloy no longer finds any counterexamples, one could then expend the considerable effort required to construct a formal mechanized proof.

Acknowledgements. I am grateful to Ganesh Gopalakrishnan and Julian Brunner for fruitful conversations on partial order reduction, to Gerard Holzmann for help with Spin, and to the anonymous reviewers for suggestions that improved this paper. This material is based upon work by the RAPIDS Institute, supported by the U.S. Department of Energy, Office of Science, Office of Advanced Scientific Computing Research, Scientific Discovery through Advanced Computing (SciDAC) program. Funding was also provided by the U.S. National Science Foundation under award CCF-1319571.

References

1. Biere, A.: CaDiCaL, Lingeling, Plingeling, Treengeling, YalSAT Entering the SAT Competition 2017. In: Balyo, T., Heule, M., Järvisalo, M. (eds.) Proceedings of SAT Competition 2017 - Solver and Benchmark Descriptions. Department of Computer Science Series of Publications B, vol. B-2017-1, pp. 14–15. University of Helsinki (2017)
2. Brunner, J.: Implementation and verification of partial order reduction for on-the-fly model checking. Master's thesis, Technische Universität München, Department of Computer Science, July 2014. https://www21.in.tum.de/~brunnerj/documents/ivporotfmc.pdf
3. Brunner, J., Lammich, P.: Formal verification of an executable LTL model checker with partial order reduction. J. Autom. Reason. **60**, 3–21 (2018). https://doi.org/10.1007/s10817-017-9418-4
4. Clarke Jr., E.M., Grumberg, O., Peled, D.A.: Model Checking. MIT Press, Cambridge (1999)
5. Courcoubetis, C., Vardi, M., Wolper, P., Yannakakis, M.: Memory-efficient algorithms for the verification of temporal properties. Form. Methods Syst. Des. **1**(2), 275–288 (1992). https://doi.org/10.1007/BF00121128
6. Etessami, K.: Stutter-invariant languages, ω-automata, and temporal logic. In: Halbwachs, N., Peled, D. (eds.) CAV 1999. LNCS, vol. 1633, pp. 236–248. Springer, Heidelberg (1999). https://doi.org/10.1007/3-540-48683-6_22
7. Holzmann, G., Peled, D., Yannakakis, M.: On nested depth first search. In: The Spin Verification System, DIMACS - Series in Discrete Mathematics and Theoretical Computer Science, vol. 32, pp. 23–31. AMS and DIMACS (1997). https://bookstore.ams.org/dimacs-32/
8. Holzmann, G.J.: The Spin Model Checker: Primer and Reference Manual. Addison-Wesley, Boston (2004)
9. Holzmann, G.J., Kupferman, O.: Not checking for closure under stuttering. In: Grégoire, J.C., Holzmann, G.J., Peled, D.A. (eds.) The SPIN Verification System. DIMACS Series in Discrete Mathematics and Theoretical Computer Science, vol. 32, pp. 17–22. American Mathematical Society (1997)
10. Holzmann, G.J., Peled, D.: An improvement in formal verification. In: Hogrefe, D., Leue, S. (eds.) Proceedings of the 7th IFIP WG6.1 International Conference on Formal Description Techniques (Forte 1994). IFIP Conference Proceedings, vol. 6, pp. 197–211. Chapman & Hall (1995). http://dl.acm.org/citation.cfm?id=646213.681369

11. Jackson, D.: Software Abstractions: Logic, Language, and Analysis, Revised edn. MIT Press (2012)
12. Peled, D.: Combining partial order reductions with on-the-fly model-checking. In: Dill, D.L. (ed.) CAV 1994. LNCS, vol. 818, pp. 377–390. Springer, Heidelberg (1994). https://doi.org/10.1007/3-540-58179-0_69
13. Peled, D.: Combining partial order reductions with on-the-fly model-checking. Form. Methods Syst. Des. **8**(1), 39–64 (1996). https://doi.org/10.1007/BF00121262
14. Schwoon, S., Esparza, J.: A note on on-the-fly verification algorithms. In: Halbwachs, N., Zuck, L.D. (eds.) TACAS 2005. LNCS, vol. 3440, pp. 174–190. Springer, Heidelberg (2005). https://doi.org/10.1007/978-3-540-31980-1_12
15. Siegel, S.F.: Reexamining two results in partial order reduction. Technical report. UD-CIS-2011/06, U. Delaware (2011). http://vsl.cis.udel.edu/pubs/por_tr_2011.html
16. Siegel, S.F.: Transparent partial order reduction. Form. Methods Syst. Des. **40**(1), 1–19 (2012). https://doi.org/10.1007/s10703-011-0126-0
17. Siegel, S.F.: What's wrong with on-the-fly partial order reduction (extended version). Technical report. UD-CIS-2019/05, University of Delaware (2019). http://vsl.cis.udel.edu/pubs/onthefly.html

Permissions

The contributors of this book come from diverse backgrounds, making this book a truly international effort. This book will bring forth new frontiers with its revolutionizing research information and detailed analysis of the nascent developments around the world.

We would like to thank all the contributing authors for lending their expertise to make the book truly unique. They have played a crucial role in the development of this book. Without their invaluable contributions this book wouldn't have been possible. They have made vital efforts to compile up to date information on the varied aspects of this subject to make this book a valuable addition to the collection of many professionals and students.

This book was conceptualized with the vision of imparting up-to-date information and advanced data in this field. To ensure the same, a matchless editorial board was set up. Every individual on the board went through rigorous rounds of assessment to prove their worth. After which they invested a large part of their time researching and compiling the most relevant data for our readers.

The editorial board has been involved in producing this book since its inception. They have spent rigorous hours researching and exploring the diverse topics which have resulted in the successful publishing of this book. They have passed on their knowledge of decades through this book. To expedite this challenging task, the publisher supported the team at every step. A small team of assistant editors was also appointed to further simplify the editing procedure and attain best results for the readers.

Apart from the editorial board, the designing team has also invested a significant amount of their time in understanding the subject and creating the most relevant covers. They scrutinized every image to scout for the most suitable representation of the subject and create an appropriate cover for the book.

The publishing team has been an ardent support to the editorial, designing and production team. Their endless efforts to recruit the best for this project, has resulted in the accomplishment of this book. They are a veteran in the field of academics and their pool of knowledge is as vast as their experience in printing. Their expertise and guidance has proved useful at every step. Their uncompromising quality standards have made this book an exceptional effort. Their encouragement from time to time has been an inspiration for everyone.

The publisher and the editorial board hope that this book will prove to be a valuable piece of knowledge for researchers, students, practitioners and scholars across the globe.

List of Contributors

Andrei Damian and Alexandru Militaru
Politehnica University Bucharest, Bucharest, Romania

Cezara Drăgoi
Inria, ENS, CNRS, PSL, Paris, France

Josef Widder
TU Wien, Vienna, Austria
Interchain Foundation, Baar, Switzerland

Sidi Mohamed Beillahi, Ahmed Bouajjani, Constantin Enea, Ranadeep Biswas and Constantin Enea
Université de Paris, IRIF, CNRS, Paris, France

Michael Emmi
SRI International, New York, NY, USA

Idan Berkovits and Sharon Shoham
Tel Aviv University, Tel Aviv-Yafo, Israel

Marijana Lazić
TU Wien, Vienna, Austria
TU Munich, Munich, Germany

Giuliano Losa
University of California, Los Angeles, USA

Oded Padon
Stanford University, Stanford, USA

Florian Frohn
Max Planck Institute for Informatics, Saarbrücken, Germany

Peizun Liu and Thomas Wahl
Northeastern University, Boston, USA

Akash Lal
Microsoft Research, Bangalore, India

Juneyoung Lee and Chung-Kil Hur
Seoul National University, Seoul, Republic of Korea

Nuno P. Lopes
Microsoft Research, Cambridge, UK

David Sanán
School of Computer Science and Engineering, Nanyang Technological University, Singapore, Singapore

Xiaojie Guo and Maxime Lesourd
Univ. Grenoble Alpes, CNRS, Grenoble INP, VERIMAG, Grenoble, France
Univ. Grenoble Alpes, Inria, CNRS, Grenoble INP, LIG, Grenoble, France

Hari Govind Vediramana Krishnan, Vijay Ganesh and Arie Gurfinkel
University of Waterloo, Waterloo, Canada

Yakir Vizel
The Technion, Haifa, Israel

Jürgen Giesl
LuFG Informatik 2, RWTH Aachen University, Aachen, Germany

Constantin Enea
Université de Paris, IRIF, CNRS, 75013 Paris, France

Kartik Nagar and Suresh Jagannathan
Purdue University, West Lafayette, USA

Yongwang Zhao
School of Computer Science and Engineering, Beihang University, Beijing, China
Beijing Advanced Innovation Center for Big Data and Brain Computing, Beihang University, Beijing, China

Lionel Rieg
Univ. Grenoble Alpes, CNRS, Grenoble INP, VERIMAG, Grenoble, France
Yale University, New Haven, CT, USA

Zhong Shao and Mengqi Liu
Yale University, New Haven, CT, USA

Stephen F. Siegel
University of Delaware, Newark, DE, USA

Index

Printed in the USA
CPSIA information can be obtained
at www.ICGtesting.com
JSHW051358221024
72173JS00006B/1314